S0-BEP-514

CHILD MIGRATION AND HUMAN RIGHTS IN A GLOBAL AGE

Human Rights and Crimes against Humanity

Eric D. Weitz, Series Editor

A list of titles in this series appears at the back of the book.

For my dear friend Norma, with so much admiration & affection over decades!

Jackie

Oct. 2014

Child Migration & Human Rights in a Global Age

Jacqueline Bhabha

Princeton University Press
Princeton and Oxford

Published by Princeton University Press, 41 William Street,
Princeton, New Jersey 08540
In the United Kingdom: Princeton University Press, 6 Oxford Street,
Woodstock, Oxfordshire OX20 1TW
press.princeton.edu

ISBN 978-0-691-14360-6

Library of Congress Control Number: 2013954741

Credits for the chapter opening photographs are as follows:

Chapter one, copyright © BID; chapter two, courtesy of KPBS; chapter three, © UNICEF/NYHQ2012-1924/Dormino; chapters three, four and seven, © International Labour Organization/Crozet M.; chapter six, Heba Aly/IRIN.

Jacket Photo: *Young Boy Carrying Plastic Bottles, La Paz* (Alto), Colombia. © International Labour Organization/Marcel Crozet. Courtesy of the Photo Library of the International Labour Organization.

British Library Cataloging-in-Publication Data is available

This book has been composed in Sabon Next LT Pro
Printed on acid-free paper. ∞
Printed in the United States of America
10 9 8 7 6 5 4 3 2 1

For my Homi, Ishan, Maria Elisa, Satya, and Leah

Contents

Acknowledgments

Any book that spans a large part of one's working life reflects the impact of relationships extending far beyond work. This book is no exception. The concerns it describes have been with me since I was a graduate student at Oxford. They developed during my years as a practicing lawyer and activist in London. They still preoccupy me decades later at Harvard. Deciding whom to thank is thus a daunting task. Stray conversations, engaging arguments, nurturing distractions, generous collaborations, insightful suggestions, probing questions, frank testimonies, rigorous critiques, and loving relationships have all played a crucial role. To avoid an endless list, I only mention a few among the very many people I am grateful to.

I owe a huge debt of gratitude to colleagues I have worked with closely on immigration-related issues over the years—Sylvia Whitfield in Birmingham; Nony Ardill, Don Flynn, Elspeth Guild, Francesca Klug, Sue Rowlands, Sue Shutter, and Nira Yuval-Davis in London; Arjun Appadurai, Bernardine Dohrn, Susan Gzesh, Rashid Khalidi, Mary-Meg McCarthy, Mae Ngai, and Maria Woltjen in Chicago; Susan Akram, Deborah Anker, Elizabeth Bartholet, Dan Kanstroom, Nancy Kelly, Gerald Neuman, Susannah Sirkin, and John Wiltshire-Carrera in Boston; Mary Crock, Nadine Finch, and Susan Schmidt on the three-country Seeking Asylum Alone project; Kate Halvorsen, Judith Kumin, Michèle Levoy, Nevena Milutinovic, Siobhan Mullaly, Elena Rozzi, Daniel Senovilla Hernandez in Europe; and, across North America, Alex Aleinikoff, Susan Bissell, Patty Blum, Linda Bosniak, Michèle Branlé, Catherine D'Auvergne, Barb Frey, Lisa Frydman, the late Arthur Helton, Kay Johnson, Linda Kerber, Stephen Legomsky, Yali Lincroft, Audrey Macklin, Susan Martin, Chris Nugent, Geraldine Sadoway, Andrew Schoenholtz, Debora Spar, Peter Spiro, David Thronson, Steve Yale Loehr, Wendy Young.

Many others have been sources of enrichment—intellectual, political, institutional, personal—over my years at both the University of Chicago and Harvard. I am most grateful to James Chandler, John and Jean Comaroff, Norma Field, Michael Geyer, Mona Khalidi, Elizabeth O'Connor Chandler, Geof Stone at Chicago; and, at Harvard, Michael Blake, Charlie Clements, Liz Cohen, Stanley Hoffmann, Steven Hyman, Michael Ignatieff, Doreen Koretz, Michèle Lamont, Margaret McKenna, Martha Minow, Gerald Newman, John Ruggie, Beth Simmons, Henry Steiner, Lucie White. Sincere thanks are owed to Gus and Rita Hauser and to the Hauser Foundation for most generous support of my work over several years at Harvard. I am also greatly indebted to many librarians, research assistants, students, and administrative colleagues for superb help on a huge range of matters, from fact checking and legal research to technical assistance and editorial work. I am particularly grateful to Trevor Bakke, Ivelina Borisova, Molly Curren, Sarah Dougherty, Susan Frick, Lyonette Louis Jacques, Adam Kern, Ita Kettleborough, Yoojin Kim, Angela Murray, Bonnie Shnayerson. My colleagues at the François-Xavier Bagnoud Center for Health and Human Rights at Harvard University—Heather Adams, Theresa Betancourt, Arlan Fuller, Liz Gibbons, Orla Kelly, Magda Matache, Anne Stetson, Aly Yamin—are much more than fellow workers; they are friends and co-conspirators in much of what I do. I would not have managed to finish this book without their generous comradeship.

I am fortunate to have had editors—Brigitta van Rheinberg and Eric Weitz at Princeton University Press—who were always there when I needed them but left me to my own devices otherwise. I am also grateful to a terrific copy editor, Marsha Kunin, and to two anonymous reviewers who provided invaluable feedback, without which this book would have been much less accurate and coherent.

As an itinerant jack of several trades and mistress of none, I have again and again depended on several close friendships for encouragement, support, and the sense of belonging that nurtures the confidence to write. I am immensely grateful to Riccardo Bottelli, Martha Chen, Ana Colbert, Nancy Cott, Caroline Elkins, Diane Fernyhough, Stephen Greenblatt, Julian Henriques, Anish Kapoor, Susanne Kapoor, Joseph Koerner, Meg Koster, Jennifer Leaning, Bikhaji Maneckji, Zareer Masani, Luigina Palmiero, Diana Sorensen, and Ramie Targoff.

Finally, my beloved family are the bedrock on which all else depends: Naju Bhabha, Oliver and Harriet Strimpel, Michal and Moshe Safdie, Shanta, and then of course, Homi, Ishan and Maria Elisa, Satya and Leah. A child and adult migrant survives and thrives because of the relationships she is fortunate to enjoy. I hope this book contributes to this same anchoring for others.

CHILD MIGRATION AND HUMAN RIGHTS IN A GLOBAL AGE

Introduction

Every year, tens of thousands of children cross borders alone. Some travel to join families that have already migrated. Others leave home to flee war, civil unrest, natural disaster, or persecution. Some migrate in search of work, education, opportunity, adventure. Others travel separated from their families but not actually alone, in the company of traffickers or smugglers, risking exploitation and abuse. The majority, perhaps, travel for a combination of reasons, part of the growing trend toward mixed migration. And yet, the complexity of child migration is a largely untold and unanalyzed story. This book is an effort to correct that omission.

Child migration is part of a contemporary phenomenon that changes and shapes the world we live in. Migration affects not just the 3 percent[1] of the global population who are migrants, but the vast majority who are not. As villages become depleted of young adults and the population in metropolitan centers changes beyond recognition within the space of a couple of decades, as schools, hospitals, workplaces, and shops cater to an increasingly diverse clientèle, so the cumulative impact of contemporary migration irrevocably seeps into the fabric of everyday life. Many stories have been told about this process, ranging from alarmist xenophobic accounts of invasion and cultural pollution to cautious academic analyses of the impact of migration flows on population stocks and domestic economic prospects. They are interspersed with a range of literary and cinematic depictions of the imaginative correlates of migration. Very few of these stories center on the experiences of child migrants, the push and pull factors affecting their movements, and the social and legal environments they populate. This deficit is nontrivial. It affects the perception of migration as a whole and the social investment it attracts. Migration is increasingly considered a voluntary adult phenomenon requiring management and control. The claim to protective intervention or fiscally backed social engagement is ever-diminishing now that concerns about the Holocaust and the brutalities of the Cold War have given way to apprehensions about terrorists and welfare scroungers. Children do not feature in this large-scale picture, except as occasional appendages to adults. But they should. The failure to attend to child migration coincides with the diffusion of confused, unsatisfactory, and frequently oppressive policies that should not stand up to careful public scrutiny.

Migration to developed states has more than doubled in the last thirty-five years. A significant proportion of that migration, recently estimated at 11 percent,[2] consists of children and young people under twenty. There is every reason to expect this trend to continue, given global inequalities and shrinking geographies. But until the late 1990s, policy makers and advocates failed to ask themselves, let alone the children and adolescents in question, what the reasons for their migrations were, or who made (or should make) key decisions concerning their journeys, their well-being, their rights, and their future. With very few exceptions, no agency, department, or expert body considered itself primarily responsible for this group or competent to address the increasingly complex dilemmas that it presented. Though children outside family care have generally lacked the attention and support required to flourish—"the rhetoric of respect is contradicted by the reality of marginalization, rejection, abuse and neglect"[3]—there has at least been long-established and dedicated institutional provision for citizen children. Not so, until recently, for child migrants. Child welfare specialists have been absorbed by their domestic preoccupations with issues such as abuse and neglect, the relative role of foster care and adoption (including, increasingly, intercountry adoption),[4] the scope of parental autonomy versus state responsibility, and the relationship between nurturing and punitive interventions for abandoned and troubled children. Immigration considerations did not feature as complicating, let alone central, issues for children in need of state protection. In many cases migrant children who did not have families to care for them became the responsibility of diasporic community organizations from their countries of origin—Ethiopia, Iran, Vietnam, Somalia, Sri Lanka, El Salvador, or Guatemala. Formal legal decisions were not taken on their behalf, and state entities did not take responsibility for their well-being.

Similarly, immigration advocates have been increasingly engaged in defending humanitarian immigration access—refugee protection—in the face of a changing refugee demographic (what David Martin usefully referred to as the "new asylum-seekers"[5]) and in challenging a growing state propensity to detain, exclude, and criminalize immigrant populations. As subsequent chapters in this book will show, children did not feature in this equation as individual subjects of immigration concern. Rather (as women before them) they were considered appendages and possessions of others—parents, families, lone mothers. Immigration specialists lacked child-specific competence, both substantively in terms of child welfare law and policy, and procedurally in terms of child-friendly operational guidelines. Where they were not entirely overlooked, decisions about migrant children's immigration status and rights were generally linked to and driven by adult entitlements and concerns. This state of affairs began to change in the late 1990s. Two factors were key to the transformation. One was population driven. It concerned the growing presence of unaccompanied child migrants manifestly requiring some form of state attention in developed destination states. There were two aspects to this newly pressing issue. On the one hand child migrants appeared to require *protective attention* because they had or were at risk of having no adults caring for them. On the other hand, child migrants seemed to some key policy makers to need *punitive attention* because their presence as suspected gang members or otherwise threatening outsiders was disruptive and posed challenges to existing state structures.

The other factor central to the changing approach to child migrants at the end of the 1990s was law driven: the increasing importance given to children in international law, thanks to the growing influence of the widely and rapidly ratified 1989 Convention on the Rights of the Child, and the foundational impact of the 1996 Graça Machel report on children and armed conflict. The public law acknowledgment that children featured as rights bearers and as subjects of concern in international law, and that noncitizen children deserved attention and state protection as much as domestic children, provided ammunition to child migrant advocates. As a result of these two developments, conceptions of migrant children began to change, to assume more importance and definition and to have a greater impact on child welfare and immigration decisions. By the beginning of the twenty-first century, the chasm between child welfare and immigration experts was starting to close, with a small group of immigration advocates, juvenile justice experts, child welfare specialists, and humanitarian activists directing attention to issues specific to different groups of child migrants.

Clear evidence of this gradual transformation in the conception of migrant children and the legitimacy of their claims to attention is the evolution of terminology dealing with child migrants, an evolution that reflects a growing sophistication in categorization and understanding. As already noted, until the 1990s[6] the vast majority of child migrants were subsumed within family immigration where they were simply "dependents." This was true both of national immigration statistics regarding family reunification claims, and of international demographic data regarding refugee processing. Insofar as any attention was paid to other child migrants, it was simply because they arrived alone. They were at first referred to as "unaccompanied children," and were generally assumed to be asylum seekers. The February 1997 Office of the United Nations High Commissioner for Refugees (UNHCR) *Guidelines on Policies and Procedures in Dealing with Unaccompanied Children Seeking Asylum*[7] was among the first of official documents to address this population.[8] The *Guidelines* targeted children under eighteen who were "separated from both parents and [were] not being cared for by an adult who by law or custom had responsibility to do so."[9] Within four months, the European Union followed suit. It passed a "Resolution on Unaccompanied Minors who are nationals of Third Countries,"[10] its only one to date focused on this issue. The assumption here too was that all these children needed to be dealt with within the asylum-determination framework. National guidelines eventually followed in the United States and the United Kingdom[11] targeting unaccompanied child asylum seekers as the only category of concern.

The inadequacy of this terminology gradually became apparent. As the UNHCR definition itself noted, children requiring attention were not just those who were unaccompanied by parents but those not cared for by a responsible adult. In other words, lack of care rather than unaccompanied status was the factor precipitating the need for public attention. The terminology changed to reflect this new conception—"unaccompanied and separated child asylum-seekers" were the new target, so that children separated from their customary caregivers but in others' company were also included. Indeed it became apparent that accompanied migrant children might be highly vulnerable, if for example they were with traffickers, military recruiters, or other exploitative individuals. What unaccompanied and separated children had in common was a protection deficit, one that the state in its role as *parens patriae* was obliged to address.

Toward the middle of the new century's first decade, around 2005 to 2006, a third development regarding child migrants appeared that coincided with the growing constriction of access to asylum after the mushrooming of applications following the Balkan War, and the expansion of independent child migration from North Africa, West Africa, and Latin America. It became apparent that many unaccompanied or separated children were not asylum seekers at all, but young migrants driven to cross borders because of a complex, mixed set of factors unrelated to fear of persecution. Fitting all these diversely driven young migrants into the asylum-determination process and the refugee definition for the purposes of securing a legal immigration status became increasingly unworkable. Most undocumented migrant children living in irregular situations who are not asylum seekers continue to fall outside domestic legislation and institutional protection in the destination states where they reside.[12]

Gradually, however, in specialist circles at least, some acknowledgment of the complexity of child migration developed, reflected in a more differentiated categorical lexicon and more thoughtful policy articulation. In France, where large numbers of North African and East European adolescents arrived during the first decade of the new century, the terminology of "unaccompanied" or "separated" was replaced by the notion of *jeunes errants*, a term that means "young wanderers" but became translated into the less pejorative "children on the move." This terminological shift reflected a new conception: child and adolescent migrants were moving in search of various key elements of a rights-respecting life absent in the home countries—safety, nurture, educational opportunity, economic prospects, and perhaps family life. The dichotomy between forced and economic migration was giving way to an acknowledgment, for children too, of the reality of mixed migration. Migration was prompted not just by persecution or by family migration but by the spread of a global social imaginary, the fall of the Berlin Wall, the dramatic curtailment of legal status for Latino populations in the United States (rendered "impossible subjects" in Mae Ngai's evocative terminology[13]), the growth of immigrant diasporas, and the proliferation of social networking through omnipresent portable and affordable personal technology. Border crossing, therefore, was no longer simply an adult or family life strategy, but one adopted by children and adolescents—independent child migrants making choices (whether experts considered them in their best interests or not) that expressed their views about their future preferences.

Greater attention to child migration is gradually bringing more sophistication to the related policy and decision-making process. As acknowledgment of the variety of the migration projects undertaken by young people has expanded, so has a more differentiated conception of the category "child." In international law, the term spans a huge capability range, from zero to eighteen.[14] It covers infants entirely dependent on adult provision, who should have a positive right to protection,[15] as well as late teens considered independent family members back home, whose capacity to make best-interest judgments for themselves should be respected. In the migration context this more nuanced understanding of the evolving capacities of the child complicates decision making about the meaning of "the best interests of the child" as applied to the child's future plans. Protective policies rub up against autonomous desires and plans that reflect an increasing capability for self-reflection and decision making. There is a growing recognition that unaccompanied child migrants are, in most cases, teenagers with complex life stories and agendas that challenge previous orthodoxies. Some advocates now insist that family unity traditionally conceived is not synonymous with the best interests of the child, and that other human rights—to education, to a reasonable standard of living, to freedom from exploitation—should complicate a simple-minded "return home" policy.

Consider the differences between the following common child-migrant situations explored in subsequent chapters. Some children who are unaccompanied or separated or in situations of "errance" are trapped by traffickers or exploitative employers unbeknown to their families, or held by smugglers refusing to hand them over to parents waiting to reunify their family: these children need positive protection by the state, including legal support, social and emotional care as a prelude to family reunification. Other children who have left home exercising their own initiative, leaving behind situations of abuse or exploitation, need to be protected from families and spared rather than forced into family unity. Policies that return these children "home" without scrutinizing the homes to which return is being effected may contribute to retrafficking or forced conscription. Even migrant children joining or living with loving families may nonetheless risk human rights violations requiring state intervention. Paradoxically, some accompanied children may face greater risks than their unaccompanied or separated counterparts. Whereas many unaccompanied children within state custody get access to education, necessary medical attention, and sometimes even regularization of their immigration status, accompanied children living in families with an irregular immigration status rarely do. As chapter 2 discusses, children living with parents frightened of being arrested and deported, as millions of US resident children are, risk being kept away from necessary medical services and other public situations to avoid potentially devastating encounters with law enforcement and immigration agents. And, as chapter 7 points out, children living with stateless parents or parents in irregular settlements, including European Roma children, are regularly denied access to necessary state services for similar reasons. Unprotected rather than unaccompanied child migrants are a new and urgent focus of concern.

Finally some advocates have adopted the terminology of "lone" or "independent" child migrants, which suggests a more recent set of issues: that child migrant advocates need to take on board the autonomy and adolescent aspirations of many child migrants who are not looking to be "rescued" into state-run facilities where their opportunities to earn are blocked, or inducted into migration itineraries where their aspirations for agency and empowerment are erased. The large-scale absconding from state shelters by children "rescued" from traffickers (discussed in chapter 4) or from a life on the streets is evidence of this dynamic. This population of child migrants requires nonpaternalistic support and advice to enable them to realize the rights guaranteed to them by international law, including the rights to freedom from inhumane or degrading treatment; to basic education; to adequate health care, welfare support, and shelter. Above all, young migrants need to be listened to, and given a voice with which to articulate their concerns and hopes. Legal protections related to migration status need to be coupled with child welfare investments related to social and economic rights. Work with these independent migrant adolescents is in its infancy in Europe, and hardly in evidence at all in the United States. These terminological journeys illustrate the complex ecology of interrelated rights and needs that child migrants present and the unfinished business of legal implementation and policy refinement that lies ahead.

At the same time as conceptions of child migrants evolved, indeed in dialogue with and response to them, domestic proceedings linked to international law began to change. The first two chapters record the process by which child migrants appeared as plaintiffs or co-plaintiffs in challenges to family deportations citing the right to respect for their family life. Chapter 6 describes how asylum applications by children started to be presented expanding the boundaries of the 1951 UN Convention's definition of a refugee to include child abuse or child trafficking as a basis for international protection. Several chapters document the evolution of child-friendly procedures in a range of immigration proceedings to facilitate children's access to some form of justice, a reflection of the increasing connection between the immigration and child welfare worlds.

The growing influence of the Convention on the Rights of the Child (CRC), with its foundational concept of "the best interests of the child" and stimulation of greater attention to the agency, views, and participation of children themselves, and with its clear articulation of the rights of refugee and asylum-seeking children,[16] has had some impact on domestic law and practice affecting child migrants. Even the US government, as chapter 6 points out, despite nonratification of the Convention, has referenced its principles, both in its child asylum guidelines, and in the regular trainings given to asylum officers adjudicating children's cases. In addition to the general force of key articles in the Convention, the work of the UN Committee on the Rights of the Child in the development of a General Comment dealing with migrant children[17] is an important contribution to an evolving rights-based adjudication framework. The General Comment provides guidance on general principles such as nondiscrimination and right to life as they impinge on states parties' treatment of migrant children, as well as on survival and development principles. It also sets out considered responses to more specific protection needs and challenges, including age determination procedures and the appointment of guardians and legal advisers.

A few of these international law principles have now found their way into state practice affecting migrant children, reassuring evidence that the time-consuming and politically costly process of norm setting can, with sufficient civil society mobilization and political will, translate into rights enforcement on the ground. By piecing together the diverse strands of policy development, law enactment, and finally institutional implementation, the book attempts to illustrate through the lens of child migration how human rights principles can move from theory to practice. Many examples of this complex and erratic process are covered in subsequent pages. Among them is the radical reform of protection and reception provisions for unaccompanied migrant children approved by the Belgian government in the wake of the European Court of Human Rights condemnation of state practice in the notorious

Tabitha case[18] discussed in chapter 7. The book also discusses the holistic age determination procedures adopted (at least in principle) by the UK immigration authorities referenced in chapter 6 in response to an assiduous and well-organized advocacy campaign against the Home Office's continuing use of discredited, one-dimensional medical measures of age. The growing international acknowledgment that detention of migrant children (including in family detention contexts) must be a last resort, used as sparingly as possible is referenced in several contexts. The move away from detention is hugely significant as a human rights principle, though, one could argue, it is a modest achievement given the manifest unsuitability of detention for nearly all children, but particularly those not charged with any criminal wrongdoing. Finally, there is reference to the increasing investment in collecting and disseminating disaggregated migration statistics detailing age, gender, and status of migrant children, a precondition for the monitoring of progress and the evaluation of the impact of reforms on child migrants' rights.

These and other related changes manifest themselves across a broad spectrum of child migration situations. For ease of analysis, rather than to suggest that each migration category is hermetically sealed from the others, the book organizes the discussion of child migration into three nonmutually exclusive groups: family-related migration (comprising family reunion, family-related deportation, and intercountry adoption); exploitation-related migration (including child trafficking and recruitment related to armed conflict); and survival-related migration (covering refugee- and asylum-driven migration, and economic migration). Each of these three migration groups presents dilemmas for child migrants, their families, and their advocates, as well as for policy and decision makers. To preview the discussion in the following chapters, I will briefly comment on each.

The first section deals with child migration for family reunion, the most familiar and well-understood aspect of child migration, and the one that has been the focus of law and policy the longest. It covers a range of different migrations, including challenges confronting children who follow to join parents who have migrated first, the dilemmas confronting citizen children whose parents are refused permission to reside in the children's home country and who thus face "constructive deportation" from their own country, and intercountry adoption, a practice that affects approximately thirty thousand children moved from the "majority" to the "developed" world each year to become part of a new family.

The second section of the book examines child migration situations primarily driven by the intention to exploit moving children. This section consists of two chapters, one on the flourishing industry in transnational child trafficking leading to different forms of exploitative child labor in peacetime, the other on the transport and exploitation of child labor in situations of armed conflict.

The third and final section of *Child Migration and Human Rights in a Global Age* covers yet another significant aspect of child migration, that primarily driven by the search for survival, opportunity, and a viable life. Like adults, large numbers of children and adolescents cross borders each year in search of a future. Some refugees and asylum-seekers travel to escape armed conflict, ethnic strife, religious discrimination, or more individualized forms of personal abuse. Others flee from destitution, unemployment, or societal disintegration. In either case, the young migrants aspire to a future that is more secure and rights respecting than the past they left behind.

A central claim of *Child Migration and Human Rights in a Global Age* is that child migrants need to be viewed as agents whose aspirations are relevant to institutional decision making. Legitimate concerns about encouraging child labor, curtailing educational opportunity, or acquiescing in forms of child exploitation are not a justification for treating migrant adolescents as elementary school children. The delicate balance between familial protection and youthful autonomy, between educational and employment opportunity must be established in partnership with the young migrants themselves. The alternatives, as I show in the book's final chapters, are incarceration or absconding and return to risky street environments.

These dilemmas associated with children's border crossing are challenging to resolve, particularly in a political climate dominated by security concerns and nativist protectionism over employment opportunities. But the instruments increasingly available through international law create opportunities for advocacy and public education that advocates have a responsibility to exploit to the full as they move on to the next set of terminological transformations in our thinking about child migrants.

What are the key dilemmas that confront child migrants and their advocates over this broad spectrum of migration situations today? Among the plethora that exist, a few are particularly critical. Most central is the continuing inefficacy of international, regional, and domestic law as an instrument to protect the human rights of migrant children. What alternatives to law making, litigation, and advocacy exist, then? How can unprotected child and adolescent migrants—the majority of whom have no access to guardianship, to legal representation, to competent advocacy—translate the principles of international law into meaningful human rights protections? For years, the preferred answer to this dilemma has been to suggest that the rights deficits are a product of the child migrants' invisibility—their in-between status, the omissions that have resulted from the gap between child welfare and immigration experts that I mentioned earlier. The implication, of course, is that visibility will correct the rights deficit. In my view this answer has been effectively discredited. For the past half-decade at least, attention has been paid to the interests and rights violations affecting child migrants—invisibility is no longer an acceptable explanation for lack of protection. I suggest in what follows that an unresolved ambivalence about the legitimacy of according protection to migrant children without a legal status provides a more convincing explanation of the policy failures that persist. As a society, we are stymied by a fundamental contradiction in our approach. We view the state as having a protective obligation toward vulnerable children in its role as *parens patriae*, parent of the nation; but we also expect the state to protect us from threatening, unruly, and uncontrolled outsiders, even if they are children. It is not that we have forgotten or missed the problems of migrant children. Rather they are a moving target, compelling but shifting, and we are deeply ambivalent about our responses. Our neglect of child migrants' rights is therefore a strategic compromise that represents our unresolved ambivalence. It has enabled us to avoid the conceptual and political dilemmas raised by child migration and to sidestep the policy challenges it presents.

At first glance, ambivalence may seem an inadequate explanatory tool. The global demand for cheap child labor is, one might argue, a product of transnational economic forces, a reflection of deeper market-driven imperatives. And the growing demand for mobility of persons to match the mobility of goods, services, and capital inevitably brings with it exploitative and irregular forms of border crossing such as trafficking. In the face of these broad and complex economic factors, why invoke the concept of ambivalence? Because, *Child Migration and Human Rights in a Global Age* will demonstrate, it provides a richer and deeper analytic framework than purely economic arguments and a more accurate explanation of current realities than the invisibility theory. Much of the theoretical work on the tension between equality and difference relies on the concept of ambivalence. Hannah Arendt for example examines the ethical dilemmas involved in dealing with groups other than ourselves in these terms: "I am not only for others but for myself, and in this latter case, I am clearly not one. A *difference is inserted into my oneness.*"[19] Her idea is that the tension between one's identification with others (e.g., the sentiments that motivate human rights principles) and one's self-interest (the sentiments that drive nativism and xenophobia) is not a contradiction that is resolved or overcome, but a deeper ambivalence that endures—the *difference inserted into oneness.* The concept of ambivalence has also been used in the political sphere for analyzing the tension between freedom and tyranny. Writing about Nazism, Theodor Adorno emphasizes the internalization of barbaric and tyrannical traits within democracy itself, pointing out that the existence of National Socialism *within* democracy is potentially more threatening than the continued existence of fascist tendencies *against* democracy. The same idea is taken up by Giorgio Agamben in his discussion of the role that the concept of the refugee plays within our contemporary political systems as an inherent part of the political framework rather than an outside challenge to it: "The refugee should be considered for what it is, namely *nothing less than a limit-concept* that, at once, brings a radical crisis to the principles of the nation-state and clears the way for a renewal of categories that can no longer be delayed."[20] Both writers stress the importance of understanding that the tension between contrasting principles is enduring *within* our own society, not external, transient, or ultimately resolvable.

The concept of ambivalence is inherent in these profound insights. But it is not only philosophers and political scientists who rely on ambivalence. Scholars working on questions of citizenship and migration in contemporary society—material close to the subject matter of *Child Migration and Human Rights in a Global Age*—also consider ambivalence an essential explanatory tool. Linda Bosniak, for example, has a similar approach to mine. Her book, *The Citizen and the Alien: Dilemmas of Contemporary Membership*, explicitly invokes the concept in its concluding chapter: "Aliens are liminal characters, subjects of contrasting and sometimes competing citizenship worlds. The worlds are *ultimately inseverable* at the point of alienage because it is alienage's very condition to be at their interface. Alienage, we might say, pits citizenship against itself. . . . Our condition . . . is one of *ambivalence* and ethical conflict." Homi Bhabha's recent work on global citizenship adopts a similar approach: "Tolerance, as a universalist principle of integration, must . . . endure the unsettling contingency of unresolved contradictions. . . . The *ambivalence* that marks the practice of tolerance . . . allows it to be effective."[21]

Let me attempt to translate these rather abstract concepts into a framework for understanding my material. I suggest that the approach to "otherness" in our societies is ambivalent—caught between an identification of the other as "human like me" and a hostility or indifference toward the other as separate or dispensable or threatening. This is particularly so for migrant children, where perceptions of vulnerability ("poor and innocent children") and otherness ("not *really* like *our* children") coalesce. So, economic and self-interested demands for the cheap labor of migrant children are in tension with uncontroversial rights that all children, including these children, now have as a matter of both law and popular belief. That is why the exploitation of migrant children in factories, farms, and sweatshops in industrialized countries continues, as does the vulnerability of the relevant industries to rights-driven lawsuits and human rights campaigns. It is an uneasy but continuing balance, reflecting society's ambivalence.

The concept of ambivalence is also useful for understanding the approach to trafficked child sex workers, child gang members, and former child soldiers. Migrant children drift into these abusive contexts as a consequence of the protection lacunae they face (albeit in very different ways). Alternative mentoring situations (boyfriend-pimps, gang leaders, military commanders) fill the gap left by ineffective or nonexistent families and state structures. The mentoring is abusive but it provides the child with a survival structure, even the possibility of some autonomy and income. Meanwhile state interventions are punitive and infantilizing. This explains why trafficked children so often escape from state institutions where they are placed after "rescue" and return to their traffickers, why girl child soldiers are hard to incorporate into the DDR (demobilization, disarmament, and reintegration) process and drift back to their bush "husbands," why orphaned or "left-behind" children of migrants repeatedly get involved in gangs. Official responses are ambivalent, mired between the pressure to protect rights and the obligation to punish juvenile offending. Should we prosecute or protect former child soldiers guilty of war crimes, should we award asylum to former gang children or deport them (regardless of whether they fear persecution from gang members if returned), should we grant permanent residence to migrant children inducted into sex-trafficking rings or cleanse our societies of this scourge and send them "home"—we are ambivalent.

Understanding the ambivalence that underlies public policy in this field is key to developing a more effective approach to enforcement of rights. We legislate migrant children's right to public education and health care irrespective of their legal status, but we erect practical obstacles to their access to these services; we accept an obligation to protect them from persecution, trafficking, and destitution, but we blame them for the risks they pose to our social fabric by finding ways to detain them or remove them from our territories. We are torn, obligated to protect migrant "children," but frightened and resentful of alien "juveniles."

The concept of ambivalence clarifies why simple "exposé" is not sufficient. Because invisibility is not the fundamental problem, these injustices are not self-correcting once they come to light. In child rights terms, we have to carefully calibrate the ongoing tension between the child's need for protection (the best interest principle enunciated in Article 3 of the Convention on the Rights of the Child) and the child's evolving ability to be autonomous (the right to voice and agency, expressed in Article 12 of the same Convention). We have to acknowledge, for example, that the problem of trafficking cannot be addressed simply as one of adult criminality. Many children choose to be smuggled or trafficked as their best exit option, as their most promising survival strategy.

This situation presents us with a different and more complex (and common) challenge than children who have simply been kidnapped by evil exploiters. Children in the former situation are both vulnerable and culpable, in need of protection but law breakers. A rights-respecting approach places the child's best interests at the forefront of the policy response. But it leaves open what that best interest is and how it should be determined. Most child migrants are teenagers between the ages of fourteen and seventeen. Their best interests must involve opportunities for both protection and exploration, dependence and independence. At a minimum these include a legal status, access to fundamental economic and social rights (education, health care, etc.), and a supportive social environment.

To translate the abstract principles of human rights law into effective policies that protect the best interests and the agency of child and adolescent migrants requires a categorical shift. The answer must lie in more creative stimulation of political will through productive, cross-cutting allegiances—allegiances between those who acknowledge the importance of adolescent agency, of opportunity for the next generation, of the right to aspire, to hope, to seek empowerment and those who acknowledge the need for trained and motivated young workers to build and sustain the societies of the future. Giving an account of the complexity and scope of child migration today is one step in this direction. As chapter 7 suggests, the thrilling but traumatic events of the Arab Spring provide some indication of the sorts of new allegiances that can be formed: an acknowledgment of the importance of young, skilled labor, of migration as an opportunity and a potential benefit for host societies as much as for young migrants themselves.

This final chapter suggests that current child-centered policies in the migration field end up targeting children for infantilizing, harsh, and punitive measures that reduce their autonomy and their scope for self-development and self-sufficiency. Drawing on the preceding discussion, this chapter shows how, by denying children the family reunion rights that their adult relatives have, by restricting the access to self-sufficiency and autonomy for children escaping situations of gross exploitation, and by misconstruing the alternatives available to autonomous child migrants moving for survival, our current interventions are at best ineffective, often counterproductive. Child migration needs to be understood in a broad context of economic and social inequality as a potentially redistributive tool that can contribute valuable resources for aging societies. Inclusive policies that foster access to opportunity and reward are more likely to yield social benefits than the current ambivalent strategies of shor-term protection followed by rejection, exclusion, and punishment.

To insist on the human rights of migrating children, then, is not to beg for the exercise of state discretion in favor of neglected or hidden foreign victims whose plight moves us, but to assert the imperative of building just foundations for an inclusive, diverse, and globally mobile future society. To tell the story of contemporary child migration is to document the extraordinary obstacles that large numbers of very young people face and overcome in the process of securing a foothold for a productive and rewarding life, a process we all have a stake in, whether we realize it or not.

PART I

The Right to Respect for Family Life?

Moving Children for Family

Dear, judge,

I miss my mom and I Really want her to come home.
It's going to be my birthday soon and I would really
like her to be there. I miss her so much when
I visit her I don't want to go home and I
cry some time because it makes me sad,
I wish she was never gone I want her
To be in my family, so please make her come
home cause I want my mom please

CHAPTER 1

Looking for Home: The Elusive Right to Family Life

> Few rights are as important as an adolescent son's right to live with his father and to take advantage of the atmosphere of affection as well as of the father's help and advice.[1]
>
> "I told him not to cry, and that soon we would be with Mommy and Daddy," seven-year-old Salvadorian child being smuggled to the United States with his brother under two.[2]

Introduction

Family life is a given, a fact of daily existence that most of us take for granted as much as the arrival of dawn after night or the taste of everyday food. It shapes the pattern of our life, the nature of our emotions and our sense of self. However complex our identification with space or place, with a nation or people, family is a critical aspect of feeling at home in the world. This is why we consider it an essential part of our children's upbringing. The basic human intuition that family life is crucial for the well-being of children is confirmed by human behavior, by the sacrifices made, the plans developed, the migrations embarked upon to secure reunification when family unity has been interrupted. Indeed one of the central reasons why people move is family—the desire or need to be with family, the aspiration to improve the prospects for family, the imperative to secure safety or care for family. The intuition about the importance of family life for children is widely supported by scholarship across a range of disciplines. In this first chapter I will be mainly concerned with legal and social structure and its impact on the exercise of family life. But the justification for starting a book about children who cross borders with the issue of family unity and family reunification[3] is not legal: it is moral and psychological. It is because of the way human beings are wired, not because of the way laws have been written, that the right to family life is a crucial bedrock of a just migration policy. This is where I start my inquiry.

Attachment and Belonging: Bedrocks of Childhood

Jean Piaget, the eminent Swiss developmental psychologist, considered the presence of parents essential for a child's development of morality. He reports an interview with a five-year-old, Fal, who could attribute morality only to his father, more authoritative for him than even God.[4] Of course in many societies, including those from which many immigrant families originate, physical and psychological nurturing tends to be more broadly distributed than the classical Western nuclear family model would assume. But the emotional costs of prolonged separation are not thereby reduced. Research on the enduring impact of separation on immigrant children eventually reunited with parents documents the complex emotional upheavals experienced by children thrust into the migration process. Clinical reports reveal substantial negative impacts on children and on family relationships both during and after the separation phase. "Once I was in the plane they told me to be calm, not to be nervous, and not to cry. I was crying because I was leaving my grandfather. I had conflicting feelings. On the one side I wanted to see my mother, but on the other I did not want to leave my grandfather."[5]

Parents forced to separate for long periods from their children may feel guilt but also expect gratitude for their sacrifices, while left-behind children often feel resentment and anger. This dynamic compounds the difficulties that flow from the young child's loss of early parental anchoring. The effects of parental migration on children are at least as complex. While migrant parents who send remittances can often improve the material well-being of their families,[6] prolonged parental absence leaves many children without the resources and support to maintain schooling and educational performance,[7] to attain adequate nutrition status and health, to achieve a standard of living that takes them above the poverty line.[8] Available research also shows that long-term separation negatively impacts the psychosocial development and functioning of children left behind, contributing to a sense of family disintegration.[9] A complicating factor in many cases is the difficulty of reunifying the family legally, once the parent is legally qualified and economically prepared to do so.[10]

A "secure attachment" is an accepted key to a successful nurturing relationship and to the child's future responsiveness to parental socialization attempts.[11] Children who move with their parents in intact families to better socioeconomic prospects when they are young typically relocate successfully and integrate into their new environment as if it had always been home. For them the danger of deportation "back home" rapidly becomes a far greater threat than a family decision to make the migration permanent.[12] But where the family is divided, the process of establishing a "secure attachment" is compromised. Disruption of this process can have long-term adverse effects. For example, as the literature on immigrant families shows, family reunification after a period of separation is often associated with patterns of inconsistent parenting (veering from indulgence to strict discipline), child insubordination, and pathological family relationships. As a self-perceptive child put it: "I don't know how to live with my parent."[13] Lengthy delays in reunification can also produce in children feelings of abandonment and rejection, especially when legal or economic hardship permits some but not all siblings to migrate. One young man from El Salvador, forced to wait over a decade to join his family in the United States, reflected:

> What do you think is worse, to share poverty [in the United States] with my half-siblings and mother and father, or not having learned how to love them because I never saw them? What would I have given for a good-night kiss from my mother, for instance, or even for a fight with a sibling! You know? That's what makes a family a family. But instead, I don't know who these people are![14]

Fraught relationships can also lead to serious individual pathologies. According to an influential American bicoastal study of adolescents separated from one or both parents for extended periods, more than the upheaval of migration, it is the preceding separation from parents that correlates with later reports of depressive symptoms, particularly among girls.[15] Studies conducted in the United States, China, Colombia, Romania, Jamaica, Trinidad, and other countries have confirmed that left-behind children also face substantially increased risks of violent behavior, drug abuse, and teenage pregnancy, as well as vulnerability to physical and sexual abuse and exploitation.[16]

Contemporary legal frameworks reflect the social and psychological importance attached to family unity: domestic, regional, and international laws consider the family the bedrock of society, and a key aspect of childhood. The US Supreme Court, to cite one domestic legal system, has established in its jurisprudence that "the Constitution protects the sanctity of the family precisely because the institution of the family is deeply rooted in this nation's history and tradition."[17] The same approach exists in Europe, home to the world's most vigorous and effective regional legal system. The European Convention on Human Rights (ECHR) requires signatory states to respect the right to family life of all persons within their jurisdiction.[18] The European Social Charter requires all European Union member states (a subset of twenty-eight of the forty-seven states that are parties to the ECHR) to protect family unity not just for their citizens but also for "foreign workers."[19] Family unity is thus highly valued in European legal thinking.[20] International law includes the same cardinal principle. According to the Universal Declaration of Human Rights: "The family is the natural and fundamental group unit of society and is entitled to protection by society and the State."[21]

What is true for society as a whole is particularly true for children. The 1989 Convention on the Rights of the Child, the most widely ratified United Nations human rights convention in the world, and the document that codifies a broad range of legal principles relevant to children, asserts in its opening preamble: "The family [is] . . . the natural environment for the growth and well-being of all its members and particularly children."[22] This principle is inclusive in its generality, across races, nationalities, and religions. We expect our social structure to enhance the strength of the family and protect it from disruption and disintegration. The centrality of institutions such as marriage and parenthood across societies, the significance of events such as adultery or child abandonment, confirm this presumption. Given this prevailing consensus, it is hard for most of us to imagine family life as a luxury, a distant goal, or a lifelong dream. And it is surprising, even shocking, to learn that state policies, rather than dysfunctional or incompatible individuals, are major sources of family separation. But, as this chapter will show, for immigrant families and for children who need to cross borders to enjoy family unity, this is the case. A leading scholar notes: "[T]he existence of even close family relationships with persons permitted to live in the United States does not inevitably or even usually provide feasible avenues for legal immigration."[23] The same is often true in Canada, Western Europe, Australia, and other wealthy migration destination states. A combination of extensive delays, exacting documentary requirements, logistical complexities, and legal barriers prevents many children from enjoying the right to respect and enjoyment of the family life to which they are entitled. The following vignette poignantly conveys a common situation:

> Irénée is waiting for reunification with his wife and six children who had to remain in Kinshasa (Democratic Republic of Congo) when he left for Canada. Since his departure the children have had to drop out of school because their mother can't pay the costs and the family have had to move away from their home. One of Irénée's children is indignant: "*Why did you bring us into the world if it is only to condemn us to becoming street kids? You abandoned us to go and live in peace in Canada while we are living here in misery, while we have nothing.*" When he heard this, Irénée burst into tears. He then tried to explain that these are administrative delays. His oldest son responded: "*Can Canadians themselves accept being separated from their children and their wives for 2 or 3 years? Dad, ask one of the officials who is married and has children if he could bear such a thing.*"[24]

The European Court of Human Rights would agree with this indignation. It found, in a 2008 case concerning Norway's imposition of a prolonged entry ban, that two years separation between mother and child violated the state's obligation to protect the best interests of the child. The International Commission of Jurists, a highly respected expert body, confirmed this assessment. It noted, in reviewing implementation of the European Union's family reunification directive, that "a waiting period of three years is capable of rendering almost void the right to respect for family life, particularly in cases involving children."[25]

Delays and other, more enduring legal obstacles to reunion unsettle the bedrock of family life on which children are meant to be raised. Out of desperation, some take foolhardy measures. Fernando Betzabel, a five-year-old Honduran, embarked alone on a journey to the United States: "I want to see my parents. My grandmother told me to get on the bus, that it would take me to where they are."[26] In 2011, Mexico's National Migration Institute reported that over 14,237 unaccompanied minors found on the US-Mexico border were returned to Mexico.[27] Data from the US Office of Refugee Resettlement indicate a 93 percent increase in the number of unaccompanied minors apprehended from 2011 to 2012, which some experts attribute to the "caging effect" of increased border enforcement, driving children to migrate to join families "locked" in the United States.[28] For those who do not embark on perilous journeys to redress the pain of separation, other problems exist. Millions of children[29] live with daily uncertainty and unpredictability about when reunification will take place, an anxiety that can precipitate lifelong detriments.[30] A fourteen-year-old Dominican girl separated from her mother conveys the intensity of emotion: "The day I left my mother I felt like my heart was staying behind. Because she was the only person I trusted—she was my life. I felt as if a light had extinguished. I still have not been able to get used to living without her."[31] The economic benefits generated by parental migration have to be set against the increased social risks and burdens placed on nonmigrant children, including the difficulty of reconstructing family life and the unfathomable emotional costs that follow.[32]

The contradiction between a universal consensus on the critical importance of family unity for children and the reality of policy-induced family separation for immigrant children calls for some explanation. At its heart lies the prerogative of the sovereign state to control its borders, to regulate the access of noncitizens to its territory, and to temper the force of human rights obligations with the exercise of exclusionary discretion. The precise basis for family reunion regulation is a complex and changing amalgam of political priorities over time and across space. At the start of the twentieth century, in the United States, for example, "policies encouraging family reunification . . . came into direct conflict with those insisting on race exclusion."[33] In mid-twentieth-century Europe, guest worker policies encouraged the migration of single workers, mainly men, as units of labor, who could be discarded without the complications and social costs that family appendages would generate.[34] More recently, economic constraints restrict migration options for immigrants seeking family reunification: obligations to demonstrate financial self-sufficiency, sometimes to a standard of living well above that customary for blue-collar or agricultural laborers or for populations in the immigrants' country of origin, interfere with the ability to satisfy entry requirement regulations.

International norms have made some inroads into unfettered state sovereignty in matters of border control and have acted as a countervailing force to migration control priorities. But, these norms have not fundamentally changed the underlying logic of restriction. Family life that spans international borders still abuts against the state's exclusionary prerogative, generating family migration policies that are inherently unstable and susceptible to the vagaries of political and economic protectionism in the domestic sphere. To quote a mid-twentieth-century US presidential commission: "Many social complications are intensified by the presence of families,"[35] complications that have repercussions on local health and education budgets, on nativist political activism, and on inner city social and cultural life more generally. But the refusal to respond appropriately not only to government priorities but to the needs of families divided by borders also generates "social complications." The reluctance of immigrant communities to accept enforced legal separation is one such complication.

Numerous examples exist of challenges to family separation practices, challenges that are most successful where human rights principles can be translated into enforceable legal entitlements. Some challenges have taken the form of grassroots mobilizations, such as the Divided Families Campaign in Britain[36] in the 1970s and 1980s targeting the obstacles to the entry of dependents of legal UK residents, and the Sans Papiers sanctuary movement in France in the 1990s[37] highlighting the impact of undocumented status on the security of immigrant families in France. From an opposing political perspective, grassroots mobilization has produced the self-appointed vigilantism of the Minutemen along the US-Mexico border, taking into private hands the job of capturing undocumented migrants attempting to evade immigration control.[38] Other challenges are precipitated by individual cases, most memorable among which was the highly contested campaign over the future of shipwrecked Cuban six-year-old Elian Gonzalez,[39] a campaign that resonated across the United States, Cuba, and beyond.[40]

Because states have the dual power and responsibility to defend family unity and national self-interest, the instability over the resolution of this tension is endemic, inevitable rather than accidental, constitutive of our system of governance rather than extrinsic to it. This instability reflects a broad social ambivalence about the appropriate prioritization of the conflicting policy imperatives that manifests itself in the handling of individual cases as much as it does in the development of broader strategic plans. Immigration and refugee law and policy is the domain in which this complex dynamic plays out. Though regional and national variations abound in this multifaceted field, there are two archetypal cases of disrupted family unity spanning international borders (as subsequent chapters will show, the dichotomy is somewhat artificial in reality since many migrants are affected by both sets of factors). On the one hand are refugee cases that result from the fallout of conflict or political persecution; on the other are immigration cases that follow from economic migration. In both situations, it may take years for families to attempt reunification. But when they do, new obstacles to the enjoyment of family life often arise. As states debate and change the rules governing lawful entry to their territory, children in families divided in either of these circumstances can experience prolonged state interference with their right to resume living with their parents or close family once again.

Refugee Families: The Struggle to Recreate Home

War, ethnic strife, revolution, or civil disturbance are major precipitators of family disruption affecting millions of children and their families. According to the UN High Commissioner for Refugees, the agency responsible for the protection of forced migrants, the number of refugees worldwide currently stands at 10.5 million.[41] Official estimates suggest that 83 percent of refugees are hosted within their region of origin, but this still leaves 17 percent who migrate further afield.[42] It is rare for all members of a refugee family to have the fortune to flee together to a place of safety and to secure protection together. Political risks, financial expense, legal and bureaucratic obstacles, health impediments, and unmovable ties such as elderly or sick relatives militate against complete family relocation. The trail blazers have to secure a place of safety, they have to get minimally established, they often have to trace surviving relatives left behind. Only then can they initiate attempts to reestablish their interrupted family life.[43] Typically adults travel first, leaving children behind with relatives or acquaintances, either in the home country or in refugee camps bordering it, planning to seek reunification as soon as possible, once legal, social, and financial hurdles are cleared. After the destruction of one's previous life, and given the hardships of most refugee camps and temporary resettlement locations, few types of family reunification are experienced as more psychologically and materially urgent, particularly for children. In practice, months, often years, pass before refugee families manage to reunify.[44] Statistical data documenting delays in reunification of children with refugee parents are not readily available, so the argument that follows relies on anecdotal accounts drawn from litigation and practitioners' experiences.

The competing policy imperatives outlined above account for the often overwhelming difficulties facing refugee families. James Hathaway, a leading scholar of international refugee law, clearly describes the inherent ambivalence underlying the protection of family unity within refugee law. On the one hand, he asserts: "There is . . . little doubt that there is ample raw material from which to derive the necessary *opinio juris* for recognition of a customary legal norm to protect the family unity of refugees." And certainly, according to widely established international law, migrants granted refugee status or asylum in accordance with the main international treaty governing refugee protection, the 1951 UN Convention on the Status of Refugees and its amending 1967 Protocol,[45] have a right to respect for the unity of their family. The Final Act of the Conference that adopted the 1951 Convention

> Recommends Governments to take the necessary measures for the protection of the refugee's family, especially with a view to:
>
> 1. Ensuring that the unity of the refugee's family is maintained particularly in cases where the head of the family has fulfilled the necessary conditions for admission to a particular country.
> 2. The protection of refugees who are minors. . . .

The 1979 UNHCR *Handbook on Procedures and Criteria for Determining Refugee Status*, a widely used and authoritative "soft law" source on refugee protection principles, further explains:

> If the head of a family meets the criteria of the definition [of a refugee], his [*sic*] dependents are normally granted refugee status according to the principle of family unity. . . .

As to which family members may benefit from the principle of family unity, the minimum requirement is the inclusion of the spouse and minor children. In practice other dependents . . . are normally considered if they are living in the same household. . . . The principle of family unity operates in favor of family dependents, and not against them. . . .

The principle of the unity of the family does not only operate where all family members become refugees at the same time. It applies equally to cases where a family unit has been temporarily disrupted through the flight of one or more of its members.[46]

These proclamations are unambiguous. However, as Hathaway further explains:

[O]n close examination, it is clear that while there is a continuing insistence that the family members of a primary applicant refugee should be admitted to protection, most refugee-specific formulations fail to define with any precision the content of an affirmative dimension of the principle of family unity. . . . In other words, the *opinio juris* which achieves the specificity and precision needed to generate binding legal duties does not include norms mandating affirmative reunification, *or even prohibiting all forms of interference with family unity* [emphasis added].[47]

This lack of affirmative obligation enables states to apply their domestic procedures in ways that, while not explicitly in conflict with the letter of the law promoting family unity, in practice pose serious, sometimes insurmountable, obstacles to it. Official intentions are difficult to read from bureaucratic practice, but certainly the urgency of family reunification does not drive the process. While families who manage to move together at least confront the trials of delay and incompetence together, children awaiting reunification have an especially hard time. Because of the absence of adult applicants in situ to move the application forward, these cases can take much longer than those involving the migration of adult refugees. From the perspective of displaced children living in refugee camps and confronting the enduring nightmare of war—physical hardship, loss, fear, and anxiety, children for whom the protective impact of family life is crucial—these obstacles exacerbate already grave situations.

The following case, depicting a scenario familiar to anyone working as a refugee advocate or protection officer, illustrates this point. It concerns an application lodged in the United Kingdom for family reunion for two Somali war orphans stranded in Ethiopia, still pending over *five years* after the date of the original request. When the children, a brother and a sister, were respectively seven and three and living in Somalia, both their parents were killed. They were adopted by their uncle and aunt, but these two adults were killed two years later. By the time they were nine and five, the children had twice experienced the death of their primary caregivers. Their cousin, the daughter of the deceased uncle and aunt, took over their care for a year until she herself was arrested and placed in a detention camp by hostile militia forces. The children were handed over to the cousin's mother-in-law. A year later, acute civil upheaval and conflict forced the mother-in-law to flee with the children from Somalia to Ethiopia. Meanwhile the cousin managed to escape detention and the sectarian carnage in Somalia and reach the United Kingdom, where she was eventually granted refugee status. She applied for family reunion in the United Kingdom with the two refugee children in Ethiopia, sent modest sums to support them, and maintained regular telephone contact with them. According to the European Commissioner for Human Rights:

> The shape of the core family differs depending on traditions and situations. In war-torn and HIV-affected areas, for instance, it is not unusual for orphaned children to be cared for by other relatives. Often grandparents, or other members of the extended family, depend on the active generation. A positive and humane policy should consider the real family pattern in each individual case.[48]

The UK government thought differently. Thirteen months after the original application to join the cousin in the United Kingdom as her dependents, the children learned that their application had been refused because the government contested the cousin's *locus standi* as a caregiver.[49] A month after the refusal, the children lodged their appeal. The UK Court of Appeal, not a body given to sharp censure of government, commented, "For reasons which again are *completely unaccounted for*, and which it has to be inferred amount to *no more than inertia* in the Home Office (the relevant government department), the papers did not reach the AIT (the appellate immigration tribunal)" until *sixteen months* later. Meanwhile the children's situation had seriously deteriorated. The cousin had been abandoned by her husband, and the mother-in-law, blaming the cousin for the breakup of the marriage to her son, had left the children—aged fourteen and ten, respectively, and now facing their third radical change of caregiver—with a friend of the cousin's. At the time of the appeal court hearing, the judge described the children as follows:

> They are not being well-clothed and sometimes money has to be begged for from neighbors. [The caregiver] is not giving the care that would be adequate for children of the appellants' ages.[50]

In child care phraseology, this situation would translate as serious child neglect. Four and a half years after the children's initial family reunion application, the case was remanded to a lower court to reconsider the merits of the original refusal. Meanwhile the judge encouraged the family to lodge a fresh entry clearance application, adding the following unusually critical comment:

> Given its serious dilatoriness in these proceedings, which has resulted in the passage of almost 5 years since the application was first made, the Home Office has in my view *a moral obligation* (and if there is further delay, arguably a legal one) to deal speedily with any fresh application made on behalf of these two children for entry clearance.[51]

What does this case demonstrate? First, it highlights the critical importance of strict time limits for substantive due process. While individual applicants seeking to enforce their rights have to comply with onerous procedural requirements, failure to comply with which leads to dismissal of their case, governments in family reunion applications of refugees have no such constraints. The passage of time, potentially life threatening to these two children, brings with it no sanctions for the dilatory state.[52] Quite the contrary: it is consistent with the ambivalent legal mandate allowing but not supporting refugee family reunification, a de facto rationing of access.[53] Second, the case demonstrates the impotence of fundamental human rights protections in the absence of competent legal representation. A recurring theme in this book is that, especially for children, principles become practice only if enforced by vigorous agents; but destitute refugee children rarely have access to those critical resources. If legislators are serious about creating actionable rights for children, they need to ensure budgetary support for competent legal representation, and for transparent procedures as part and parcel of a meaningful and concrete right. Procedural defects quickly translate into substantive violations; in this case troublesome domestic legal procedures had the effect of trumping international and constitutional mandates protecting the children's right to family life. Third, an ambivalent legal mandate can be more deleterious for the protection of fundamental rights than no mandate at all, because it suggests no cause for concern or reform. Even though on the one hand the family reunion policy remained, in the case cited, unquestioned in principle, government procrastination and intransigence attracted no effective sanctions, while the children in question were reduced to the status of beggars and were separated from the only caring relative willing and able to provide a vestige of family life. If the children ever reach the United Kingdom to effect family reunion, their childhood will be largely over, and their recollection of family life nil.

This case is typical of the complexities facing families ravaged by war and death. As caregivers die or disappear, so the job of parenting moves to available relatives, a social reality that is at odds with a rigid system of migration management. The central purpose of family reunification, to provide safety and nurture for children, becomes obscured by rigid, culturally limiting assumptions about what constitutes family. But complexity alone does not explain the ubiquitous delays and incompetence jeopardizing refugee children's reunification with family. More straightforward cases than the one just discussed are also subject to extensive delays and illustrate the impact of administrative indifference and political ambivalence about migrant children's claims to protection. The sad saga of a Somali refugee in Ireland who complied with all the requirements to bring her three young children to join her is instructive.[54] For three years, the mother tried to ascertain the status of her application, only to receive the same boiler plate letter back from the Irish Department of Justice advising that the case was under consideration. Eventually it transpired that the children's applications had in fact been approved a month after the mother arrived in Ireland but the authorities had failed to communicate this. Even after the family was given the good news about their visas and told to collect them from the Irish embassy in Addis Ababa, no visas were found. It took court proceedings against the Minister of Justice to finally rectify the situation, and three years of unnecessary family trauma. Would that the case were a one-off "gross act of maladministration." In fact the Irish government estimates a backlog of two thousand applications merely awaiting government approval, but leading to average family separations of two years.[55] For any family this is an inordinate trial; for refugee families and children subsisting in poverty- and disease-ridden refugee camps with manifold dangers, it is a human rights outrage.

Time is not the only issue in family reunification. Cost can also present a hurdle to realization of this basic right. According to a study cited in the United Nations Human Development Program's (UNDP) 2009 *Human Development Report*, the average cost of a passport in fourteen countries surveyed exceeded 10 percent of the annual income per capita,[56] a statistic that throws into sharp relief how qualified the "right" to mobility is. In addition, refugees attempting family reunification have to cover additional administrative charges, which can be substantial, as the following account of a Somali refugee in New Zealand awaiting reunification in the United Kingdom demonstrates: "First, the cost of lodging an application under the humanitarian category with the New Zealand Immigration Service in London—$1,000. There is a separate fee for each adult member of a family. Then, an applicant must have a psychiatric report—$800. A one-way air ticket costs about $2,500."[57]

Children pay a different price for the "privilege" of family unity. Adult detention facilities, quite unsuited to housing children, have repeatedly been the setting in which asylum-seeking children and their parents live while the authorities determine the outcome of their cases. Instead of conceding that families with minor children should be accommodated in child-appropriate facilities and devising creative solutions to address official security or absconding concerns (such as regular reporting obligations or dedicated staffing to monitor presence), immigration authorities in a range of countries have opted to willfully ignore the needs of children in their custody. They have conveniently assumed that the protective mantle of family unity cancels out the traumatic impact of incarceration and makes it acceptable to place children in an adult detention facility. This approach ignores explicit international legal obligations,[58] and has the effect of placing accompanied children in a worse living situation than their in-country unaccompanied counterparts who are not generally placed in adult institutions. States, through these detention policies, exact a high tariff for the privilege of family unity, and deflect their child-protection obligations onto vulnerable parents themselves in a compromised legal status. We will again encounter this paradoxical relative disadvantage of accompanied migrant children when we consider the situation of undocumented migrants in chapter 7.

Among the most egregious examples of this problematic family unity practice for asylum seekers was the long-term detention of families by the Australian authorities in remote jails situated in the Australian outback during the first years of this twenty-first century. Predictably, the results were catastrophic for some among the hundreds of children detained. A twelve-year-old girl incarcerated for months in the Woomera detention center, the most notorious of these facilities, and a remote jail far from legal advocates or potentially supportive immigrant communities, told interviewers: "I am getting crazy. I cut my hand. I can't talk to my mother. I can't talk to anyone and I am very tired. There is no solution for me—I just have to commit suicide—there is no choice." This was no idle threat. An investigation into the circumstances of detained children in Woomera found a series of serious incidents of self-harm: an attempted hanging, five incidents of lip sewing, thirteen threats of self-harm, and many responses that "indicated a propensity for self harm and suicidal thoughts."[59] Public outrage eventually forced the Australian authorities to abandon this family detention policy.

But others have continued similar policies. The Belgian authorities detain asylum seekers, including families with young children, in closed transit centers. One of these, "Transit centre 127 bis," near Brussels airport, is notoriously unsuitable for children, as established by several public investigations. According to a 2007 French Children's Commission report on the center: "The rooms look more and more like prison detention cells (graffiti, odors . . .). . . . Men in the courtyard peered in through the barred window several times (during the interview with the young girl); . . . [T]his secure establishment . . . is not a place suited to the well-being or the healthy development of a child, or where any child should be placed." Another official audit concurred: "None of these centers is adequately equipped for receiving families and children; . . . The punitive character (barbed wire, uniformed guards, group discipline), lack of any freedom of movement or outside recreation space, no privacy, inadequate space or daytime light, the impossibility for families placed there to . . . share any intimacy . . ."[60]

Detainee hunger strikes (on occasion involving minors) protesting inadequate food, and three suicide attempts in 2006, confirm the terrible personal cost of this oppressive detention environment. Nevertheless the Belgian authorities detained a Chechen domestic-violence victim and single parent fleeing the carnage of war in Grosny and her four children under eight—the youngest a seven-month-old baby—in the center for over a month between

December 2006 and January 2007, despite persistent legal challenges to that detention. Eventually the European Court of Human Rights in Strasbourg ruled on the case. It noted, in addition to the generic reports about detention conditions, specific medical reports presented to the authorities two weeks after the family's detention. These documented serious psychiatric and psychosomatic symptoms among the children, particularly in the five-year-old girl Khadizha. She was diagnosed as suffering from post-traumatic stress disorder, manifesting serious anxiety abnormal for a child her age, nightmares that caused her to wake up screaming, persistent shouting and crying, hiding under the table when a uniformed guard appeared, and head banging. The six-year-old was reported to suffer from breathing difficulties. A subsequent medical report prepared the following week documented medical deterioration among the children and acute stress in the mother too—this latter aggravating the children's distress as it conveyed the sense that she was incapable of looking after them. The Court concluded that the children had been subjected to inhuman and degrading treatment in violation of Article 3 of the European Convention on Human Rights and awarded the family 17,000 euros by way of damages against the Belgian government.[61]

Many refugee families, despairing of the possibility of finding a lawful route to safety for their children, engage smugglers to secure their journeys to safety. War-torn Somalia is a good example. And indeed Somalis have long comprised one of the largest groups of unaccompanied children in Europe. According to a UN information bulletin, about 250 Somali children were being smuggled out of the capital Mogadishu every month before the events of September 11, 2001. A year later, "traffic out of Mogadishu was said to be picking up again with the most resourceful agents opening up different routes . . . to South East Asia or previously unexplored countries in the Middle East" rather than to American and European destinations. But by then the price had more than doubled and the odds of success had shrunk, leading families to demand the return of one third of the smuggling fee in the event of a migration failure. The brunt of the repercussions of failure, however, is often borne by the children themselves: smuggling agents tend to abandon them at the first sign of trouble. In one case, airport officials found six young Somali children abandoned at the Istanbul airport with no identifying documents or other indicators, the children having been terrorized by the smuggler into staying silent.[62]

Together, these disparate stories suggest a worrying lacuna in protection. While many refugee children do eventually manage to reunify with their parents without having to resort to litigation, much precious time is wasted and stressful administrative hurdles burden already debilitated groups with demanding procedural challenges. The reality of endemic delays, administrative complexities, and a pervasive atmosphere of indifference, even suspicion, belies the expectation that humanitarian child migration of this sort would be facilitated, indeed fast-tracked by an ethical migration system. Citizens in implicated countries fortunate enough to enjoy normal family life are in dereliction of their humanitarian duties when they ignore the failings of their governments in this sphere.

Divided Immigrant Families: Looking Back to the Mid-1970s

The second common context in which children seeking reunification with families encounter problems concerns immigrants who leave home to improve their economic prospects. Here too the numbers are significant. The UN estimates that 3.1 percent of the world's seven billion inhabitants live outside their birth country.[63] In developed countries the proportion is even higher—about 9 percent of the population is foreign born.[64] This is, perhaps, not surprising. Whatever the emotional, cultural, and social costs of leaving home (and they are many), the economic benefits are, statistically speaking, significant. *The Economist* reported in 2002 that a California think tank conducting a survey of new immigrants to America concluded: "They gain on average $20,000 a year, or $300,000 over a lifetime in net present-value terms. . . . Not many things you do in your life have such an effect."[65] More recent data is equally compelling. According to the 2009 *Human Development Report*, "Migrant workers in the US earn about four times what they would earn in their developing country of origin." This is the context that generates the other archetypal case of disrupted family unity. It occurs when migration is prompted by economic factors rather than political necessity, by the quest for enhanced opportunity rather than bare survival. The distinction, of course, is not a clear one—migration compelled by persecution or political upheaval often includes economic desperation, and economic migrants are frequently members of discriminated-against or marginalized populations. "Sending a family member elsewhere allows the family to diversify against the risk of bad outcomes at home"[66]—a pragmatic survival and development strategy for impoverished communities. But though there is a continuum in real life, the legal framework, both international and domestic, is predicated on a dichotomy: the assumption that "economic migration" is not coerced but chosen, that the economic migrant is exercising a free choice while the refugee is not.

As with refugees, so with economic migrants—many breadwinners set out on the journey alone, leaving dependents behind in the hopes that the family can reunify quickly, once the breadwinner is established in the new country. In practice, the obstacles to realizing this often turn out to be considerable. Again the result is that children separated from their parents pass years without the benefit of their love and care, often formative years when future aspirations and affective bonds are most deeply formed. Sometimes delays, whether caused by the migrants or by government red tape, prevent family reunification altogether.

Historically for migrants, economic activity and family reunification were thought of as taking place in separated spheres: contract work in the destination state, family reunification back home.[67] In part this was a response to state policy and practice, an approach well captured by a 1911 US Immigration Commission report: "In the case of the Mexican, he is less desirable as a citizen than as a laborer."[68] Correlated with this approach is the emergence of a view of migrant workers as inherently "temporary," "biologically destined" to return home, as one scholar has perceptively observed, after completing his (and the "temporary Mexican" was overwhelmingly male) natural role: "The Mexican is adapted for that special character of labor. . . . [He is] specially fitted for the burdensome task of bending his back to pick the cotton and the burdensome task of grubbing the fields," as Representative Carlos Bee, a Democrat from Texas put it to the 1920 US Congressional Hearings on the "Temporary Admission of Illiterate Mexican Laborers." A key policy assumption underpinning this approach is that the economic migrant is always "free" to go home, to exercise his or her family life where the family is. So, the reasoning goes, the destination (sometimes called "host") state has no overriding obligation to protect the right to family life, because there are other alternative sites where it can be exercised, namely back home. The ability of migrants to participate and contribute fully to the society they work in is strongly influenced, of course, by the public portrayal of their role and status: groups identified as "temporary" are likely to experience obstacles to rewarding development of a full life in their new environment.[69] As chapter 2 will demonstrate, this approach persists even where "returning back home" in fact means moving a child born to workers abroad away from the child's home to a new country, simply because it is the parent's home country. The child's interest in family unity is assumed to be value free as regards location. This conveniently matches the pervasive bias in states' immigration policies.[70] Referring to US citizen children born in the United States to Mexican laborers participating in the Bracero contract work program, the Immigration and Naturalization Service argued: "As small children, they are much better off with their parents whom they have every legal and natural right to accompany to their homes in Mexico."[71] Many states today have restrictive policies that mirror the earlier, more exploitative and instrumental approach to migration. Temporary worker programs in the Gulf States, where the contemporary rate of increase in economic progress and migration exceeds any other area, are a dramatic case in point—the opportunities for family reunification "in country" are severely restricted.[72]

Economic migration often takes place against a backdrop of suboptimal home circumstances and powerful push factors. A contrast is instructive. Consider corporate transfers, where the executive, the spouse, the family members, and sometimes nannies or other staff are all relocated together, to a well-appointed house, with guaranteed employment, schooling, health care, immigration status, even social introductions, all prearranged. Apart from the adjustment to food, language, and perhaps weather, few challenges present themselves. By comparison, the much more common blue-collar or unskilled economic migration is little if not a series of challenges, before, during, and after the migration itself. The migrant leaves behind unemployment, debt, unmet medical needs, housing repairs, educational aspirations, and travels in search of work, hoping to establish a viable base and then eventually to reunify. "[M]oving is commonly described by the poor as both a *necessity*—part of a coping strategy for families experiencing extreme hardship—and an *opportunity*—a means of expanding a household's livelihoods and ability to accumulate assets."[73] Dixie's case is typical:

> I was a single mother raising two children, so the financial squeeze continued to worsen as my pay shrank. My children grew older. They had greater needs. . . . We were all living together—my parents, my kids, me,

> and my mentally disabled sister. Then disaster struck. My father came down with cancer and suddenly we had huge medical bills. . . . We simply didn't have enough money to make ends meet. . . . I began to think that moving to America was an answer to my problems.[74]

An autobiographical diversion describes my introduction to the notion that family life is a precious but scarce resource. Though this narrative relates to events that took place over thirty years ago, in my first job, it is uncannily replicated in events taking place at the time of this writing. I was first brought face-to-face with the elusive quest for family life when I started working in the large working-class city of Birmingham, in the British Midlands, as a recent graduate in the mid-1970s. At the time, I worked on an Oxford University action research project in Saltley, an inner-city area in Birmingham with tiny brick-terraced houses that had for centuries been occupied by coal miners and their families. For several years prior to my arrival, parts of Saltley had been settled by Pakistani immigrants from the remote Mirpur District of Azad (meaning free) Kashmir. Mainly young men, these immigrants had been forced to leave their villages and fields, because a huge national dam had flooded vast tracts of Mirpur including their lands, reducing them to landless and unemployed laborers. To survive and support their families, the men followed the entrepreneurial co-villagers before them and traveled to the booming postwar industrial heartland of the United Kingdom. Today we might call them environmental refugees, but in the 1960s and 1970s, they were considered migrant workers, immigrating for economic reasons. For years these former peasants worked day and night shifts in factories, often using beds alternately in multioccupied apartments in the brick terraces, living frugally and sending nearly all their income home to their families. Every three or four years, each worker would travel back to the village, and there, finally, have the luxury of a few months of family life before returning to the factory floor. This pattern might have continued undisturbed until the men were ready to retire and enjoy the fruits of their years of labor back home with their families. (Fast-forwarding to today and shifting countries, we can easily transpose this scenario to Eighteenth Street in Chicago, and Michoacán in Mexico, to the outskirts of Paris and villages in Mali, to Brussels, to Rome, to New York, to hundreds of other metropolitan centers to which impoverished young migrants have migrated, in complex stages and with similar obstacles to those I am about to describe.)

But my arrival in Birmingham coincided with radical changes in British immigration law. In the early 1970s, from a period of rapid postwar industrial growth and labor shortage, the country was moving toward an economic downturn, and, as we witness to this day, immigrants became a convenient scapegoat. As unemployment rose, so calls for immigration restriction and border controls increased, resulting in radical changes in migration law that hindered frequent trips to and from Pakistan for Saltley's Mirpuris and drastically tightened the immigration rules regarding family reunion.[75] The relatively straightforward circular migration pattern that had become the norm for thousands, became impossible. Much like Mexican and other immigrants in the United States and Europe in the early twenty-first century, the hardworking Pakistani factory workers realized that the relative freedom of movement they had once enjoyed could no longer be relied on. Instead, to ensure continued access to employment and at the same time the continuation of their family life, they had to take at face value the family unity rights enshrined in law. The United Kingdom, like all members of the Council of Europe, has ratified the European Convention of Human Rights, a cardinal article of which protects the right to respect for family life. This right applies not only to citizens but to all residents. The Pakistani immigrant workers therefore applied under UK immigration law for "entry clearance" or immigration permission for their wives and dependent children.

This is where my education started. What was a fundamental human right, the right for a father to live with his dependent child, the right for a child to grow up with his or her parents, turned out to be a Kafkaesque nightmare. In order to qualify for "entry clearance" to the United Kingdom, the village wives and children had to prove they were "related as claimed," that they were indeed the wife and children of the applicant in the United Kingdom. Consular offices were instructed to scrutinize cases carefully to ensure that false claims were detected and refused, and that only people who were "genuinely related as claimed" received the coveted entry certificates. They also had to prove that they could "support and accommodate their dependents without recourse to public funds," the latter term defined increasingly expansively to include a wide range of welfare benefits to which the immigrants themselves were, as a matter of law, entitled. The complexity of the procedure, the documentary requirements, and the other procedural difficulties became a Sisyphean challenge.[76] The delays in processing applications (likely the product of an informal and unacknowledged quota system) rapidly escalated to a point where four to six years became a normal waiting period. In the process, babies became children, children became teenagers, teenagers became young adults. Meanwhile of course childhood was passing without enjoyment of family life.

Once a family's application reached the head of the queue, other problems presented themselves. How do you prove a family relationship across thousands of miles? The standard method of proof of course relies on documents—marriage certificates, birth certificates, passports, letters, affidavits, photographs. And indeed the British immigration authorities required all of these, as do immigration authorities in the United States and Europe today. But in remote villages, where most of the population is illiterate, where birth registration is intermittent, where government services are nonexistent and documents scarce, unreliable and heavily dependent on expensive bribes, this method presented significant difficulties. Birth certificates were unavailable or unreliable (scarcity producing a lively market in expensive forgeries that were easily discredited), records of engagement or marriage dates were inconsistent and hard to retrieve (chosen and remembered by astrological criteria, not Western calendars), proof of a child's age was often nonexistent. Where birth certificates did exist, they tended to record everyone as having been born on January 1 (a bureaucratic convenience for village scribes that prior to UK government scrutiny, had no significance) and were therefore suspect even if they were original and genuine reflections of birth registration. Relying on documents to prove demographic facts was therefore problematic, as indeed it still is today for thousands of immigrant families whose children's births have not been registered, whose marriages are not officially certified, who live outside a paper (let alone electronic) economy.

What other methods exist to prove one's entitlement to family reunion? A second strategy, often supplementary to the first but in the case of documentary scarcity a key stand-alone tool, is oral testimony that one is indeed "related as claimed." Convincing and "consistent" storytelling can paint a coherent picture of family life and relationships as a substitute for documentary certainty. But this storytelling does not take place in the village square, at the well, or in the mosque. Nor does it unfold between peers, or between members of a broadly shared communicative universe. Instead, it has to be performed, in interview form, through poorly trained but often arrogant interpreters loyal to their employers and impatient with, even contemptuous of, their less educated, nervous fellow citizens. A cumbersome and extended procedure developed, with interpreters translating questions from British government officials at the embassy in Islamabad (the capital of Pakistan) to villagers reporting for their scheduled interview, then translating the villagers' answers back to the officials. Officials too had a vigorous skepticism, sometimes bordering on contempt, toward their rural clientèle. And so it was that women, children, and babies, from the small villages of Mirpur, left their home territory for the first time in their lives to undertake the long, exhausting, and expensive journey to the Pakistani capital, to be interviewed by British consular visa officials in the massive edifice of the British Embassy. Many families had to make the journey multiple times, as appointments they were given often turned out to have been canceled at the last minute, documents they had to produce were not considered adequate, family members required for interview were not notified that they had to accompany the main applicants, village scribes misread or mistranslated interview dates. The journey from village to embassy lasted several days, starting with a long walk to the bus stop, and continuing with crowded and uncomfortable but costly bus rides and multiple stops along bumpy and dusty roads, to the alien and intimidating city.

Most daunting of all however was the interview. In an attempt to chart family relationships that formed part of a foreign and largely incomprehensible cultural tradition, British consular officials devised long and detailed questionnaires to test the accuracy and "consistency" of the narratives offered. Always on the lookout for cheats, for bogus applicants attempting to secure the coveted entry clearance by deceit or fraud, the officials subjected the villager applicants to interviews sometimes lasting entire days. Women who had never met a foreigner, let alone answered questions through an interpreter or been alone in a room full of men, had to engage in an utterly unfamiliar social exchange—direct question and answer. Failure to look the questioner in the eye was interpreted as evidence of shiftiness, not shyness. The applicants were asked questions that sought to test knowledge of the family-tree names and dates of birth of children, cousins, aunts, uncles, grandparents, great-aunts and -uncles on both sides of the family. Questions included tests to ascertain knowledge of shared daily rituals: "Where do you eat your meals?"; "Where do you hang your clothes to dry?"; "How many sheep/cows/goats do you have and where do you keep them?" Some questions were designed to reveal distinctive family details—"What was the weather like on your wedding day?"; "Where were your children born?";

"Who was present?"; " What did your spouse wear?" After months, sometimes years, the translated and transcribed answers were transmitted, by diplomatic box, to the Home Office, the government department in the United Kingdom responsible for immigration control.

Eventually, the "applicant" or sponsor—typically the husband/father resident in Saltley—was questioned, again through interpreters, by immigration officers at the Birmingham immigration office, and asked the same questions. Different answers to the questions—"discrepancies"—were seen as inconsistencies, proof of lies. So families struggled to memorize together correct family trees, to learn dates that had no meaning in their recording system, to practice correct answers to questions like "where do you keep your string beds?" or "how many goats do you have?"—the equivalent of where do you park your car, or how many apples do you have, questions that could have several correct answers, and often made no sense to migrant workers living away from village life for years. But the methodology was followed relentlessly—and thousands of children were denied permission to join their fathers because of alleged inconsistencies. As a history of the period documents:

> There has been a high rate of refusal of applications for entry [from families] from the Indian subcontinent each year since 1977. . . . More than half (56%) of the applications from wives and children in Bangladesh were refused during 1983. . . . The figures . . . reflected the entry clearance officers' practice . . . of refusing the whole family if there was any doubt about the identity of even *one* member.[77]

The advent of DNA partly solved some of the problems of proof, where cost, access to efficient blood collection, transport and lab analysis did not impede the effective use of the test to compare blood samples drawn from village children to those of their father thousands of miles away. But by then generations of children had turned eighteen and missed an opportunity to be reunited with their families.

The Right to Respect for Family Life? The Hurdles of Reestablishing Unity

My experience goes back decades. But the drivers of contemporary family separation are remarkably similar. Take the situation of Mexican and other Central American immigrants in the United States. Many, like the Mirpuri emigrants from Pakistan to the United Kingdom, left home to escape poverty and unemployment, natural disasters, or shrinking agricultural yields. Throughout the twentieth century, they left families behind in the hopes of finding employment—earning, saving, and eventually comfortably supporting their families and a family life back home. To do this, like the Pakistanis, they worked long hours in the classic "DDD" (dirty, dangerous, difficult) jobs, for low wages and in poor working conditions, filling jobs left vacant by the more prosperous or protected domestic work force.[78] And like the Pakistanis, they traveled home from time to time, to enjoy family life, to savor some of the fruits of their labors. But in the United States, as in Europe, migration laws changed in the latter part of the twentieth century, and what had been a fairly easy trip to and from Mexico across the border became increasingly perilous and costly. Workers in the United States therefore decided to bring their families to join them.[79] Again, this was easier said than done. Problems of proof, of access to affordable and competent legal help for the complex bureaucratic procedures involved, of securing resources to comply with documentary and fee requirements prevented immigrant parents from bringing children to join them, even where they could prove their relationships were genuine. These problems persist to this day. Securing birth and marriage certificates and other identity documents that the authorities accept as genuine can be a challenge, even for families with some members born in developed countries. In some US states, for example, children of Mexican descent born with the help of midwives have had difficulty convincing the authorities to grant them passports because of suspicions of birth certificate fraud.[80]

Several other obstacles regularly prove insurmountable and perpetuate the division of families. One is the reliable proof of age, for only children under a certain age—the exact age ceiling varies from country to country but is typically somewhere between twelve and eighteen years—are admissible as dependents of their parents. Establishing age recalls the difficulties mentioned earlier about proving that one is "related as claimed." The absence of reliable documentary proof often leads to the use of other techniques for estimating age—techniques immigration officials slavishly follow as scientific evidence, but pediatric experts frequently discount. A range of tests is used across destination states—wrist or dental X-rays in the United States, clavicle X-rays in the Netherlands, dental and wrist X-rays in the United Kingdom. Medical bodies have for decades challenged before parliamentary and congressional authorities the reliability of all these one-dimensional physical strategies of age-determination tests, asserting that a two-year margin of error must be assumed. They have confirmed that malnutrition and dietary differences can interfere with standardized testing assumptions,[81] and that population differences jeopardize the reliability of the whole exercise. Nevertheless immigration authorities still regularly refuse entry on the basis that child applicants have exceeded the age ceiling. In August 2011, Thomas Hammarberg, the Council of Europe Commissioner for Human Rights, urged relevant authorities to improve their age-determination methods, to use these tests only in cases of "serious doubt," and to adopt a multidisciplinary approach, combining "physical, social and psychological maturity assessments, which respect the child's culture, dignity and physical integrity." In the absence of "serious doubt," he argued, authorities should rely on documents submitted by the migrant.[82] As a prominent doctor publicly commented, referring to US immigration authorities' practice:

> I am extremely troubled by the inaccuracy of the current . . . practice of using bone age and dental age standards to judge chronological age among undocumented immigrants. . . . This practice imparts an unwarranted scientific legitimacy to what I understand to be a social-political-legal problem.[83]

For effected families, refusals based on unfavorable age-determination tests are costly, time-consuming, and legally complex to overturn. But they are not the only technical hurdle facing children left behind.

Another equally unpleasant device for complicating the reunification of children with immigrant parents forced to leave them behind is the so-called sole responsibility rule, a British rule that is widely applied against single parents. It does not take much thought to realize that a requirement that an immigrant parent have "sole responsibility" for a child in another country (even continent) amounts to a comprehensive reunification ban. To be sure, the immigrant parent might bear the primary economic responsibility for the child by regularly sending maintenance money home. But inevitably the day-to-day responsibility for the child's safety, school attendance, nutrition, medical care, and other critical aspects of responsible parenting will fall on local caregivers. And yet, British governments continue to refuse family reunification because the UK-based parent has not successfully demonstrated his or her "sole responsibility" for the child back home. A case that has laboriously been working its way through the British courts for over three and a half years poignantly illustrates the point. A Bangladeshi immigrant, long legally settled in the United Kingdom, applied to sponsor his three daughters to join him on the basis that there was no one in Bangladesh to care for them. At the time of the initial application, the children, to whom the sponsor was regularly sending financial support, were being cared for only by their elderly paternal grandmother, having been separated since childhood from their mother, who suffered from mental illness. The sponsor even stated that one of the three girls was not able to attend school because the journey alone from their remote village to the school was too dangerous.[84] Yet the application was initially refused by the entry clearance officer, and though this finding was reversed by a tribunal of first instance, a second instance appellate court found in favor of the government and reinstated the refusal order. It fell to a third appellate court to review the evidence and the law—by which time the sole carer, the elderly grandmother, had died. The courts had throughout the case accepted that the family in the United Kingdom, the father and his sons, had sufficient means to support the three girls were they to be admitted. The relationship between father and daughters was also not in question. What the case hinged on, however, was whether the evidence of the mother's mental illness was adequate to establish the father's sole responsibility, and whether the financial contributions made to the girls by their working brothers in the United Kingdom, vitiated the father's claim to have "sole responsibility" for the daughters.[85] The legal technicalities need concern us no further. What is remarkable is the fact that three indigent girls in a remote village in Bangladesh, one of whom was unable to safely attend school and all three of whom wished to be reunited with their only healthy parent, were separated from him for three years after he applied to bring them to join him. In this subtle, often invisible way, without the need for public racist pronouncements or explicit quota systems, the political reluctance to support the legitimate immigration of uneducated foreign children and unskilled adolescents trumps the principled modern support for nondiscriminatory human rights. Without the benefit of hands-on legal advocacy or a careful analysis of reported cases, the resulting ambivalence in government policy escapes public attention.

The obstacles to family reunification for underrepresented immigrant populations are at their most perverse, perhaps, when families are permanently separated because the migrant parent's means are considered inadequate to support family reunification. Exploitative labor contracts, where blue-collar immigrant workers are paid minimal wages, even after years of service, become the basis for enforced separation, or the false option of returning home to unemployment and destitution. Various international bodies have criticized unreasonable financial burdens, be they administrative fees or income requirements imposed on immigrant sponsors seeking to exercise family reunification rights.[86] But this remains a popular immigration control device. The case of Mr. Ali, a British citizen of Bangladeshi origin living in the United Kingdom and attempting to bring his wife and six children in Bangladesh to join him, illustrates this point. He had to demonstrate that the family could be "supported and accommodated without recourse to public funds." To discharge his burden of proof, Mr. Ali argued that earnings from his eldest son and accommodation provided by his brother, both also legally residing in the United Kingdom, should be factored into the calculations. The government disagreed, insisting that this joint family's proof of ability to cope financially was not adequate and that complete self-sufficiency of the individual sponsor was essential.

As a matter of social justice, one might question why a law-abiding resident, indeed citizen, who had paid all his taxes should not be entitled to social welfare benefits irrespective of where his family lived. But the policy reflects the ambivalence toward the rights of immigrant children—their right to family life can be nullified by fiscal considerations, in circumstances where nonimmigrant children would not have to face separation from their parents. The stark reality is that this approach frequently prevents children moving from extremely resource-poor settings to situations where their access to basic amenities such as health care, education, and shelter would be greatly improved. Fortunately the (then) House of Lords disagreed with the culturally myopic interpretation of family support and the insistence that Mr. Ali support his family without the assistance of his relatives. After eight years of delay, the wife and children joined Mr. Ali, and the family was eventually permitted to look after their financial needs in the United Kingdom as they saw fit.[87] But many other families (according to an April 2012 briefing paper, up to 50 percent of the working immigrant population in the United Kingdom) whose means do not satisfy the authorities' definition of self-sufficiency, risk being forced to live apart.[88]

Other potentially devastating obstacles exist. In several European countries, cultural factors are used to justify questionable selection criteria for immigrant admission, criteria that can militate against family reunification. I have already cited international authority affirming that immigration authorities should adopt a broader, more culturally inclusive concept of the family than the predominantly biological, nuclear Western one. This approach protects the rights of children to live within the "functional families" to which they are accustomed[89] and encourages the authorities to conform their reasoning to developments in domestic family law and current international human-rights-law understandings of family.[90] However the question of cultural integrity, and what reasonable criteria for inclusion might include, goes beyond the inquiry into the composition of the family. Other requirements increasingly compromise older children's access to family life, as states explore the viability of a series of "integration conditions."[91] A common assumption is that teenagers, particularly those over fifteen, have less compelling needs to reunify with parents than younger children. Age-based discrimination of this sort has rightly been criticized: adolescent girls, in particular, may be most vulnerable to early marriage or other adverse circumstances, where they are compelled to live without close parental defense of their interests.[92] Another assumption is that older children should be required to demonstrate their aptitude for cultural adaptation as a precondition to securing the right to reunify with immigrant parents. In the Netherlands, for example, since 2006, prospective immigrants over age sixteen have to prove knowledge of the essence of Dutch language and culture to be admissible.[93] This is not as extreme as the process for obtaining Dutch citizenship (which at one stage included being questioned about a video showing homosexuals kissing in public and women sunbathing topless to confirm the acceptance of such conduct supposedly associated with "Dutchness").[94] Nevertheless this process of enforced cultural assimilation indirectly discriminates against immigrant children's ability to exercise the fundamental right to family life. Why should a teenager seeking to join a parent have to learn, *before* being granted admission, about customs such as leaving house curtains undrawn or bringing gifts to birthday parties?[95]

The use of cultural assimilation to drive immigration restriction is not limited to the Netherlands. In France, hostility to young immigrant populations in the urban centers has led to proposals to eliminate family-based immigration altogether.[96] And in Germany, a residence permit is conditional on proof of knowledge of German and of a capacity to integrate into the "German way of life." Increasingly, immigration law is being used as an instrument for controlling religious and cultural diversity, a role better suited to vigorous and frank discussion between those living together within the community, whether citizens or residents. To be sure, as Orgad suggests, states have a legitimate interest in ensuring that immigrants comply with a minimal set of fundamental principles prohibiting violent or intolerant behavior just as states have an interest in ensuring that residents and citizens comply with such norms.[97] As the 2003 European Union Directive on Family Reunification mandates, states may "deny entry and residence [to] family members on grounds of public policy, public security, or public health."[98] This affords states considerable leeway. But several states now violate the tolerance they claim to insist on by requiring that immigrants, including adolescents seeking family reunification with parents, espouse a narrowly tailored concept of what is good or that they demonstrate at interview a broad range of progressive liberal opinions. With these requirements, cultural assimilation becomes an exclusionary and discriminatory precondition to enjoyment of the right to family unity, given that no such cultural or political tests are imposed on the domestic population as necessary hurdles prior to their enjoyment of family unity.

Children's Right to Family Reunion and European Human Rights Law

International courts, charged with balancing the rights of states against those of individual children, have often deferred to immigration-control exigencies and sidestepped children's strong claim to family life. A survey of decided cases indicates a deep-seated ambivalence within judicial thinking, reflected in sharply contrasting judgments by majority and dissenting judges. Torn between the sovereign state's prerogative to exercise border control and the human being's right to respect for family life, courts have had difficulty reaching unanimity. The following cases illustrate this dynamic.

One case concerns a Turkish family in Switzerland, a member state of the forty-seven-country-strong Council of Europe covered by the 1950 European Convention of Human Rights. This Convention is quite similar to the Universal Declaration of Human Rights (UDHR) in the scope of its rights protection but it is much more effective in terms of enforcement because it is justiciable: claimants have rights of action they can exercise through individual litigation in courts. However, precisely because the ECHR is a binding treaty that creates state obligations and affords individuals the opportunity to enforce their individual rights, unlike the UDHR, many of its articles are qualified rather than absolute. They reflect the tension between rights entitlements and state interest, the pressure to balance principles that may conflict, or to establish a mechanism for introducing pragmatic governance considerations as a qualification on individual rights. This is true of the right to respect for family life. Contrast the generic terms of the UDHR statement with the much more nuanced and qualified articulation set forth in the Convention. Article 16(3) of the UDHR states: "The family is the natural and fundamental group unit of society and is entitled to protection by society and the State." By contrast, Article 8 of the ECHR states:

1. Everyone has the right to respect for his private and family life, his home and his correspondence.
2. There shall be no interference by a public authority with the exercise of this right except such as is in accordance with the law and is necessary in a democratic society in the interests of national security, public safety or the economic well-being of the country, for the prevention of disorder or crime, for the protection of health or morals, or for the protection of the rights and freedoms of others.

A European Court of Human Rights (ECtHR) case illustrates the consequences that flow from this qualified legal approach, the way it translates into judicial ambivalence, and the practical impact it has on the right to family reunification. A Turkish couple consisting of a disabled husband and a severely epileptic wife with a baby placed in a children's home in Switzerland sought to bring their seven-year-old son from Turkey to join them. The case included undisputed evidence that the wife required medical treatment unavailable in Turkey, from which it followed that family reunion with the seven-year-old was only possible in Switzerland. The Swiss government argued that the family's reliance on state welfare benefits disqualified them from bringing their son in to join them. It emerged in the court proceedings that the child in Turkey was not attending school on a regular basis due to the absence of financial resources and adult care and that the parents, long settled in Switzerland, had no means of changing this situation while the child remained in Turkey. Taking judicial note of the fact that, as the government counsel pointed out, "in Switzerland immigration is a particularly sensitive subject," the Court upheld the Swiss government's refusal of entry permission to the child to join his parents. The dissenting judge commented critically on the Court's failure to effectively enforce respect for the family life of this unit: "The European Court of Human Rights has to ensure, in particular, that States interests do not crush those of an individual, especially in situations where political pressure—such as the growing dislike of immigrants in most Member States—may inspire State authorities to harsh decisions."[99] In the final analysis, the Court accepted the government's arguments that a clear distinction between nationals and non-nationals in terms of access to the territory and its resources was fundamental and that the distinction justified privileging immigration control over human rights–based arguments.[100]

It is not just permanent resident immigrants who have found their family unity rights trumped by their long-term home state. Even nationals have found their rights of citizenship subordinated to border-control concerns. This is particularly so, as is often the case, when the "real" identity, that is, the racial or ethnic identity, of the national suggests a cross-border affiliation that the court can cite to strengthen the legitimacy of an argument in favor of the exercise of family life elsewhere. The increasing salience of dual nationality has led some to look behind the acquired nationality (the return by the United States of Maher Arar,[101] a Canadian citizen of Syrian origin, to Syria, where he was tortured and illegally detained for a year, is the most egregious case in point). With this devaluation has come skepticism about the significance of nationality for naturalized immigrants. In some cases it is hard to avoid the inference that racialized decision making plays a key part in the administrative or judicial outcome. An ECtHR case on family reunion for immigrants illustrates this problem clearly. A father, who had dual Dutch and Moroccan nationality, and had settled in the Netherlands for some years, applied for family reunification for his ten-year-old son. He had not done so earlier because he and the child's mother, with whom the child resided in Morocco, were divorced and the boy was living in Morocco with his mother. However, once the mother died, the only alternatives for the boy were boarding school in Morocco or family reunification with the father in the Netherlands. The Dutch immigration officials, and later the Dutch judicial authorities, decided against the applicant. He appealed to the European Court of Human Rights. The court upheld the Netherlands government decision to refuse the child permission for family reunion with his Dutch father. It made its decision on the basis that the child had strong links with the country of origin and the father had no entitlement to choose the place where family reunion should take place—he had, the court pointed out, the option of leaving his business interests and life in the Netherlands and moving to Morocco to be with his son. The interesting question in this case was why the fact that the applicant father had acquired Dutch nationality did not immediately rule out this discussion. The answer is not hard to find: the Dutch father was called Ahmut. Had he been called Peters or van Peters the ECtHR's judgment might have been different. This is what the dissenting judge had to say about the decision:

> The arguments in support of the Netherlands authorities' decision to separate the son from his father do not weigh very heavily and even reflect a restrictive spirit incompatible with the very meaning of the Convention and the concept of human rights. . . . The father had acquired Netherlands nationality, and in any country, a national is entitled to have his son join him, even if the son does not have the same nationality. How does it come about that in the present case this right was refused him? I cannot think that it is because the Dutch father was called "Ahmut." However, the suspicion of discrimination must inevitably lurk in people's minds.[102]

Family reunification for children left behind by immigrant parents, even in countries governed by a vigorous and effective system of supervisory human rights norms, is fraught and problematic. Where no such international oversight exists, as in the United States, the situation of children seeking to join their parents abroad is no easier, as the next section demonstrates.

Reunifying with Parents in the United States: The Human Cost of Political Procrastination

In the United States today, cultural tools such as those described above are not used to restrict immigrant entry. Given the accepted heterogeneity of American life, such narrowly crafted conceptions of expected social behavior would be intolerable. But egregious obstacles to family reunion for children seeking to join their immigrant parents exist in the United States too, suggesting the same ambivalence about the importance of protecting immigrant children's rights in the United States as in Europe, even if instrumentalized differently.

Family reunion has long been and remains the primary source of legal migration into the United States, accounting for nearly 65 percent of the immigrant entry visas granted in 2011.[103] Yet the system of preferences that determines family reunion for everyone except "immediate"[104] relatives of US citizens is marked by extensive delays, suggesting a low government priority attached to protection of a child's rights to enjoyment of family life. Authorities typically process the visa petitions of spouses and children of lawful permanent residents (F2A visas) filed two years previously,[105] contributing to reunion delays of four or more years. At present there are approximately 400,000 spouses and dependent children waiting to be granted family entry visas.[106] The human cost of these procedures emerges from interviews with affected family members. As a child from El Salvador put it: "I was four years old, and I wanted a bicycle. My mother told me she was going to go work at another job to get me a bicycle, and she would be back soon." He was eventually smuggled into the United States when he was twelve: "There is still a distance. . . . [T]he early years are when you get attached to your parents. I got attached to my grandparents."[107] And of course grandparents suffer too: "I couldn't eat or sleep in the days that they were gone. . . . It was their parents' dream to have their kids with them, and I couldn't refuse them. They are their parents, and they wanted the best for them," recounted a tearful Salvadorian grandmother, whose grandchildren were eventually intercepted by smugglers and returned to her.[108]

But immigrants who manage to file family reunification petitions before their children turn twenty-one are relatively fortunate. More troubling, is the situation of the thousands, blocked by unseemly administrative delays, who only become eligible to lodge family reunification petitions after their children have "aged out" beyond twenty-one. The delay for these "sons and daughters" seeking to join (noncitizen) immigrant parents is far longer than the delay for younger children, stretching to decades. Evelyn Santos, a Filipina supermarket clerk living in Northern California, is only too familiar with this. Having started her quest for family reunification in the United States over two decades ago, she still has her two older sons stuck in the queue waiting in the Philippines. The fifty-five-year-old mother jokes with her son: "Am I still alive when you come here?"[109]

Because of these inordinate delays, some families have tried suing the federal government to take advantage of the 2002 Child Status Protection Act,[110] passed to prevent family separation caused by administrative immigration delays. A case in point is the sad decision in *Matter of Xiuyi Wang*.[111] Mr. Wang, a Chinese national, was the beneficiary of a family-reunion visa petition filed in 1992 by his US citizen sister; Mr. Wang's wife and three minor children, including his ten-year-old daughter, were derivative beneficiaries. Twelve years after the petition was filed, Mr. Wang finally became eligible for an entry visa; but by then his daughter was twenty-two, not a "child" and was no longer able to acquire beneficiary status under the original petition. So in 2006, less than a year after entering the United States, Mr. Wang filed a petition for his daughter. This was approved but the authorities refused to retain the 1992 priority date for visa eligibility and instead they set the clock ticking from the 2006 filing date. At the time of the decision, petitions filed five years earlier were being granted for this category of beneficiary.

The decision therefore condemns Mr. Wang's daughter to years of separation from her parents and siblings, to a wait of approximately *eighteen years* from the time of the original immigration petition and to remaining unmarried unless she is willing to sacrifice family reunification in the United States altogether. The government's justification for this divisive policy: "avoiding open-ended petitions with no timeliness considerations."[112] The parents and child pay the emotional price of prolonged family separation because of the low political priority of family unity,[113] like the UK-based Mirpuri workers from Pakistan applying for family reunification in the 1970s. The misery caused by long delays in securing legal family reunification visas is compounded by the increasing concern that many immigrant parents feel about making the trip back home, particularly to Central America, including the fear of possible exclusion when reentering the United States. As a result even documented parents arrange for third parties to bring their children across the border.

Reunification via Smugglers: The Hazardous Route to Family Unity for Children of Irregular Migrants

Poverty is often the driving force propelling family separation; and it is the most important factor preventing compliance with government family reunification requirements. Poor families do not qualify for reunification as easily as wealthy ones because provisions prohibiting reliance on public funds militate against them, because priority visas reserved for entrepreneurs or high net worth individuals are inaccessible, and because competent legal advice is scarce. As a result, less systematic and reliable strategies than securing entry visas often become central to the migration process. Stories of extreme exposure are commonplace. Here is one:

> "In May 2003, nineteen migrants, including a five-year-old child, died of asphyxiation, heat exposure, and dehydration in the back of a smuggler's truck in South Texas. The smuggler had fled leaving the immigrants to die. One of the dead had worked five years in the United States before he returned to Mexico to fetch his children, hoping to provide them comforts he could not give them in Mexico."[114]

Undocumented migrants[115] face particularly severe hardships in the process of family reunification. Their irregular status effects their earning capacity, their access to secure accommodation, and of course the legal basis on which to seek entry for dependent children. In the United States, immigrant workers without legal status—a growing number, as opportunities for unskilled legal migration have shrunk[116]—have little alternative but to try and bring their families in if they want to maintain their jobs and enjoy family life.[117] Increasingly militarized and heavily policed southern US borders[118] make the prospects of reentry for irregular migrants ever more uncertain. So growing numbers of undocumented immigrant parents are making risky arrangements for their children left behind to join them in the United States.

> [C]hildren can no longer simply be brought over the border by an aunt or a fellow villager and then delivered to the parents. Despite this, parents sometimes send for very young children—the youngest child in a seven bus convoy headed for the US "was a one and a half year old boy named Diego, who was traveling with his 7 year old brother, Eduardo, and a 5 year old cousin."[119]

"[A]nd there have been some notorious cases of busloads of children being transported to the US-Mexican border."[120] This phenomenon is not confined to Mexican parents—it affects all Central American migrant communities and is at least a decade old. In April 2002 the *New York Times* reported that

Guatemalan authorities had intercepted forty-nine children, "from toddlers to teenagers, who were being illegally transported from El Salvador to the United States," reportedly part of a highly organized smuggling network charging $5,000 per child. Another Central American child-smuggling ring broken up by the authorities in 2002 was estimated to have smuggled one hundred children per month into the United States.[121] Some of the children involved are extremely young—Victor Flores, "four years old, maybe five, was abandoned on a bus by a female smuggler."[122]

"Any human being wants to be with family. . . . What is happening with the smugglers is just a form of family reunification." Certainly, for parents seeking to bring over children without visas, it has become necessary to hire travel professionals, smugglers, or coyotes to ferry children across safe border-crossing points. The professionals also have to secure effective documents, bribe relevant border control agents, and use safe routes through the desert at appropriate times. "The growth in child smuggling . . . reflects how difficult it is to get into the country."[123] These increasingly specialized and costly services cater to a growing demand for assistance with unaccompanied-child border-crossings.

Some estimate that over 48,000 children a year,[124] make the dangerous trek from Central or South America to the US border with smugglers and traffickers of various sorts. As chapter 4 describes, this phenomenon is associated with increasing criminality, including a rising incidence of robbery, physical assaults, and accidents. Reported rates of sexual violence against girls along the migration routes are extremely high.[125] According to Sonia Nazario, whose compelling story of the cross-border journey of a Honduran child, Enrique, received a Pulitzer Prize: "The journey is hard for the Mexicans but harder still for . . . the [children] from Central America. . . . They are hunted like animals by corrupt police, bandits and gang members deported from the United States."[126]

Some children have described these journeys as "an adventure that would carry them back to their parents' embrace . . . [noting] how long it had been since they had last seen their mothers and fathers."[127] But for many the journey is a nightmare, and sometimes it ends in tragedy. According to one study, "Most [children] are robbed, beaten or raped, usually several times. Some are killed."[128] On May 21, 2003, the US Border Patrol "received an anonymous telephone call" about a girl who fell ill and died trying to cross into the United States with relatives after she was abandoned by her smugglers.

Eventually her body was found: "That was an especially tragic case, because some members of the group that were traveling with the minor and later abandoned her were her relatives."[129] Some run out of money along the way and are forced into prostitution. Smugglers have been known to abandon children when they fear detection, and to "deprive them of food or water so that they won't ask to go the bathroom."[130] Sometimes smugglers hold on to children to extort more money than originally agreed, and even threaten abuse. According to court documents in a case involving smugglers and two Salvadorian boys transferred across the border to Houston in October 1999, when the family failed to produce the fee demanded, the boys were taken away in the trunk of a van: "If we don't get our money, we're going to use you like girls or send you back to El Salvador," one of the boys reported being told.[131] Yet worse, some children simply vanish altogether.

Sometimes the family must borrow money to pay the smugglers.[132] Often the money invested by parents in this hazardous form of family reunion is wasted. The trip is intercepted, the child detained by the authorities and then summarily sent back across the border to Mexico or to a government-run children's shelter in Mexico. Here the child anxiously waits for contact from parents, and the parents desperately seek access to the child, sometimes for days, weeks, or even months on end. Noé, age eleven, and Moises, age thirteen, waited for two weeks in one such shelter for "a call from the mother they haven't seen in 8 years."[133] They are not alone. On occasion, during the summer months in these Mexican shelters, "the staff puts extra mattresses on the floor to accommodate the crush of children." Children intercepted on their way from farther south through Mexico as they head for the US border can experience terrifying and squalid journeys. The following report describes a common situation: a group of Salvadorian children found by a joint El Salvador, Guatemala, Mexico, and US law-enforcement effort were being held in "deplorable conditions" in a safe house outside Mexico City while "another handful were being kept at the airport in Tijuana."[134]

A reliable estimate places the number of unaccompanied, undocumented children removed from the United States across the southern border each year at 43,000.[135] If the child is stopped by immigration officials, "the family incurs a massive debt and the child feels a double sense of failure—for not making it across the border and because the family is now worse off economically than it was before."[136] Removal and repatriation of children unsuccessful in reunifying with their families is a painful and often traumatic process.[137] In the United States, the Mexican children get removed hastily and returned across the border. Sometimes these children fail to find relatives or to be traced by them, and, tragically, they end up in long-term foster care organized by the Mexican authorities. Children of other nationalities face US detention and other forms of hardship as the authorities decide whether to return them to their countries of origin or trace relatives in the United States, the latter complicated by the fact that children are regularly used as bait to find irregular parents. When this happens, parents are detained and eventually the whole family is removed.[138] In other cases, to avoid this drastic outcome, parents decide not to claim children when they arrive. A case in point is that of a Nigerian girl of seven, brought to New York by smugglers paid by her father to bring her in. Though her undocumented mother was waiting for her when she arrived at Kennedy Airport, the mother did not claim her because the child was in the custody of the immigration authorities. The child spent the next fifteen months in a children's detention facility with no contact from anyone in her family. It took media attention to persuade the authorities to eventually release her to relatives.[139] Legally resident relatives are not allowed to claim unaccompanied children if the authorities are aware of the presence of undocumented parents within the country. Children with no relatives coming forward are removed across the border by plane. "Those caught before crossing the border are sent home on a bus—a dangerous journey in reverse. The bus sometimes travels onto the Mexican-Guatemalan border, stranding the children there with no means of returning home."[140]

This sorry chronicle of the obstacles and hardships associated with the exercise of family reunification through domestic immigration procedures demonstrates the extremes to which families will go in search of reunification. But it also illustrates the ideological distance between current US policy and a fundamental tenet of international children's-rights law, widely accepted though not binding on the US government. According to Article 9 of the CRC, "a child *shall not* be separated from his or her parents against their will, except when competent authorities subject to judicial review, determine . . . that such separation *is necessary for the best interest* of the child."[141] Current US immigration policy is deeply ambivalent about the importance of protecting immigrant family life. On the one hand, family visas represent the overwhelming majority of lawful permanent migrations, a reality no politician can afford to publicly challenge. On the other hand, immigrant children, through no fault of their own but with no political muscle, continue to be subjected to excruciating delays and hardships in the quest for reunification.

Conclusion

Though the right to respect for family life is a fundamental human right, enshrined in domestic and international law, in practice, necessity—whether economic, political, or both—compels sizable populations of migrants to temporarily separate from their families. The hardship of separation may be alleviated by occasional visits back home, where the political situation in the home country, the immigration restrictions in the country of immigration, and the migrant's employment and financial situation permit this. But visits are temporary, and a pale substitute for fully fledged shared family life. So as soon as migrants are economically and/or legally able to exercise their right to family life, they usually attempt to do so.

Despite the apparent simplicity of the rights apparatus, the exercise of family reunification is fraught with complexities for most immigrant families. As this chapter has shown, the complexity affects all family members—because legal restrictions, delays, disruptions, and upheavals are inherent in the process. But for children, the process of family reunion can be particularly painful and dangerous. As immigration restrictions increase, as crossing borders becomes increasingly militarized and criminalized, as xenophobic pressures restrict immigration quotas and produce increasingly restrictive requirements for reunification, so growing numbers of children find themselves involved in processes of family reunion that are traumatic and hazardous, rather than celebratory and reassuring. This chapter suggests that family reunification is viewed merely as a desideratum and a prerogative of parents, awarded as a trophy for responsible income generation or diligent documentary compliance. Meanwhile children only exist as parental possessions or rewards, not as active holders of the right to family life themselves. Recall the Somali children still stranded in desperate life-threatening conditions despite the willingness of their cousin to support them in the United Kingdom, the Bangladeshi girls stuck in their village without an adequate caregiver while their father and brothers seek to facilitate reunion, the Mexican and other Central American children summarily separated from caring parents and returned across the border, the Moroccan child refused access to his only surviving parent by the Dutch authorities, the Turkish child indefinitely separated from both his parents by Swiss nativism.

Family life, at its best, is a unique and scarce commodity in a fast-paced, turbulent world. While its disruption is frequently unavoidable in situations of conflict and economic necessity, its long-term severance because of unresolved ambivalence toward adult immigrants and their rights of inclusion in the state is an underappreciated consequence of contemporary immigration control. For children to leave the homes they have known all their life, the family members they have been most intimate with and grown up with, the languages, food, and friends that make them who they are is bad enough. But when the process of reunifying with the closest relatives is deferred, delayed, complicated, and ultimately predicated on perilous and long-drawn-out journeys, then family life really does become an elusive holy grail that threatens to overshadow the enjoyment of any other fundamental aspects of life. And yet, the imperative to reunify continues against all the odds. "Grandma, I'm leaving," Enrique says. "I'm going to find my mom."[142]

CHAPTER 2
Staying Home: The Elusive Benefits of Child Citizenship

Introduction

On July 27, 2002, two contrasting immigration stories appeared in the US press. Both concerned families of US citizen children[1] and noncitizen mothers facing an identical dilemma: the choice between family separation and exile from their family home. One story reported on the British widow of a trader killed in the World Trade Center on September 11, 2001, and her two US-citizen children ages seven and four. A textbook case of "family migration," the woman had left her country and moved because of her husband's job. As a result, her US visa was dependent on that of her British husband. Following his death, the United States Immigration and Naturalization Service took steps to deport her.

Her role as a full-time caretaker of young US-citizen children did not afford her the immigration benefits that flowed from her former role as spouse of a noncitizen worker. Following intensive lobbying, including support from Prime Minister Tony Blair and former first lady Hillary Clinton, however, the authorities granted the British mother a Green Card under an exceptional provision in the USA Patriot Act allowing foreign-born spouses of 9/11 victims to apply for residency.[2] High-profile leverage, British heritage, and the sympathy surrounding the events of September 11 resulted in the sparing of these two American children from the trauma of being uprooted from their country or separated from their mother.

The other story concerned a Guatemalan woman, "handcuffed and arrested in front of her stunned husband and sobbing eight-year-old daughter," both of whom were US citizens. Though the news report does not contain details, it seems probable from the sparse facts available that this woman did not follow her husband but set out on her own or with her birth family, probably in search of an unskilled job in the informal economy, jobs for which visas are not available. While the British male trader secured a lawful immigration status that was derivatively transmitted to his wife, the female migrant became an undocumented worker. The woman was deported to Guatemala after spending seventeen days in jail. She had missed a hearing date to regularize her status in immigration court because the notification sent to her had listed the date incorrectly. At a subsequent interview she was told the deportation order had already been signed. Lobbying by the Parent Teachers Association at the child's school and by a Latino organization, were to no avail. The woman's lawyers requested a waiver to allow her to return to the United States as a legal resident; such requests can take years to process. Without a waiver, the woman would have to attempt to have her deportation case reopened, an arduous legal challenge. Meanwhile, following deportation she had to stay with a friend in Guatemala City since no family resided there any longer. The daughter complained, "I can't sleep, I can't eat, I can't do my work or my arts."[3] In neither case did the citizen child have an enforceable right to preserve family unity at home. Nor did the mother have any recourse based on her critical relational role as parent within the family. From the perspective of international human rights,[4] both the mothers and the children experienced a radical rights deficit. In one case, government discretion was exercised in favor of family unity, in the other case it was not—a bonus for the privileged white family but a casualty for the working-class Latino one. In both cases, the parent's legal and social credentials rather than the child's nationality were the deciding factor.

Now fast-forward ten years and switch from the *New York Times* to the *Wyoming Tribune-Eagle*. Consider two other stories concerning citizen children and their noncitizen parents. The first concerns a Mexican mother, Erica Delgado, living in a trailer in Wyoming with her eleven-year-old US-citizen daughter Miriam. Her violent husband had left for Mexico some years earlier (whether deported or voluntarily is not clear); an irregular migrant, she worked to support her daughter until her trailer was raided by ICE, the US Immigration and Customs Enforcement Agency. Erica was questioned about the false Social Security identity number she used and taunted about a return visit by ICE officers. A week later, on February 3, 2012, Erica set fire to her trailer, killing Miriam and herself.[5] Another family of irregular Mexican migrants was raided on the same day as Erica and Miriam. Two sisters, Irma Meija and Irma Avina, were living with their five children. Here is an eyewitness account by one of the children:

> When imagration [*sic*] got to my home they started to kick the door. My sister and I got up really scared my sister was crying a lot she is only five. . . . [T]hey all came in and they did not tell us anything. . . . [T]hey were screaming at my mom a lot. . . . [T]hey told [my mom] to get ready because she was going to go with them.

A month later, the children involved had not seen their mothers since the night of the arrests.[6]

The events of September 11 led to the detention and deportation of many hundreds of thousands of permanent-resident foreign nationals, long settled in the United States but with old criminal convictions. And the deportation fury has not abated as the trauma of 9/11 has receded,[7] but continued, indeed accelerated, with strong bipartisan political backing and new targets. Until 2008, nationwide workplace raids were pervasive; more recently, stepped-up postentry immigration enforcement has targeted immigrant communities in their homes. The pervasive use of deportation as a visible domestic tool in the war on terror is not surprising: as Judith Butler has pointed out, citing Hannah Arendt, "The exemplary moment of sovereignty is the act of deportation."[8] But its abuse as an instrument engendering terror in highly vulnerable populations is deeply concerning.

The US-government measures just described have resulted in the destruction of family life for hundreds of thousands of US-citizen children. The reason is simple: US law requires parents attempting to secure cancellation of their removal order from the United States to prove their removal will result in "exceptional and extremely unusual hardship" to their US-citizen or lawful permanent-resident immediate relatives.[9] Between 1998 and 2007, ICE deported over 100,000 noncitizen parents of US citizen children.[10] In the first six months of 2011 alone, ICE deported another 46,486 parents,[11] and thousands more may be affected in the future.[12] Very few noncitizen parents manage to secure "cancellation of removal" under the very high hardship standard set for remaining with their children in the United States.[13] Despite a 2011 policy memo issued by ICE, urging immigration officials to refrain from prosecuting aliens who are "primary caretakers of children,"[14] immigrants undergoing removal are rarely asked if they have children.[15]

Faced with bleak alternatives, many families take their US-citizen children with them when they are forced to leave the United States, but others leave the children behind[16] to finish their education and benefit from the security and familiarity of the environment in which they have grown up. In a recent Seventh Circuit case, a Mexican father challenging his removal described the untenable situation his three citizen children would face: poverty, educational exclusion, and threats of violence in Mexico, or economic hardship if forced to rely on the single income of their mother in the United States. His challenge was unsuccessful.[17] Advocates of immigration restriction polemicize that "Mexico is not Auschwitz"[18] but a middle income country with infrastructure and employment opportunities, suggesting that deportation should occasion little real hardship. Accounts provided by deportees contradict this glib argument.[19] American children ripped out of the only home they have known endure traumatic experiences that can create lifelong scars. Removal decimates family earnings and jeopardizes human security at many levels. Typically, where families are forced out, the choices they confront are "excruciating."[20]

Some parents, as Erica's story illustrates, are so despairing at the prospect of family separation or survival back home that they commit suicide. Others lose all contact with their children, because sudden arrest and removal prevent them from making care arrangements.[21] Tragically, deportation may even result in loss of parental rights altogether: state child-protection authorities are legally required to terminate parental rights if a child has been out of parental custody for fifteen of twenty-two months. One organization estimates that at least 5,100 children with a deported parent are currently in foster care, and the numbers are likely to grow. [22] The emotional and psychosocial toll placed on children affected by a parent's deportation is equally catastrophic.[23] In 2007, Representative Jose Serrano of New York introduced a bill to give immigration judges discretion in stopping the removal of citizen children's parents.[24] He reasoned: "*If, in fact, some (children) were left behind here, then you have the sad tragedy of breaking up families. If they were taken back, I would argue the direct result of our actions is the deportation of our citizens. How do you deport a U.S. citizen?*"[25]

How indeed and why? Chapter 2 addresses this question. Part of the answer is to be found in a deep-seated modern ambivalence about what it means for a child to be a citizen.[26] In 1930, launching his Children's Charter, President Hoover stated: "The rights of the child [are] the first rights of citizenship."[27] In 1996, contributing to a symposium on the meaning of contemporary citizenship, Bill Bell, a respected historian, commented: "The assumption that children are not citizens is deeply rooted in our civic traditions."[28] President Hoover's claim reflects the liberal conception of citizenship as a bundle of rights and obligations that is universal and inclusive—and that sets no age limit, no mental or physical competency requirement. From this perspective, chronologically, and morally, the first claim to citizenship's rights lies with the child, starting from the moment of birth, which is also the moment of greatest vulnerability and dependence on others. But there is another, complementary modern conception of citizenship, the republican view, which goes back to Aristotle and Rousseau. Citizenship here entails the ability to participate in public deliberation. It is this perspective that informs the assumption Bell describes—the influential notion that children, especially young children, are not able to contribute to the *res publica* and are therefore not citizens.

Both these perspectives inform our current approach to citizen children. The liberal approach is implicit in nondiscrimination law and policy, and consistent with the principles enshrined in the 1989 UN Convention on the Rights of the Child. It vests citizen children at birth with the full panoply of human rights entitlements derived from enlightenment thinking about human dignity and equality, the rights to state protection from harm, to welfare and educational services, to personal and social respect increasing in line with growing capabilities. The republican approach is implicit in much domestic family and social-welfare practice. It subordinates citizen children's independent interests and agency to those of their adult mentors, reflecting the view that children belong to their families and depend on their protection, mentorship, and judgment. Together, these two frameworks generate the complex and ambivalent legal framework shaping the entitlements of citizen children in contemporary immigration and nationality law, entitlements that continue to be contested and unstable.

The ambivalent conceptual framework has many unambivalent consequences. In the United States, it has resulted in the destruction of family life for many tens of thousands of citizen children. They include the three Miguel children, ages eleven months, seven, and twelve—all American citizens and each requiring extensive medical attention because of a genetic defect necessitating liver transplants. Their father, a longtime legal resident, was deported because of an old conviction. His American-born wife had to quit her job as a farm worker to care for the three sick children alone.[29] They also include the two American-citizen Andazola-Riva children, ages eleven and six. Their single-parent mother, who had lived undocumented but fully employed in the United States for fifteen years with her entire family, was unable to prove her removal from the United States would result in "exceptional and extremely unusual hardship" to her two children. The children had to leave their home, their school, and their friends for an insecure future with an unemployed parent in Mexico—the alternative would have been to stay on in the United States without their sole caregiver.[30] Approximately 4.5 million US-citizen children have at least one parent in the United States without a regular immigration status;[31] tens of thousands each year experience the deportation of a parent.[32]

Citizenship: A Social Fact and a Genuine Connection

Little political consideration has been given to what it means for a child to be a citizen.[33] This is surprising given that many of the cardinal formal attributes of citizenship—including the right to vote, to serve on a jury, and to stand for public office—are denied children. No other group of citizens in the developed world today has such legally sanctioned partial access to the benefits of membership. In other societies, and during other historical periods, as suffragettes[34] and Islamist feminists[35] have forcefully demonstrated, the same has been true of women. But the inequities of that discrimination are considered increasingly indefensible. Age-based discrimination, by contrast, is universal and relatively unquestioned. And it has dramatic consequences given the centrality of citizenship to the organization of social life.

Citizenship is a fundamental, constitutive social fact. It governs the relationship between the individual and the collectivity—does one "belong" or is one an "outsider"? It may or may not affect the actual emotional attachment a person feels to the place he or she lives in (residence, the presence of family networks are other key factors) but it certainly regulates and stimulates the insertion of the personal into the public—access to an effective voice in local or national government.

Citizenship defines the framework in which the balance between self-interest and public concern is negotiated, both by the individual citizen and by the polity, because citizens' interests are central to the assessment of what is a public good. Citizens have a privileged claim to public concern and expenditure where noncitizens do not; citizens exemplify the norm, the standard, the instantiation of national interest where noncitizens do not. In short, through their vote, their agency in public office, their civic participation, their clout as primary addressees of politicians, citizens have a role in shaping the society they live in that is radically different from noncitizens.

A key consequence of this collection of social facts is that public life is dominated by and organized around the perspectives of citizens. Groups excluded or marginalized from membership find their interests subordinated and their point of view neglected, even ignored. To establish their "genuine connection" to the polity and to achieve their political goals, those who are excluded have to garner the support of citizens. This political process requires an engagement in the public sphere that may present an insurmountable hurdle—for example, for a young citizen child of undocumented parents. The ambivalence toward children's interests exemplifies the kind of difficulties that may arise in the framing of public policy and is a point that will be returned to below.

Citizenship is not only a social fact. It is the legal correlate of territorial belonging. It signifies official recognition of a particularly close relationship between person and country, typically characterized as a bundle of reciprocal rights and duties, a set of entitlements owed to the citizen by the country, and of duties owed to the country by the citizen. The International Court of Justice (ICJ) articulated a classic definition of citizenship in the famous *Nottebohm* case: "a legal bond having as its basis a social fact of attachment, a genuine connection of existence, interest and sentiments, together with the existence of reciprocal rights and duties."[36]

Domestic constitutions also enshrine the special status of citizens, as members of a community that is privileged precisely because it is exclusive. The Fourteenth Amendment to the US Constitution, for example, states: "All persons, born or naturalized in the United States, are citizens of the United States and of the State wherein they reside. No State shall make or enforce any law which shall abridge the privileges or immunities of citizens of the United States."[37] Article 2 of the Irish Constitution reads: "It is the entitlement and birthright of every person born in the island of Ireland, which includes its islands and seas, to be part of the Irish nation. That is also the entitlement of all persons otherwise qualified in accordance with law to be citizens of Ireland." As a matter of constitutional law, therefore, citizenship is distinguished as a marker of belonging from other close relationships between person and country also based on "the social fact of attachment," most significantly indefinite or permanent lawful residence. Though generally not an immediately visible or audible marker of belonging in multiethnic societies, it becomes salient as an aspect of someone's identity at key moments—on election day, in the choice of queue at international borders, as a trump to possible deportation proceedings.

As a marker of identity, citizenship signals "belonging" and "insider-status" in a privileged way. Yet the cluster of "reciprocal rights and duties" attached to citizenship is surprisingly unclear: no constitutional statement enumerates them, nor is there complete consistency across states. What is clear, however, particularly since 9/11, is that the border- and mobility-related entitlements owed by a country to its citizens have become highly significant. They include the entitlement to a passport, the right to consular protection abroad, the right to move in and out of the country freely and to reenter at any time irrespective of the length of absence abroad, and the entitlement—in some countries such as the United States or EU member states—to privileged family reunification opportunities.

Arguably the most significant citizen-specific entitlement today is the guarantee of nondeportability, irrespective of criminal offending. Even treason cannot lead to deportation of a citizen. And yet, for all intents and purposes, some of the American children described above were de facto—or constructively—deported. If a young child's parents are forced to leave a country, so in effect is the child. This is an extremely severe sanction inflicted on an innocent party, a vivid example of the lack of importance attached to the child's perspective. For what could be more devastating for a child than the loss of a parent or a home? From a child's perspective, parenting should be regarded as a critical activity capable of qualifying the impact of a deportation order. But family separation is viewed primarily through the lens of its impact on the adult deportee.

The Primacy of Nondeportability as an Incident of Citizenship

In contemporary society, citizenship is a demographically inclusive status—not generally determined as it was in antiquity and other earlier periods, as recent as the nineteenth century, by race, gender, class, or age.[38] It is a status that has no minimum age requirement—children are citizens as are adults. Indeed the vast majority of people acquire their citizenship at birth. But children cannot vote, stand for public office, serve on juries, or (according to international law)[39] be called to bear arms in defense of their country. Thus the special attributes are reduced in the case of children to the migration/border-crossing rights of protection, particularly the entitlement to reside in their country indefinitely without risk of deportation.

These residency rights are no less vital for children than they are for adults, though this point is usually ignored. They may be as critical as the much more widely acknowledged dependence on and need for consistent parenting. Institutional acceptance of the fact that separation from close relatives can cause permanent psychological damage is pervasive, a bedrock of international law as much as it is a core principle in the immigration systems of developed states.[40] There is more disagreement about how and where family unity is to be achieved, but the principle itself is universally accepted.

By contrast the importance of residency rights for children is scarcely considered. Yet, the ties and influences that result from belonging to a particular territory are critical, even for very young children. The place of residence has pervasive impacts and lifelong consequences: it affects children's life expectancy, their physical and psychological development, their material prospects, their general standard of living. Belonging to a particular country determines the type of education the child receives, the expectations regarding familial obligations, employment opportunities, gender roles, and consumption patterns. It determines linguistic competence; social mores; vulnerability to discrimination, persecution, and war. It affects exposure to disease, to potentially oppressive social and cultural practices, to life-enhancing kinship, and to social and occupational networks. In short, the fact of belonging to a particular country fundamentally affects the manner of exercise of a child's family and private life during childhood and well beyond. Yet children are often considered parcels that are easily movable across borders with their parents and without particular cost to the children—and the younger the child, the easier the relocation.

Family Mobility: A Mismatch between Theory and Practice

What determines who moves with whom? The sovereign prerogative of states to control their own borders and to regulate the admission and residence of aliens on their territory explains the traditional limitations on the right to freedom of movement that underpins all legal migration. Israel is an extreme case in point. It ignores the residence or "private life" rights of children born in Israel to parents without legal status: however long the child stays in Israel, he or she never qualifies for citizenship. As a fourteen-year-old Israeli-born Ghanaian girl who had spent her whole life in Tel Aviv said when challenging removal from Israel: "We should not be punished for the mistakes our parents made."[41]

The sovereign border-control prerogative of states does not, however, explain the striking asymmetry in the family reunification rights of similarly placed adults and minor children, just like it did not explain the gender bias of earlier immigration rules relating to married couples, which accorded primacy to the interests and life choices of men over women. Parents with claims to asylum can travel across borders with children and subsume them in their applications whether the children have valid claims to asylum or not; immigrant parents can generally (subject to the delays and other hurdles considered in chapter 1) bring their minor children to join them once they have established themselves in a new country. Parents, if they defeat attempts at deportation or removal directed against themselves, can thereby also prevent the removal of their minor children, whether the latter are independently eligible for settlement or not. Parents, as will be discussed in chapter 3, can even obtain residence and citizenship for biologically unrelated children whom they choose to adopt transnationally. And a noncitizen but legal permanent-resident parent can, in some countries, transmit citizenship of the country of residence to his or her children.[42] Yet children cannot exercise such choices. A citizen child cannot generally[43] use the fact of citizenship to block the removal of parents facing deportation or to secure entry for a parent abroad.

This approach has much more far-reaching consequences for family security and public policy than has been acknowledged. Massive contemporary global migration has multiple and complex impacts on the conduct of family life. The assumption of a unitary family, all of whose members share the same nationality, live in the same country, travel together, or, following the (male) breadwinner, have the same short- or long-term interests, with easy access to one another, is outmoded. It is disrupted by intricate and rapidly changing patterns of mobility. These new patterns include children born in host countries to parents with different nationalities and immigration statuses, or complex new parenting roles rendered possible by advances in birth technology and fertility outsourcing. In the majority of situations, parents provide the anchor to which children are attached. This is a consequence of widespread state policy to support (with some qualifications considered in chapter 1) family unity by providing a means to keep children with their parents, particularly their mothers. But contemporary migration patterns also result in many situations where children have a more secure status than their parents and where it is the children who are in the best position to provide a point of migration stability for the family. Were it not for the asymmetry in allocation of citizenship benefits, many of these children would be the legal justification for enforcing family unity in their place of residence.

This approach should not be dismissed as fanciful: it is uncontroversial that many immigrants, whether in temporary or irregular immigration status, derive a sense of purpose in trying life circumstances from the prospect of generating better life chances for their children than those they had themselves. Nancy Villeda, a high school senior born to undocumented parents facing removal, described the pressure on her to maintain her 3.9 grade point average: "The reason my parents came here was to start a new future, have something better. I felt like if I gave that up, their hard work would be in vain."[44] And yet, precisely because they are children, these youngsters do not generally have the legal capacity to solidify the family's future prospects, to "earn" the full attributes of citizenship.[45]

In the worst cases, families can become permanently divided because of differences in immigration status. A case in point concerns an Ecuadorian woman who left her one-year-old US-citizen daughter in the care of a friend while she went home to Ecuador to pick up her undocumented son. On their return to the United States, both mother and son were arrested. After her release from detention nine months later, the mother could not trace her daughter.[46] In this case the separation was accidental, though no less tragic for being so. In other cases, separation is by design, the result of court judgments depriving undocumented parents of the custody of their US-citizen children. An undocumented Guatemalan mother lost custody of her child after she was detained in a raid in a Missouri processing plant, and incarcerated. The circuit court judge granting custody to a local couple making a comfortable living found that the biological mother "had little to offer: The only certainties in the biological mother's future is [*sic*] that she will remain incarcerated until next year, and that she will be deported thereafter."[47]

Much more common than permanent separation is the situation where citizen children in mixed-status families grow up in poverty, with all the inevitable consequences for access to medical care, educational achievement, and career prospects that poverty entails. The 4.5 million US-citizen children growing up with at least one undocumented parent are close to twice as likely to face poverty as other citizen children;[48] they thus experience a form of de facto "semi-citizenship."

The assumption that children's native citizenship cannot alter parents' immigration status highlights a striking divergence between the foundational assumptions of family and immigration law. Where families are divided by marriage or relationship breakdown, courts traditionally allocate the family home to the party with custody of the children—home is where the children are, the custodial parent's residence deriving from the child's.[49] But if families face separation because of immigration law, the presumption is that the anchoring role of the children must give way, their primacy evaporating. If children have no right to use their citizenship as a basis for exercising family reunion or shoring up family unity, then—if their parents face deportation—the children too risk constructive deportation, despite being citizens.

The Attack on Birthright Citizenship

In recent years and especially in the post-9/11 period, as immigration battles are more frequently fought out on the terrain of citizenship, so the citizenship rights of children, and birthright citizenship in particular, have come under political and legal attack in the United States[50] and elsewhere. The citizenship benefits that a child acquires because of birthplace (jus soli) are singled out as a self-evidently arbitrary basis for the acquisition of an important civic and political status.[51] This critique is particularly targeted at children born to illegal or undocumented migrants who acquire citizenship by territorial birthright despite their parents' compromised legal relationship to the state. A US appeals court judgment reflects this widely held perspective:

> A minor child who is fortuitously born here due to his parents' decision to reside in this country, has not exercised a *deliberate decision* to make this country his home, and Congress did not give such a child the ability to confer immigration benefits on his parents. It gave this privilege to those of our citizens who had themselves *chosen* to make this country their home and did not give the privilege to those minor children whose noncitizen parents make the real choice of family residence.[52]

Which minor children, one wonders, are in a position to make deliberate decisions about the country they reside in or call home? And yet, since the turn of the century, supreme courts in the United States,[53] Canada,[54] and Ireland,[55] to name but three, have all attacked the alleged arbitrariness of birthright citizenship. The challenge to birthright citizenship captures the ambivalence of our attitudes toward children's claims to citizenship more generally—the tension between the universalist model embedded in the liberal approach to rights where children, like adults, are rights-holders, and the more republican approach related to the deliberative and participatory model where children belong to the adults who decide for them.

The attack on birthright citizenship has several sources. One is exclusionary—a desire to restrict eligibility for community membership. This approach has a long history in the United States. Martha Gardner documents the gender and race-based assumptions underlying US citizenship. She demonstrates that, despite the well-established legal principle of jus soli (literally law of the soil) or birth on the territory as an avenue to citizenship,[56] children who do not prima facie appear to belong have long had difficulty establishing their claim to membership. The following case is illustrative. In 1897, Leong Quai Ho attempted to return to San Francisco, her city of birth, after a stay in China. But the San Francisco immigration inspectors challenged her birthright citizenship. They asked: "In what part of China were you born." "I was not born in China," Leong explained for the second time, "I was born in California." "Well go on," frustrated inspectors prodded, "give us the rest of your story, let's have it." Though a citizen, she did not look like one. Eventually Leong Quai Ho was admitted. Other children also born in the United States fared less well. Returning to the United States after seventeen years in China, Lee Sing Far failed to establish to the satisfaction of the Ninth Circuit Court of Appeals that she was born in San Francisco despite having four witnesses testifying for her: their evidence was discounted because "enforcement of the Chinese exclusion laws," the court argued, "necessitated that the testimony of Chinese witnesses be held in some doubt." There was no doubt, by contrast, that Gina Missana's baby was born in the United States. But because the mother was inadmissible, both mother and baby were removed from the United States back to Italy: "While this child was physically born in the United States," officials concluded, "it was not born to a Mother who was lawfully domiciled in this country."[57] Gardner concludes:

> Under the Fourteenth Amendment, every child born in the United States was a citizen. The civic status of two groups of children, however, revealed significant practical limitations to the law's embrace. Children born outside the black and white limits of naturalization law and those born in the space between arrival and admittance [i.e., where the mother occupied this space] were beyond the race and place assumptions of citizenship.[58]

This historical antecedent has a contemporary legacy. The American Civil Liberties Union (ACLU) recently filed a law suit alleging that the government unfairly targets some Mexican American communities, "essentially reducing them to 'second class citizenship status.'" Heightened suspicions about birth-certificate fraud, particularly for children born with the assistance of midwives in southwestern border states (whatever the immigration status of their parents), result in requests for excessive numbers of documents (including baptismal or school records that may never have existed) once these children come to make passport applications. These requests can block the issuing of passports for years.[59]

This practical example of skepticism about the legitimacy of birthright-citizenship claims from border communities has a doctrinal counterpart. One influential strand of the challenge to birthright citizenship relies on the irregular status of the parents to disqualify the children. According to Peter Schuck, birthright citizenship is an "infringement of consensualism" because "illegal alien" parents with very little effort or commitment and no enduring ties to the United States are able to secure citizenship for their children by mere border crossing. The "powerful lure of the expanded entitlements conferred upon citizen children and their families by the modern welfare state" constitutes, it is claimed, an incentive to illegal migration.[60] However, as Bonnie Honig points out and as business-sector support for the Obama administration's comprehensive immigration-reform proposals confirms, the premise that undocumented migrants are present in the United States without consent is questionable. Significant economic advantages to the nation accrue from their presence;[61] steps to remove illegal migrants have been erratic and inconsistent, suggesting a lack of serious political will to eject this key element of the US work force. The claim that "illegal alien parents" have made little effort, or exhibited little commitment or enduring loyalty to the United States, is also deeply flawed, as the recent activism of the undocumented-migrants movement, anxious to consolidate their ties to the U.S., demonstrates. Far from being a security threat as some have claimed,[62] many children born to undocumented parents identify deeply and actively with their birth country, including enlisting as members of the military and standing for public office.[63]

Another line of criticism, building on Schuck's argument, attacks birthright citizenship through textual analysis. Lino Graglia argues that it stems from a "misinterpretation" of the Fourteenth Amendment's first sentence, "All persons born or naturalized in the United States, and subject to the jurisdiction thereof, are citizens of the United States." He claims that when the amendment was drafted and ratified in the mid-nineteenth century, the phrase "subject to the jurisdiction thereof" could not have been intended to include children of undocumented migrants, because (in the absence of any laws restricting immigration) no such population existed. "There cannot be a more total or forceful denial of consent to a person's citizenship than to make the *source* of that person's presence in the nation illegal,"[64] he writes. This argument is illogical. Unless they are diplomats or Native Americans governed by tribal law, all persons in the United States, whatever their legal status, are subject to its jurisdiction.[65] As Gerald Neuman has pointed out, "[t]he word 'jurisdiction' has various meanings in American law, but it has never been defined in terms remotely resembling the elaborate construct"[66] suggested by Schuck. The plain meaning of the sentence is unambiguous. What is more, the argument depends on eliminating the independent claim to protection and personhood that every child has, as a human being. Presumably a child born through rape or appropriation of stolen sperm also comes from an illegal "source" yet one would not support depriving him or her of citizenship.

These arguments may seem contrived. But, the attack on birthright citizenship is not purely academic. Politicians have vociferously criticized the birthright citizenship rule. Congressman Gary Miller has been outspoken: "You have many people coming to this country illegally. They come to this country and have babies. The children are citizens. The children are eligible to go to school, they receive food stamps and social programs, the American taxpayers are paying for it."[67] But it is not just Americans or lawful residents who are taxpayers. According to the 2009 *Human Development Report*, "[i]llegal immigrant workers provide around US $7 billion annually to the US Treasury."[68] Nevertheless influential opinion leaders, including prominent judicial figures, have weighed in to attack birthright citizenship. The chief justice of the Seventh Circuit Court of Appeals and an influential legal scholar, Judge Richard Posner, delivered the following opinion in a 2003 asylum case:

> [O]ne rule that Congress should rethink . . . is awarding citizenship to everyone born in the United States (with a few very minor exceptions . . .) including the children of illegal immigrants whose *sole motive* in immigration was to confer U.S. citizenship on their as yet unborn children. This rule . . . makes no sense.[69]

Opponents of birthright citizenship, however, have a hard time proving what the "*sole motive*" of immigration is. Citing the number of births to undocumented mothers[70] without comparable statistics for similarly placed documented or citizen mothers proves nothing. Moreover, the argument seems to ignore the economic roles that migrant women play, casting them essentially as breeders. In fact, migration is a multifaceted human activity: survival or economic advancement, protection from persecution or enhanced personal security, adventure, career development, family reunification, keeping up with neighbors or relatives may all be part of the purpose of migration, and identifying a single factor across a large and diverse population is problematic.

The British government discovered this in the 1980s when it used equally simplistic and discriminatory assumptions about immigration to curb the rights of some groups. It legislated to restrict the entry of young South Asian men applying to join their British-born wives or fiancées and settle in the United Kingdom by establishing that only marriages where the "primary purpose" was NOT the fiancé's or husband's immigration into Britain would be considered valid. The British government, over a period of ten years, used the rule to refuse approximately half the entry clearance applications from these South Asian men. Indignant judges criticized the sexist and racist assumptions behind the primary-purpose rule. In the words of one judge, "Where arranged marriages are the norm, the fact that a marriage is an arranged marriage . . . does not show that its *purpose* is or was to obtain admission to the United Kingdom."[71] Another judgment highlighted the Eurocentric and gender biases in the refusal decisions of immigration officers by posing a culturally contrasting hypothetical:

> [I]n the context of arranged marriages in Muslim society, the absence of . . . a passionate relationship or indeed of being "in love" [is] not itself indicative of [immigration] being the primary purpose of a marriage. . . . To draw an analogy with English society at the turn of the century, the fact that an American heiress was so keen to be a duchess that she was prepared to marry an Englishman whom she did not love would not lead one to suppose that the primary purpose of the marriage was for her to obtain admission to the UK. She may have been after his title and he after her money.[72]

Eventually, protracted criticism from civil society, advocates, and the European Court of Justice persuaded the British government to moderate the application of the rule. In doing so it had to concede that immigration decision makers could not unquestioningly apply their stereotypes and biases to assess the motivations of populations they had little understanding of.

By analogy, the argument of critics such as Schuck and Posner against birthright citizenship is grounded in a worldview that considers the intruding "other" immoral and set on securing benefits he or she is not entitled to. It is also completely adult-centric. Schuck defends the proposal to remove birthright citizenship on the basis that this does not interfere with moral obligations, such as they may be, to illegal aliens: "Citizenship status is not necessary to afford illegal aliens and their children at least minimal protection and public benefits."[73] But what of the state's moral obligations toward its own citizens? Attention to the claims of the citizen child is displaced by a focus on the noncitizen parent. In fact all non-naturalized citizens acquire their privileged insider status and their associated claims on the state through the accident of birth, not through the moral obligations owed their parents or other relatives. No child consents to his or her citizenship at birth or closely thereafter. Consent to citizenship, in the sense of personal commitment and affirmation of a common historical or cultural project, only develops cumulatively, gradually, and with maturity—citizen children have the incipient right to consent as they reach adulthood. Depriving a subset of children born within the state of that right on the basis of parental immigration status places an extra burden of active consent on one category of children, penalized because of the parent's behavior.

The attack on birthright citizenship also stems from another, quite different set of preoccupations, centered on questions of social justice and concern for equity across groups. Seyla Benhabib, for example, argues that "*territoriality* has become an anachronistic delimitation of material functions and cultural identities; yet, even in the face of the collapse of traditional concepts of sovereignty, monopoly over territory is exercised through immigration and citizenship policies." She calls for much greater acknowledgment of the interdependence of different "peoples" and suggests that "the right to membership [in a society] ought to be considered a human right, in the moral sense of the term and . . . ought to become a legal right as well."[74]

From this, more inclusionary perspective, the legitimacy of birthright citizenship as the basis for allocating valuable resources is questioned because it is an irrational basis for allocating such resources. Following a related line of argument, Ayelet Shachar argues that citizenship is akin to a property right that must be distributed according to systematic, not arbitrary, criteria: "When our citizenship laws effectively become intertwined with distributing shares in human survival on a global scale . . . we can no longer silently accept this situation. . . . The problem of unequal allocation and transfer, which has gained plenty of attention in the realm of property, is, in fact, far more extreme in the realm of birthright entitlement to citizenship."[75] In theory it sounds laudable to call into question the legitimacy of borders as fences between rich and poor and to reconsider the equitable basis of access to the privileges associated with the citizenship of developed states. But in practice, requiring an evaluation of "the significance of *actual membership* in the community" is a perilous strategy in times of rampant xenophobia and nativism. In the absence of an alternative set of viable proposals, it is likely that successful attacks on birthright citizenship will result in citizenship proposals that increase rather than reduce inequality.

The attack on birthright citizenship is, first and foremost, an attack on the existing rights of citizen children. But it has not been discussed in those terms. In debates on the allocation of entitlements to citizenship, the perspective of the citizen child is remarkably absent. Concerns about differential or discriminatory access to the benefits of citizenship and about asymmetries in the flow of citizenship rights have typically focused on questions of race and gender, not age. In the case of gender, in particular, the parallels are dramatic. Obliteration of the woman's perspective was justified by assumptions about her dependence—social, political, economic, and personal—on male relatives, typically her father first and her husband second. Since she was considered an appendage of male agency and dependent on male protection, her legal status, and with it her citizenship and immigration rights, flowed from those of her male relative. Nineteenth-century British nationality law exemplifies this approach. The 1844 Naturalisation Act granted any foreign woman married to a British subject automatic British nationality; conversely, the 1870 Naturalisation Act deprived British-born women marrying aliens of their British nationality. These laws simply codified long-standing gendered assumptions. As Judge Lord Hale had held as early as 1664: "It is without question that if an English woman go beyond the Seas and marry an Alien, and have Issue born beyond the Seas, the Issue are Aliens, for the wife was *sub potestate viri* [under the power of the man]."[76]

It took decades of concerted pressure from suffragettes and their supporters to dislodge these deep-seated prejudices, and to replace them with gender-neutral citizenship laws. Not until 1948 were British women finally allowed to keep their nationality following marriage to a noncitizen. And yet, over thirty years earlier, the problem underlying the gross gender inequality had been clearly identified by a member of Parliament: "We must feel that there is something ironical in a Parliament of men, elected by men, settling once and for all the citizenship and civic rights of women who have no voice in the matter directly at all."[77] The parallels with age discrimination are dramatic. Adults are discussing the citizenship and civic rights of children who have no voice in the matter directly at all. And so, by a strange twist of logic, the claim that children exercise the normal rights that flow from citizenship, including security of home, family, and residence, is cast as an "abuse."

The so-called abuse of birthright citizenship to secure immigration advantages for undocumented or criminal alien parents—to act as "anchor children"—is a prime contemporary concern, not limited to countries such as the United States that have jus soli laws. Children's citizenship may differ from one or both parents' in other circumstances too—for example, when parents have different nationalities,[78] or when the child has acquired citizenship through residence and the parents have not. But the focus on citizenship disparities and their consequences for the enjoyment of family relationships is firmly adult focused. Public concern centers on inequalities between adults (mothers versus fathers, women versus men), rather than between adults and children.[79] There seems to be an assumption that children's disabilities as citizens are self-evidently justified, a consequence of the fact that they are citizens in the making, "future"[80] rather than actual citizens. The one-way descending flow of familial transmission of citizenship, from parent to child rather than from child to parent, is accepted as a natural rather than a constructed asymmetry, just as its gendered antecedent was. A consequence of this approach is that retrospection rather than prospection dominates the discussion about justification for access to citizenship: the importance of connection to a community or territory is assessed in terms of the length and depth of past association, rather than the salience or value of future connection. This perspective thus privileges the existing connections sustained by adults or parents over the potentiality for future connections of babies or children.

Child Citizens: A Rights Deficit

It is a strange paradox of modern public policy, that children are considered to have a fundamental right to family life[81] and yet no legally enforceable right, unlike their adult counterparts,[82] to initiate family reunion or resist family separation where a family is divided by national borders. Most notable is the disparity in the position of citizens. In the United States, nondeportability and preferential access to family reunification with immediate relatives are considered among the most significant attributes of adult citizens, distinguishing them from legal-resident aliens who, in many other respects, share the benefits of modern "postnational" welfare entitlements—access to education and social security, for example.[83]

For US children, however, these cardinal attributes of citizenship are not available. Citizen children are not entitled to any preferred immigration status for their immediate relatives until they reach majority and can demonstrate links of marriage or, in the case of elderly parents, dependency. Though not deportable themselves, citizen children are constructively deportable when their alien parents face deportation. As shown earlier in this chapter, their right to permanent residence in their home country does not extend to an entitlement to protect other necessary aspects of that residence, such as the continued presence of parent caregivers. Deportation of parents, particularly of mothers, usually amounts to a de facto or constructive deportation of dependent minor children—a reality that is obscured by the extreme option of placing citizen children with guardians or others in the home country.

Countries adopt differing criteria and standards in balancing their ambivalent mandate between family protection and border control. At one end of the spectrum are policies that unambiguously enact the presumption that immigration-control considerations are paramount and that children have no independent claim to full enjoyment of the attributes of citizenship: in these situations, only exceptional and unusually compassionate circumstances can militate against the deportation of a citizen child's parent, and then only if such circumstances relate directly to the citizen child, not the parent or the family as a whole. At the other end of the spectrum are policies that privilege the citizen child's right to enjoy family life in the home country, a right that trumps immigration-control considerations unless there are serious exclusion considerations, implicating national security or comparable threats to the state. In between these two extremes are policies that require a balancing of citizenship and immigration considerations to determine whether the justifications for deportation override the child's best-interest rights. The contrast between European and American approaches is illustrative.

Balancing the Individual's Right to Family Life and the State's Interest in Immigration Control: The European Approach

The European approach has been governed by the European Convention on Human Rights and the jurisprudence of the Council of Europe institutions that have regulated implementation of the Convention: the European

Commission[84] and the European Court of Human Rights. Article 8 of the ECHR establishes that the right to respect for one's family or private life can only be interfered with by the state where this is the result of a lawful and legitimate government aim and is "*necessary* in a democratic society." The first qualifier does not assist families attempting to challenge separation or deportation, as the implementation of immigration laws has been considered a legitimate goal because it aims to promote the economic well-being of the receiving country. So, the critical question, including for citizen children opposing the deportation of noncitizen parents, has been whether the test of necessity has been met.

To determine what is necessary, the European Court of Human Rights has resorted to a balancing exercise: deportation is necessary when the interests of the state seeking to enforce immigration control are more compelling than the interests of the family resisting it. To make this assessment, the Court has articulated a demanding standard for states, insisting on a robust enforcement of the right to respect for the family life of deportable aliens.[85] However, for the most part, the perspective of the citizen child has been strikingly absent.[86] The Court has tended to focus on the equities involved in the alien parent's behavior and status, in particular asking: how worthy or deserving is the relevant deportable adult? In all but one of the reported court decisions developing this approach, the citizen child is not a co-applicant to the proceedings. The impact on a young child of long-term separation from a parent is ignored in favor of an emphasis on rights of parental access to the child. Parents—in nearly all the reported cases, fathers—who have been law abiding, solicitous toward their children, and who have diligently pursued their child-rearing responsibilities have been rewarded for their behavior by being allowed to reside in their child's home country. Parents who have committed serious criminal offenses, or who have been erratic in their exercise of "parental obligations" as understood by the Court have been penalized, even where no threat to state security exists and where they have close and loving relations with their citizen children. Family unity and the right to respect for family life have thus generally been viewed as a privilege of parents, earned by good or reasonable behavior, rather than as a right of children, or an aspect of citizenship independent of parental conduct.

Several cases are illustrative of a long line of decisions, dating back to the leading 1988 case of *Berrehab v. the Netherlands*,[87] a case in which a Moroccan father who lost his right of residence in the Netherlands following the breakdown of his marriage to a Dutch citizen was found by the court to have had the right to respect for family life violated by his ensuing expulsion, since this prevented him from regular contact with his Dutch child. The court noted that the father had lived and worked "without reproach" in the Netherlands for six years prior to his expulsion, had seen his daughter four times a week since her birth, and had contributed to her education and maintenance. The rights of the citizen child to the continuing presence of her father were not addressed, nor was the child a party to the proceedings. Rather, the father's irreproachable behavior was rewarded.

By contrast, in *Yousef v. United Kingdom*, a strong loving relationship between a Kuwaiti father and British son was restricted to limited access arrangements because of the impending threat of the father's removal from the United Kingdom following the breakdown of his marriage to a UK citizen. A matrimonial-court welfare report described "a strong and affectionate bond between the father and the child" and commented that it would have "been beneficial to the child if that could be maintained in more normal circumstances, i.e. without the threat of the applicant's removal from the United Kingdom which effectively prevented his reasonable access to the child." But the European Commission on Human Rights found no violation of the right to respect for family life: the fact that the father had a minor criminal conviction (for wrongly appropriating 100 UK pounds-worth of electricity), was unemployed, and had failed to maintain consistent contact with his son "because of [his] preoccupation with [a] second British woman"[88] meant that his conduct compared unfavorably with the irreproachable behavior of *Berrehab*. The decision has strong moralistic overtones about the father's less than exemplary conduct; the rights of the citizen child to continue his strong and affectionate bond with his father, again, were not addressed.

Parental equities rather than children's rights were once again the basis for the later decision of the European Court of Human Rights in *Ciliz v. the Netherlands*. In this case, the facts resembled those in *Berrehab*, except that in *Ciliz*, the Turkish father had had less opportunity to develop and establish an ongoing relationship with his Dutch son because his expulsion had prejudged the outcome of access proceedings. The father was expelled "at the moment when the official investigation into the closeness of the ties between father and son had not yet been concluded, and . . . he was subsequently denied an entry visa allowing him to take part in the proceedings concerning access."[89] Since his removal from the Netherlands was not warranted by any criminal proceedings but simply by the breakdown of his marriage and his subsequent unemployment, the court found a violation of his right to respect for family life. In these cases, blameless parents were rewarded with the right to remain close to their citizen child, but the child's right to family life and the impact of deportation on the citizen child was not part of the decision.

A welcome departure from this line of cases is the approach adopted by the European Court of Justice (ECJ), the court that regulates the implementation of European Union law. Not to be confused with the European Court of Human Rights which oversees the implementation of the European Convention on Human Rights in the forty-eight states of the Council of Europe, the ECJ is an institution of the European Union and is responsible for ensuring that the extensive and growing body of community law (on free movement, on the elimination of trade barriers, on a range of other economic and social matters) is appropriately implemented by the twenty-seven member states of the EU.

By contrast with the cautious jurisprudence of the European Court of Human Rights, deferential to the immigration-control agendas of national governments, the European Court of Justice has recently articulated a bolder set of principles prioritizing citizen children's rights to enjoy the care of their parents in their own countries over States' interests in restricting those parents' residence rights.[90] Two ECJ cases provide an interesting model for future policy and a challenge to the adult-centered thinking that dominates the ECtHR case law just described. They illustrate the practical applicability of the following child-rights principle enshrined in Article 24 of the Charter of Fundamental Rights of the European Union:

1. Children shall have the right to such protection and care as is necessary for their well-being. . . .
2. In all actions relating to children, whether taken by public authorities or private institutions, the child's best interests must be a primary consideration.
3. Every child shall have the right to maintain on a regular basis a personal relationship and direct contact with both his or her parents, unless that is contrary to his or her interests.

The first landmark case is *Zhu and Chen v. Secretary of State for the Home Department*.[91] It concerns the rights of an EU citizen child to have her noncitizen mother reside with her in an EU member state. Though the case turns on the rights to free movement and residence enjoyed by EU citizens as a result of European community law, its exploration of the relationship between age and the exercise of citizenship rights has much wider resonance.

The facts of the *Zhu and Chen* case can be simply summarized. Man Chen and her husband, prosperous Chinese nationals with a controlling interest in a successful company with a significant presence in the United Kingdom, decided, after the birth of their first child, to avoid the negative repercussions of having a second child in China in violation of the one-child population policy, by arranging for a foreign birth and residence rights. Accordingly, Catherine Zhu was born in Belfast, Northern Ireland, and when she was six months old, mother and daughter moved to the United Kingdom mainland. Northern Ireland is part of the United Kingdom, but because neither of her parents had a lawful permanent status in the United Kingdom, when Catherine was born, she did not, as required by British law,[92] acquire British citizenship by birth. Northern Ireland is also part of the Irish island, and the Irish Constitution protects the right of everyone born on the Irish island to citizenship at birth. So Catherine acquired Irish citizenship by virtue of her birth on the island.[93] Because of her birthright Irish citizenship, Catherine was entitled as an EU citizen to exercise her free movement and residence rights within the European Union. She traveled with her mother to the mainland United Kingdom.

Mrs. Chen applied for residence permits for both Catherine and herself. Catherine was covered by private health insurance and supported by her parents' ample resources; she therefore fulfilled the residency requirements of EU law. However, the British government refused the request. Before the ECJ, the government argued that the deliberate choice of Belfast as a birthplace, to generate Irish nationality and thus immigration entitlements in Britain, was an abuse of EU law—neither Ireland nor the United Kingdom had consented to this. This argument closely matches the Schuck and Posner critiques of US birthright citizenship described earlier.

The Irish government also participated in the proceedings before the ECJ and advanced the additional argument that, because of her age, Catherine lacked the capacity to exercise EU rights: "While a minor, and unable to exercise a choice of residence, Catherine cannot be a 'national' for the purposes of Article1(1) [of the Council Residency Directive]."[94] It followed from this that Mrs. Chen had no claim to residence rights within the EU either.

The ECJ disagreed. It held that "a very young minor who is a Community National" and fulfills the legal insurance and resource requirements for residency, enjoyed "a right to reside for an indeterminate period" within the EU and that it was not for the court to *look behind the reasons* why the family decided to arrange their affairs in this way. What mattered was whether the legal requirements for citizenship (as determined by the individual member state, Ireland in this case) and for residency (as determined by community law) had been met. Moreover, to enjoy the residency right that Catherine was entitled to, the Court determined that she needed the continued presence of her primary caregiver; without this, her right of residence would be rendered ineffective. In the Court's words, "Refusal to allow the parent . . . would deprive the child's right of residence of any useful effect."[95]

A second ECJ decision develops this rights-based approach to child citizenship a step further. In the case of *Zambrano v. Office national de l'emploi*,[96] the Colombian parents of two Belgian children were held to have rights of residence in Belgium because of the children's fundamental right to family life and to protection of their rights as children, which included their continuing right to future residence anywhere within EU territory. In a momentous and far-reaching judgment, the Court considered the meaning of EU citizenship as a vehicle for the realization of fundamental and nondiscriminatory human rights. It rejected the argument that this citizenship depended for its efficacy on prior transfrontier movement—the children had never traveled outside Belgium, their country of birth. Endorsing the approach taken in this chapter, the Court held that citizenship (in this case EU citizenship) looks to the future rather than merely to the past to define the rights and obligations it confers.[97] This is critical for children because state actions against parents can radically alter the course of a child's entire life:

> If Mr. Ruiz Zambrano were to be deported, then so, too, would his wife. The effect of such steps on the children would be radical. Given their age, the children would no longer be able to live an independent life in Belgium. The lesser evil would therefore, presumably, be for them to leave Belgium with their parents. That would, however, involve uprooting them from the society and culture in which they were born and have become integrated.[98]

The reasoning developed in Zambrano confirms another proposition advanced in this chapter: that children can transmit the benefits derived from citizenship to relatives just as adults can if this transmission is necessary for the enjoyment of the citizens' fundamental rights: derivative rights, in other words, can move in an ascending as well as a descending line. Expanding on the *Zhu and Chen* ruling, *Zambrano* asserts that this nondiscriminatory rights transmission applies even when, as in the case: (a) children acquire their citizenship by naturalization (to avoid statelessness),[99] (b) children have not yet exercised freedom-of-movement rights (but preserve the option to do so in future),[100] and (c) the parents support their children's needs by relying on their entitlement to state tax and other economic benefits.[101] These judgments illustrate the impact of an approach to citizenship that explores the substantive meaning of a right from the perspective of the citizen affected, even when the citizen happens to be a baby or a naturalized child—with little or no past history of lived experience to link him or her to "home"—rather than only from the standpoint of a generic adult claimant with long preexisting ties.[102]

The US Approach to Deportation of Parents of Citizen Minors

The US approach to removal of alien parents of citizen children provides a dramatic contrast. Though the impact of removal on the citizen child is listed as a relevant factor in the immigration regulations, in practice the outcomes of appeals against deportation of noncitizen parents reflect profound disregard for the fundamental rights of citizen children. By contrast with the ECJ process, the US system does not offer the child an opportunity to be a party to the proceedings. The citizen child's interests are thus represented, if at all, only indirectly through the alien parent, as a subsidiary consideration. International human-rights norms relating to children's rights play no direct role in the US decision-making process, and as a result no meaningful balance is struck between state interests in exclusion and child citizens' interests in stability and the protection of family life. Indeed the concept of proportionality, so central to the evaluation of these competing interests in the European system, is effectively lacking from the US approach, its place taken by an increasingly inflexible enforcement of postentry immigration control.

The US approach has been governed by a series of legislative acts impinging on the relief available to aliens seeking to resist deportation. The contemporary system is rooted in US government practice of earlier decades. The effect of official deportation policy is best illustrated by its impact during the years of the Great Depression of the 1930s: "Historians have estimated that close to a million Mexican American citizens and Mexican immigrant noncitizens, adults and children were repatriated during the early 1930s."[103] Among this population were many thousands of US-citizen children, forced to leave their home in order to remain with parents. As Dan Kanstroom notes, this approach has accelerated over subsequent decades. Today

> the size of the deportation system is impressive. . . . Since 1925 . . . [m]ore than 44 million people [have been] ordered to leave. From 2001 through 2004, the total number of formal removals . . . was over 720,000, while those expelled [by the more informal procedure of "voluntary departure"] exceeded four million.[104]

Until 1996, US immigration law provided some opportunities for *discretionary relief from deportation* for aliens who were lawfully admitted as permanent residents but faced removal because they had criminal convictions. Section 212(c) of the Immigration and Nationality Act (INA) enabled aliens with substantial ties to the United States to prove to an immigration judge that the negative aspects of their convictions were outweighed by their US connections. Moreover, an undocumented alien without any criminal convictions and seven years continuous presence in the US could receive a *suspension of deportation* if he or she could establish the deportation would result in *extreme hardship* to the deportee or a US citizen or permanent resident spouse, parent, or child.

Though both of these remedies had similarities to the European approach of balancing the interests of individual and state, in practice neither was at all easy to obtain. "Illegal aliens" faced particular difficulties. For them, the critical question revolved around demonstration of "extreme hardship," a term that was not defined by the Immigration and Naturalization Service (INS) or by the Supreme Court, but that was left to the attorney general to construe, "narrowly should [he] deem it wise to do so."[105] By definition, the normal, intense hardship that separation from a parent or enforced deportation from one's home country entails for a child was not sufficient to enable the parent of a citizen child to resist removal. In practice, the vagueness surrounding the term worked against the interests of citizen children and their immigrant parents, and led to "practically unattainable relief for the citizen child whose parents [were] subject to deportation."[106]

According to the Board of Immigration Appeals (BIA), "The mere fact that an alien's child is born in the United States does not entitle the alien to *any* favored status in seeking discretionary relief from deportation."[107] Economic loss, inadequate medical care in the country to which deportation was to occur, and lower standards of education have all been considered insufficient to establish extreme hardship. The impact of economic difficulties combined with language problems facing two children who had spent their whole life in the United States, only spoke English, and faced constructive[108] deportation to the Philippines were found not to constitute extreme hardship. Only exceptional cases, raising life-threatening medical conditions or unusually pressing individual circumstances, could benefit from the narrowly drawn provisions. So, for example, suspension of deportation was granted in the case of a Colombian mother of a citizen child who claimed deportation to Colombia would put both of them in mortal danger because of risks from the husband who had severely abused her repeatedly and was serving a sentence for shooting two men who had tried to restrain him from attacking his wife and daughter. But in other cases posing extremely negative results for citizen children, the deportation of long-settled parents was not considered an extreme hardship.

A case in point is *Hernandez-Cordero*: a Mexican couple who had lived continuously in the United States for twelve years prior to their deportation proceedings—with three US-citizen children who could not read or write Spanish, substantial assets, and strong credentials as an exemplary family—were denied suspension of deportation. It was held the children would not suffer extreme hardship, which the court defined as hardship that is "uniquely extreme, at or closely approaching the outer limits of the most severe hardship the alien could suffer."[109] In a case difficult to reconcile with this Mexican case, a Taiwanese couple were granted relief because their fifteen-year-old US-citizen daughter was not fluent in Chinese.[110] Judicial decision makers clearly adopted a different approach to devising a standard that reflected their ambivalent legal mandate—to respect the child's best interests within the confines of an extremely limited scope for discretion.

Given the facts of *Hernandez-Cordero*, and the gloss on "extreme hardship" just quoted from that case, it is surprising the US government considered it necessary to further restrict the exception to mandatory deportation of irregular migrants. But they did. Since 1996, the seriously limited forms of relief for criminal and undocumented aliens just discussed have been even more severely curtailed. The *Antiterrorism and Effective Death Penalty Act* and the *Illegal Immigration Reform and Immigrant Responsibility Act* together have stripped aliens convicted of a large number of offenses defined as "aggravated felonies" from the relief they were eligible for under Section 212(c). And the statutes have extended from seven to ten years the continuous residence requirement for eligibility for discretionary relief for undocumented aliens. As noted at the beginning of this chapter, discretionary relief from deportation is now only available in the "most extreme and unusually compassionate circumstances." If the earlier relief was considered "practically unattainable," its more recent substitute is all but illusory—requiring proof that the hardship caused by deportation is "substantially different from, or beyond, that which would normally be expected from the deportation of an alien with close family members here."[111]

The impact of these measures has been devastating for thousands of families and their US-citizen children. In a decision issued the same day as the successful Taiwanese appeal against deportation just discussed, but covered by the new and harsher cancellation of removal standard, the BIA upheld the deportation order of a thirty-four-year-old Mexican father[112] who had lived in the United States since the age of fourteen and who had three US-citizen children. The Board held that deportation would not result in "exceptional and extremely unusual hardship" to his wife and children in part because the wife and children were able to speak and write in both English and Spanish, which would facilitate their integration in Mexico.[113] More recent cases have followed this harsh trend. The Court of Appeals upheld the immigration judge's decision to deny cancellation of removal to a family with three citizen children, one of whom had a "problem with speech," because the father had previously failed to find treatment for his daughter's "serious speech issue";[114] and it denied cancellation of removal to parents of four US-citizen children, one of whom had a speech disorder and required special education.[115]

In these situations, where the parent's alienage trumps the right of the citizen child to parental care and companionship at home, citizenship loses all effective meaning for children.[116] Over the years, applicants and their advocates have attempted to argue that these harsh standards are unconstitutional, in that they deprive US citizens of the equal protection of US law to which they are entitled. Reducing the citizen child to a "mere bystander" in his or her parent's deportation-suspension proceedings denies the child constitutional due process rights as an American citizen and rights to parental companionship that have been recognized by U.S. courts in other areas concerning children. But these critics have had no success. In one case, the deportable parents of a US-citizen child argued that the de facto deportation faced by their child amounted to discrimination on the basis of her alien parentage;[117] in another, parents challenged the difference in the rights of under- and over-twenty-one-year-old US citizens, since the latter but not the former can transmit immediate immigration benefits to their parents.[118] Constitutional challenge has not advanced the position of citizen children on this issue.[119]

Ambivalence over Neglect of Child Citizen's Rights

The draconian regulatory framework has caused judicial disquiet among American judges, reflecting the impact of the ambivalent legal framework. In *Beharry v. Reno*, a New York district court judge granted a writ of habeas corpus to a convicted Trinidadian permanent resident seeking relief from deportation on the basis of his strong familial ties to the United States including a six-year-old citizen daughter. The court held that to do otherwise would be to contravene American obligations under international law. Drawing on international-law provisions protecting the right to family life and the child's best interests to challenge US statutory provisions, the court held that "forcible separation of a noncitizen legal resident [of the US] from his citizen child or spouse implicates this right to familial integrity."[120] However, this decision was reversed on appeal.[121]

In a second case, *Nwaokolo v. INS*, the Seventh Circuit Court of Appeals granted a stay of removal proceedings to the parent of two citizen children, because the immigration authorities had failed to consider the likely consequences of enforced removal on the citizen children. In this case, the parent had sought to resist removal from the United States by claiming that she and her two daughters would be subjected to female circumcision (often referred to as female genital mutilation or simply FGM) if she were returned to Nigeria. Both the INS and the BIA failed to consider the irreparable injury that the citizen children would suffer.

Reversing, the Seventh Circuit commented: "The record before us offers no reason to believe that the BIA *even considered* the threat to Victoria [the four-year-old citizen child] from the widespread practice of FGM in her mother's home country of Nigeria." Neither child had ever been represented by counsel or had had their interests directly considered by the authorities. "The government could never do to these girls in this country what the INS seems all too willing to allow to happen to them in Nigeria."[122] The court concluded that the BIA abused its discretion by failing to consider the relevant factor of the hardship to US-citizen children that would result from the deportation of the alien parent.

However, the impact of this decision too has been circumscribed by subsequent judicial pronouncements on deportation of citizen children's parents. Like the European Court of Human Rights decisions discussed earlier, most US judgments focus on the parent's behavior and how "deserving" he or she is, rather than on the impact on the citizen child. In *Oforji v. Ashcroft*,[123] the Seventh Circuit refused to reverse a decision denying asylum to the Nigerian single-parent mother of two young US-citizen girls. The court distinguished the case from *Nwaokolo* because the mother in that case had, unlike in *Oforji*, initially entered the United States legally and resided here continuously (albeit unlawfully as an overstayer) for over seven years, thus qualifying to make an "exceptional hardship" claim for her children under the terms of the regulations discussed earlier.

The *Oforji* court acknowledged that "as United States citizens, [the two children] have the right to stay here without [the mother], but that would likely require some form of guardianship—not a Hobson's choice but a choice no mother wants to make." The citizen children's likely choice was not even considered: "Undoubtedly, any separation of a child from *its* mother is a hardship. However, the question before us is whether this *potential hardship* to citizen children arising from the mother's deportation should allow an otherwise unqualified mother to *append to the children's rights to remain* in the United States. The answer is no."[124] The contrast with the ECJ's approach could not be clearer.

Citizenship Rights and Nondiscrimination

The position adopted by the European Court of Justice in *Zhu and Chen* and in *Zambrano* reflects the traditional view that citizenship signals a particularly close connection between person and territory. This view is trivialized when young children are given the "option" of staying in their home country only without their adult caregivers, or when, as with the US rules, child citizens have no impact on the deportability of their parents unless they face extreme medical emergencies or the threat of torture.

Birthright citizenship should bring with it a presumption of nondeportability for children just as it does for adults. In fact, a fortiori, given the significance of developmental experiences, of educational access, and of the powerful resource implications of continued residence within a developed country, the arguments for not deporting citizen children would appear to be even stronger than those for not deporting citizen adults. This is true from the viewpoint of the child's best interests. It is also true from the viewpoint of equity and nondiscrimination; for why should the right to family unity, to enjoyment of family and private life of the child, be less enforceable than the corresponding right for adult citizens? Why, as the ECJ wisely recognized in *Zambrano*, and the UK Supreme Court held in *ZH (Tanzania) (FC) v. Secretary of State for the Home Department*[125] should past time spent in a country rather than the prospect of future time enjoyed be the determining criterion of connection? What does citizenship bring to a child, if not the right to grow up in his or her country in the company and with the care of family?

The realist answer lies in the dichotomy between the child's best interests and the parent's just deserts. Punishing or excluding a parent may be socially and politically justifiable even if the consequences for his or her child are devastating and contradict a just approach—imprisonment is the clearest example of this. Moreover, the fear of perverse incentives—that attaching parental immigration rights to children's birthright citizenship produces undesirable migratory outcomes—militates against the *Zambrano* approach. Yet, the child's citizenship rights are irreparably (not temporarily, as often suggested) damaged when family-unity decisions are made only on the basis of the parent's immigration status and equities. Citizenship for a child quickly becomes a denuded status. In the absence of the other cardinal civil and political attributes of citizenship, citizenship for the child effectively means the entitlement to enjoy permanently and indefinitely the attributes of social and private life in the home country. Since, increasingly, permanent residents are also entitled to the full range of social provision, it is the *permanence of access* to these social goods, the fact of nondeportability for now and the future, that distinguishes the rights of the citizen child from the noncitizen child, not the access itself. A just legal framework incorporating a child's perspective would, like the ECJ has done, acknowledge this and increase the burden on the deporting state to demonstrate that the benefits of parental removal outweigh the costs of child separation, institutionalization, or disorientation. In short, a new set of variables would have to enter the reconfigured calculation of what is just, equitable, and proportional in a democratic society.

Birthright citizenship is an ascriptive status, not chosen or consented to, that provides the basis for future assumption of the obligations and responsibilities of adult citizens: the civic responsibilities, the legal benefits, the affiliative identifications. As the child develops and his or her capabilities evolve, so the balance between ascriptive status and consensual identification shifts—the child changes from a repository of protective concerns, a recipient of enabling inputs to an active participant, an autonomous contributor, a member of the community with an investment in its future harmony and vibrancy.

For children, then, citizenship like childhood itself is a status in process.[126] Initially, it has to be conceived of principally in terms of rights rather than obligations—rights to family life, to traditional civil and political freedoms as they apply, to education, social support, and protection from exploitation. Decisions about accessing and enforcing these rights are vested in the child him- or herself, insofar as the child is a "mature minor" capable of so doing; otherwise parents, or failing that the state in its capacity as *parens patriae*, have the responsibility. But access to these rights paves the way for the assumption of obligations on majority—the child is an adult in process, entitled to a "moral minimum" in order to be apprenticed into future effective participation in the citizenry.[127] Ability to enter into this apprenticeship and enjoy its attributes is a prerequisite for the assumption of the obligations of citizenship on majority. Citizenship, to be meaningful, then, is a civic practice that has to be lived and experienced and requires participatory presence and engagement; it is not simply a juridical status that is learned by watching from a distance.[128]

What sort of juror or voter with a contribution to make to his or her peers is one who has been forced to live outside the community during the pre-majority period? How is such a person to engage with the concerns of the polity in a meaningful and contributory, rather than hostile or resentful way? The child's enduring presence in the home country is thus not simply an important guarantee for the child of access to the rights and benefits of the community's social goods; it is also a prerequisite for the mature exercise of the obligations of citizenship as an adult. Excluding a child should thus be a last resort option, chosen only when overwhelming considerations of state security or public interest require it. It certainly should not be a convenient subsidiary instrument of defective immigration control.

Conclusion

The poignancy of this situation is well illustrated by the case of the undocumented, so-called *sans papiers* in France.[129] The sans papiers are parents of children born in France who are considered "nonexpulsables" because of their French-born children, but are also considered "nonregularizables" unless they have spent ten years on French soil, because no amnesty procedure has been afforded them.[130] As a result of their indeterminate status, they have faced constant state harassment.

In response, some of these parents organized politically, becoming involved in a hunger strike in 1995, in order to draw public attention to the impossibility of their situation—long-term, settled "irregulars" with strong moral obligations and claims to remain in France but no legal remedies to enable them to do so.[131] An Aliens Bill, approved on its first reading in July 2003 and signed into law on November 26, 2003,[132] allowed parents of French-born children the right to apply for a residence permit if they had had at least five years of uninterrupted undocumented residence in France, or at least two years of residence since the expiration of a temporary visa, provided they could prove "exercise of parental responsibility" and financial support for the child.[133]

This is a far cry from focusing on the child's interest in having the care and company of his or her parents in the home country irrespective of the official acceptability of the parent's behavior. However, this approach did provide an avenue for short-circuiting the painful limbo of insecurity and discrimination that citizen children of alien parents were otherwise subjected to. The law was a response to the strength of public feeling about the injustice of penalizing citizen children for the immigration irregularities of their parents. Given the volatile racial politics of contemporary France, however, the prospects of longevity for this progressive legislation were poor. And indeed only one year after its enactment, the law was amended to deprive parents of citizen children of access to regularization of their immigration status, the amendment taking effect on March 1, 2005.[134] For an excluded and marginalized group such as the children of sans papiers to have received, albeit for only a year and a quarter, the right to legitimate their parents' stay because of their citizenship, was a dramatic and inspiring achievement. For it to have lasted such a short time is a sobering illustration of the tenuous access to just public policy this group has. But the vision of a rights-respecting approach to the interests and needs of child citizens is there, in the record. And the European Court of Justice, to its great credit, has begun to flesh out what such a vision might mean for a just and nondiscriminatory society. All that remains is for this vision to be realized more comprehensively, through the force of persuasion and political mobilization. Since children have to rely on the political clout of their more powerful elders, perhaps adult self-interest in avoiding deportation, rather than adult dedication to protecting children's rights will turn out to be the most promising engine of change.

CHAPTER 3
Family Ambivalence: The Contested Terrain of Intercountry Adoption

> Poor parents see foreign adoption as one of the few ways to give their children a decent life.[1]
>
> No child should have to grow up in an orphanage. . . . The answer is not to whisk children away to a new life thousands of miles from where they were born, unless as a very last resort. The answer is *far simpler.* Families need help to get themselves out of poverty, so they can feed, educate and protect their children in a loving, family environment.[2]

Star Power

On April 3, 2009, Judge Esme Chombo of the Malawian Family Court rejected an application by pop superstar Madonna to adopt CJ, known as Mercy, a three-and-a-half-year-old Malawian child. The child had been placed in the orphanage shortly after her birth. Her mother, a fourteen-year-old girl who became pregnant while in secondary school, had died a few days after giving birth; her father was unknown. Mercy was initially cared for by her sixty-seven-year-old maternal grandmother, whose circumstances were described as follows by the Malawian Supreme Court: "She is very poor and depends on subsistence farming. . . . [T]he area where the grandmother lives is frugal, squalid and desperate and poses health hazards to normal life for people living in this community."[3] Because of her circumstances, including the absence of any family support, the grandmother together with other members of Mercy's extended family asked an orphanage to take over care of Mercy. At the time of Madonna's application, Mercy was a social orphan who had spent her life in the orphanage; no extended family member or foster caregiver visited or came forward for her. Given these bleak circumstances, why did Madonna lose her first application to adopt Mercy?

The technical reason was clearly articulated by the judge in the Family Court. Madonna had failed to comply with a residency requirement for prospective adoptive parents: "According to information from the global media the Petitioner jetted into the country during the weekend just days prior to the hearing of this application." Reflecting on the dangers of "opening the doors too wide," the judge explained her concerns about intercountry adoption in general: "By removing the very safeguard [the residency requirement] that is supposed to protect our children, the courts by their pronouncements could actually facilitate trafficking of children by some unscrupulous individuals who would take advantage of the weakness of the law of the land."[4] Judge Chombo's court verdict unleashed international headlines and a lineup of sharply opposing viewpoints on what constituted "protect[ion of] our children." International agencies, represented by Save the Children UK, defended the court's decision to allow the child to stay in her original community, close to relatives and familiar cultural, linguistic, and ethnic practices. Intercountry adoption advocates, including the Center for Adoption Policy, criticized the court's decision to favor institutional care over the possibility of nurture in a nuclear family: "Each child deserves a permanent family," they said. Popular opinion mirrored this line-up of specialist opinion: while some expressed outrage at what they considered neocolonial exploitation to "save" poor black children, wresting them from their communities, others bemoaned the myopic stance of a court more interested in asserting proprietorial ownership of children as national assets than in ensuring access to the precious enjoyment of family life for a destitute and abandoned child.

The family court decision did not end the controversy. Two months later, following a determined public campaign, substantial financial investment in Malawi's child welfare system, and a carefully prepared legal appeal, Madonna appeared in Malawian court again to try and reverse the original judgment. She succeeded. By June 2009, Malawi's Supreme Court had given permission for the adoption to go ahead. Between April and June, nothing much had changed regarding Madonna's Malawian residence; her sojourn in Malawi still had none of the attributes of permanence that the judge at first instance had deemed essential. Nor had the generic threat of predators from outside intent on profiting from opportunities for child trafficking changed. But the Supreme Court placed itself on the opposite side of the polarized line-up. It reinterpreted the meaning of residence: "Appellant is not a mere sojourner in this country but has a targeted long-term presence aimed at ameliorating the lives of more disadvantaged children in Malawi. . . . [S]he is not here only to adopt CJ but to also implement her long-term ideas of investing in the improvement of more children's lives." The Supreme Court criticized the lower court's generic reference to potential outside threats: "[W]e think [the judge] fell in error by looking beyond the particular petitioner and the particular benefactor that were before the court and basing her decision on some imaginary unscrupulous individuals allegedly involving themselves in child trafficking."[5] After a high-profile media battle and vigorous legal intervention, Madonna succeeded in adopting Mercy.

Only one year before the Mercy adoption saga, Madonna's application to finalize another Malawian adoption begun two years earlier had proceeded without any hitches despite noncompliance with the same residency requirement. The adoption involved a three-year-old Malawian boy whose mother had also died within days of childbirth but whose father, unlike Mercy's, had been identified and was alive. In that case, the judge noted approvingly that Madonna and her then-husband "were not motivated by any material gain other than the joy of open arms." And he construed the residency requirement expansively as part of an integrated set of considerations rather than as a condition precedent to adoption: "[T]he requirement as to residence . . . is intended to protect the child, and to ensure that the adoption is well-intended. . . . [It] . . . is merely a means to an end. I . . . have no doubt in my mind that the 'end' is the best interest of the child."[6]

Public Ambivalence and a Contested Terrain

As chapters 1 and 2 have shown, the assumption that children belong within a nurturing family environment forms a bedrock of international human rights law. It is also a key feature of immigration and citizenship law. Children with no other legal claim are allowed to immigrate permanently, and citizen children are assumed to be constructively deportable because of the importance of family unity. Family protection through intercountry adoption is different, as the Madonna adoption saga illustrates. "Social and legal regulations vis-à-vis non-European immigrants and adoptees differ enormously, as do the attitudes of the native-born population."[7] In the immigration context, families make the primary decision about where the child should live, in the adoption context, as in international divorce situations, states do. Only intercountry adoption gives rise to heated public controversy over what constitutes the "best interests of the child."

The contrasting trajectories of Madonna's two attempts at adoption are emblematic of a multifaceted oscillation in intercountry adoption, "between the advocacy of 'child saving' and the condemnation of 'child trafficking,'"[8] between the search for a permanent home for abandoned children and the emphasis on strengthening vulnerable families. This oscillation belies a deep ambivalence that spans law, politics, and culture. It has an impact on the scale of intercountry adoption and the assessment of its legitimacy. Consider the question of scale. Over the last twenty years, the instance of intercountry adoption has more than doubled. Total intercountry adoptions in the countries with the highest numbers went from over 16,000 in 1980 to nearly 44,000 in 2004. In some countries the increase was even more spectacular: in Spain, the intercountry adoption rate more than trebled between 1998 and 2004.[9] In many European countries intercountry adoptions represent over half the total adoptions in the country.[10] But the upward trend is not consistent. Over the past five years, the numbers of intercountry adoptions in the United States have declined for the first time since World War II, from a high of over 22,000 in 2005 to under 13,000 in 2009.[11]

Public opinion about the legitimacy of intercountry adoption is a major factor in these oscillations. During the twenty-year period just described, by contrast with the unqualified approval of adoption following political upheavals in South Korea, South Vietnam, and Romania, a vociferous lobby critical of intercountry adoption has developed. UNICEF has raised concerns about predatory practices leading vulnerable and poor mothers to relinquish their babies in return for small monetary payments. Researchers have documented "child laundering" networks that supply well-intentioned adoptive parents with children "available" for adoption from orphanages as a result of strong-arm, financially lucrative deals.[12] Many destination countries have prohibited adoption of children from specific origin countries until adequate procedures and safeguards against such practices are in place.[13] At the same time, several origin countries have also responded to high-profile cases of abuse or maltreatment of adopted children by restricting or closing down their intercountry adoption processes.[14] Russia, the third largest source of adopted children in the United States,[15] has banned adoptions to the United States[16] following two incidents in 2010 and 2011.[17] Adult intercountry adoptees have also begun talking and writing about their unsettling, fractured, even traumatic experiences,[18] challenging the earlier orthodoxies that described intercountry adoption as a win-win process.[19] In response, pro-adoption advocates have insisted on the urgent need to enhance the availability of intercountry adoption for the millions of babies and young children who face precarious and destitute lives in institutions or on the streets. Rightly (but without justifying why they are the best interlocutors), they point out that this is the only constituency whose voice in the raging adoption debate is more or less completely absent.[20] And they challenge critics to produce evidence to substantiate some of the "urban myths" about adoption-related child abuse.

At the heart of these oscillations are contested understandings of "the best interests of the child," understandings that are informed by different human rights principles and evaluative frameworks. Some of these contestations stem from unresolved philosophical questions. Robert Mnookin asks, "How is happiness at one stage to be compared with happiness at another?"[21] There are differing answers to the inevitable indeterminacy of outcomes and the counterfactuals they raise—how will a child exercise his or her ability to choose life's goals in the future, and what course of action is likely to be most conducive to an enabling outcome? And there are different evaluations of the relative importance of cultural as opposed to distributive-justice considerations, the impossibility of arriving at an agreed universal checklist for what constitutes "best interest."

I first started researching and writing about intercountry adoption about eight years ago. At the time I was struck by the plethora of evidence of poorly supervised adoption procedures and of improper financial arrangements involving destitute birth mothers and middlemen supplying babies to orphanages. A careful report by UNICEF about adoption in Guatemala was representative of many exposés of adoption rackets, and baby-selling schemes. The report described Guatemala, at the time among the top three countries of origin of children adopted by American parents, but with no indigenous tradition of adoption, as follows:

> In Guatemala, two parallel systems for processing intercountry adoptions are in use, the judicial and the extra judicial, both are legal. Only one percent of intercountry adoptions are carried out under the judicial procedure. The remaining 99 percent are handled under the extra-judicial process [which] is so lacking in transparency that it is impossible to determine, with certainty, the origin of the child, under what conditions the child was given up for adoption, whether or not the lawyer is involved in facilitating the trafficking of children, whether his fees represent "improper financial gain" or whether the character witnesses for the adoptive parents are even known to these parents. . . . Under this system it is impossible to ensure that the best interest of the child is being served.[22]

The risks of trafficking and abuse seemed to me to warrant considerable skepticism about the human rights justifications for intercountry adoption. I wrote: "The growing market in babies is a relatively new form of commodification of human beings. It shares many features with the more widely recognized market of trafficking in persons, particularly women and children."[23] Returning to the topic more recently, I am even more alarmed about the very unequal playing field on which intercountry adoption is transacted, the inadequacy of family support to poverty-stricken families, and the dramatic rightlessness of most birth mothers.[24] But, as this chapter will demonstrate, I also note the risks of inadequate domestic and international attention to incidents of institutionalized abuse and to endemic and extensive child neglect and deprivation. Because the voice of the child outside family care is completely absent from the discussion, the impact of long-term institutionalization is easy to neglect. It is also very hard to remedy. Some of the institutionalized children, those not permanently disabled by mental illness or drug addiction,[25] eventually opt for unaccompanied international migration as a survival strategy, risking their lives in precarious journeys. I will return to these situations in subsequent chapters.

Since my first work in this field, two welcome developments in scholarship on intercountry adoption have appeared: the proliferation of writing by transracial intercountry adoptees themselves, and deconstruction of "plenary adoption" as the only alternative to child abandonment and institutionalization. Both these inputs complicate the assessment of the impact of intercountry adoption on the best interests of the child. They also suggest as yet unexplored overlaps with policies and solutions related to domestic adoption and to child migration and immigration for family reunification. Questions of open adoption and the appropriate place of birth families that inform domestic adoption practice have direct relevance to intercountry adoption; understandings about bi-national or hybrid identity and about membership in diasporic communities that are helpful to construal of "best interest" for children in migrant families also apply to intercountry adoptees. I will suggest that the field of intercountry adoption would benefit from being brought out of its narrow ghetto into a more direct engagement with these related topics.

From "Win-win" to Contested: Changing Assessments of Intercountry Adoption

Though "transnational adoption has been on the margins of cultural consciousness for many generations"[26]—the transport of institutionalized British children to former colonies,[27] the removal of indigenous children from their homes to be relocated within "mainstream" society,[28] the large-scale "kindertransport" of Jewish children before the outbreak of World War II[29]—its dramatic expansion is relatively recent. When the contemporary phenomenon of intercountry adoption first took shape in the aftermath of World War II it was perceived as a well-intentioned and positive response to the need for care of war orphans: "Parents and adoption agencies did not question that their acts were good deeds."[30] Over the years, however, the source countries for intercountry adoption have changed radically, "[f]rom the predominance of war-torn and defeated countries after World War II through the long period of adoption from South Korea after the Korean War to the emergence of Latin America as a major source in the 1980s and the recent dominance of China and Russia, with brief periods of high levels from Vietnam and Romania."[31]

The primary impetus for intercountry adoption has changed too. Though contemporary adopters from faith-based communities (many of whom already have children themselves) may be motivated by the desire to "save souls for the Lord,"[32] saving war orphans has generally given way to providing a permanent home for social orphans. Intercountry adoptees are frequently described interchangeably as orphans,[33] but the literature suggests that a significant proportion are not orphans at all: "[t]he fact is that the vast majority of children living in orphanages aren't orphans. Most have at least one parent. And those that don't almost always have extended family that could give them the loving home they need—with the right support."[34] Today parental destitution or social/political pressure rather than death or disappearance appears to be the prime factor motivating relinquishment.[35] The impetus to adopt, and its timing, are increasingly adult- not child driven. While some adopters are proselytizing evangelists, most adults engage in intercountry adoption as part of a family-building and family-sustaining exercise. In the process, intercountry adoption has come to resemble family-driven child migration much more than it once did.

Concerns about Abuse

This is not to suggest that physical or manmade emergencies play no part in the decision to adopt internationally or that child protection does not form a central part of the motivation to adopt in a significant minority of cases, whatever the background circumstances. But these interventions no longer generate an unequivocally positive attitude, because the background assumptions and contexts have changed. Consider the rapid turnabout in attitudes to intercountry adoption following the devastating earthquake in Haiti on January 12, 2010. Within days of the disaster, several governments, including the United States and Canada, announced expedited procedures for facilitating the family "reunification" with prospective adoptive parents of hundreds of Haitian children in adoption proceedings legally under way before the earthquake. Public opinion was uniformly positive across the religious and political spectrum. Roman Catholic leaders in Miami applauded the plan unveiled by US Homeland Security Secretary Janet Napolitano;[36] the liberal opposition in Canada endorsed the government's new fast-track adoption process to welcome children who had survived the earthquake "to enter Canada as quickly as possible."[37]

But the dangers of fast-tracking adoptions, even in acute emergencies such as Haiti, rapidly surfaced. Less than a month after the earthquake, ten American missionaries trying to leave Haiti with a group of thirty-three undocumented Haitian children were arrested and detained on charges of illegally transporting children. Contested accounts immediately spread: some of the American travelers described their intentions as "upright and pure," designed to "help the children start a new life." Haiti's prime minister, however, characterized the incident as "a kidnapping case." A complex and troubling story emerged, suggesting that many of the children rounded up were not orphans at all as had been claimed, and that some of the adults involved in the transport had checkered prior histories.[38] The attitude toward fast-tracking and airlifting of Haitian children rapidly changed, leaving a confused and ambivalent global public torn between the desire to provide humanitarian assistance to acutely vulnerable children, and realization of the dangers of unregulated child appropriation, including the ever present risk of exploitation and abuse.

Half a year after the earthquake, with over one thousand Haitian children whisked off to the United States (a figure that exceeds US adoptions from Haiti over the previous three years), some of these apprehensions about risk were confirmed: children had been sent away without proof that they were orphans or that surviving relatives had consented, adopting parents had received children without prior screening, some airlifted children had ended up in juvenile detention centers because no matching family was arranged prior to their transport. However, other children, already certified as "adoptable" but stuck in orphanages for months due to administrative delays, suddenly and miraculously found themselves transferred to families that had been waiting for them.[39] A case study in mixed outcomes.

While procedural safeguards are essential, they must reflect the urgency of securing appropriate child care—they need to be expeditious not dilatory. They also must be monitored and transparent rather than labyrinthine and arbitrary. The availability and suitability of local and international care options can be investigated concurrently.[40] Speedy access to foster care pending background checks and investigation of alternative child care options can be promoted as an alternative to long-term institutionalization and concurrently with procedural investigations or compliance with lengthy parental residency requirements. Especially for very young children, time spent in institutions threatens their well-being and should connote urgency. In practice, however, current procedures including checks with no time limits, politically driven moratoria, and compulsory waiting periods to seek out local-care alternatives, compound the delays. According to the US State Department, it takes an average of 254 days for an adoption from China to be completed.[41]

The Haiti adoption scandal was not the first of its kind. Just two years earlier, a French volunteer group called Zoe's Ark traveled to the Chad/Darfur border to "save" over a hundred Chadian "orphans" caught up in the protracted Darfur conflict by airlifting them to France where adoptive families were waiting. This incident too attracted huge attention. Evidence again emerged that many of the children were not orphans at all, and within days, the president of Chad publicly condemned the act as clear evidence of kidnapping, trafficking, or even potential organ harvesting, though (as in the Madonna case) no specific evidence was provided to substantiate these extreme allegations.[42] Similar accusations surfaced in the aftermath of the Asian tsunami and the Rwandan genocide, with humanitarian workers emphasizing the risks posed by predatory outsiders gaining custody of available children, whether or not they were really "adoptable," in order to profit from the demand for adoptees. After the scandals subsided, so did public concern with the reality of child destitution and family insecurity, and the support for family protection and *in situ* child welfare. The radical mismatch between the substantial resources spent on the (relatively) few children adopted intercountry and the utterly inadequate socioeconomic engagement with millions who languish in intolerable conditions continues to provoke a widespread ambivalence about the intercountry adoption project as a whole—a growing malaise over "implicit neocolonial overtones."[43]

Deconstructing "Plenary Adoption"

So, over the years, what seemed like an example of disinterested transnational engagement and straightforward human solidarity has become less easy to distinguish from some of the most ethically complex migration patterns of our age. Concern about abusive adoption procedures and investment disparities are not the only causes for skepticism about the value of intercountry adoption. Another reason for the shift in public attitude is increased uncertainty about the unqualified benefits of "plenary adoption," that is adoption that irreversibly severs the child from the birth family and places the child in an unrelated nuclear family.[44] The uncertainty stems in part from concern that "plenary adoption," and the radical break in contact with the birth family that ensues, may suit adoptive parents in search of a child better than it suits other members of the adoptive triad ("adoptable" children and birth parents).[45] While growing numbers of intercountry adoptees insist on their rights to (and the psychological importance of) information about their birth origins,[46] the voices of birth parents are also increasingly heard, with some speaking about the enduring trauma of their loss.[47]

Questions about "plenary adoption" also stem from growing skepticism about how appropriate the standards of First World child-rearing norms are for measuring child care in societies with more flexible and extensive kinship networks.[48] Where children have living parents and/or relatives, when are professional decision makers justified in considering them "social orphans" or "socially naked" children whose best interests lie in intercountry adoption?[49] Placement in an institution often accelerates the social stripping that precedes adoption: "By entering the anonymous non-kin world of an institution, usually an orphanage, the abandoned child who is earmarked for adoption overseas enters a liminal world, awaiting a new set of kin."[50] Uncertainty about the "adoptability" of destitute children stems in part from concern about where to draw the dividing line between child neglect and poverty, between parental incompetence and despair. In Peru, for example, according to Jessaca Leinaweaver, "[w]hile the law carefully asserts that 'the lack of material resources in no way justifies the declaration of abandonment,' in practice, poverty is translated into [i.e., interpreted as] malnutrition and ill health among children and psychological incapacity among parents."[51]

Where children are placed in or abandoned to institutions by their families[52] because of disease, disability, or family destruction, it is likely that adoption (including intercountry adoption if domestic adoption is not available) will further the child's best interests better than the other available child care options. Procedures guaranteeing and facilitating this must be encouraged and supported; concerns about abuse should not eclipse this central and critical role for intercountry adoption.[53] But other apparently clear-cut situations of institutionalized children voluntarily abandoned by their families, turn out on careful inspection to be murky, complicated by a close relationship between the economic enticements generated by the intercountry adoption market and the production of "adoptable babies."[54] In China, for example, the one-child policy together with the cultural "need" for a son[55] has created powerful disincentives to family retention of "over quota" children, especially daughters, born in contravention of family-planning regulations. The situation has led, in some reported cases, to forcible snatching by local officials of children from indigent families unable to pay fines[56] that would permit baby retention. This process of baby confiscation feeds the strong, financially backed demand for intercountry adoptees and deflects future adoptees from a domestic child-support system into orphanages that prepare these children for foreign adoption.[57]

The Demand for Healthy Babies, the Imperative of Best Interest

Though millions of children lack adequate care, intercountry adoption today is probably[58] largely driven by a family formation strategy for adults who want to raise children but are unable to give birth themselves because of infertility, sexual orientation, or other family circumstances (e.g., being single). This skews the demand toward healthy babies, and away from the disabled, older, or other "harder to place" categories of rejected or otherwise needy children. The top source countries for intercountry adoptees today are not "postconflict" states but rather countries such as China, Ethiopia, and Russia with large numbers of institutionalized children and weak systems of family protection and support.[59] Thus the child-protection crisis generating a need for adoption is no longer, primarily, the result of family destruction caused by conflict or disaster, but of family destitution or disintegration caused by poverty, addiction,[60] and lack of rights (including reproductive rights). "In most cases it is poverty, and the ensuing hunger and lack of opportunity, that forces parents to give their children up in the hope of giving them a better future."[61] A central question therefore is how the "best interests of the child" principle should be construed in relation to questions of distributive justice.

As has been remarked, "If the best interests of the world's children are a primary consideration, rich nations will have to re-examine many of their policies."[62] Not only rich nations, one might add. The desire to adopt, to create "new geographies of kinship"[63] immerses adoptive parents in questions of global inequality and in moral dilemmas that resemble the complex weighing of incommensurable factors in immigration and deportation contexts. Whereas decision makers in the latter cases have to compare the possible detriment to the state with the likely benefit to the individual, adoptive parents have to evaluate the legitimacy of engaging in a process that produces "adoptable" children shorn of familial embedding. They also have to make decisions about the relative weight they accord to their desire for a baby that is healthy, newborn, and perhaps racially similar to themselves, versus the urgency of the baby's need for a nurturing home: generally, these two sets of factors are inversely related. The decisions involve the evaluation of general data and case-specific information, an assessment of complex counterfactuals, and, in the end, the exercise of discretion.

Information on some relevant matters is plentiful. A widely cited study notes that children in Russian orphanages have a grim prognosis: one out of three become homeless, one out of five commit crimes, one out of ten commit suicide. In 2006, according to official Russian figures, about 800,000 children were without parental care.[64] There can be no doubt about the effect of deprivation in many orphanages. An important longitudinal study of Romanian orphans in state care has shown that institutionalized children may experience stunting unrelated to malnutrition. They may also experience reduced intelligence, reduced language development, and greater psychiatric disorders. The same study showed increased physical growth and psychosocial well-being for children placed in (very well-supported) foster homes at a young age.[65] As the judge in the first Madonna case rightly commented:

> The reality of the situation in Malawi is that a lot of children are in dire situations of material deprivation characterized by poverty, lack of access to essential nutrition, lack of access to education, lack of access to proper sanitation and lack of access to adequate health care. This is the inescapable reality in Malawi as in most third world countries. And to argue that we will soon find adequate solutions for all our deprived children is to assert a shameless and insolent lie.[66]

Babies and children orphaned by the AIDS pandemic, the overwhelming majority of whom live in Africa,[67] are the clearest example of urgent need and inadequate provision. According to the United Nations, global adoptions would need to increase by a factor of sixty to provide families to all AIDS orphans. This claim ignores the reality of extended family or other forms of informal care that most AIDS orphans grow up with, but it does draw attention to the huge strain on traditional care mechanisms generated by the pandemic.[68] Meanwhile intercountry adoption has not been part of the solution. To quote one observer: "Though it is not explicitly U.S. policy to exclude HIV positive adopted children, and these children generally respond rapidly to the onset of medical treatment in America, the immigration paperwork is more complicated, and few families step forward for these youngsters."[69] The case of Ethiopian adoptions is illustrative. In 1999 there were nearly 16,000 intercountry adoptions in the United States and only 42 were from Ethiopia,[70] a country with an estimated 800,000 AIDS orphans.[71] By 2002 Ethiopia accounted for a quarter of all African orphans adopted into the United States, but still only ranked seventeenth among countries of origin (with 105 adoptions, in contrast to some 5,000 each from Russia and China). But this situation is changing. According to the US State Department, adoptions from Ethiopia to the United States increased from 284 in 2004 to a peak of 2,511 in 2010, dropping to 1,732 in 2011. Whereas in the early 1990s Ethiopia was not among the top twenty countries of origin of orphans adopted into the United States, it has been every year since 1997, and is among the top five countries since 2007.[72]

This growth in the number of Ethiopian adoptees each year is noteworthy, given that an estimated 5.5 million Ethiopian children are orphans, 16 percent having lost one or both parents to AIDS.[73] (Russia by contrast, which also did not feature in the top twenty countries of origin until 1992, was first on the list in 1998 and 1999 and has, until the recent ban, been a close second to China since. Russia has consistently been the third largest source of children adopted into the United States since 2007.)[74] As elsewhere, the growth of intercountry adoption has had a mixed response in Ethiopia. According to an Ethiopian expert: "Public opinion seems ambivalent, undecided and of two minds. While some perceive international adoption as 'manna from heaven' for the adoptive child, others look at it as a disgrace for the country of origin and an act of profiteering at the cost of vulnerable children."[75] Meanwhile it appears that domestic adoption in Ethiopia is a much more laborious and complicated procedure than intercountry adoption, a troubling reflection of the broader context within which intercountry adoption often takes place.

The Baby Market—A Case of Trafficking?

Public ambivalence toward intercountry adoption is, primarily, the result of concerns about the context within which the process takes place, not the motives of adoptive parents. This is an important distinction. Well-meaning adopters can fuel processes that are abusive rather than protective of children's best interests. The availability of a lucrative intercountry adoption market distorts child-welfare policy and individual family decision making in many developing countries. Where political capital for child protection is limited, choices have to be made about the central focus of child-rights policy. Several poor states have chosen to acquiesce in rather than aggressively tackle child relinquishment in the knowledge that obligatory donations to the domestic child-welfare system by adopters[76] replenish their depleted coffers while foreign homes are found for many of the children who are abandoned (with welcome foreign-exchange benefits from fees paid to local handlers). As anthropologist Pauline Turner notes: "Adoption across political and cultural borders may simultaneously be an act of violence and an act of love, an excruciating rupture and a generous incorporation."[77]

Over the years, a range of adoption subcultures defying effective regulation have flourished. Mexican babies have been rented by smugglers assisting Central Americans to cross the border into the United States by posing as bona fide families.[78] Trafficked Chinese babies have been gender segregated—the boys sold for the domestic market to couples anxious to have a male heir (an aspect of the dramatic rise of a market economy in China),[79] the girls supplied to orphanages that service the international market of religiously motivated "rescuers"[80] or Western couples unable to have biological children.[81] Post-Communist Russia, with spiraling destitution, addiction, and failing state-welfare infrastructure is a plentiful source of white babies. Sometimes the differentiation within the baby market is even more specific than simply race: "'I know one with blonde hair, green eyes, very beautiful, you will love her.' The price? £70."[82] At its worst, in countries from Guatemala to Ethiopia to Tajikistan, babies have become big business, a commodity that is openly exchanged to satisfy a Western market where the child has become, literally, "priceless." There are remarkable parallels to the United States in the 1930s, where "childless couples were paying large sums of money to purchase a black market baby."[83] The fact that childless couples today are willing to pay substantial fees to secure a suitable adoptable child is not per se a sign of abuse—after all, intercountry adoption is a complex transaction involving multiple actors who can legitimately claim a fee. But the contested boundary between payment for services and commodification of children raises concerns. According to UNICEF: "While a good many intercountry adoptions are completed in good faith, increasing commercialization and the lack of adequate safeguards are resulting in criminal abuses including trafficking in, abduction, and sale of children."[84] How valid is this claim?

As the next chapter will explore in greater detail, to be trafficked, according to international law, is to be moved for the purposes of exploitation.[85] Typically it is a brutalizing experience that destroys most aspects of the life of the trafficked person—health, self-confidence, family life. Trafficking poses serious challenges for law enforcement because it is carried out by a constantly evolving, sophisticated transnational network that defies national policing capabilities while generating huge profits.[86] Given that trafficked children are moved to be exploited whereas adopted children are moved to be nurtured, what features might intercountry adoption and trafficking have in common?

Here are some. Both phenomena involve the globalized and commercially mediated transport of individuals accompanied by strangers[87] across continents. Both have been enhanced by advances in global information technology because they rely heavily on the internet to match demand and supply.[88] Both reflect a crisis in family relations and economics driving the supply of transportees: the inability of birth families to sustain all their members, driving some to desperate migration strategies (that end in trafficking), driving others to abandon babies, and yet others to seek out babies they cannot give birth to themselves. This much should be noncontentious. What is strongly disputed, however, is the degree to which coercion or exploitation plays a part in intercountry adoption, as it does by definition in trafficking.

Clearly the babies have no say in the matter—a central stakeholder is silent. The agency of another central stakeholder, the birth mother, is circumscribed by pressure, either direct (from families or coercive laws) or indirect (from financial incentives, social and economic hardship). Just as young women frequently agree to travel with traffickers in return for enticing gifts and the promises of flattering romantic attention and rosy opportunities abroad, only to find themselves trapped, so, it is suggested, young mothers frequently agree to part with their babies in return for desperately needed financial inducements and/or the promise of prosperous futures for their children. Where basic and essential welfare resources for family care are lacking,[89] this may be a sad but rational decision driven by the "best interests of the child." Over the last two decades, like trafficking, intercountry adoption has been driven by demand as much as by supply. The market in babies exists because there are prospective parents dedicated to making a lifelong contribution to the lives of some of the world's most deprived children—but only if they can care for them as their own children. The same funds are not offered as financial assistance to needy birth families. As a BBC talk show about the Madonna adoption put it: "adoption and charity are not synonymous. They arise from completely different impulses. . . . People do not adopt because they feel sorry for children."[90] The market strength of potential consumers or customers has driven the expansion and differentiation of the trade,[91] not the availability of ample supplies of very needy children, which had long existed independently.[92] As Guatemala's prosecutor for crimes against women and children, engaged in investigating 110 cases of adoption irregularity, noted: "The money tempts everyone."[93] Every one of the babies adopted intercountry every year is part of a transaction that includes a range of fees and expenses. This does not contradict the possibility of nonpecuniary benefit on both sides of the transaction—assurance of a loving and well-supported home for one's child in the case of the birth mother, and of an adoptable baby in the case of the adoptive parent. Not so different, one might say, from the nonpecuniary benefit accruing from the consciously chosen exit strategies selected by young women seeking to improve their future prospects: "Marriage migration is one of the best options for a girl who wants to leave China."[94]

The market concept also applies to another aspect of intercountry adoption. Price is, as with all markets, a relevant factor. The executive director of the Adoption Council of Ontario attributes China's popularity partly to the fact that the intercountry adoption program "carries a relatively low price tag."[95] But how much does this matter? According to an adoption advocacy organization: "Ultimately the amount intermediaries are paid for their services really is not the key issue. The basic concern is whether financial means unduly influence intermediaries to act in a way that is illegal or against the best interest of the child. Of utmost concern in relinquishment adoptions is whether the birthmother was coerced."[96]

Situations where babies are transferred internationally under market arrangements may be mutually advantageous, motivated as much by genuine concern for the best interests of the disadvantaged child from both the birth family and adoptive parents, as by the desire to earn an income by the adoption experts. The payment of fees to cover transport, medical checks, administrative processes, expert advice and consulting, orphanage fees and government taxes and related charges is not ethically problematic either—if it is indeed true they are fees. But there is a clear moral difference between the payment of service fees and a commodity price. Everyone[97] agrees that babies should never be sold. Teasing out the difference between a service fee, a voluntary present, and a payment in exchange that commodifies babies, however, is not always straightforward, as this news story illustrates. A Tajik midwife, given a suspended sentence for selling a baby, wept as she described how she had looked after the abandoned baby in hospital for a month before she helped a couple to take him: "They did give me money but I didn't ask for it. They slipped the money to my pocket."[98] Was the baby sold? The same question has arisen in the Chinese context, where the "cost" of delivering babies from poor and remote rural areas to orphanages that cater to intercountry adoption includes more than the transport expenses or other disbursements.[99]

Just as it is difficult to draw a bright line between service fee and sale price, so problems arise in establishing a clear dichotomy between coercion and consent,[100] abuse and individual advantage, though the extremes on the continuum differ dramatically. To distinguish clearly between a coercive "threat" and a consensually accepted "offer" requires identification of a subjective boundary, a threshold of baseline expectations for each individual: anything below the threshold counts as a threat, anything above an offer. For people in dire poverty, for example, the possibility of giving up all contact with their baby in return for an assurance that the baby will thrive, or even that they will be relieved of all financial and social obligations for this child, may seem like an offer worth consenting to, rather than a coercive alternative. This may be true even as the players participate in a broader process that Richard Falk has called predatory globalization[101]—in which persons (in this case babies) from very disadvantaged backgrounds are commercially moved across borders to satisfy (in whole or in part) the interests of others.

Intercountry Adoption as a Form of Child Migration: The Development of International Legal Regulation

As the first two chapters explain, a series of human rights concerns arise when children migrate from home—to reunify with immigrant parents abroad or to travel with noncitizen parents facing deportation. These concerns are compounded when children leave both family and home, as is the case with adoption, particularly when international border crossing is involved. Legal regulation is required to facilitate access to suitable care and block other types of outcomes.

Concerns about the risk of abuse in the intercountry adoption process are not new. Many of the countries that generate "adoptable" babies are poorly regulated, vitiated by official corruption, degrees of lawlessness, and widespread poverty. The opportunities for profiteering and for abusive production of children for adoption are considerable. Sensationalist reports abound: in Albania a poverty stricken Albanian family exchanged the youngest of their seven children for a TV from a childless Italian couple;[102] in India,

> After Rukkibai . . . gave birth to her fifth daughter, a woman from a nearby village came and offered her 1,100 rupees—roughly $20—for the girl. . . . The same woman from the nearby village also bought other newborns from families here. But she was only a link in the chain. For a small amount . . . she passed the baby to others. Eventually the infants were taken to orphanages and then adopted, almost all by Westerners.[103]

Other stories feature Cambodia,[104] Korea,[105] or Guatemala.[106] Romania's flouting of a moratorium on out-of-country adoptions nearly threatened its accession to the European Union.[107] Star power has intensified media interest. Over the past few years, the intercountry adoption strategies of the likes of Angelina Jolie and Madonna (taking the lead from Audrey Hepburn and Mia Farrow years earlier) have been publicly debated at great length.

The first authoritative analysis of the dangers that an unregulated procedure could engender was provided by the Indian Supreme Court judge Justice Bhagwati in the famous 1984 case of *Lakshmi Kant Pandey v. Union of India and Others*.[108] The case paved the way for a new international regulatory approach. Prefiguring subsequent controversies, the court reviewed reports of fraudulent adoptions fueling racketeering and heard nationalist sentiments linked to descriptions of foreign childless couples benefiting from the destitution of Indian families. The facts of the case were certainly disturbing. Two young Indian sisters from a rural area, found alone and distraught on the streets of Bombay (as it then was), were placed in a remand home (a detention center) in the city and eventually declared destitute. A Swedish couple was granted guardianship of the children, and, after a successful High Court petition, was given permission to take the children to Sweden, where in due course the children were legally adopted and granted citizenship. Six months after the adoption was finalized, the birth mother, a laborer from a village some distance from Bombay, made a court application seeking custody of the girls. This was the outcome of two years of searching for her daughters, who were nowhere to be found one evening when she returned home late. She had filed a missing persons report at the local police station the following morning, but it was never connected to the two destitute girls found on the streets of Bombay a day later. Eventually the mother's quest resulted in proceedings seeking directions that the girls be returned to her or, as an interim measure, that the girls be brought from Sweden to Bombay to meet their birth parents. The Indian court held that the birth mother's claim was "totally untenable," that it would not best serve the interests or welfare of the girls to grant any of the relief sought by the birth mother. The court held that "only in exceptional cases, where it was established that the adoption was secured by fraud or misrepresentation, and the fraud or misrepresentation was *at the instance of the adopter*," should the adoption be set aside or ignored. Enabling the birth mother to visit the girls in Sweden was not considered an option.[109] The court having given consideration to the circumstances in the home country decided that "in spite of the sympathy one might feel for the natural mother, the effect of removing the girls . . . from the care and control of their adoptive parents would lead to disastrous consequences."[110]

Clearly the court was concerned about unsettling a permanent and well-functioning arrangement that appeared to have served the children well. The court's difficult choice arises in a range of situations in which birth parents unwittingly lose their children to the care of well-meaning strangers through complex processes of intermediation. These situations include the well-known example of Argentinian and Salvadorian children "disappeared" during the dictatorships of the 1980s and early 1990s, often abducted after their parents were arrested or murdered, and then placed in orphanages and given up for intercountry adoption to well-intentioned parents unaware of the antecedents. Michael Kennedy is one such case:

> What Michael Kennedy remembers from his childhood in El Salvador comes to him in flashes: picking coffee with his father; felling into the mountains with his family; hiding with his mother and sisters in a shelter dug into the side of a mountain during a raid, while his father, a guerilla, was off fighting. He remembers seeing his mother shot. It was then that Michael, six at that time and named Jose, was carried off by Army soldiers. The American family who adopted him soon after was told he was an orphan. That's what Michael thought too. . . . But last week Michael, now 26, did go back—for a reunion with his biological father, who has spent years working with a local private organization to find his children.[111]

Several human rights organizations, including Physicians for Human Rights in the United States and Pro Busqueda in El Salvador, have wrestled with the tension between the compelling claims of the birth families intent on tracing and reestablishing contact with children stolen from them decades earlier, and the legal and emotional claims of adoptive parents, and frequently (though not always) of adopted children too, resisting disruption of well-established family lives.[112] Recent reports of cases where children of undocumented migrants have been taken into care following the arrest and detention of their parents, discussed in chapter 2, have raised similar concerns. Advocates recount cases where their clients face termination of parental rights because of their inability to trace their children while they are in custody pending deportation.[113]

In the *Pandey* case, two issues were presented: a nationalist concern about the large numbers of Indian children being taken out of the country, never to return, and a child-welfare-driven anxiety about the safety and life prospects of the child in the new home. In a farsighted judgment, prefiguring the architecture of contemporary intercountry adoption law, the Indian Supreme Court mandated a clear division of labor between the receiving and sending countries: certification of the adoptive parents' suitability to adopt by a recognized agency in the receiving country, confirmation of the child's adoptability by a similar agency in the sending country, and relevant background information to enable the court to ascertain whether adoption would be in the child's best interests.[114]

The 1989 Convention on the Rights of the Child, the landmark international treaty consolidating children's rights, drew heavily on the scheme developed in the *Pandey* case five years earlier, endorsing the complementary partnership between countries of origin and receiving countries and prioritizing domestic over transnational placements to preserve cultural heritage: "States Parties . . . shall . . . recognize that intercountry adoption may be considered as an alternative means of child care, if the child cannot be placed in a foster or an adoptive family or *cannot in any suitable manner* be cared for in the child's country of origin."[115] Thus, under the CRC, intercountry adoption appears to be a last-resort option.

The phrase "in any suitable manner" denotes ambivalence. "Suitable" according to what metric? Might it include a month in an institution while the child's caretaker attends drug rehabilitation? Or living one's whole childhood as an "illegal" child, kept out of school because of parents' defiance of rigid birth-control policies? In what circumstances, if any, might intercountry adoption be considered less preferable than in-country institutionalization? The CRC's approach to legal regulation of intercountry adoption reflects public concern about the unequal purchasing power of birth and adoptive parents, and the exploitative mechanisms this can fuel, but it leaves open the relationship between "best interest" and suitability. It is an attempt to address the previous failure to devise ethical and effective procedures to rid intercountry adoption of its abusive elements, and to facilitate genuinely transparent and rights-respecting adoption.[116] But does it water down the primacy of the "best interests of the child" principle?

The CRC's approach has had a mixed reception. According to UNICEF, families needing support to care for their children should receive it, and alternative means of caring for a child should only be considered when, "*despite this assistance*, a child's family is unavailable, unable or unwilling to care for him or her."[117] But even this statement is ambiguous. Is provision of parental assistance a necessary precondition to adoption? A demand of this sort would eliminate intercountry adoption in the vast majority of cases. As a pro-adoption agency, Families Without Borders, has pointed out, in relation to Guatemala:

> For the past few years, efforts by the intercountry adoption community to promote and increase the numbers of domestic adoptions have been unsuccessful. . . . While in theory we would not fault UNICEF-funded

> education aimed at popularizing national adoption, we believe that funding needs for other relief programs are so overwhelming (for example, providing food and basic medical care to the Guatemalan children who live in dire poverty) that such a program of adoption education must be given relatively low priority.[118]

In Guatemala, where no indigenous tradition of adoption exists, the dramatic explosion of three hundred private foster homes, in effect private orphanages (as opposed to four state orphanages), prior to the current shutdown of adoptions evidenced the impact of private money on the rate of child relinquishment and on the development of a market.[119] By contrast, in countries emerging from colonialism and poverty into a global market economy with a growing middle class, domestic cultural attitudes toward adoption transform themselves to resemble those in the West, with increasingly sizable numbers of domestic adoptions taking place.[120] In South Korea, for example, 69 percent of all adoptions prior to 2004 were intercountry adoptions, but since 2007 the majority of adoptions have been domestic.[121]

Endorsement of the Convention's conservative approach to intercountry adoption also draws on anthropological data on the variety of child-rearing practices, including forms of "circular" child rearing in which different parties play a role at different times, as alternatives to childhood in an orphanage or on the streets. Claudia Fonseca interrogates the legitimacy of policies that "cast . . . aspersions on a wide array of options for childcare that [fall] outside the polarity of birth family versus adoptive family."[122] In her view, in the Brazilian context at least, a more careful assessment of the role of foster care and children homes as composite solutions is called for to evaluate where the best interests of the child may lie. Barbara Yngvesson relates the international endorsement of plenary adoption to Western demand:

> This form of adoption began in the 1950s as falling birth rates in the overdeveloped world and a scarcity of children available for domestic adoption created an opening for children in the so-called developing world to become resources for individuals and couples who wanted to become parents and were unable to bear a child. *Transnational adoption was conceptualized as simultaneously solving the adults' desire for a child and a child's need for a family, but in both cases the solution—"a family"—was the same.*[123]

Supporters of this approach point to rash of "child saving" adoption schemes instead of the rigorous development of sustainable family protection and child-support policies in country. International attention and goodwill are scarce commodities, they suggest, so if emphasis is placed on intercountry adoption, the needs of the majority of vulnerable children and families untouched by it are more likely to be overlooked.

But the CRC also has its fierce critics. Some see its restrictive approach to intercountry adoption as a gross overreaction to a few egregious cases of abuse, an approach that lamentably coincides with complacency about the widespread neglect of very large numbers of children. According to Elizabeth Bartholet, "[t]he law focuses on the bad things that might happen when a child is transferred from a birth parent. . . . [As a result] even when international adoption is officially allowed, it is in effect not allowed, except for a tiny percentage of children in need, leaving the rest to grow up in institutions or on the streets." If needy children themselves had an effective voice, she argues, they would contradict the prevailing orthodoxy that relegates them to "the horrors of institutional and street life"[124] and emphasizes state-centered solutions. Signe Howell also questions the CRC's essentialism that renders kinship and place of origin "integral to a genealogy that can only be based on biology,"[125] challenging the assumption that "blood is [always] thicker than water," and pointing out that many intercountry adoptees have flourished. An interesting aspect of this approach is that it moves the responsibility for child protection out of a purely domestic legal framework, envisaging solutions to problems of poverty and lack of opportunity that intersect with other aspects of contemporary child migration. Families with children (as chapter 1 noted), and children without families (as chapter 7 will discuss) often choose the uncertainties of migration over the economic miseries and lack of opportunities back home.

Criticism of the CRC's restrictive approach to intercountry adoption has had an impact on the development of subsequent international law. Four years after the CRC was signed, a new international treaty dealing with intercountry adoption, the 1993 Hague Convention on Inter-country Adoption was enacted. Instead of mandating the CRC's unequivocal preference for care in the country of origin, the Hague Convention requires a more nuanced decision-making procedure. An explanatory note to the Convention sets out the "subsidiarity principle" that addresses head-on the tension between in-country and family care.

> Subsidiarity in the Convention means that Contracting States recognize that a child should be raised by his or her birth family or extended family

> whenever possible. If this is not possible or practicable, other forms of permanent care in the state of origin should be considered. Only after due consideration has been given to national solutions should inter-country adoption be considered, and then only if it is in the child's best interests. As a general rule, institutional care should be considered a last resort for a child in need of a family.[126]

The emphasis here is somewhat different from the CRC's. Permanent care may not always imply adoption—a range of extended-family arrangements may also qualify. Thus, context and variations within domestic care-giving regimes have to be carefully considered before intercountry adoption is approved as the only viable permanent solution for a child. But under Hague, unlike the CRC, the sending country cannot refuse to consider intercountry adoption simply because "suitable" in-country institutional options are available. Instead the relevant question for the decision maker is whether a "suitable *family*" or other form of permanent care is available to provide for the child in the home country.[127] And even this does not prevent the possibility of intercountry adoption. The decision maker must simply give "due consideration" to adoption within the state of origin[128] when child-care choices are made. In practice, this approach has paved the way for a somewhat more international conception of the equivalence of placement destinations. Calibration of the relative benefits of different elements of child care is left to the decision maker. Some adoption advocates still counter that the Hague Convention, like the CRC before it, is too narrowly focused on preventing abuse than on promoting child protection, emphasizing violations against children—abduction, sale, trafficking [129]—and mirroring international institutional priorities. They note that, since 1994, the UN has had a Special Rapporteur on the Sale of Children and an Optional Protocol to the Convention on the Rights of the Child on the Sale of Children, Child Prostitution and Child Pornography, but no special focus on the hardships of institutionalized children.[130]

Modernizing Intercountry Adoption: Learning from Other Contexts

The regulatory framework for intercountry adoption established over the last twenty-five years has addressed many of the concerns about abuse raised in 1984 by Justice Bhagwati. From the vantage point of the migrating-child adoptee straddling two worlds, however, several fundamental improvements to the current system remain to be addressed. Two issues in particular stand out. One is the failure to secure accurate birth records that are retrievable as of right by the intercountry adoptee and, related to this, the insistence on "closed" adoptions when open adoption is more and more accepted in the domestic context. The other issue is the reductive understanding of cultural identity in the adoption context when decades of immigration have produced more differentiated, hyphenated, and capacious conceptions that enable child migrants to explore different facets of their lives and affiliations.

The Lessons of Domestic Adoption

Domestic adoption, first established in the United States in the 1920s and 1930s, reached its height in the 1950s and 1960s.[131] At this stage adoption was based on the *"as-if" model*: the adoptive family was constructed to be as similar to the biological family as possible, with a "clean break" from the birth family, secrecy about the baby's origins, sealed records, and a changed birth certificate. Of course this "as-if" model of adoption depended on a reasonable physical resemblance between baby and adoptive parents.

Gradually, as parents by choice or necessity moved to adopt children of different races and backgrounds from their own, the as-if model gave way to a *difference model*, an acknowledgment that the adoptive family was not a replica of the biological one. Indeed the whole concept of "the family" was challenged—paving the way for other challenges to follow and reflecting the increase in step-families, single-parent families, unmarried and gay-parent families.[132] Interracial adoption brought with it huge controversy about the appropriateness of moving poor black children into middle-class white families. Black community leaders and social workers decried this form of racial erasure and theft, as they saw it, and pressed for children to be adopted only by same-race parents. Prefiguring arguments in *Pandey*, these cultural-preservation advocates depicted interracial adoption as a form of illegitimate colonization, reminiscent of some of the worst horrors of slavery. Adoption advocates, by contrast, pointed to the oppressive conditions in which all children in institutional care in the United States were kept, and condemned the inevitable lengthening of such care that the race-matching adoption policies led to. They also criticized the essentialist (and patently false) assumption that people, including very young children, can only "belong" to same-race communities. Similar arguments and line-ups of opposing views have, as already noted, come to the fore in the international context.

Interracial and international adoptions have continued and so has discussion about the cultural issues that arise. In the domestic context, the development of a "difference" model of adoption opened the door for a challenge to the earlier "clean break" approach, and with it a challenge to the obliteration of the birth mother's presence. Gradually the secrecy and shame surrounding adoption has begun to give way to a more open engagement with the ambivalence generated by different types of family form. Recognition that a radical break from every aspect of the child's past life was not necessary had several important and beneficial consequences, including providing birth mothers with a voice, a role, a presence—however complex—in their children's new world. In the words of one birth mother: "I guess I expected her to know me, and she didn't, and it was like, she wasn't *my* baby any more, I mean, she's my baby but—but she's Joan and David's baby now. . . . I know she'll know who I am, and I still love her, and she knows, or will know . . . I'm her mother, but Joan's her mommy."[133]

The move away from the "clean break" approach also facilitated a more open discussion of racial difference. Adoptive families no longer looked as if they were biological families (of course biological children may also look different from their parents, particularly if the parent they resemble more is absent). The "secret" of adoption could no longer be concealed. Familiarity gradually reduced the "stare" factor for intercountry adoptees. According to one account:

> Five years ago, Ann Tollefson notes, her family was constantly stared at. Nobody was openly hostile, but often enough they'd point to her children—adopted from China, India and Vietnam—and ask, 'How much did they cost?' Today it is a different story. There are more mixed-race families in America than ever before. Hers was the only mixed-race family [in her St. Louis suburb] when she and her husband first adopted in 1995. Today, three other families have adopted kids from China, several more from Guatemala.[134]

Although the rates vary substantially from state to state, approximately one-fifth of all adoptions in the United States are transracial adoptions.[135]

Familiarity may reduce the hostility or novelty factor that intercountry adoptees encounter, but it does not necessarily resolve deeper issues, about belonging and origin. The words of a Swedish adoptee, of Ethiopian origin, are telling: "It is annoying . . . to always be met with questions about me and my origins. [As though] it is not natural that I am here," and

> Because of my exterior, the foreigner, the unknown is always with me. . . . When I try to gather together all the bits of myself, I easily lose myself. . . . When I walk by a mirror I see something exotic that I barely recognize. . . . [M]ost often the reflection in the mirror evokes questions that have no simple answers. I have tried to absorb the black but then I have difficulty holding onto the Swedish. I have tried to absorb the "Swedish" but then I haven't understood what I see in the mirror . . . almost an immigrant even though I felt myself to be extremely Swedish. And the immigrants thought I was like them. And my Swedish friends thought I was like them. And I couldn't really decide where I belonged.[136]

Many intercountry adoptees report the opposite reaction—a feeling of rejection from both their natural constituencies.

The ambivalence inherent in the adoptive transaction cannot be willed away, particularly when racial difference constantly exteriorizes it. Traces of origins are not obliterated by a clean break without the risk of doing severe injustice to at least one of the parties,[137] and perhaps to several. Domestic moves toward open adoptions, greater access to birth records, and easier communication between adoptive and birth families are consistent with these insights. But, as yet, the international legal framework is not. Somewhat paradoxically, the Hague Convention recognizes only plenary adoptions, replacing the child's original identity with a new one. Acknowledgment of the adoptee's origins is confined to his or her cultural roots while requiring legal termination of the relationship between the child and the family of origin. According to the Hague Convention, then, the historical anchor for the child is not a family but a nation or culture. As Yngvesson points out, "Tensions between sending and receiving nations . . . were finessed by [these] conflicting stipulations."[138]

Each of the three parties to an adoption is a stakeholder in questions of openness and closure. A measure of legal security is essential to support the adoptive parents' emotional and material commitment to wholeheartedly raising a child. Similarly, while many birth parents yearn for information about or contact with their relinquished children, some dread the potential disruption of the new life they have managed to construct and stick to their original insistence on anonymity as a condition of relinquishment—no one knows in what proportion[139] Certainly the interests of adoptive parents (rather than birth parents) have driven the pressure for legal closure.

For the adoptee, erasure of birth kin is a radical step, not self-evidently aligned to the "best interests of the child" under any credible psychological theory. The late Betty Jean Lifton, one of the first adoptees to write about adoption, claimed that it can lead to "genealogical bewilderment,"[140] since every adoptee wants to know where he or she came from and why he or she was "given up." Domestic adoption procedures now acknowledge that the child's best interests depend on attaching importance to the inevitable questions of origins, belonging, and rejection,[141] and that, as children grow up, their right to an "open future" should be enhanced, with the exercise of choice in selecting "life-goals."[142] The failure to maintain accurate birth records militates against this. Why is intercountry adoption different from domestic adoption?

International law acknowledges every child's right to a name, a family, an identity, and a record of his or her birth.[143] But the exact contours of the "identity" that is protected are ambiguous. International law does not, for example, stipulate exactly what "identity" information must be preserved for the child or by whom. It is left to each country to establish domestic procedures, and as a result, there is no uniformity or minimum standard. In practice, "[c]ountries that maintain reliable records . . . remain the exception." In China, for example, child abandonment is illegal and child relinquishment hard to justify officially: as a result, orphanages generally characterize adoptees as having been "found" rather than "left," though the reality is that the latter is a precondition of the former. It is well known that, over the years, Chinese families have placed their newborn girls in front of village police stations with surrender notes pinned to their clothes—to ensure that they will be "found" promptly and will qualify for adoption.[144] A fairly streamlined process, which has left the population-control policy in place while generating a steady supply of healthy adoptable infants for the burgeoning intercountry adoption market, is the result. Meanwhile there are substantial disincentives to transparency about the birth mother's identity and the child's birth details. Parents are only allowed to place a child for adoption in China if they are "unable to rear their children due to unusual difficulties." And if they do place a child for adoption, they are prohibited from having other children "in violation of the regulations on family planning." Even those who are permitted to place a child for adoption, including guardians and social welfare institutions, may do so in secret, and their wish for secrecy must be respected.[145] Advocates of intercountry adoption have not so far challenged these provisions, presumably in the interests of not interfering with the smooth functioning of the adoption process. But from the perspective of adoptees, and birth mothers, this is regrettable. Thousands of Chinese birth mothers must long for information about their daughters, and conversely, many adoptees would likely welcome access to information about the young women compelled by circumstances largely outside their control to relinquish them.

Information is a necessary but not a sufficient condition for addressing the ambiguity of an adoptee's identity. As noted, the Hague Convention, while legalizing the obliteration of birth-family ties, acknowledges the importance of cultural linkages. This emphasis is consistent with the development of "roots tourism," and other culturally inflected practices within the world of contemporary intercountry adoption that cultivate a sense of belonging to the "home country" among adoptees.[146] This is already a move away from a completely "clean break" or from guilty secrecy about the fact of adoption. But it generates other ambivalences. In what sense are children, adopted at or shortly after birth and raised in a developed country, "returning" to a "home" culture as opposed to an unknown and foreign country? Just as this question has been raised to challenge the legitimacy of deporting back "home" second-generation immigrants[147] who migrated from their countries of origin in their early childhood,[148] so similar considerations apply to intercountry adoptees and their "return" journeys. Such travel can emphasize a sense of displacement and hybridity rather than belonging. But not always. "Roots journeys" for some confirm a feeling of belonging. A spectrum of reactions has been documented: from huge emotion, relief, and delight at the opportunity to connect with biographically significant places and people, through bewilderment and ambivalence about the "home" culture, to outright "disidentification"[149] and rejection of any relevant connection.[150]

The Lessons of International Child Migration

There is growing investment in the creation of community among the diaspora of adult adoptees of similar background now living in the receiving countries, an investment enormously facilitated by global information technology. Korean adoptees, one of the earliest and largest modern intercountry adoptee groups now reaching adulthood, are the most organized, though groups of Vietnamese, Chinese, and Latin American adoptees are also noteworthy. Over the last twenty years, Korean adoptees have built up a well-developed network of organized groups spanning three continents: Asia, Europe, and the Americas. Their organizations function not only as forums for psychological support and exploration of often ambivalent emotions, but also as advocacy agencies highlighting concerns about racism in the receiving community and lack of access to birth records and other information about the family of origin. Korean adoptees have rewritten the historical record of their migration to some extent, moving away from an earlier "saving" narrative to an account that critically highlights South Korea's reliance on intercountry adoption as a mechanism for exporting deep social-welfare problems, with no attention to the needs or rights of the disempowered and voiceless birth mothers. The South Korean government has not directly challenged this account but has responded by consciously reaching out to include the adoptee diaspora within an enlarged, global "Greater Korea." Through the Overseas Korea Foundation, the government has sponsored motherland tours and homecoming conferences targeted at overseas Korean adoptees, with a view to enhancing their identification with the "home" country. As Eleana Kim, points out, these initiatives are based on the contradictory assumptions that adoptees both "have a Korean identity" and yet are culturally incompetent tourists when they visit "their" country.[151]

Similar issues have come to the fore in immigrant organizations that have flourished over the years since large-scale migration to Western countries. Immigrant diasporas, and the artistic, scholarly, and entrepreneurial activities associated with them, have also spawned radical contemporary challenges to earlier understandings of identity, belonging, and affiliation.[152] They have questioned simplistic accounts of the givenness of race or ethnicity, of the unitary nature of the self.[153] These conceptual moves speak to the ambivalences faced by intercountry adoptees, though of course the analogy between family migration and intercountry adoption only goes so far. "Whereas the diaspora communities of transnational migrants are replete with significant others in their new country of residence, their country of origin, and many corners of the world, the significant others of adoptees are their adoptive family and its kin. By and large, adoptees are "socially naked" in relation to their country of origin."[154]

Some suggest that these differences delegitimize the comparison between immigrant and adoptee diasporas or migrations altogether. According to Signe Howell, "Transnationally adopted persons are anomalous within the diaspora community of their birth country. . . . To characterize [their] international organizations . . . as a manifestation of diaspora would be to extend the meaning of that concept beyond the limits of its usefulness."[155] In a similar vein, Eleana Kim notes: "Although similar to 'exiles' or 'refugees,' adoptees are distinct because of their emigration as children. The aspect of agency that grants a measure of rational choice to exile, even under extreme duress, is arguably of a lesser degree and kind for the adoptee."[156]

But the differences are perhaps not as great as suggested. As this book shows, very sizable numbers emigrate alone as children, in different ways, and there are significant similarities between young migrants who cross borders, with or without their families, and intercountry adoptees. Both groups leave their birthplace without any meaningful opportunity to make a choice, both move to live in new contexts where their race, ethnicity, and/or religion may render them minorities. Both groups belong, in a sense, to two communities, a "home" in the developed state and a "family" or homeland far away. Like intercountry adoptees, child migrants are a very diverse group including asylum seekers, children smuggled or trafficked across borders, and economic migrants.

Like intercountry adoptees, these children straddle different ethnic, religious, and cultural worlds, many without their birth parents close by as anchors or nurturers. Like adoptees, many migrant children experience a high degree of "social nakedness"—as unaccompanied refugees, as victims of trafficking, as deportees back to countries with which they have little or no connection. The challenges of dealing with hyphenated identities and a sense of belonging are in some ways common to both. And yet, intercountry adoption law addresses the question of cultural belonging through a time warp, based on dichotomies of self and other, on plenary adoption within the nuclear family, and on radical severance from the birth family, far removed from the nuances of contemporary discussions of the psychological and social correlates of migration and the acknowledgment of new modalities of belonging and identification. While child migrants and their advocates have for some years noted the problem of engaging in a valid "best interest" calculation without a careful exercise of individualized discretion,[157] supporters of intercountry adoption have yet to incorporate these important complexities into current practice. Best-interest calculations concerning Moroccan child migrants smuggled into Spain, Chinese unaccompanied asylum seekers in the United States, Albanian or Afghan independent children arriving in the United Kingdom may encompass valuable insights for decisions concerning the long-term interests of their intercountry adopted counterparts. In the introduction to this book, I noted that domestic child-welfare specialists and immigration experts failed to share their expertise and communicate about the needs of migrant children for decades, to the great detriment of the children concerned. Intercountry adoption experts and international child-migration advocates, and especially the children they represent, might benefit from promptly avoiding a similar silo effect where each set of experts ignores the complexities raised by the other's work.

Consider some of the similarities that might emerge from an integrated consideration of children's best interests in these two fields. First, there are many situations involving both smuggled child migrants and adoptees, where money is exchanged as a fee for services; and there are some situations where money is handed over in abusive and coercive ways. Exchanging ideas might assist with better delineation of trafficking in the adoption context. Second, many of the same international and advocacy bodies are engaged with both sets of issues, the same child-rights framework, but quite different priorities. They stress the continuing importance of the birth country in the adoption context as a source of cultural belonging, but in the child-migration context, they emphasize the importance of enabling full integration into the destination country to anchor security. Exploring this difference might spawn less polarized debate over the spectrum of best interests that affect moving children. Third, for unaccompanied migrant children held in institutions opposing return home, the centrality of immediate economic and social factors to "best interest" decisions about the children is stressed by advocates over the claims of repatriation back home. Echoing the insight of feminists like Susan Muller Okin, the child migrants and their advocates point out that family is not an unequivocal good or a guarantee of nurture and care.[158] Russian authorities might sympathize with this sentiment, given recent tribulations over US adoption placements. And yet for intercountry adoptees, some of the same advocacy organizations discount similar factors in favor of a long-term societal vision of economic development and family support in the home country. Does the age difference between the adolescent migrant and adoptee baby make the critical difference here because of the possibility of child consent in one case and not in the other? Child migrants, such as those discussed in chapter 7, who decide to embark on international journeys are making a considered choice; adoptees are not. But the child's role in decision making may not be a convincing difference: institutionalized children would, in the short term and if given a voice, likely choose intercountry adoption over continuing institutionalization for themselves.

Children need a sense of belonging to family and community, the possibility of sustained individualized care, nurture, and social and economic rights to thrive, wherever they are. Whether one's primary focus is on the life prospects for individual children or the structural problems of disenfranchised communities, these criteria apply. Reductive notions of "home" introduced as a proxy for careful assessment of the possibilities for nurture by family or within a "home country" context do not advance the development of a proper best-interest judgment in either context. Following the 2010 earthquake in Haiti, many spoke of the importance of "reunifying" children caught in the adoption process with their adoptive families—whom they may never have lived with before. The dangers of this rushed approach to child protection have already been discussed.

Conclusion

Child migrant advocates look closely at the family and broader social context when making decisions about the future of children who have crossed borders alone—they consider the social supports, the political dangers, the long-term prospects of the child. By contrast, the factors that fuel intercountry adoption such as gross economic hardship among birth families, punitive population policies, gender disparities, and violence are generally given less attention than sensationalized accounts of baby selling, child trafficking, or even organ harvesting by critics of intercountry adoption. Focusing exclusively on abuses[159] in intercountry adoption markets is not an adequate engagement with the problems of desperately poor communities where large numbers of children are institutionalized.

A starting point, I have suggested, is to introduce more vigorously into the intercountry adoption movement the progressive changes percolating in the domestic sphere. Years of experience suggest that the "baggage of birth" cannot be obliterated. Moves toward open adoptions and away from the clean-break approach in the domestic adoption market acknowledge this. Access to information about birth parents is increasingly considered an adoptee's right.[160] Many advocates in the domestic sphere also consider the ethnic and cultural mix of the adoptive family's home community important: adopted children, they argue, should live in neighborhoods where they do not stand out as uniquely different. Yet much intercountry adoption takes place in a time warp with little evidence of this newer approach. Obliteration of the birth mother's identity is still generally considered a *sine qua non* of adoption success.

These differences are hard to justify. They stem from pragmatic rather than ethical considerations, the poverty of information systems in the countries of origin, the weak leverage of birth families, the self-protective interests of adoptive parents. These realities bolster the accusation that intercountry adoption is primarily a transfer of babies from poor to rich countries, and from poor to rich families.[161] These concerns have led countries as different in their political systems as Romania,[162] South Korea,[163] Cambodia,[164] Guatemala,[165] Russia,[166] China,[167] and India[168] at varying times to denounce intercountry adoptions, defend state ownership of their children, and even close their doors altogether.

Current immigration and citizenship laws bolster the finality of the "clean break" approach.[169] Adoptive parents are fully fledged legal parents, entitled to pass on their citizenship to their adopted children without delay,[170] and to secure the child's legal immigration status, a necessary condition of family unity and permanency. This is an improvement over the previous state of affairs, which often resulted in prolonged uncertainty and bureaucratic entanglement for adoptive parents seeking to regularize their new child's status.[171] In fact once adoption formalities are completed, immigration requirements are generally hugely simpler and speedier for adoptive parents bringing in their new children than for the immigrant families trying, as discussed in chapter 1, to reunify with children left abroad.

There is another discrepancy that raises equity issues. Most intercountry adopters are middle class white adults who navigate immigration systems with ease and confidence, including professional single women "forging new territory in the changing landscape of the American family"[172] with the benefit of education, access to legal skills, and financial resources. Birth parents by contrast typically have dramatically inferior economic resources and legal access to valuable immigration and citizenship benefits. Usually[173] they are citizens of states that require visas for any type of cross-border access. Migration abroad may be dependent on dangerous and expensive smuggling routes. Birth parents have no privileged immigration access to their children adopted abroad and no enforceable rights to information or connection of other sorts. To be sure, many adoptive parents provide truthful information to their children and, on occasion and where possible, to the children's birth parents. But the initiative and the permission lie exclusively with the adoptive parents.

More openness and access for the noncitizen birth parent, and an immigration status that reflects the family link and the complex nature of the child's parentage would seem important next steps. If adoptive parents could bring themselves to press for this redistributive set of demands, and international human rights organizations could add to their agenda demands for greater transparency about birth registration, more flexibility in child-care options, and immigration benefits for birth parents, each moving toward a less one-sided framework, the disadvantaged children who need family and family life would be the biggest beneficiaries. In an era where mixed identities are starting to be celebrated rather than disavowed, adoptive children have much to gain from being in touch with two different family types. The testimony of some intercountry adoptees who after years of separation have, through DNA testing and vigorous human-rights work, reestablished contact with their birth families, suggests that such contact can be enormously beneficial and healing.[174]

Let us return to the Madonna adoption saga that this chapter opened with. A focus on the best interests of the adoptable child was clearly the primary focus of Judge Nyirenda when he finalized Madonna's first adoption petition. Despite the fact that the star was not "resident in Malawi" as required by Malawian law,[175] the judge found in her favor. Residence, he argued, was not to be considered an end in itself but a means to "ensure that the adoption [was] well-intended" and in the child's best interests, particularly as the intercountry adoption was not "in the way of any permanent domestic solution for the infant." David's father was never produced before the court, no domestic alternatives to prolonged institutional care were explored or suggested; schemes for strengthening the capacity of indigent Malawian families to care for child survivors of maternal mortality were never even discussed. The final order was approved. On the available evidence and given the child-welfare policies in place at the time, it is hard to question that this order was in the best interests of this particular child.

By contrast the second Madonna adoption case raised a more complex and contested set of "best interest" questions. The judge at first instance rejected the star's petition to adopt because the domestic alternatives available were considered adequate and complied with the CRC requirement that the child be cared for "in any suitable manner." The suitability of child care, she argued, had to be assessed in relation to "the style of life of the indigenous or as close a life to the one the child has been leading since birth." By this definition, then, all institutional provision would pass the suitability test—it would simply become a lowest common denominator assessment of what was available.[176] This argument is very similar to the argument I discuss in chapter 2 and used by Western courts to justify deportations of children back to very poor countries of origin: there is nothing exceptionally compassionate let alone cruel about living in very deprived circumstances, if one is used to them or they constitute the norm. Deporting a child back to these circumstances is therefore justified, as is leaving a child in them if a child has never known anything else. Some defend this position by claiming that to argue otherwise is to make poverty a justification for adoption. Writing about Peru, Leinaweaver argues: "International middle-class values have been so normalized in connection with children's welfare, health, and nutrition that those whose poverty prevents them from attaining those values are demonized. This strategy deflects attention from Peru's inability to provide basic social services for its citizens."[177]

This argument is unacceptable. The inability to provide basic social services for children and the absence of a non-institutional framework of care for raising children are profoundly harmful conditions that urgently need to be addressed.[178] As suggested earlier, if children in these situations had an effective voice, they would clamor for something else, something better. Human-rights and child advocates ignore the threat of that clamor to our shame and the children's great peril. Domestic forms of child care are preferable to options that remove children from their birth families only if they guarantee rights-respecting and life-enhancing conditions. Of course the primary responsibility for securing children's rights lies with the domestic authorities. But, as with other human-rights challenges, borders and nationality alone do not justify standing idly by when the domestic authorities fail their populations, especially when those populations have no voice or leverage. While intercountry adoption is not the primary answer to child destitution any more than migration is, to deny it any role a priori is not in the best interests of children who stand to benefit.

According to Save the Children:

> No child should have to grow up in an orphanage. . . . The answer is not to whisk children away to a new life thousands of miles from where they were born, unless as a very last resort. The answer is *far simpler.* Families need help to get themselves out of poverty, so they can feed, educate and protect their children in a loving, family environment.[179]

But is this solution really "far simpler" than would be the linking of adoptive parents to adoptable children? If simpler is a proxy for quicker, it would seem not; if it is a proxy for more feasible, it would seem not either; if for more ethically straightforward, undoubtedly yes.

Perhaps the ultimate legitimacy of intercountry adoption can be probed by testing its defense against arguments that support the legal and growing practice of child surrogacy. Childless couples are allowed to enter binding contracts (in some jurisdictions, for financial consideration) with surrogates overseas to provide eggs or gestate new babies.[180] As these avenues to securing children are streamlined and simplified, it is possible that the challenges inherent in intercountry adoption may increasingly deflect infertile adults toward this alternative source. Adoption might then become a default option for those unable to secure a baby through artificial means.[181] From the perspective of child protection and the needs of destitute children, this is alarming. It suggests to me that the ethical distinction between providing a home to an institutionalized or homeless child and securing the birth of a child through surrogacy be marked in law.[182] Child-rights advocates have an urgent obligation to develop and improve measures to identify genuinely adoptable children, not only to prevent the abuses discussed in this chapter, but also to prevent the risk that children who really do need caretakers, including international ones, become less and less likely to receive them. An essential element of this agenda is development of a more elaborate regulatory and supplementary system of information and documentation than presently exists. Each child has a right to know about his or her origins, birth parents, and early history[183] because no child and indeed no adult flourishes in a biographical knowledge vacuum. Adoptees in this sense are no different from all children, including other child migrants: their social, cultural, and emotional identity depend on a firm anchoring in a legal identity that renders them fully fledged persons before the law in the multiple communities they may straddle in the course of their life journey.

PART II

Youthful Commodities: Moving Children for Exploitation

CHAPTER 4
Targeting the Right Issue: Trafficked Children and the Human Rights Imperative

> *Austrian Times* reports that Italian police caught a child trafficking gang that purchased children from Romanian orphanages and brought them to Italy, forcing them to beg and steal.[1]
>
> The frameworks we use determine how good our work is.[2]

Introduction

Trafficking is not one phenomenon but many. For the trafficked child, it is at times explicit, brutal, and sudden; at other times, invisible, incremental, and insidious. For the witness, it can manifest in blatant and gruesome incidents, or in social situations that are difficult to decipher, and whose full meaning emerges only later. I recall having had the latter experience.

In the late 1990s, I attended a human rights meeting convened to address legal strategies for improving the circumstances of migrants and asylum seekers in Chicago. I have attended many such meetings over the years, but I remember that meeting distinctly. A colleague, an experienced immigration attorney, presented a problem to the assembled experts. He had just returned from visiting a closed shelter facility for unaccompanied migrant children who had arrived in the United States without a parent or a legal immigration status. There he had met a tiny, pencil-thin six-year-old girl from India. The shelter director asked whether the attorney might consider representing her. Not a specialist in child abuse, contested custody, or juvenile justice, the attorney hesitated—he had no experience working on behalf of someone so young, who could not speak a word of English. He was told by the shelter staff that the girl—let us call her Tara—arrived at New York's John F. Kennedy airport accompanied by an Indian man claiming to be her uncle, who on inspection turned out to be unrelated to her. The immigration authorities detained man and child separately and proceeded to question the former. It emerged that he had bought the child from her destitute parents, in order to supply her as a domestic servant to a wealthy Indian family in Manhattan, in return for a fee.[3] After further investigation, the man was refused entry to the United States and put on the next plane back to Mumbai. Meanwhile Tara was transferred to the shelter facility in Chicago. More details of her story emerged over time: she came from a remote area in Gujarat, a large state in North West India bordering Pakistan and increasingly desertified as a result of global warming and failed monsoons. She had been brutalized by her parents (severe burn scars still evident on her back). My colleague was perplexed: what claim to stay in the United States might she have? Who should give him instructions on the child's behalf? Alternatively, could this six-year-old be his direct client without an intermediary or a guardian?

Protecting Trafficked Children through the Asylum System

After some discussion, the group decided the best course of action would be an asylum application, based on the child's "well-founded fear of persecution" if she were returned home (the test that applies under the 1980 Refugee Act, now incorporated into Section 101(a)(42) of the Immigration and Nationality Act). The elements of applicable persecution might include exposure to the risk of further physical abuse from her parents, and of being sold again to another domestic-servant recruiter. The refugee protection system, established after the atrocities of World War II and codified in the 1951 UN Convention on the Status of Refugees, still constitutes one of the most effective human rights delivery systems of our time (as discussed in chapter 6). But remarkably, given the child's age and recent exposure to trauma, this case dragged on over many months. A central obstacle was the dominant, adult-centered conception of persecution, which is based on state oppression (such as torture and imprisonment) targeted at political opponents. (It would take child-rights advocates years to establish that child abuse might count as a recognized basis for being granted asylum.) Substantive legal doctrine was not the only obstacle. Tara was in no position to give a convincing account of the negotiations leading up to her journey to the United States or whether she was likely to face continuing persecution if returned to India. Procedurally, therefore, the case was complex because without the "victim's" compelling testimony, there was a yawning deficit in its evidence base.

With hindsight it is clear to me this was a case of child trafficking. Tara had been sold and then transported from India to the United States for the purpose of exploitation, to work as an unpaid domestic servant. But this perspective did not strike me or any of my colleagues at the time, and indeed she was never identified as a trafficking victim, even though several state officers—at the airport, at the shelter facility, at the immigration court—and experienced pro bono attorneys spent time on her case. This identification failure had several serious consequences. First, Tara spent over a year in the "shelter" (a detention facility, in reality), not going to regular school, not being cared for in a family setting, not receiving the medical and psychological attention she needed. Second, the trafficker was never charged with an offense; the main concern of the immigration authorities was to remove him from the United States, because he had no legal claim to remain, rather than to secure a conviction against him or extract information about the trafficking network of which he was a part. In all likelihood on return to India he resumed his exploitative business, finding other children to traffic. Third, no investigation was carried out into the home circumstances that gave rise to the abusive relationship and trafficking arrangement—the parents' brutality, the grinding poverty contributing to the predisposition to sell a child, the risks to other children in the family, the recruitment networks operating with impunity in Tara's home community.

And yet, despite these problems—child abuse, a terrifying trafficking journey, and prolonged incarceration in a strange country where she did not speak the language—Tara was relatively fortunate. She was not immediately returned "home," one of the most common outcomes for trafficking victims, despite the known risks.[4] According to an authoritative multicountry report, "Immediate repatriation of . . . victims of trafficking [is] often the beginning of a vicious circle. Studies confirm that up to 50 per cent of those immediately deported are re-introduced into the . . . cycle."[5] To quote one agency, "The question is not whether retrafficking takes place, but how fast."[6] What's more, Tara was not placed in an easily identifiable children's home where members of the trafficking network could find her.

Others are not so fortunate. In Albania, a known target country for child traffickers, 131 out of 228 residents in a shelter for trafficking victims reported having been trafficked at least twice.[7] Traffickers are known to exploit domestic immigration laws, including the asylum system, to secure entry into the destination state for their child victims.[8] Once children have passed through the initial legal formalities, the traffickers reclaim them and put them to work, often in street prostitution.[9] The exploiters regularly outsmart the child-welfare staff, even in relatively well-supported child-welfare systems. In Sweden, eighty-seven refugee children in the custody of the local authorities simply went missing in 2001.[10] In the United Kingdom, sixty-six unaccompanied West African children placed in the care of social services disappeared over a period of years in the late 1990s: "The children would remain in care for one day to several months before disappearing; authorities suspected that a trafficking route from West Africa to Gatwick, then to London, Belgium, and finally northern Italy had developed. Once in Italy, authorities suspected that the girls were forced into sex work."[11] Since 2000, 503 unaccompanied children have vanished from child-welfare centers in Ireland,[12] and in 2009, another 173 unaccompanied children went missing from state care in one English county alone.[13] Nearly 20 percent of children known or suspected to have been trafficked in northern England vanished from state care over an eighteen-month period, and recent investigations have found that many are being located and reenlisted by their traffickers—they completely slip through the cracks in the protection system.[14]

My colleague, Tara's immigration attorney, realized that representing a traumatized six-year-old required expert assistance. He invited a social worker friend trained in child protection to mentor Tara (pro bono) and successfully applied to the immigration judge to have the social worker appointed as Tara's guardian for the duration of the asylum proceedings. Other attorneys at the time were not so creative. In the immigration court in Chicago, I observed many children's cases where adult detainees in prison garb, handcuffs, and shackles sat on benches surrounding the child giving evidence. In some cases children were also shackled. A less appropriate forum for eliciting a child's painful and intensely personal testimony would have been hard to imagine.

Many of the faltering steps we discussed at the meeting, described at the start of this chapter, later became flashpoints for advocacy and change. Without knowing it, we were at the cusp of a new movement, both in North America and in Europe. Our engagement with children's cases made us question some of the simple dichotomies that dominated antitrafficking discourse—coerced versus consensual movement, protection from traffickers versus protection from persecution, smuggling versus trafficking. To us many of these categories did not seem separated by bright lines.[15] It is now commonplace to realize that children who may need to flee persecution end up doing so through the manipulations of traffickers. Families make arrangements for a child to be smuggled across a border but the process of repaying the smuggling debt often results in the child's being trapped in an exploitative labor or sex situation. A journey precipitated by a trafficker's intention to secure an exploitable child worker may end in a detention facility where an asylum claim is made on behalf of the child. As a June 2009 UNHCR report states: "The growing scope, scale and complexity of population movements have multiplied the points of intersection between refugee protection and international migration."[16] This changing appreciation of the context in which child trafficking occurs has led to important innovations in the representation of trafficked children who use the asylum protection system to secure a lawful permanent status. The evolution of the child asylum system, described in more detail in chapter 6, now incorporates a series of features responsive to children's circumstances. Also relevant is the substantive expansion of the concept of asylum—to child trafficking.[17] A good example of the enduring and cumulative impact of our movement's grassroots advocacy on behalf of trafficked child migrants within the asylum system is the development in recent US legislation of protective provisions that cover many of these concerns. The Trafficking Victims Protection Act, also known as the William Wilberforce Act,[18] expands the protections (both in immigration law and welfare services) available to trafficked children, including eligibility for indefinite legal residence in the United States. European and international bodies have also elaborated regulatory frameworks encouraging the expansion of protections for trafficked children within domestic asylum systems.[19]

Protecting Trafficked Children Outside the Asylum System

Progress in dealing with child victims of trafficking outside the asylum system has been much less pronounced in the decade and a half since Tara's case. Policy priorities remain unsatisfactory, and essential resources are still lacking. To be sure, many states have accepted a wide range of legal obligations to protect trafficked children. They have ratified the CRC and its Optional Protocol on the Sale of Children, Child Prostitution and Child Pornography;[20] they have ratified the Protocol to Prevent, Suppress and Punish Trafficking in Persons, Especially Women and Children, which references the "special needs of children."[21] In Europe, states have adopted the European Convention on Action against Trafficking in Human Beings[22] and the 2011 Directive on preventing and combating trafficking in human beings and protecting its victims,[23] both of which emphasize the need for development of a "child sensitive approach."[24] Nevertheless, law enforcement, both crime- and border-control-related, remains the primary driver of policy and practice in migration-destination states, foregrounding convictions and removals of unauthorized migrants, including children, to the detriment of victim protection and social-justice enhancement.[25] In the words of one expert, "Illegal migrants are more often targeted by law enforcement than the smugglers and traffickers who exploit them."[26] Meanwhile child-protection systems remain poorly developed,[27] particularly in many of the critical areas where trafficked children are recruited in the first place.[28] The public energy that has been directed at decrying the perfidy of traffickers has not been matched by creative problem-solving efforts targeted at unprotected and often desperate children. To be sure, an absence of viable life opportunities is a complex problem to tackle. It requires holistic solutions that are costly fiscally, politically, and in terms of skilled implementers across multiple governance areas. But these are the first priority of an effective trafficking-prevention strategy. In their absence, need breeds abusive adaptation. The problem of resource scarcity manifests itself in direct pressures on families to sell or otherwise exploit their children.[29] It is also reflected in weak governance structures; radically underfunded public services; unmonitored, even absentee, state employees; and the disintegration of public ethics, which results in impunity for corrupt officials and inadequate protection for the most vulnerable state-dependent citizens, including exploitable children. An extreme example of the problem is the situation in Eastern Europe. "Some recruiters in Russia and other post-Soviet states have an ongoing relationship with specific orphanage directors who regularly deliver 18–year-old 'graduates' of the children's homes into the hands of traffickers." Some of these children end up for sale in markets in Turkey and farther afield.[30]

Apart from endemic problems of corruption and poor governance, access to protection for trafficked children and adolescents is elusive because initial identification is complicated and fraught with errors. The problem of age determination, discussed elsewhere in the book, arises here too: in the absence of reliable documents and corroborated oral testimony, ascertaining whether a suspected victim of trafficking is a minor may be impossible. This complicates the protection challenge. As I will explain later in this chapter, someone who *consents* to migration for exploitation is not a trafficking victim unless he or she is under eighteen. So government officials have to prove that a person voluntarily migrating to seek exploitative work is a child before antitrafficking-protection obligations arise. Even if age determination is not a problem, accurately assessing the purpose of the child's journey and his or her relationship with any accompanying adult may be. It requires time, experience, and skill to establish whether the child is traveling with a relative, for a family holiday, to study, to avoid danger back home, to reunify with relatives, to engage in exploitative work, or for several of these reasons combined. But these attributes are little known at the first point of official contact with a trafficked child, whether at the border, at a hospital outpatient clinic, or at a homeless shelter. An important, perhaps *the* most crucial, link in the chain to securing protection, is thus highly defective.[31]

Some states have cut corners and tried to reduce the chances of non-identification of trafficked children by experimenting with migration-prevention strategies designed to block the travel of vulnerable groups—Nepali girls being taken to the brothels of Mumbai,[32] Pakistani or Bangladeshi boys traveling to the United Arab Emirates to be camel jockeys, Laotian children being moved for forced labor and sex work in Thailand.[33] The results are not encouraging: thousands of children continue to be trafficked, while discriminatory immigration-control strategies expose vulnerable groups such as girls and young women—who already encounter greater hurdles to migration than their brothers and fathers[34]—to additional obstacles. These blanket solutions are generally frowned on by human rights advocates who argue that increasing the cost of exit from a country tends to generate more clandestine routes, exposing children to greater danger and higher repayment "debts."[35] This strategy reduces rather than increases a child's agency, replacing provision of information about risks, legal entitlements, and services that might be available,[36] with discriminatory curtailment of the option to exercise free movement.[37] For the same reasons, there has been criticism of the work of antitrafficking organizations that concentrate on "rescue and return" strategies to "save" girls from the horrors of sexual exploitation by moral reeducation and return "home" rather than by investing in more long-term and sustainable empowerment options that afford children who need to earn rights-respecting choices, affording them some control.[38] Because child trafficking intersects with child abuse, domestic violence, economic destitution, and gender-based persecution to create the labor supply on which the exploitation industry feeds, multidimensional strategies are essential to the search for solutions. Mechanistic border-control bans targeted at certain demographically defined sections of the population are likely only to contribute to the problem if they are used short-term, for example in response to specific intelligence reports.

So far I have discussed some of the complexities involved in curbing the "supply" of trafficked children. Official understanding of the "demand" for the services of trafficked children is also unsatisfactory.

> Frequently it is assumed that the only demand to be addressed is the demand for commercial sex by men and boys. However, the main "demand" for children who are trafficked actually comes from those who can potentially make a profit out of them, either in the course of recruiting and moving them or once they are exploited and earn money.[39]

So there are several quite different sets of "demands" that need to be targeted, spanning both "process" and "result":[40] an immediate consumption demand, for child sex or child labor; a short-term profiteering demand, for delivery of an exploitable child (recall Tara's case discussed earlier); and a more long-term investment strategy, in the repeatedly exploitable labor of a child. The emphasis of antitrafficking work to date has been on penalizing demand, especially the first two types just outlined.[41] Less attention has been paid to the third type of demand—the long-term investment in child exploitation, and the supply of destitute children that feeds it. Yet, this type of demand and supply nexus goes to the heart of today's child-trafficking problem. Understanding its drivers explains why demand-based antitrafficking interventions to date have been so ineffective.

Questions of Magnitude and Strategy

There is no public disagreement about the gravity of human trafficking. At issue is how best to counter it. Those who are critical of the missionary zeal of prostitution abolitionists and the dramatically different level of public interest in abolishing sexual as opposed to labor exploitation among children[42] rightly note the hypocrisy associated with the neglect of child labor exploitation when contrasted with the militant call to "rescue" all child sex workers. From the opposite end of the political spectrum, constituencies overtly hostile to irregular migration and the tolerated presence of undocumented immigrant populations nevertheless call for state protection for trafficked children.[43] And yet, this broad public consensus between child-rights activists and immigration restrictionists, bolstered by a robust international-law edifice, has not solved or reduced the problem of child trafficking.

The numbers of trafficked people, including children, appear if anything to be rising. While reliable quantification of the phenomenon is problematic, because of clandestinity, official corruption, the lack of effective monitoring mechanisms, inadequate victim protection, and definitional complexities, there is no dispute that it affects millions of people, particularly young women and children (66 percent women and 13 percent girls)[44] every year. The ILO (International Labour Organization) reports that there are 20.9 million victims of forced labor/trafficking worldwide.[45] The US Department of State estimates some 800,000 individuals are trafficked each year, with as many as 27 million trafficking victims at any given time.[46] The general difficulties of documenting irregular and complex behavior of this sort are compounded by the unfortunate tendency to group women and children together, as if they are one entity, "women-and-children." As one report notes:

> It is interesting that women and children are lumped together in anti-trafficking legislations and the dominant trafficking paradigm when in all other instances, including labor laws, great care is . . . taken to separate child labor from adult labor. Many writers use the word "children" but focus on young women—and research on trafficked boys is non-existent.[47]

Data on trafficked children is no more precise or satisfactory. The frequently cited ILO figure of 1.2 million child-trafficking victims per year, relied on by UNICEF and others, dates to 2002.[48] More recently the ILO has estimated that children account for 26 percent of all forced labor/trafficking victims (5.5 million children).[49] Reports suggest that trafficked children span the gamut of work-related activities. As already noted, sexual exploitation attracts most public attention and legislative focus,[50] but researchers disagree about whether it is more or less prevalent than labor exploitation. The most recent ILO figures indicate that there are 4.5 million victims of forced sexual exploitation: 21 percent are children (945,000) and 98 percent are female (4.4 million). By contrast, there are 14.2 million victims of forced labor exploitation: 27 percent are children (3.8 million) and 40 percent are female (5.7 million).[51] In the United States, however, the overwhelming majority (98 percent) of confirmed child-trafficking cases involve the commercial sex industry as opposed to labor exploitation (2 percent).[52] Child trafficking for sexual exploitation includes both short- and long-distance journeys, both same-sex and heterosexual sex, both younger and older children of each sex, and a vast array of different contexts, from highly organized international criminal networks that use a web of intermediary locations and facilitators, to localized rudimentary contexts yielding much lower earnings.

Labor exploitation of trafficked children also includes much work and geographical variation: agricultural labor, domestic servitude, begging, a range of criminal activities, armed conflict, and forced marriage. Children work in agriculture and food processing in America and Brazil, clothing sweat shops in France and Argentina, mining in Angola and the Democratic Republic of the Congo, brick and carpet industries in Afghanistan and India, electronics in China, child soldiering in Sri Lanka and Colombia, and a range of other activities in the informal and black market sectors, including begging, street peddling, drug smuggling, and petty shop theft.[53] Asia has by far the largest percentage of working children. IPEC (the International Programme on the Elimination of Child Labour), the UN office addressing child labor exploitation, estimates that an astounding 18.8 percent of five- to fourteen-year-olds (amounting to some 650 million) are working full-time,[54] though of course many do so in their home regions and are not trafficked.

Moral outrage about the perfidy of the exploiters who generate the demand for trafficked children needs to be supplemented with systematic grassroots economic- and social-development policies that tackle the supply and the fundamental and enduring source of the problem. A necessary condition for embarking on this approach is to revisit one of the conceptual cornerstones of current antitrafficking work, the assumption that trafficking is simply a form of modern-day slavery.

Trafficking as a Form of Slavery

On January 4, 2010, President Barack Obama made the following statement: "Fighting modern *slavery* and *human trafficking* is a shared responsibility. . . . Together, we can and must end this most serious, ongoing criminal civil rights violation."[55] President George W. Bush had made similar pronouncements during his terms in office,[56] as have a host of other heads of state. Continuing in the steps of the Bush administration, the Obama government has published an annual Trafficking in Persons (TIP) Report ranking countries, including the United States for the first time in 2010, on their efforts to contain "this [universal] human rights abuse."[57] But the analogy between trafficking and slavery is partial and misleading.[58] It has generated priorities that have not been optimal from the perspective of trafficked children.

Many commentators and advocates use contemporary slavery as a synonym for trafficking.[59] The rhetorical advantage is obvious—no other word signals extreme exploitation so dramatically. Moreover, slavery is universally prohibited as a matter of customary international law, which gives all states the right to bring suit against perpetrators. It is not difficult to see why the slavery analogy has purchase. This is an excerpt from the story of

Isabel, a girl from Moldova, who responded to an ad for a $500-per-month housecleaning job. Speaking to Siddharth Kara, the author of *Sex Trafficking: Inside the Business of Modern Slavery*, Isabel had this to say:

> In Istanbul, a man named Uri met us at the station. He took us to a hotel called Meke. I will never forget that hotel. Uri took our passports and said, "You must shower and get dressed. Tonight you will go on your first program." I thought he meant we will go for house cleaning, so I did as he said. That night, Uri sold us to a German man. He raped us in the hotel with five other men. They made us have sex with many men that night. The Germans made me work like this for sixteen months. I was kept locked in a hotel room with three other girls.[60]

But using slavery as the dominant framing concept is problematic. "As a matter of international law, the link between trafficking and slavery is not well understood."[61] Slavery and trafficking are not synonyms. First of all, the equation is inaccurate. Slavery, strictly speaking, refers only to situations where a human being is legally owned by another; in this sense, its scope is narrower than that of trafficking, which includes situations where persons, with a legal identity of their own, are transported to be exploited. Second, not all slavery-like situations fall within the definition of trafficking; sometimes the scope of trafficking is narrower. The most common type of slavery, bonded labor,[62] where the creditor exercises powers of ownership over the debtor, is handed down from parent to child. It is not a form of trafficking because child bondage is caused by inheritance of an oppressive and illegal contract.[63] It does not require a specific preceding act targeted against a specific child, and, as the discussion below will clarify, it lacks a constitutive ingredient of trafficking, for instance, recruitment, transport, or harboring of the bonded person. Third, the equation obscures a highly significant and distinctive element of many trafficking but no slavery situations: they are initiated by the trafficked person. While this point is more applicable to adults than children, because most life decisions for children are taken by adults, it remains the case that some trafficked children, particularly teenagers, in some ways seek out or solicit the relationship, unaware that it will end in trafficking because they view it as a conduit to otherwise unavailable opportunities. In general, a substantial proportion of trafficked persons in Europe and Latin America first enter into the relationship with their trafficker on the basis of a seemingly consensual agreement—"a pragmatic response to a limited range of options"—to quote a global study.[64] In other words, they "agree" to the offer of work that eventually turns into the trafficking relationship. I will argue that understanding and engaging with this "voluntary" element in trafficking relationships affecting children is critical to developing lasting solutions.

The analytic confusion can be simply stated. The slavery model views human trafficking, including child trafficking, along a single vector of demand, delivery, and supply. The *demand* for exploitable individuals comes from a broad range of exploiters—brothel owners, pimps, cleaning contractors, agricultural landowners, organ harvesters, criminal gangs, abusive employers, corrupt government and border-control officials, child sex consumers, opportunistic relatives. These may be a handful of collaborating individuals, as in the case of Tara, or consortia, small or large, as in the case of Isabel. They may be based in the same country as the trafficked person, in a neighboring country, or on a distant continent. The *delivery* of exploitable individuals, according to the slavery model, comes from traffickers—intermediaries who recruit, transport, harbor, or receive victims—in order to secure a fee for their illicit labor and maintain a lucrative client base. The *supply*, finally, comes from vulnerable, ill-informed, impoverished, and often displaced individuals and communities, many of them already compromised by war, natural disaster, economic destitution, social exclusion, physical or sexual abuse, poor or nonexistent parenting, inadequate child-welfare provision, or other forms or combinations of trauma.[65] According to the model of trafficking as slavery, these victims are pawns in the hands of the exploiters and their intermediaries, the traffickers who ensnare them into an exceptionally vile situation. This model focuses on three critical remedies: first, criminalization of the traffickers and suppliers; second, protection of identified victims; and third, preventive public-information campaigns directed at alerting unsuspecting victims.

Criminalization determines the space in which all antitrafficking work based on the slavery model takes place. Its targets are the traffickers, not the institutions—political, legal, economic—that drive the value systems sustaining the practice. Supporters of the criminalization approach argue that, to be effective in countering the enormous profits generated by the trafficking business, the penalties and the resources dedicated to arrest and prosecution must be increased.[66] Assistance to trafficked persons is typically short-term, victim oriented, and remedial in nature. It aims to make good the damage done by the trafficking experience through trauma relief, rather than through engaging with long-term survival and empowerment options for the trafficked person. Finally, public information campaigns are directed at "warning" potential victims about latent dangers around them, through TV ads, educational programs, and other dissemination strategies. The intervention strategy, to borrow from Carole Vance speaking in a different context, is akin to a melodrama in which there are three characters[67]—the victim, the villain, and the rescuer or hero. Readers familiar with Nicholas Kristoff's work on buying out young trafficking victims[68] will see the validity of the analogy.

The Law Enforcement Approach

The most influential antitrafficking initiatives are closely related to this model. They are governed by a law enforcement approach addressing transnational organized crime. The policies build on linkages, first established in Europe through the 1990 Schengen Convention, between drug smuggling, weapons dealing, and irregular migration as salient and connected aspects of globalized crime, often reliant on the same transnational networks for their operations. Ten years later, the international community as a whole, meeting in organized crime's legendary birthplace, Palermo, the capital of the Italian island of Sicily, signed the 2000 United Nations Transnational Organized Crime Convention,[69] and appended to it three protocols, two of which deal with issues directly relevant to child migration—trafficking in persons, and human smuggling. The distinction between these two activities revolves around a dichotomy between coerced and consensual illegal migration, and a corresponding moral dichotomy between innocence and guilt. Trafficking involves an innocent, coerced victim; smuggling involves a guilty, consensual immigrant.

The UN Protocol to Prevent, Suppress and Punish Trafficking in Persons, Especially Women and Children, also known as the Palermo Trafficking Protocol, came into force in 2004. It sets out a now widely adopted, though cumbersome and complex definition of the crime of trafficking in human beings:

> Trafficking in persons shall mean the recruitment, transportation, transfer, harboring or receipt of persons, by means of the threat or use of force or other forms of coercion, of abduction, of fraud, of deception, of the

> abuse of power or of a position of vulnerability or of the giving or receiving of payments or benefits to achieve the consent of a person having control over another person, for the purpose of exploitation.[70]

Essentially the definition specifies three crucial ingredients for the crime of trafficking in persons: first, *some action* is taken, which can include induced (or assisted) movement (not necessarily cross-border); second, *except in the case of children*, some means such as the *use of coercion or deceit* is used to recruit the trafficked person; and third, *exploitation* is the purpose of the action and the coercion being undertaken. Whether they consent or not, children are considered trafficked whenever two of these conditions obtain: some action is taken, and there is an intention to exploit them.[71] The term "exploitation" is intentionally not defined in the Convention (since the signatories could not reach agreement on its scope), but it covers forced movement for both sexual and labor exploitation. Given that coercion is not required to prove the crime of trafficking against children, the distinction between smuggling and trafficking children revolves around the intention to exploit—if irregular border crossing is arranged to secure a nonexploitative objective, typically an immigration advantage for a child (e.g., family reunification), then the child is considered smuggled. If irregular border crossing is arranged to exploit the child, to extract a profit from child labor or sex work, then the child is considered trafficked.

Another way of characterizing migration status is based on the division between regular (or legal) and irregular (or illegal or undocumented) migrants. On which side of the divide do trafficked children fall? Technically children trafficked for labor exploitation are irregular migrants subject to removal because they enter without a visa or other legitimate immigration status. And indeed, as discussed in chapter 6, in many countries, including the United States and EU member states such as Spain and Italy, trafficked children do face the prospect of removal or deportation, often after periods of harsh detention and stressful legal proceedings. As discussed at the beginning of this chapter, a compelling argument can be made for the claim that this approach violates international law. Penalizing trafficked children because of their irregular entry ignores the explicit protective injunctions of refugee and children's rights law. Because they have a strong claim to being accepted as bona fide humanitarian beneficiaries or asylum seekers with a demonstrable, well-founded fear of persecution, trafficked children should benefit from the opportunity to be considered refugees[72] or asylum seekers,[73] including receiving "appropriate humanitarian assistance" and assistance in attempting to secure long-term residence and legal status.

Trafficked children and their advocates have, for some time, advanced arguments to support the claim to refugee protection of trafficked children.[74] But mapping exploitation, a central element in the legal trafficking definition, onto persecution, a central element in the legal refugee definition, can be challenging: whereas the main focus of the trafficking definition is on the motivation of the violator (moving a child in order to exploit him or her), the main focus of the refugee definition is on the motivation of the victim (resisting repatriation home in order to escape a well-founded fear of persecution). Some states have taken the decision to foreground child victims' protection needs, regardless. This is the approach in Belgium, for example. An International Organization for Migration (IOM) report states: "An intercepted minor is a priori entitled to the status of victim of trafficking in human beings and is thus supported."[75] Other jurisdictions are less protective, preferring to simply return child victims of trafficking to their home countries because of their irregular migration status, irrespective of the risks faced.

Establishing that a trafficked child qualifies for the opportunity to secure a stable immigration status free of control by the trafficker is not the only legal challenge. Another difficulty is distinguishing legitimate forms of children's work (whether as part-time trainee, or apprentice) from illegitimate child labor. Are all forms of child work inherently exploitative, or only some? Recall that movement for exploitation is a critical element in the trafficking definition, but that a child does not lose access to protection merely because he or she cannot demonstrate coercion, duress, or fraud. In other words, if a child arranges to be transported across a border for the purposes of exploitation, say from Cambodia to Thailand to beg by the roadside, or from Mexico to the United States to pick grapes, that child is ipso facto a trafficked child—his or her consent (or the parents' consent) to the migration is irrelevant.[76]

But what are the outer boundaries of "exploitation"? Consider the situation of unaccompanied minors transported from the port of Wenzhou in China to Paris: their families agree to a journey fee of between 20,000 and 30,000 euros, and the children, once in France, work several years in small workshops to repay the fee.[77] Are they "smuggled" because they agreed to the migration contract and subsequent working arrangement, or are they "trafficked"—transported for purposes of exploitation? Myron Weiner suggests that all work interfering with schooling is exploitative because states have a duty to ensure children receive an education:

> [E]ducation should not be regarded merely as a right granted by the state, but as a duty, imposed by the state. When education is made a duty, parents, irrespective of their economic circumstances and beliefs, are required by law to send their children to school. It is the legal obligation of the state to provide an adequate number of schools appropriately situated, and to ensure that no child fails to attend school.[78]

Others would disagree and assert that the notion of exploitation be limited to the "worst forms" of child labor, as codified by the 1999 ILO Convention No. 182. If not, then all child migrants who are found working in destination states, including those who made the arrangements themselves, should count as trafficked children. If, on the other hand, exploitation is construed in accordance with the ILO's "worst forms" definition, then only those child migrants found working in harsh contexts count as trafficking victims, leaving other child workers ineligible for the protections associated with being trafficked. I will return to these points in chapter 7.

The Palermo Trafficking Protocol established an internationally agreed-upon definition of trafficking. Prior to its enactment, an inordinate amount of policy time and energy had been spent on definitional battles[79] to the detriment of effective interventions to protect trafficked children. As Anne Gallagher notes, whatever the qualms of human rights and antitrafficking advocates about the dominance of the criminalization approach, " there is no way the international community would have a definition and an international treaty on trafficking if this issue had stayed within the realms of the human rights system."[80] Definitional clarity is a necessary condition for accurate data collection and for effective Interpol coordination between states across whose borders trafficked children are transported. Thanks to the Protocol, law enforcement officers across borders at least have a common set of goals, even if efficient operational collaboration still seems to lag behind the traffickers' highly professional global networks.[81] Annually consolidated international figures provide an ever-improving basis for monitoring and evaluating programmatic interventions and better targeting policy responses. Recent advances in information technology, and their application to tracking the electronic footprint of traffickers, are also promising avenues for future intervention.[82] Most progress has been made in the area of trafficking for sexual exploitation. IOM has established an international case management database to store individual data and facilitate intercountry collaboration; European initiatives bring together EU justice ministries with EUROPOL and international organizations; the US Department of State commissions and disseminates data on trafficking on an annual basis and operates a ranking system for evaluating countries' compliance with minimum standards to eliminate trafficking. These developments provide an annual baseline against which policy measures can be evaluated, trends assessed, and innovations encouraged. For example, if as the UN Office of Drugs and Crime claims, sexual exploitation accounts for 79 percent of global trafficking, and labor exploitation for 19 percent,[83] then policy initiatives targeted at economically disadvantaged young girls are unarguably a top antitrafficking priority. This sets a different agenda from the indiscriminate immigration-control priorities of antitrafficking policies to date. I will explore this point in more detail below.

The Protocol definition is important in another respect. It includes an expansive notion of coercion beyond physical pressure, acknowledging that brute force is not necessary to ensnare vulnerable individuals into exploitative situations. The Protocol recognizes that force exercised through the abuse of a position of vulnerability may be an act of coercion as decisive as a physical kidnapping or the administration of a date-rape drug. This accords with the reality of trafficking today. According to one expert: "The patterns of exploitation and abuse are changing. The use of . . . overt violence is decreasing, while psychological abuse and manipulation is increasing." Even though coercion is not required to prove trafficking of children, it is helpful to understand how broadly the concept is now construed, so that trafficking cases in which there is an age dispute about the victim are pursued despite no evidence of the use of force or deceit. Examples include the use of voodoo rituals to terrorize young Nigerian girls into loyalty to their traffickers despite grueling prostitution regimes in Northern Europe; and the use of "debt"—the obligation to "repay" the costs of the trafficking journey and accommodation rental[84]—as a mechanism to ensure continued service by trafficked children, anxious to get to the point where they can keep the earnings from their labor. The Protocol's insistence that trafficking may stem from fraud-induced consent as well as from coercion, reframes the "blame game" for young women who "agree" to cooperate with their exploiters, or who have previous histories of sex work. These trafficked persons can no longer be dismissed as undeserving or of bad character,[85] or as appropriate targets for criminalization (still a serious problem in many countries). Instead of punishing trafficked persons, the Protocol encourages states to provide at least short-term assistance, counseling, and support.[86]

The protection approach in the Palermo Trafficking Protocol has been adopted more vigorously in some jurisdictions than others. The Council of Europe Convention on Action against Trafficking in Human Beings, for example, *requires* states parties to afford comprehensive support, *including residence permits*[87] to trafficked persons, irrespective of whether they cooperate with law enforcement officials prosecuting their traffickers. The US Trafficking Victims Protection Reauthorization Act (TVPRA) also mandates protection for trafficking victims. The Act includes a protection mechanism, the "T visa" that guarantees long-term legal residency for victims of serious forms of trafficking. However, unlike the EU approach, US law excludes victims with a history of sex work from protection, and makes victim protection a reward for providing criminal evidence against the trafficker. Fear of retaliation against oneself or family members back home, who are beyond the reach of antitrafficking enforcement agencies, acts as a strong deterrent to giving evidence. Children are exempted from these provisions but they may also be affected by the impact on related adults.

Despite the Trafficking Protocol's impact on international, regional, and national efforts, its overall legacy has been disappointing. Far from evidence of a decrease in trafficking, a senior UN antitrafficking official comments: "We fear the problem is getting worse,"[88] despite the fact that more and more countries recognize trafficking as a crime. Between 2003 and 2008, the numbers of countries with a specific offense of trafficking in persons on their books rose from 35 percent to 80 percent of those investigated,[89] but law enforcement outcomes have been derisory. Although the number of *identified* victims of labor trafficking worldwide rose from (a mere) 33,113 to 42,291 (a growth of 27 percent) between 2010 and 2011, the numbers of prosecutions barely changed, from 6,017 to 7,909 (under 19 percent). In 2011, *under two percent* of identified labor trafficking cases resulted in convictions. Forty percent of countries covered by the 2009 UN Office of Drugs and Crime (UNODC) report had recorded no trafficking convictions during the 2003–2007 period; 58 percent of countries had fewer than ten trafficking convictions per year.[90]

These conviction rates call into question the validity of the law enforcement model as a preventative antitrafficking strategy.

Limitations in Provision of Protection to Trafficked Children

The second, "rescue" prong of antitrafficking intervention—assistance and protection for trafficking victims—has not been more successful than the first. Part of the problem goes back to the difficulty of victim identification. Even in countries where domestic legislation encourages protection of victims, there appears to be little ability to actually deliver it. In the United States, for example, while the Department of Justice estimates that between 14,500 and 17,500 foreign nationals are trafficked into the United States every year,[91] the Department of Health and Human Services identified and certified a grand total of 2,617 trafficking victims between 2001 and 2010.[92] This gives an annual average of 261, well under 2 percent of the numbers estimated to have been trafficked.[93]

Another obstacle to effective protection of victims, even where they have been identified, is the ambivalence of states toward fully acknowledging the human rights and needs of trafficking survivors, including children. Fears of incentivizing irregular migration, and of encouraging people to use traffickers to enable them to secure access to lawful immigration status, are a constant impediment to fully fledged commitment to victim protection. This ambivalence is apparent in both international and domestic law. Consider the international legal framework. While the Palermo Protocol forcefully *requires* states parties to enable identified victims to participate in criminal proceedings against their traffickers (some states insist on this as a condition of assistance), it weakly *advises* states to "*consider* implementing measures to provide for the physical, psychological and social recovery of trafficking victims in persons."[94] States are left to decide whether victim support will be part of their antitrafficking domestic policy. Consistent with this approach, much more emphasis is placed on procedures to *facilitate repatriation* of victims than regularization of temporary or permanent immigration status.[95] It is sobering to analyze how this international advice translates into domestic interventions in the United States, one of the countries that has paid most political and rhetorical attention to human trafficking. As I have already noted, the US Congress, on a regular basis, oversees passage of antitrafficking legislation and annual preparation of the TIP Report. No fewer than six federal agencies are responsible for collecting and disseminating statistics on trafficking.[96] Many more have other antitrafficking-related responsibilities. Congress has approved a non-immigrant "T visa" (set at an annual quota of 5,000) to enable "victims of severe forms of trafficking" to remain in the United States pending investigation and prosecution of their traffickers. If they manage to stay in this capacity for three years after the T visa is issued, they are then entitled to apply for permanent residence. This is a generous and rare state acknowledgment of the immigration–related needs of trafficked persons.

Most countries with protections for victims fail to consider long-term, let alone permanent protection options, preferring temporary benefits for recovery or "reflection" following the trafficking. In a 2009 pilot survey a colleague and I conducted for the United Nations High Commissioner for Refugees, out of eleven countries surveyed, only one—Norway—had a system for referring trafficked children automatically to the international protection system for a consideration of their eligibility for asylum. All others simply dealt with trafficked children alongside trafficked adults as victims with short-term welfare needs, in some cases with a right to a short legal status while they participated as witnesses in criminal proceedings against their traffickers, but no long-term entitlement to a secure immigration status. In all these states, the long-term remedy of choice for trafficked children was repatriation back to the country of origin.[97] Often this is no remedy at all, as the case of Katya, first trafficked to the United Kingdom from Moldova when she was fourteen, illustrates:

> When they assessed her case, British immigration officials knew that Katya, a vulnerable 18-year-old from Moldova, had been trafficked and forced into prostitution, but ruled that she would face no real danger if she was sent back. Days after her removal from the UK, her traffickers tracked her down to the Moldovan village where she had grown up. She was gang-raped, strung up by a rope from a tree, and forced to dig her own grave. One of her front teeth was pulled out with a pair of pliers. Shortly afterwards she was re-trafficked, first to Israel and later back to the UK.[98]

A leading British charity working with trafficked girls notes that 21 percent of those seeking their help have already been sent home and retrafficked once.[99] Immigration-control goals are a driving force in this process.

According to the former head of the London Metropolitan Police vice unit, friction between the immigration service's desire to remove irregular migrants and the police's wish to interview potential victims contributed to speedy removal in unwarranted cases.[100] But the claim that family reunification is in the trafficked child's best interest is also regularly advanced to justify return. The justification for sending trafficked children back is that speedy return is in the best interests of the child, because home is where a child belongs. It relies on Article 3 of the CRC, which expresses the best interests principle, and Article 9, which emphasizes the importance of ensuring that a child is not separated from his or her parents. This justification is problematic given the known and serious risks of retrafficking, the common reluctance expressed by trafficked children to be returned to their countries of origin, and the frequent absence of evidence of a supportive family environment back home. To quote a research study on trafficked children in Germany:

> [I]t is clear that these children almost exclusively come from poor, economically less developed and/or conflict regions, such as Romania, Kurdistan, the NIS States or African countries. Most of them come from family structures that are breaking up or have already done so as a consequence of high unemployment, low wages, social insecurity, high conflict potential or child overpopulation. Often the minors have experienced a high degree of violence, frustration or disappointment.[101]

This explains why many children, placed in reception centers after they are identified as having been trafficked, view their stay there with considerable ambivalence and run away rather than risk repatriation. As one report notes,

> Alien minors may not always correctly interpret the meaning of measures [to remove them to a place of safety]: the presence of a uniform, the identification procedures to which they are subjected and their accompaniment to "first reception centres" may be perceived less as protection and more as a form of punishment (a sort of "arrest").[102]

Escape from these centers may expose the children to further risks of exploitation, compounded by their irregular immigration status. In some cases, parents are directly involved in the trafficking transaction. A study carried out in big Greek city centers ten years ago found that the "vast majority [of unaccompanied street children] . . . were brought to Greece by a third person, who had 'rented' them from their parents. The 'rent' usually amounted to a certain share of the child's expected earnings in Greece."[103] Sending children "home" to destitute and/or abusive family situations is not likely to be in their best interests.[104]

Some countries have formally acknowledged the importance of creating legal mechanisms to facilitate permanent residence and protection for trafficked children.[105] As noted above, the United States makes available five thousand T visas each year for the benefit of trafficking victims, including children. Between 2000, when the TVPA was first introduced, and 2011, only 2,635 trafficking victims received the T visa altogether,[106] whereas 55,000 visas were statutorily allocated.[107] Given current US government estimates of 14,500 to 17,500 trafficked individuals into the United States each year,[108] the annual average of 219 T visa recipients demonstrates the failure rather than the success of the protection program. Given the absence of age breakdown in the T-visa recipients data, it is not possible to determine how many children have benefited. Meanwhile other systems that require individualized targeting of government policies applicable to noncitizen individuals seem to work much more effectively. Whereas well under 300 T visas are issued every year for victims of "one of the great scourges of our time," the numbers of people removed or deported from the United States are over three thousand times that amount: around 390,000 for both FYs 2010 and 2011.[109]

So, poor identification of trafficking victims is one obstacle to protection, and political ambivalence toward the importance of protection is a second. It is widely assumed that "if there is any group around which most societies can mobilize to protect it is children."[110] But the evidence regarding trafficked children suggests this is not the case at all. In most European countries, trafficked children are eligible for short periods of government-sponsored services after identification. In some countries, such as the United Kingdom, Spain, Italy, and the Netherlands, they may be granted a humanitarian leave to remain lawfully in the country until they reach the age of majority, but thereafter, they lose any legal claim to remain. Similarly, in France, a foreign minor already within the territory cannot legally be deported, whether or not in possession of a residence permit; though they are meant to be cared for by Aide Sociale à L'Enfance, the child-welfare agency, in practice, many of the child shelters are overcrowded, and so, migrant children are often released into the community (and often into the clutches of traffickers) by the courts. In some countries, however, such as Belgium, children who are identified before the age of sixteen are typically given permission to stay in the country indefinitely once they turn eighteen, though older adolescents are repatriated once they turn eighteen.[111]

Explanatory Frameworks

This set of policies seems contradictory. How is it that society proclaims itself eager to protect trafficked children, and at the same time routinely denies them the fundamental human right to long-term protection? A common answer is that their needs have been invisible and unarticulated and that this is why they "fall through the cracks." A second and related explanation is that children's needs are already catered to by current policies—where children are accompanied, their protection needs are subsumed within those of their parents; where children are not accompanied, current policies of repatriation are in their best interests since they promote family reunification. The suggestion is that nothing additional is required.

My research suggests that neither of these responses is adequate, and that a more nuanced set of explanations than mere "invisibility" or the perception that effective protection already exists, needs to be advanced. For one thing, children who are identified as trafficked are no longer invisible—even if they once were. There are numerous examples of public outrage at child-trafficking incidents—relating to sex, begging, domestic service, to name just three. A child who refuses to stay in a reception center for trafficked persons and insists on the right to work in order to support his or her family is liable to be denied the right to remain, to be incarcerated as a "flight risk" pending decision making, and eventually, as a matter of conscious government decision, to be sent home.

Second, children's needs are not always met when subsumed within those of the family as a whole: the abuse of West African children trafficked to the United Kingdom under so-called private-fostering arrangements with uncles or other relatives, frequently a screen for round-the-clock domestic work, is one example among many of familial exploitation of children.[112] Daughters in particular are a commodity that poor families draw on or "cash out" for purposes of survival. In some cases a desperate utilitarian strategy drives the decision: "[T]he Hill Tribes of Northern Thailand . . . stateless and lacking Thai citizenship, are not granted access to social services, education or state employment. . . . Daughters are often sold into prostitution because families cannot survive through legitimate means." Statelessness and related legal problems also drive parents to place their own children at risk. Desperate migrants from Central Asia and the Caucasus "often are forced to abandon the children they cannot sustain in Russia. . . . [M]any of these children have no identity papers, and with a poor knowledge of Russian are even more vulnerable to exploitation." In other cases, however, the decision to sell a daughter is less a matter of immediate survival. "Trafficking their daughters is one way that Southeast Asian families generate funds to make capital improvements to their home and their land."[113]

There is yet a third obstacle to protection. Even when victims are identified, and are granted protection, the facilities and services to which they are entitled are so hard to access that in practice they are illusory. Inadequate resources are allocated, there is little monitoring of on-the-ground services, and support for community-based and -targeted youth projects directed at trafficked children are scarce and inconsistent. This is true in Europe, Asia,[114] and North America.[115] Lack of consistent support affects all areas, but none more clearly and dramatically than access to reliable and affordable health care. A study conducted in India, where large-scale trafficking both international (particularly from Nepal) and domestic takes place, reports that "sex-trafficking victims are severely restricted in their ability to seek health care services."[116] In the richest member state of the European Union, the situation is also unsatisfactory. According to IOM, "[r]eception facilities and aid organizations agree that in Germany, security for [trafficked] minors falls well below an acceptable level."[117] According to a recent study of trafficking victims' access to medical services in New York City,

> the health system response . . . to sex trafficking victims [is] . . . extremely limited. . . . Free outpatient medical services are reportedly extremely limited, as there is [only] one free clinic in each borough. . . . According to one informant, "There are no specific, unique providers of health care to victims."[118]

The situation on the West Coast is not better. A study in Los Angeles found that even where health care facilities are available, other barriers prevent victims from accessing appropriate services, including lack of privacy during visits, mistrust of providers, and the cost of medical treatment: "Most survivors explained that their traffickers charged them for the cost of their medical care and added the incurred debt to their overall debt burden."

Health care providers in turn lacked necessary training and awareness to identify trafficking victims.[119] These deficits impinge heavily on the future prospects for trafficked children and on their capacity to survive and thrive.

Educating At-risk Children about the Danger of Being Trafficked

Public education campaigns geared to prevention constitute a third, "victim centered" prong of international antitrafficking intervention. The Palermo Protocol encourages state parties to engage in these measures: "State parties shall endeavour to undertake measures such as research, information and mass media campaigns . . . [t]o prevent and combat trafficking in persons."[120] Across Eastern Europe and throughout Asia, antitrafficking education campaigns have been widely adopted in schools, on public transport, radio and television, and in other forums where young people can be targeted.

This strategy is based on the notion that lack of knowledge is a significant contributor to the supply of trafficked persons, and that public information can change the incentive structure leading to the establishment of exploitative relationships. If young girls and women were more aware of the dangers lurking behind the seemingly innocent offers of jobs as dancers, waitresses, or housecleaners, or if they were alerted to the nefarious intentions of potential "boyfriend/traffickers" plying them with gifts, compliments, and exotic travel opportunities, they would, so the theory goes, turn away from traffickers. The recent revelation that, unlike in any other area of large-scale transnational crime,[121] a "disproportionate number of women are involved in human trafficking," many of them former victims of the business themselves, adds fuel to the claim that ignorance (the target of public education campaigns) rather than force is a major source of recruitment. For example, in Latvia, whereas women constitute 53 percent of those convicted of trafficking, they constitute only 9 percent of persons convicted of crimes overall. This is true for every European country reported on by the United Nations.[122] More sensitization to the psychological manipulations of traffickers, male and female, is obviously important. This is how one informant described a common strategy:

> These [vulnerable] girls run away, they go to shelters, train stations—and this is where the guys are that pick them up and tell them *what they want to hear* [emphasis added]. Then there is what I call the honeymoon period

> of about two weeks, and this is when these men collect as much information as they can about the girls, their lives, and their families. This is how they can keep their hold over the girls, and create fear in them—they know where to find their families, and how to harm them if the girls don't do what they say. They talk of threatening family members if they ever do run away.[123]

So far, attempts to raise alarm bells for vulnerable girls do not seem to have deflected them from dangerous choices or naïve exit strategies—as the quote just cited put it, they hear "what they want to hear." Well-intentioned and highly visible poster advertisements and radio warnings have not stemmed the flow. Consider the case of La Strada International, one of the best-known European women–led organizations working at the grassroots on antitrafficking. A large, well-organized, and well-supported network that has grown out of national antitrafficking organizations, La Strada has energetically developed public education initiatives to highlight the dangers of trafficking across nine European countries, both EU and non-EU, for well over ten years.[124] During its early years, much of its activity focused on public education. It led social awareness, training, and prevention campaigns to alert the public, teachers, social workers, health officials, and other relevant parties to the pervasive risks of trafficking. And yet, because the exploitation landscape has not significantly shifted, La Strada now supports a wide range of victim-support programs, including help lines (most recently an EU-wide antitrafficking hotline), victim shelters and reintegration programs, and a human-rights impact-assessment tool to monitor the usefulness of these programs.[125] The Polaris Project in the United States has implemented a comparable range of policies.[126] Despite these important practical strides, progress in stemming the flow of trafficked children and developing viable alternative survival strategies remains painfully slow.

What Is the Alternative?

A more effective return on resources dedicated to the issue of trafficking is urgently needed. Promising strategies include the development of incentives for more effective collaboration between police forces across countries, including whistleblowing rewards and guarantees, the promotion of cross-border partnerships between national police forces, and clear checklists promoting victim identification. At the same time, paltry financial penalties and lenient criminal sentences fail to communicate a vigorous deterrent message to those who profit hugely from the trafficking business—this is still the most lucrative low-risk crime. Many vigorous contemporary commentators rightly continue to emphasize the importance of radically reforming and strengthening these two strategic prongs of antitrafficking policy.[127]

Moreover, social-welfare spending on child trafficking victims needs to be increased and more effectively monitored. Targets for grants of T visas or humanitarian- or asylum status need to be more consistently set and realized, if the promise of top-down antitrafficking interventions for the benefit of victims is going to be credible. The same is true of public education and community-based awareness raising: these strategies can adopt tools facilitated by advances in information technology to target, expose, and monitor potential dangers much more effectively than ever before, to make hotlines and dedicated text-message codes widely known and usable, and to support trafficking survivors in a range of chosen strategies.

However, even if these strategic changes to current policies were energetically implemented, the fundamental inadequacies of current programs would not be substantially overcome without a change of direction. The dominant theory of causation used to explain trafficking is flawed and with the wrong framework come ineffective policies. What is wrong? My answer is that the single-vector theory of trafficking as fueled by demand from exploiters, delivery by traffickers, and supply of victims is inadequate. It leaves out a second equally crucial demand-delivery-supply chain in which the demand comes from victims of structural inequality who have no choice but to seek opportunity, escape, income, security, and hope elsewhere. The delivery comes from migration professionals—smugglers and traffickers—who exploit the need for migration. Meanwhile the supply of funds fueling this lucrative migration business comes from exploiters waiting to prey on exploitable migrants. An additional set of antitrafficking strategies is needed for success in reducing the numbers of children trafficked for exploitation and trapped in rights-violating lives. This explanation is at odds with the slavery model and the "villain, victim, savior" dynamics discussed earlier in the chapter.

My alternative suggestion is—and this is not an original insight—that poverty, lack of opportunity, social disintegration following conflict, gender inequality and its omnipresent correlate domestic and child sexual abuse, and the indomitable human search for survival and self-advancement opportunities are central drivers of human trafficking. So too is the demand for exploitable children from adult consumers of child sex and child labor. But this is not the only demand driving the trade.

A huge demand for solutions to endemic poverty and lack of local opportunity comes from impoverished and disenfranchised communities themselves, including children emerging into adolescence and adulthood. This demand takes the form of a search for *exit* (to use Hirschman's famous concept)[128] across the border between the developing and developed world, whether this means rural to urban or transcontinental migration, and toward work opportunities. This search links the demand for mobility to the supply of mobility. According to IOM: "In the case of the Albanians, particularly the boys, there is definite family pressure on them to emigrate in order to work and send money back home. It could, therefore, be concluded that Albanian minors bear similar characteristics to adult migrant laborers." Domestic exploitation of girls follows the same pattern as for women. According to a study in France, 76 percent of people trapped in domestic exploitation were female, and a third were minors: over 15 percent of the minor girls were under ten when they arrived in France, another 60 percent were between ten and fifteen, and were mainly from Western and Central Africa. Child domestics were found sleeping on the floor in the employers' children's room or in box rooms, subjected to various forms of punishment including food deprivation. Their average working day—doing cleaning, washing, baby-sitting, and cooking—was thirteen to eighteen hours, seven days a week.[129]

The very fact of being a child creates perverse incentives: labor recruiters have been known to take advantage of the fact that children are less likely to be prosecuted for drug dealing, stealing from parking meters, or pickpocketing than adults, and that undocumented and unaccompanied children are less likely to be summarily removed or denied an opportunity to apply for asylum than their adult counterparts. Lengthier stays and reduced chances of incarceration guarantee a better return on money spent transporting exploitable children than adults. According to one report, "The French legislation on minor protection (which protects children under thirteen from criminal prosecution) is used by criminal organizations, which thus act with impunity, using children . . . as free and available labor."[130]

Adolescents too aspire for mobility when other options seem foreclosed, and sometimes trafficking is what enables border crossing. "Despite more restrictive immigration policies on unskilled labor in the EU member states, many economic sectors are seeking cheap *casual* labor. Migrants, including minors, are keen to seize these opportunities."[131] This widespread youth exit strategy is a critical but under-attended factor in the child trafficking equation. It drives the growing supply of children and youth who can be recruited for trafficking. It fuels the supply of child soldiers (discussed in chapter 5) for use on the battlefield, or as porters, cooks, bush wives, and other forms of exploitative work associated with armed conflict. Research has also confirmed that childhood experiences of violence, including sexual violence, are precipitating factors that accelerate the risk of being trafficked.[132] Young girls who have already been raped or otherwise brutalized within the family, the war zone, or the refugee camp are more available for sex trafficking than their luckier and healthier counterparts.[133] Neither immigration control nor repatriation are appropriate responses to the protection needs that arise in these cases.

Taking the Question of "Root Causes" Seriously

If there are not one but two primary vectors of demand for the services of traffickers—one from would-be exploiters and one from communities seeking exit from poverty and violence—then it makes little sense for antitrafficking strategies to be overwhelming targeted at only one source—traffickers—and for the vast majority of resources to be allocated in only one direction: criminalization. Yet, this is where we are at at the moment. We lack a clearly articulated demand that trafficked persons, particularly children, be permanently loosened from the clutches of traffickers (who hold their passports, control their wages, and restrict their access to protection). We minimize the importance of income generation, educational access, and other root-cause projects targeted at communities known to supply large numbers of people for the trafficking industry. Attention to fundamental economic and social-justice imperatives is typically an afterthought or an add-on to antitrafficking strategies, not a central focus.[134] It is not the target of antitrafficking budget lines.

Reducing the lure of abusive "exit" for exploitable children must become a key antitrafficking goal. For this, solutions for two groups of children must be found. One group is trafficked children who have already migrated and are trapped by their traffickers, children who need to free themselves from exploitative control but cannot. The other group consists of the millions of potentially trafficked children who have no good alternative options and long to migrate, children who are locked in by oppressive social conditions that make their future look unlivable. Without some success on these two fronts, antitrafficking public education and law enforcement campaigns will not significantly reduce child trafficking.

Children Already Trafficked

Several pragmatic steps suggest themselves as elements of a measurable anti–child trafficking strategy for already trafficked children. Full allocation of protective visas or other available remedies for child victims of trafficking is a priority. The current situation in the United States, where less than 1 percent of available T visas or permanent residence permits are awarded to trafficked children is intolerable. Antitrafficking departments should simplify the procedures, increase the expertise available to constituencies trying to access the protections, and regularly publish numbers of visas granted to demonstrate their commitment to translating protection entitlements into reality. Departments that fall below an established grant threshold should be called on to provide an explanation; departments that exceed the grant threshold should be rewarded as antitrafficking champions (with bonuses or promotion or both). Moreover, trafficked children and adolescents who do receive a permanent immigration status should be provided with full documentation and referred to trauma experts to address past brutalization and generate future resilience. Implementing programs of this sort requires ongoing monitoring to bring to an end the current hypocrisy of having child-trafficking protections on the books but scarcely anywhere else.

A second, critical step in loosening the ties between trafficked children and their exploiters is to radically improve victim identification.[135] As long as the vast majority of trafficked children are unidentified, exploitation will continue unabated. At present, less than 5 percent of children estimated to be trafficked are actually identified, suggesting either gross incompetence on the part of immigration, labor, and health and safety inspectors or significant complicity between traffickers and law enforcers. Again, benchmarks must be set at the local and national levels, and effective monitoring of official initiatives must be instituted. Improving the identification of trafficked children is a multifaceted and challenging goal. Children do not self-identify as trafficked at the border or point of initial contact; nor do they look different at first sight. Persistence and expertise must be built within a cadre of trafficking watchdogs armed with well-devised identification screens, as has been successfully done for the detection of survivors of domestic violence and child abuse. This strategy implicates a broad range of entities, from professionals such as school teachers, doctors and nurses,[136] immigration officers, youth and social-work staff, to law enforcement agencies, health and safety factory inspectors, municipal planning officials, law professionals working in employment regulation, agricultural and dairy boards. Wherever child exploitation occurs, those responsible for the context need to be alert to its existence and the form it takes: massage parlors; clothing sweatshops; takeout joints; blueberry orchards; carpet, clothing, textile workshops; begging crews; shoplifting gangs; brothels; escort services; brick-making kilns; salt mines—the list is endless. To a large extent, the challenge is one of profile raising and political will building: antibullying and broadly based reproductive-rights campaigns are also useful for establishing urgency around these fundamental child-rights issues.

Effective programs to identify trafficked children require a two-pronged strategy: a leadership obligation to generate the political will for the strategy and a managerial obligation to mobilize relevant agencies on the ground. The most critical current impediment is not ignorance, resource scarcity, or complexity. It is the ambivalence of policy makers to the project itself, to the unsettling of powerful vested interests tied to highly placed, corrupt officials deriving hugely lucrative payoffs, to the political risks of appearing to condone irregular migration (even if the migrants are trafficked), to the long-term desirability of providing indefinite protection and residence to destitute, young noncitizens. There is no quick-fix answer to this problem—but ignoring it spells defeat for an effective anti-child-trafficking strategy.

If trafficked children are going to be separated from their traffickers and discouraged from relying on them and collaborating in future trafficking contracts, services targeting their needs must reach them. Just as protective visas must be allocated to reach a high threshold quota, so medical, psychological, housing, educational, and employment training services also must be allocated. Public expenditure quotas for ensuring that trafficked children benefit from the facilities they are promised in legislation must be established, monitored, and published, as much for permanent visas as for victim-support services.

Children at Risk of Being Trafficked

The hardest and most critical antitrafficking challenge is addressing the root causes of trafficking by instituting effective prevention strategies, before children are ensnared in exploitation. This is not a new insight. Every antitrafficking statute and report includes a recitation of the importance of targeting root causes, as a preamble to a convention, as a climax in a speech, as a concluding paragraph to a report.[137] But at the moment, and this has been the case for years, these are largely empty mantras. A 2008 UN study is typical of many. It cites "economic crisis in the trafficked person's home country, social exclusion, gender discrimination . . . and [absence of] a legal or social protection system" as underlying factors propelling trafficking."[138] The Palermo Protocol notes these factors too: "State Parties shall take or strengthen measures, including through bilateral or multilateral cooperation, to alleviate the factors that make persons, especially women and children, vulnerable to trafficking, such as poverty, underdevelopment and lack of equal opportunity."[139] But, by contrast with the detailed articulation of criminal law enforcement and repatriation procedures, the Protocol says nothing further about implementing this root-causes strategy. It is essentially a window-dressing exercise.

Policies specifically targeted at children also address the issue of root causes. A May 2010 European Union Action Plan for Unaccompanied Minors invites

> Member States . . . to continue their efforts to integrate migration, and in particular the migration of unaccompanied minors, in development cooperation, in key areas such as poverty reduction, education, health, labour policy, human rights and democratization and post-conflict reconstruction. These efforts will help to address the root causes of migration.[140]

The Action Plan's determined focus on development issues is welcome. However this emphasis has not been translated into practice, as escalating trafficking and irregular migration figures demonstrate. The policy implementation wing responsible for carrying forward the Action Plan, the Justice and Home Affairs (JHA) Council of the EU, in its conclusions on unaccompanied minors subsequent to publication of the Action Plan, largely focuses on the implementation of "managed return" of unaccompanied minors. For trafficked children, this amounts to repatriation into a trafficking cycle. The JHA Council urges both the Commission and member states to encourage the voluntary return of minors to their countries of origin, and recommends the establishment of "operative networks to facilitate" this.[141]

Emphasis on the importance of returning unaccompanied minors to their countries of origin only addresses the EU concern to reduce immigration. Without investment in income-generating programs, the return migration plan does little to shore up a more secure future for the young returnees. A related criticism can be made of the education agenda. Much more effort has been made to develop educational campaigns targeted at preventing the migration of vulnerable communities than has been dedicated to more general educational innovation, skill training, gender-equality promotion, or other interventions that work *with* rather than *on* victims or potential victims of trafficking. It is easy to dismiss these broader educational aspirations as unrealistic pie in the sky. But the resources currently allocated to law enforcement would make an enormous impact on impoverished European source countries for trafficking, such as Moldova. Isabel should not have to consider cleaning jobs abroad that interfere with her university education. The problem in Moldova is not a lack of public information about the risk of being trafficked, it is a deficiency in international and European engagement with the drivers of trafficking. According to the latest available data, only 42 percent of the population over fifteen years old is employed and of these, over a third are employed in the informal economy, where jobs are less well remunerated, less secure, less healthy and safe, and less linked to employment benefits.[142] Small wonder that the lure of foreign employment attracts large numbers of Moldovans into trafficking networks each year.[143]

A similarly bleak picture can be painted in many areas of the world recently affected by economic, civil, and political turmoil. In Morocco, about 20 percent of youths aged fifteen to twenty-four are unemployed (23 percent of males and 19 percent of females).[144] The World Bank estimates that among the fifteen- to twenty-four-year-olds who *are* employed, only 35 percent are considered to be engaged in "decent" (i.e., rights-respecting) work within the meaning of Millennium Development Goal 8, Target 16.[145] In the conflict-ridden countries of Somalia, Iraq, and Afghanistan, recent unemployment data for youths aged fifteen to twenty-four is unavailable. However, the World Bank estimates that among those with jobs in this age group, few are engaged in "decent work": just 58 percent in Somalia, 23 percent in Iraq, and 47 percent in Afghanistan.[146] Observers fear that political instability and drought could exacerbate the humanitarian situation in Somalia and reverse recent economic growth.[147] Meanwhile, overall unemployment has reached nearly 18 percent in Iraq. In Afghanistan, only a third of females age fifteen and over participate in the labor force, compared with 85 percent of males.[148]

In Tara's region of origin, Gujarat, India, rural literacy rates are 62 percent for females and 83 percent for males.[149] Ninety-two percent of all workers are employed in the informal economy (with relatively little difference between women and men). Informal workers are unable to access the benefits and protections available to formal or organized workers, contributing to a "huge gap between the wages, terms of employment and working conditions." The recent global economic crisis has disproportionately affected girls and women in Gujarat, many of whom have taken on low-wage work to cope with a shrinking economy. Despite the perception that Gujarat is an example of India's success as an emerging BRICS (Brazil, Russia, India, China, South Africa) global economic powerhouse, the past few years have seen the state suffer. This is true not only absolutely but also in relative terms: Gujarat has fallen in rankings related to rural poverty, health status, and food insecurity compared to other Indian states.[150] The prospects for traffickers look increasingly good.

Tackling Root Causes in Practice, from the Bottom Up

I started this chapter with a personal anecdote related to Gujarat, India. I conclude with another personal anecdote from the same part of India. I have recently co-founded a nonprofit organization, the Alba Collective,[151] both to increase financial autonomy for girls and women living in rural communities and to increase educational and vocational resources for children, particularly girls, in those communities. Alba partners with India's largest women's trade union, the Self Employed Women's Association (SEWA) and other organizations, to develop sustainable (and scalable) income-generating projects for rural artisan women, the "poorest of the poor" as SEWA describes its members. I have done this in part because of growing disenchantment with top-down law-reform approaches to protecting vulnerable migrant children—good laws and good precedents still depend for their efficacy on good and affordable advocates, but they are in ever shorter supply and increasingly embattled as they confront public funding cuts and calls for fiscal conservatism. Another factor is my increasing skepticism about the human rights efficacy of postmigration intervention for trafficked children. Throughout this book I argue that ambivalence toward the legitimacy of child migrants' claims for robust human-rights protections permeates our system and vitiates comprehensive and effective intervention. After over thirty years of migration-related human-rights legal practice and advocacy, I co-founded the Alba Collective in part to practice what I preach. My hope is to pilot an intervention that is an effective and scalable antitrafficking prevention strategy.

The Alba Collective links rural artisans to high-end global designers to secure a premium price for handmade work and remove it from an "ethnic ghetto." Without the added value of high-end design, rural women and girl artisans are doomed to earnings below subsistence level. But an effective and constant link to the global marketplace triples, at a minimum, the daily income of the artisans from 100 rupees to 300 rupees ($2 to $6) and creates a larger, more predictable and better paid source of income. The expectation is that this female economic improvement will impact the prospects of the next generation of girls, enhancing educational and employment opportunity and reducing the pressure to migrate and the risk of trafficking and exploitation far from home. And there is urgent room for improvement. Our research to date includes the following findings in the villages where we are working:. whereas girls attend primary school at roughly the same rate as boys, their attendance falls off dramatically after the age of eleven.[152] Even when girls are attending school, during their time at home, when boys report doing homework, girls report doing housework. Early marriage is a constant threat.[153] Exacerbating this picture are macroeconomic upheavals. Distress migration, once limited to males searching for seasonal agricultural work, has become a matter of survival for entire families seeking to escape drought, environmental degradation, and rural economic collapse. Thirty-five percent of girls interviewed in our study said they had left school because they were needed for family chores,[154] a figure that includes cases where migration is a contributing factor—families are forced to move, girls are pulled out of school to look after young siblings as their parents migrate to salt mines, to the big cities, to jobs in the United Arab Emirates or farther afield. The lack of sustainable opportunity drives some families to exploit their girls and women, to secure desperately needed ready cash. Convicting Tara's trafficker would have prevented him from immediately returning to Gujarat to recruit another child domestic worker to replace Tara, but it would have done nothing to stem the supply. It is worth noting the desperation that lies behind the abusive family decisions. Two weeks before we launched our Alba Collective village survey in July 2010, we learned of the suicide of the daughter of one of our Indian team—a sixteen-year-old girl called Shanu had hung herself. We were told that despair over the migration of family members in search of work, and fear following reports of domestic violence in the family into which her marriage had been arranged (since childhood) were the precipitating causes. But the lack of viable income-generating opportunities combined with no secondary schooling and the prospects of a homebound existence could have been added to our informant's list of suicide precipitating factors. The goal of this phase of our project is to document the factors that trigger educational success and those that do not appear to, and to craft recommendations for state government reflecting our findings. Eventually female income generation opportunities and sustained educational access will reduce the desperation that propels dangerous 'exit' strategies.

Conclusion

Models such as the Alba Collective have a future wherever poor women and girls have insufficient earning capacity, underutilized but marketable traditional skills, and the desire for greater agency—which is to say, most places where trafficking is a problem. A greater focus on root causes, on working closely with local actors, in education, employment, and government is an absolutely essential and urgent priority. I suggest that many antitrafficking activists might do well to move away from their exclusive focus on the migration and postmigration context and on policy forums condemning trafficking, and instead prioritize grassroots intervention in poor communities, mainly in developing countries, where trafficking looms as a real threat for many children.

Antitrafficking work must pair up much more closely with work to develop communities from which trafficked children and adolescents originate, so that experts from each field can influence one another. At present the two worlds are quite separate. Development experts look at aggregate performance and impact, at improving school enrollment, housing stock, health access, and financial security; they do not identify the most vulnerable within the target communities—families with histories of domestic violence, forced migration or bonded labor—the most likely sources of trafficked children. Interventions that fail to reach the entire community are likely to miss precisely those sections that most need the support. Antitrafficking experts focus on penalizing the traffickers and on supporting the "victims" after the fact, rescuing them, protecting them, retraining them, and sometimes returning them. By the time they are in contact with trafficked children, it is likely that huge damage has been done, physically, psychically, and socially.

While both spheres of work are constructive, they do not add up to an effective antitrafficking strategy. Development work should be more informed by what is known about the roots of trafficking vulnerability to more appropriately fine tune on the ground interventions and monitoring and evaluation exercises—making this happen is the responsibility of antitrafficking experts, advocates, and networks. Conversely, antitrafficking work should refocus its priorities so that work within at risk communities is not solely focused on educational campaigns and warnings, but rather includes concrete alternatives to migration and exploitation in the areas of education, social support, work, and future aspirations. Only by working with those engaged in large-scale development projects can these alternatives be suitably tailored and made accessible to the communities that most need them. To improve the efficacy of antitrafficking measures and give better options to children and young people at risk of trafficking now, new frameworks and priorities must be embraced by both the antitrafficking and the development constituencies. This is the challenge we should set ourselves.

CHAPTER 5
Under the Gun: Moving Children for War

> On any given day in the center of Freetown, crowds of amputees jostle with polio victims and the destitute—both young and old—to beg for money. The government, they say, gives them nothing and the court, they argue, is not really for them.[1]
>
> [W]ell-intended targeting can create a potentially dangerous privileging of former child soldiers over equally needy villagers. One elder in Sierra Leone asked me, "Why should the soldiers who attacked us get all the assistance, when we all have suffered?"[2]

Introduction and Context

On June 20, 2007, for the first time ever, former military leaders were convicted of the international crime of recruiting child soldiers. Alex Tamba

Brima, Brima Bazzy Kamara, and Santigie Borbor Kanu, three senior figures in Sierra Leone's brutal, eleven-year war, were found guilty by the UN-backed Special Court for Sierra Leone and sentenced to between forty-five and fifty years in prison.[3] Moving children for exploitation in the course of war had become a judicially sanctioned international crime just as moving children for exploitation in the course of trafficking had become some years earlier. Eleven other defendants have since been tried for recruiting and enlisting children into armed conflict.[4] Nine have been convicted, including former Liberian President Charles Taylor, accused of aiding and abetting the use of child soldiers in Sierra Leone.[5] Meanwhile, between 2004 and 2007, children were engaged in active combat in government or rebel forces in twenty-one countries.[6]

The conscription and use of children in the country's armed conflict formed a key and novel part of the Special Court's 2007 indictment. That these convictions should happen first in Sierra Leone was no coincidence. The scale and ferocity of the use of children was notorious: 15,000 to 22,000 children were used in the war,[7] including an estimated 10,000 as combatants, and nearly half of the rebel forces consisted of children.[8] The brutality inflicted on and by them was extraordinary, even by the standards of contemporary warfare,[9] as the following brief quotation illustrates:

> I was on my way to the market when a rebel demanded I come with him. The commander said to move ahead of him. My grandmother argued with him. He shot her twice. I said he should kill me, too. They tied my elbows behind my back. At the base, they locked me in the toilet for two days. When they let me out, they carved the letters RUF across my chest. They tied me so I wouldn't rub it until it was healed.[10]

According to current estimates, there are at least 300,000 children involved in armed conflict around the world.[11] The term "child soldier," used throughout this chapter, refers to boys or girls under eighteen "compulsorily, forcibly or voluntarily recruited or used in hostilities by armed forces, paramilitaries, civil defence units or other armed groups"[12] *in any capacity*, including as "cooks, porters, human shields, sexual slaves, messengers, spies, or frontline combatants."[13] This broad definition underscores the reality that child soldiers experience multiple violations of their rights, regardless of their actual role in the conflict.[14] As with child trafficking so with child soldiering: research shows that children who have experienced economic and social exclusion, trauma, violence, or displacement are more susceptible to recruitment as child soldiers.[15] Children are frequently recruited first by tyrannical leaders because they are "more obedient, do not question orders and are easier to manipulate than adult soldiers."[16] Brutal indoctrination is geared to the transmission of barbarism and absolute obedience. As one sixteen-year-old youth described:

> I was forced to do amputations. We had a cutlass, an ax and a big log. We called the villagers out and let them stand in line. You ask [the victims] whether they want a long hand or a short hand [amputation at the wrist or at the elbow]. The long hand you put in a different bag from the short hand. If you have a large number of amputated hands in the bag, the promotion will be automatic, to various ranks.[17]

Children are moved for exploitation for a wide range of reasons. The previous chapter explored market-driven exploitation. This chapter is also about moving children for exploitation—but exploitation of a different sort, the recruitment and use of children in armed conflicts. Beyond financial gain, primary motivating factors are military advantage and political power. Instead of transcontinental journeys, the movements are to regions or countries neighboring the child's home. Instead of global criminal chains linking a range of actors from relatives to remote international mafia bosses, the key players driving recruitment are nationals, domestic military chiefs, and members of their forces or groups. Instead of deceit or the manipulation of naïve aspirations, the primary strategy to enlist the children is simply brute coercion.

> Children of this country were forced to fight for a cause we could not understand. We were drugged and made to kill and destroy our brothers and sisters and our mothers and fathers. We were beaten, amputated and used as sex slaves. This was a wretched display of inhuman and immoral actions by those who were supposed to be protecting us. Our hands, which were meant to be used freely for play and schoolwork, were used instead, by force, to burn, kill and destroy.[18]

Child trafficking and the recruitment of children for armed conflict are very different phenomena. They do however share a number of critical factors. Many of the actual tasks performed by the children are the same, including hard physical labor and forced participation in abusive sex.[19]

Children's malleability is attractive to both sets of exploiters, who use terror, brute force, drug addiction, and loyalty to ensure obedience and work performance. Many of the predisposing factors that characterize the children's lives before recruitment overlap—social and economic deprivation, the absence of strong, nurturing family structures, and prior exposure to abuse or violence. Indeed many children trafficked for labor exploitation end up being recruited for combat.[20] Conversely child soldiers are liable to be abducted and forced into exploitative labor.[21] The consequences of the exploitative experience are often similar—stigma and rejection from the home community, deep trauma and enduring psychosocial disturbance, an absence of local structures to sustain long-term recovery and integration.[22] Finally, the immediacy of the violence perpetrated on trafficked children and child soldiers alike frequently overshadows the complex underlying conditions giving rise to both types of exploitation.[23]

In this chapter I argue that child soldiers, like trafficked children, have not received the social, economic, or political support they need despite the extensive recent public interest in the phenomenon. I suggest that the concerted focus on justice and accountability, while visible and valuable, has failed to feed into more structural and enduring development strategies that are less easily compatible with the time-bound interventionist international humanitarian agenda that has been the primary context for attention to the needs of child soldiers. An emphasis on criminal prosecutions, truth telling, and short-term reintegration has substituted for desperately needed long-term inputs into family, community, employment, and strengthening of the social infrastructure, rather like the emphasis on criminalization in the trafficking sphere has trumped creative engagement with skill building, vocational training, and employment creation for trafficked children. In the case of trafficked children, human-rights-based interventions have largely failed because they have been secondary to an immigration-control and criminalization agenda. As a result many trafficked children are retrafficked after they have escaped the first time. In the case of child soldiers emerging from situations of conflict (whether international or internal), humanitarian interventions have had little enduring impact because such interventions have been tied, even subordinated, to the short-term geopolitical agendas of states.[24] As a result, former child soldiers face precarious and difficult futures and many drift back to engagement in armed combat. This is particularly true when the stigma they face is layered with a belief that they are "spiritually contaminated"[25] and ill prepared for any other activity.

> [The UN Special Representative for Children and Armed Conflict] described the ordeal of a former child soldier in Sierra Leone who left his community because he felt "haunted by bad spirits" and was re-recruited to fight for rebels in Liberia before working as a mercenary in Côte D'Ivoire. He said he left Sierra Leone because there is peace there now, explaining: "what I really know how to do well is fight and be a soldier."[26]

This humanitarian and development failure, like the human rights lacunae discussed earlier in this book, is not plausibly explained in terms of ignorance about the problem of child recruitment or invisibility of the affected population.[27] For several decades now, concern about the recruitment and deployment of child soldiers has been voiced in military and diplomatic circles. Of course humanitarianism has a bifurcated heritage. As the ethicist Sissela Bok has pointed out:

> The word humanitarian . . . has inherent moral connotations. . . . It evokes helpfulness, benevolence and humane concern going to all who are in need, without regard to person. . . . [But] in the nineteenth century when the word first came into common usage in English, the adjective "humanitarian" was nearly always contemptuous; the word conveyed *deep rooted suspicion* [emphasis added].[28]

The lack of political will to make systematic interventions in the lives of former child soldiers—despite these expressions of concern and some highly successful individual writings by former child soldiers,[29] which have served to raise the political profile of the problem—calls for a more convincing explanation than ignorance of the problem. A shift in the view of children, from "innocent victims of warfare" in the beginning of the twentieth century to more visible participants by the end, is relevant.[30] Does "deep-rooted suspicion" of child soldiers' protection claims translate into indifference to their human suffering? Responses to former child soldiers in Sierra Leone reveal the ambivalence of current child-protection policy in practice. They include a broad range of recovery strategies and humanitarian failures that affect moving children brutalized by some of the worst man-made disasters of our time.

Bringing Children within the Scope of International Criminal Law

Efforts to bring to justice political leaders and senior military figures responsible for war crimes have a long history, dating back to the end of World War I.[31] These efforts have focused on the establishment of an international legal framework with widely agreed norms leading to prosecutions and convictions of prominent individuals. The process complements the older framework of international humanitarian law, including the four Geneva Conventions of 1949,[32] which sought to prevent atrocities in times of war by establishing an agreed-upon set of principles and minimum standards for the conduct of armed conflict.

The contemporary movement for individual criminal responsibility gained momentum following bloody conflicts in Eastern Europe and Africa in the early 1990s and produced the International Criminal Tribunal for the former Yugoslavia in 1993 and for Rwanda in 1994.[33] The progression from accepted rules of wartime engagement and proscriptions on behavior to a system of international legal accountability for violations of those rules was painstaking and arduous, confronting as it did states' fears about curtailment of their sovereignty, and leaders' apprehensions about potential future liability.[34] The outcome is a victory for transnational, organizing and advocacy, an object lesson in transformative social activism at the highest levels.[35] The two ad hoc tribunals, for all their inefficiencies, costliness, and delays, have established a new principle of accountability for leaders of regimes involved in crimes against humanity and war crimes, including genocide and rape. They have also highlighted the exploitation of children in modern warfare.

The creation of the first permanent International Criminal Court (ICC) in July 1998 generalized and institutionalized this process of international accountability, bringing within the framework of international justice an ever growing number of states (currently 121).[36] As of summer 2013, the Office of the Prosecutor is engaged in investigations in seven countries and is conducting preliminary examinations in another seven.[37] As chief prosecutor Luis Moreno Ocampo commented when the first defendant, Thomas Lubanga Dyilo from the Democratic Republic of the Congo, was handed over to the court's custody in 2006: "For 100 years, a permanent international criminal court was a dream—this dream is becoming a reality."[38]

The Court issued its first conviction on March 14, 2012: Lubanga was found guilty of enlisting children under the age of fifteen into the Patriotic Force for the Liberation of Congo.[39] While some were disappointed with his modest sentence of fourteen years, human rights advocates nonetheless applauded the message it sent: "The International Criminal Court is putting military commanders around the world on notice that sending children into war could put them behind bars for a good while."[40]

The process of including children in the movement to establish and expand effective international criminal responsibility has proved complex and lengthy. Though acknowledgment of the distinctive status of children and their need for priority attention started with the Geneva Conventions, it took nearly thirty years to legislate an international prohibition of the recruitment of children under fifteen and their participation in hostilities.[41] Even after the consolidation of earlier laws into the widely ratified CRC,[42] it took high-level political action in the form of a report on children in armed conflict produced in 1996 by Graça Machel, a visible and respected international expert, to galvanize the international community into more concerted engagement with the problem. Among other measures, the Machel report recommended appointment of a Special Rapporteur on Children in Armed Conflict.[43] Two years later the Statute of Rome established the ICC, which included under the rubric of serious crimes the conscription and use of child soldiers under fifteen.[44] This was followed in 2000 by a Convention on the Worst Forms of Child Labour that prohibited "forced or compulsory recruitment of children for use in armed conflict."[45] In 2002, an Optional Protocol to the CRC, prohibiting the participation of children under eighteen in hostilities, was signed.[46] The final step in the momentous process from human-rights principle to practice was described at the start of this chapter—the first conviction by a UN-approved criminal-justice body of defendants found guilty of the recruitment and use of child soldiers.

The progression from condemnation of child recruitment to binding international law to effective practical implementation of a serious sanction against violators took decades: sixty years in all. A similar process is required for war-affected children. Societies committed to building robust and effective postconflict peace must advance from the intention to rehabilitate former child soldiers to the realization and building of enduring structures and mechanisms that will transform the circumstances placing child combatants and their peers at continued risk of exploitation. Despite awareness of children's heightened vulnerability to war, postconflict reconstruction does not automatically cater to these urgent needs. In one recent analysis of eight truth commissions, the authors found repeated failures "to recognize or address grave violations suffered by children," "to consider and define crimes in ways that include children," and "to conduct targeted outreach to child survivors."[47] As well, legislation and prosecution alone cannot be relied upon to produce results on the ground for children caught up in war. As the following case study of Sierra Leone shows, innovative approaches beyond criminal prosecutions and multistakeholder partnerships are needed to ensure children's access to substantive postconflict justice and opportunity structures that promote their ability to thrive as autonomous adults.[48]

Framing Transitional Justice: The "Hybrid" Special Court for Sierra Leone

The Special Court for Sierra Leone ("Special Court" or SCSL) was established in 2002 to investigate crimes committed in the brutal eleven-year war that left some 50,000 people dead, 20,000 people mutilated, and three-quarters of the population displaced.[49] According to some estimates, 64,000 women and girls were raped and a quarter of victims were under the age of thirteen.[50] The Special Court's mandate explicitly included the abduction and forced recruitment of children under fifteen.[51] The SCSL was set up by statute under a special treaty agreed upon between the UN and the Sierra Leone government, but it is independent of both. "It is not grafted into the Sierra Leone justice system, but rather hovers outside the national court system, having concurrent jurisdiction with, and primacy over, the domestic courts."[52] Such hybrid courts[53] combine domestic and international elements and supplement the work of the ICC, which is circumscribed by capacity and by jurisdictional limitations,[54] and the work of purely domestic courts that are often immobilized by the scale of the task and the dire paucity of their resources.[55] Several of the Special Court's practices suggest a possible precedent for the development of a framework with lasting impact on child soldiers' future prospects. For example, the Court applies a blend of international humanitarian and domestic law: it is responsive to local customs and knowledge but at the same time incorporates relevant international principles and precedents. To gauge the efficacy of this approach, consider the Court's handling of a cultural-relativism defense argument in relation to the role of children in Africa, advanced by the legal team representing the accused defendants in the child soldier cases. The argument was that "the concept of childhood is related to the ability to perform tasks, not to age" and that the practice of using children as combatants was "a practice established in Sierra Leone" long before the recent conflict.[56] The court held that the rules of customary international law were "not contingent on domestic practice in one given country."[57] Local custom could not trump international law establishing that recruitment of combatants under fifteen was a war crime. At the same time, the chief prosecutor of the Special Court established, as court policy, that no children under eighteen would be prosecuted because they were not those "most responsible" for the violence, despite the fact that the Special Court had jurisdiction over anyone fifteen years and above.[58] A similar approach could be applied to arguments about the culpability of teen mothers or rape victims rejected by their communities after years as bush wives because of customary insistence on virginity before marriage.[59] A mixed international/domestic adjudicatory body is well positioned to resist opportunistic relativism or dogmatic universalism in favor of more situationally sophisticated techniques of rights enforcement.[60]

The Court has also implemented a number of innovative measures designed to draw on local expertise and promote the engagement of the domestic community in the judicial process. A majority of the staff are drawn from the local population,[61] with the result that capacity building and human-rights training have been promoted through collaboration between local and international staff within the court itself. The Court has also conducted substantial outreach to make its activities accessible to affected communities in Sierra Leone. Though Charles Taylor, the former head of state, was considered too destabilizing a political presence to try locally in Freetown, the transfer of proceedings to the ICC's facilities in the The Hague did not reduce extensive dissemination across Sierra Leone. The Court collaborated with local and international stakeholders to transmit information about the proceedings to the public, including radio broadcasts, video screenings, and ongoing interactive forums in Sierra Leone, and to facilitate visits to The Hague by local civil leaders.[62]

The Special Court's proceedings have not been without significant institutional drawbacks, including financial instability, procedural delays, and the complications inherent in managing complex criminal trials.[63] Moreover, early concerns over the slowing pace of convictions[64] appear to have been justified, as, for now, no further indictments beyond those already initiated are expected.[65] Nevertheless, the Court's achievements have done much to strengthen the rule of law and undermine a culture of impunity in Sierra Leone. They have generated substantial local engagement with postconflict reconstruction along a broader and more inclusive range of approaches than is often the case after brutal civil war. This precedent suggests strategies that could be transposed to the benefit of former child soldiers in other jurisdictions. Instead of the adversarial reporting process where domestic civil servants record their ministries' achievements against benchmarks derived from international human-rights-treaty obligations, only to be challenged and cross-examined by outside international experts (as in the case of the treaty bodies that oversee the International Covenant on Civil and Political Rights and the Convention on the Rights of the Child),[66] a hybrid structure including national and international economists and policy experts might be more productive and politically palatable as a mechanism for engaging in complex priority setting and national reconstruction.

From Legal to Social Justice—An Unbridged Gap

The 2007 conviction of the three former Sierra Leonean rebel leaders represented a significant milestone in the campaign to ban the use of child soldiers in armed conflict.[67] It succeeded in placing children's-rights issues at the core of the international criminal justice project. It also represented an important victory for the complex and multifaceted human rights movement (dating back to the post–World War II Nuremberg and Tokyo trials)[68] to establish the international criminal responsibility of political leaders for crimes perpetrated by states against their own citizens, now extended to politically powerless groups such as children. The Special Court achieved another landmark victory on April 26, 2012, when Charles Taylor became the first former head of state since Nuremberg to face a verdict before an international court.[69] His conviction signaled a benchmark in the law-driven curtailment of state sovereignty and reinforced the continuing ideological and political shift in the standards of acceptable modern warfare.

These legal landmarks shed a stark light on the dramatic protection deficits affecting children forced to move for war. Despite the victories for international justice scored against recruiters of former child soldiers, these children's access to substantive justice has languished. It is not surprising that young people themselves express a strong sense of grievance about postwar opportunities and dynamics. A small vignette from Freetown, the capital of Sierra Leone, illustrates the point.

While the compound of the Special Court has airconditioners, water, and light, outside the compound these basic commodities are lacking. The Court's expenditures and contributions to the local economy benefit a small, already relatively privileged section of the population, some of which is involved in the corrupt resource-extraction industry (especially diamond mining) that underpinned much of the past crisis and contributed to its continuation.[70] Meanwhile thousands of amputees are desperate for sustenance,[71] huge numbers of children lack access to schooling,[72] and the business of government scarcely gets done.[73] Creative thinking about the rights and needs of children engulfed in the horror of child soldiering has stalled. As with child trafficking examined in the previous chapter, so with child soldiering: long-term and sustained structural intervention is elusive.

The Human Rights Entitlements of Former Child Soldiers—A Complex Mandate with Negligible Impact

To move beyond the ravages of war, children recruited for conflict require accountability for harms done, protection to address immediate needs, and support to realize opportunities ahead. Interventions driven by the obligations of international human rights law do not integrate these agendas coherently. The range of violations experienced by Sierra Leone's former child soldiers demonstrates the divergence of the two, allegedly "indivisible," arms of the human rights project—the realization of civil and political rights on the one hand, and the achievement, progressively, of economic, social, and cultural rights on the other.

As other chapters in this book have noted, both sets of human rights are covered by international law. Children are entitled both to equal treatment and nondiscrimination in the application of general civil and political rights and to special protection given their particular status. They must have their best interests taken into account as a primary consideration in all matters that affect them, and their opinions solicited and attended to where they are in a position to effectively articulate them. At the same time, they are entitled to access to primary education without discrimination; to the highest attainable standard of health care; to protection from harmful traditional and customary practices;[74] to special protections in relation to military recruitment,[75] sexual abuse,[76] exploitative labor,[77] and other oppressive practices.[78] This much is clear as a matter of normative universal human rights.

The international framework establishes a complex set of mandates. A universal definition of childhood—any person under eighteen—applies irrespective of local understandings or cultural variations, unless legal provisions establish majority at a lower age;[79] at the same time, individual developmental variation must be taken into account in assessing the importance of a child's views and the related obligation to promote child participation in decision making. Children are citizens with equal rights to some protections, special claims to others, and a progressive and changing right to autonomy.[80] They are also agents who gradually and imperceptibly move from passive vulnerability or victimhood to active responsibility, from simple claims to protection as young children, to more complex positions as adolescents where the relative impact of guilt, responsibility, coercion, and the mandates of universal personhood must be determined.

In Sierra Leone, acknowledgment of the special status of children before the law, demonstrated by the criminalization of their forcible conscription, has not so far been matched by an effective commitment to the realization of their economic and social rights. A decade after the end of hostilities, Sierra Leone's children and youth[81] are among the most vulnerable in the world. The country ranks 180 out of 187 in the United Nations Human Development Index[82] with the majority of the population living on less than $1 US per day.[83] It has the fourth highest under-five mortality rate in the world,[84] with one in four children classified as underweight and one in three children experiencing stunted growth.[85] Forty percent of girls under eighteen have given birth,[86] and teenage pregnancy accounts for 40 percent of maternal deaths.[87] Education and employment outcomes are similarly dire: just 11 percent of boys and 7 percent of girls complete secondary school;[88] only 5 percent of youth ages fifteen to twenty-four are employed.[89] Within this context of hardship, the special needs of many child soldiers remain unattended to. Local society struggles with questions of their guilt, responsibility, and victimhood, responding with a complex blend of forgiveness and stigmatization, inclusion and exclusion. At the same time, violations sustained during war—including the loss of educational opportunities, inadequate social assistance, and family breakdown—have contributed to "a grim world of deprivation, boredom and poverty."[90] Like the child-trafficking survivors described in the previous chapter, many former child soldiers have been driven to engage in risky income-generating activities, including, in the Sierra Leone context, diamond mining and reenlistment in armed conflict. In the words of one child miner, "I have had no achievement; nothing really good has come in my life—I make just enough for survival, some food."[91]

The separation between Sierra Leone's litigation-based court achievements and its economic and social reforms suggests a troubling disparity. Pursuing the conviction of individual recruiters of child soldiers, primarily funded by the international community, cost an estimated $28.2 million from July 2003 to July 2004.[92] Contrast this with the investment in strengthening systems in the health and education sectors in 2004. The convictions cost 84 percent of donor expenditures for health ($33.6 million)[93] and 41 percent of all donor expenditures for education ($69 million).[94] They represented 19 percent of donor expenditures for all human development activities in 2005 ($145 million).[95] Bringing to justice recruiters and abusers of former child soldiers is one element in restoring order to society and in deterring future abuse. It sends a deterrent message, it publicly signals condemnation, it establishes a retributive process. "It lays the groundwork for a rights-based approach to post-conflict recovery."[96] Beyond laying the groundwork, does it have a multiplier or trigger effect on other basic and critical processes that enhance the prospects for conflict-affected children and youth?

At issue here is the impact of litigation on broader social change. Despite the fact that this question is difficult to investigate empirically—it is impossible to test an appropriate counterfactual—it has been explored frequently. One context involves the impact of the "activist" US Supreme Court, many decades ago. The question then was: "When does it make sense to litigate to help bring about significant social reform?" The answers are contested. One controversial study of the impact of some of the most significant Supreme Court cases such as *Brown v. Board of Education* and *Roe v. Wade* concluded that courts have little independent effect but rather reflect changes already achieved in the political, social and, economic spheres. They "may be more a reflection of significant social reform already occurring than an independent, important contribution to it."[97] A more encouraging assessment is that litigation, if creatively conceived in harmony with social movements and other grassroots organizing, may make an important contribution to leveraging change.[98] However, even this more optimistic view acknowledges that on its own, litigation never "solves the problem"—the partnership with effective entities promoting a civil society is critical to the translation from legal theory to social reality.[99]

Given the partial realization of children's rights in Sierra Leone today, similar questions about the translation from courtroom to classroom or marketplace are in order. Why have national, regional, and international resources been concentrated on postwar accountability for, inter alia, child soldier recruitment but neglected the equally urgent economic and social-rights issues that underpin the ability of children to take long-term advantage of those security gains? The disparity between the progress in tackling civil rights as opposed to socioeconomic need reveals weaknesses in the normative approach that has dominated international human rights work for the past half century.[100] Perhaps criminal litigation has been so heavily used, in spite of its obviously limited impact on economic and social issues and in spite of what some consider its frustrating and costly dimensions, because social-justice advocates have viewed it as "the only act in town."[101] Legally and intellectually, high-profile criminal litigation is appealing, stimulating to a varied constituency of experts, and reasonably expeditious in its delivery of results.

The convictions handed down by the Sierra Leone Special Court represent significant moments in postconflict reconstruction. A domestically based but internationally backed court, straddling the dichotomy between local justice and transnational human rights, achieves two critical goals: a visible outcome to a specific case (conviction of a war criminal for the conscription of child soldiers) and revitalization of a system of local justice. Court-based remedies, however, remain inadequate to address the ongoing and systemic violations of the rights of former child soldiers. Have other areas of public activity generated a more enduring local reconstruction legacy in Sierra Leone for the benefit of conflict-affected children?

Implementing Transitional Justice: The DDR Process

An accurate assessment of the international community's impact on enhancing the human rights of children affected by armed conflict must take into account a second important postconflict development in Sierra Leone—the disarmament, demobilization, and reintegration process. Intended as a mechanism for paving the way for a rights-respecting transition to peacetime life for those caught up in the war, it consisted of a vigorous partnership between international and local stakeholders. It directly targeted key social and economic issues facing former child soldiers, including access to education, rehabilitation from trauma, and skill development. The reintegration prospects of Sierra Leone's war-affected youth were a central concern. A short history of the establishment of this process precedes an evaluation of its economic and social legacy.

On July 7, 1999, all parties to the long conflict in Sierra Leone signed a peace agreement in Lomé, designed to conclude hostilities and establish a government of national unity. Several months later, the UN Security Council authorized the establishment of UNAMSIL, the UN Mission in Sierra Leone, which, with progressive increases approved by the Security Council, reached the size of 17,500 military personnel.[102] UNAMSIL's role was to assist the national unity government in both peace keeping and peace building. A key element of this role was to assist with the implementation of the DDR process, first started in 1997 but continued in a second phase after the 1999 Lomé peace agreement and extended to a final, third phase from May 2001 to January 2002. According to the World Bank, which together with the British Department for International Development (DFID) supported the program over the three phases and four years of its existence, the Sierra Leone DDR program succeeded in demobilizing and disarming 72,500 combatants and in collecting 42,330 weapons and 1.2 million pieces of ammunition. Out of the estimated 48,000 child soldiers, approximately 7,000 children (or roughly 1 in 7) were officially included in the DDR program, in a special process.[103]

Many stakeholders participated in the DDR process. The model, supported by the World Bank and DFID, was to emphasize government ownership of the process but to combine this with close coordination between international and local partners, and consistent outside support in the form of funding and technical advice. This is an interesting adaptation of the hybrid model adopted by the Special Court. A Multi-Donor Trust Fund that committed $31.5 million was established by the World Bank; in addition a wide range of civil society organizations, NGOs, and donors participated in a comprehensive reconstruction and community-driven recovery event. Eventually (unlike the Special Court), in order to avoid one-off relief-and-recovery measures in favor of more long-term impact, the program concentrated on national capacity building to strengthen local leadership and increase efficiency and transparency in government implementation of rehabilitation programs.

As in the judicial prosecutions, special attention to the needs and vulnerabilities of child soldiers formed a key part of the Sierra Leone DDR process. Between 2000 and 2002, when the official program was put into effect on the ground, about 48,000 children were demobilized. For children, the DDR package consisted of a set of options. In general, in return for handing over a weapon, children could elect to receive a set of learning materials (books, pens, a school bag, school uniform, and advance payment of three years of school fees) or a skills-training package, which included a training course and a "start-up kit" to enable them to put their training into practice.[104]

These programs achieved some notable successes. According to the US Agency for International Development's (USAID's) Displaced Children and Orphans' Fund (DCOF), which between 1999 and 2004 invested over $6.7 million on projects for Sierra Leonean former child soldiers, 98 percent of children who passed through the DDR process were reunited with parents or relatives in the immediate postconflict period.[105] The injection of funds on this scale was in and of itself a dramatic statement of international engagement with the problems of the country. But it was not just a question of scale. Qualitatively, too, the DDR process applied insights from the international child-advocacy movement, much as the SCSL process built on evolving international criminal-justice principles. The DDR process acknowledged the centrality of education and training as part of the tool kit for children's future healing and self-reliance: the program assisted some children in securing skills and in taking on income-generating activities.[106] Reintegration was a central concern for all participants. A study conducted by Save the Children involving 211 ex-soldiers and other separated children adopted a multidimensional definition of reintegration. It included "being loved and cared for by their families, being accepted and welcomed by the community, living in peace and unity with others." Access to school and skills training, and factors linked to livelihood, access to food, and antipoverty measures formed part of the children's notion of reintegration. This complex definition captures the important link between healing past wounds and building a secure future that lies at the core of the postconflict challenge. As a fifteen-year-old male ex-soldier put it, focusing on his peer group: "[Reintegration means] . . . no more grumble, no more harassment, and no more *ton det* [reprisals]. Work together with them and share fun with one another."[107]

For the first time ever, reintegration measures also addressed the importance of transitional justice for children through the establishment of programs to support child participation in the Sierra Leone Truth and Reconciliation Commission (TRC).[108] The Commission had been legislated into being by the Sierra Leone Parliament in 2000, with special attention and assistance to enable the participation of children who had suffered sexual abuse during the war.[109] Even families initially skeptical about the risks of prosecution their children might face if they gave self-incriminating statements to the Commission were persuaded that the Special Court and the Commission were quite distinct entities and that the Court would abide by its policy not to prosecute anyone under eighteen. Many children, for the first time in years, found themselves in an environment where they could begin to address the trauma of the preceding years, to pick up the threads of a broken education, to rediscover support systems to help them break their drug or alcohol addiction and their physical and mental entrapment by lethal commanders.

"The role of children in the Sierra Leone TRC was . . . groundbreaking in setting precedent and developing policies and procedures." Over three hundred statements from children were taken by people who traveled the length and breadth of the country; over 350 children attended the hearings. Because of the particular difficulty of talking about sexual violence, a lower proportion of war-affected girls participated in the process than boys, even though all the children's hearings were closed to the public, and those dealing with sexual violence were held in the presence of exclusively female staff. The full impact of children's participation in the Sierra Leone TRC has not yet been studied, and may turn out to be short-lived. But the process establishes an important benchmark for postconflict interventions acknowledging the distinctive harms inflicted on children. The very fact that children's testimony was considered important and that efforts were made to elicit it in a supportive and child-friendly way is noteworthy. As an interviewed child commented: "If asked to go [to give a statement] again, I would go. It was okay. I felt protected."[110] More generally, the rehabilitation aspect of the DDR process enabled many damaged children to re-envisage the possibility of a rewarding life.

How did she know I loved to write song lyrics? I thought, but didn't ask. Later, after I had been rehabilitated, I learned that [nurse] Esther knew

> what I was interested in through the informal schooling at the [DDR] center. In the short classes that we attended, we had been given questionnaires as a form of exam. The questions were general in the beginning. They didn't provoke any difficult memories. What kind of music do you like? Do you like reggae music? . . . These were the sort of questions we would either discuss in class or write a short answer to. . . . I began to look forward to Esther's arrival in the afternoons. I sang for her the parts of songs I had memorized that day. Memorizing lyrics left me little time to think about what had happened in the war.[111]

Gaps in the DDR Process—Structural Difficulty with Short-term Interventions

For all its strengths and achievements, the DDR process had some serious shortcomings. Injection of substantial funds on a one-off basis and adoption of human-rights principles as part of a top-down managerial process in the absence of radical institutional innovation, economic redistribution, and political change did not create sustainable social and economic protections for children. Many of the children involved in the DDR process drifted away from their families after the initial reunification, in search of educational or livelihood opportunities. "Home" for many turned out not to be a panacea, either because of the lingering resentment and stigma arising out of their wartime activities, or because of the dramatic lack of educational or employment opportunities enabling young people to sustain a self-sufficient life: "[P]eople were disgruntled about them because according to the popular opinion these children have destroyed our lives, houses and property. Therefore these ex–child combatants were called different names. There was total rejection of them, some people even disowned their own children."[112] As a fifteen-year-old former child soldier put it: "Normally when you come back into the community people say 'that child killed my brother.'" Other child beneficiaries of DDR program subsidies commented that their handouts were referred to as "blood supplies" and that discrimination in the allocation of resources between active participants in the war and other child soldiers created deep resentment within the community and threatened friendships. Particular hardships faced returning children who did not have parents to live with but had, instead, to stay with extended family: many reported being discriminated against by comparison with the biological children of the head of household. According to Save the Children, "mistreatment of children living in extended families took many forms, including being provided with inadequate food, having to work long hours rather than go to school, not feeling loved and being beaten."[113] Children who were known to have taken active part in combat and the perpetration of atrocities fared particularly badly within their communities on return.

A temporary, short-term "reintegration" process is no substitute for a sustained, Marshall Plan–like investment in long-term reconstruction and state building. It is not clear that the DDR process seriously engaged with the structural innovations necessary to create an enduring legacy of change and progress. There is an important difference here between the impact of international criminal and social-justice initiatives. Whereas the former achieve a permanent and enduring result by the very fact of a one-off act (a finding of guilt is indefinite, whatever the length of the sentence), social and economic-justice initiatives need structural underpinnings to last—otherwise they risk being merely palliative or symbolic. One-off educational or social-welfare inputs generally leave no lasting trace. The legacy of creative use of hybrid procedures combining international and local actors, and a determined focus on the needs, best interests, and rights of children are precedents that must be translated into long term implementation of social and economic rights.

Even within the framework of the innovative DDR process, some serious limitations became apparent. One of the most evident was that the process had a gender-unequal impact. Of the sample of demobilized children reported on by DCOF, 92 percent were boys. Only a few of the estimated 8,600–11,400 girl soldiers benefited from the DDR program. One of the most vulnerable and rights-deprived groups of child soldiers—girls subjected to rape, to servicing militias as "bush wives," to sexual slavery—was substantially left out of the benefits of the humanitarian engagement. A key reason for this limited impact on girls was the fact that handing over a weapon was an entry ticket to the DDR program, a precondition that excluded girls drawn into the conflict in noncombat capacities.

> Eligibility for DDR became more stringent over time. Initially, all those who could prove during interviews that they had been with armed groups or forces, as combatants or in another capacity for at least one year were

eligible. This then changed to two years with armed groups or forces in any capacity, and eventually to being able to dismantle and fire a gun.[114]

Apart from this exclusionary qualifying requirement, two other factors contributed to the low impact of DDR on girl soldiers. Stigma arising out of the sexual abuse endured during the war (sometimes compounded by pregnancy and childbirth) prevented many from coming forward. According to boy respondents in one study, their raped sisters were ostracized on an ongoing basis by the community, "who believed that their contact with the rebel forces had left them with sexually transmitted diseases and unsuitable for marriage."[115] In some cases, continued enslavement by commanders was a factor, while in other cases, those administering the programs did not make it clear girls were eligible.

The limited nature of the DDR process also fostered resentment in the immediate postconflict period, compounded as the months passed by the fact that only child soldiers were catered to. "Because of the DDR, I wore nice shoes and new clothes. I was very grateful because I could never have come out of the bush in the state I was in. But other youths had no nice shoes and clothes. I became stigmatized for a different reason."[116] While the desire of funders to target the most needy group in order to limit expense is comprehensible, the consequences of this selective approach are complex. In a context of extreme resource scarcity, preferential treatment for a section of the population is always problematic. Such targeting or selection is not peculiar to the postconflict situation—it applies to all social-welfare programming. But it gives rise to particular problems in situations of community polarization. In Sierra Leone, many of the fruits of DDR selectively benefited perpetrators of grave human-rights violations, inevitably giving rise to sharp questions of equity. What notion of citizenship underlies a system in which child soldiers get free education but indigent children who, for whatever reasons, did not participate in or perpetrate violations during the war, are denied education?

Though problematic as an overall strategy, targeting is appropriate for the special needs of particular, carefully selected groups. As Wessels rightly points out: "Reintegration is a dual process of individual adaptation and community acceptance and support." There are special needs that do require targeted attention and a narrowly focused intervention.[117] A majority of former child soldiers, like the broader population of children in postconflict settings, function effectively with access to general social provision. A second group, including orphaned and disabled children, require some targeted support to address their heightened needs and enable them to take advantage of general opportunities. But, a small residual group, sometimes estimated at approximately 10 percent of the former child soldier population, do indeed have long-term special needs as a result of their trauma, both during and after conflict.[118] A serious deficiency of the short-term DDR process is the absence of effective and enduring engagement with the rehabilitative needs of this most seriously traumatized group of child soldiers, those who perpetrated the most egregious acts of violence, both in kind and over time, and those who were victims of enduring abuse and trauma. Several studies point to the worrying finding that, if untreated or if not catered to specifically, the consequences of serious conflict-induced trauma increase. Not only does this leave an enduring legacy of personal tragedy—depression, anxiety, aggression, suicidal tendencies, serious risk-taking behavior, such as drug or alcohol addiction. It also creates a public policy time bomb as a generation of ex–child soldiers grows up unable to integrate or contribute productively to their society, destined to reenlist as mercenaries or fighters.[119]

Post Postconflict—Long-term Social and Economic Rights Enforcement for Former Child Soldiers

No criminal justice system alone can reduce the chances that children will be vulnerable to conscription. For that outcome, a different sort of rights project is necessary, one that not only disarms former child soldiers, but that rehabilitates them in a holistic and long-term manner. This *necessarily includes* protecting them against economic deprivation. A project that aims to improve the lives of children and youth formerly engaged in armed conflict must start with the needs of the children themselves as rights-holders and citizens, rather than with the guilt of adults as victimizers and abusers of children. Institutional innovation is a key part of this process: new forms of national and international collaboration, new structures of engagement, new specially crafted procedures to secure local sustainability and the institutionalization of new forms of political agency. The redistribution of social resources is central to the enforcement of the rights of former child soldiers. Like the criminal-justice project, this economic and social child-rights project asks how formal legal obligations set out in binding international instruments can be translated into substantive justice for a radically disenfranchised community. In 2005 Save the Children addressed part of this issue. They noted that, to deter re-recruitment, societies had to ensure family unity and ability to nurture and protect, a reduction in household poverty, and career opportunities for young people facilitated by education and vocational training.[120]

At the same time, the problems with the implementation of DDR illustrate a structural difficulty with short-term interventions. Despite the substantial investment—of both domestic and international entities—in the DDR process for conflict-affected children, many of the problems that precipitated their recruitment and participation in war remain unaddressed, in some ways exacerbated by the legacy of the conflict. Pervasive poverty and lack of opportunity undermine piecemeal strategies to support reintegration. They also limit the effectiveness of many community-building interventions and projects initiated by partnerships between local groups and international NGOs. Feelings of disenfranchisement, stigma, and exclusion from society, compounded by endemic problems of poverty and lack of opportunities for education and employment, generate the possibility of re-recruitment and of long-term youth marginalization. Though criminalization of adult-rights violators is an important achievement, without complementary social and economic interventions, it is inadequate to sustain reintegration and deter future child enlistment.

Some aspects of an ambitious social and economic-rights project have been initiated in postconflict Sierra Leone. On June 7, 2007, the Sierra Leone government announced the adoption of a Child Rights Act, a national government measure incorporating into domestic law provisions of international children's rights law from the CRC and the African Charter on the Rights and Welfare of the Child. The Act included clauses mandating protection of the rights to education and to the highest attainable standard of health. Set against the backdrop of very difficult socioeconomic circumstances, the adoption of this ambitious bill signaled an important domestic determination, and provided, in the words of the local UNICEF representative, "an operational framework for the roll-out of children's rights in Sierra Leone."[121]

At the time the Act was announced, Sierra Leone had made some progress in ensuring the welfare of its children, despite the recent history of conflict: an increase in immunization rates and a gradual recovery of the educational system, with 4,600 primary schools operating across the country. Yet ongoing problems included exposure of children to violence and abuse, child exploitation and deprivation—"about half of the children between 5 and 14 are engaged in some form of child labor"—and an ongoing, radical protection deficit: "about 11 percent of children are orphans and 20 percent do not live with their biological parents. Sexual and gender-based violence remains a serious concern."[122]

Seven years after passage of the Child Rights Act, the challenge of realizing legislative promises remains. Sierra Leone continues to have low life expectancy (forty-eight years), a low adult literacy rate (41 percent),[123] and incomplete access to education. Despite the entitlement to free schooling through age fifteen, many parents are unable to afford the costs of sending their children to school, and pregnancy prevents many adolescent girls from completing their education. Despite a prohibition against forced labor, government enforcement is poor, and almost half the children aged fourteen and fifteen are engaged in exploitative or age-inappropriate labor, often under hazardous conditions. A recent UNICEF study found that over 50 percent of street children in Sierra Leone engage in prostitution to feed themselves, and that many, especially those separated from family or otherwise displaced, are at heightened risk of violence, abuse, trafficking, and exploitation.[124] This grim assessment suggests that the creative partnership displayed by the international community in the creation of the SCSL has not had significant ripple effects beyond the legal sphere. As one NGO worker stated: "Donors don't normally go for long term projects. But problems can be very long term."[125] What measures could be developed to advance economic and social rights for Sierra's Leone's former child soldiers?

To start with, comprehensive postconflict peace building involves a restructuring of international development aid.[126] It requires a radical transformation of global trading agreements, including those relating to the lucrative extractive industry that yields huge profits from diamonds and other minerals, profits that flow into private coffers creating the notorious "resource curse" phenomenon.[127] Effective peace building requires an investigation into regional trade and migration patterns, which exacerbate the domestic strains of postconflict societies by stimulating disinvestment in local industries, brain drain, and the progressive impoverishment of state structures—to the point where the government is ineffective as a structure mediating citizenship rights.

Solutions to these vital and foundational questions underpin the possibilities of success in the reconstruction process. A small part of this overall picture involves the realization of economic and social rights directly relevant to conflict-affected children. And one part entails a sustainable plan to work both backward and forward: backward to tackle the specific child-related issues that resulted in the possibility of child-soldier recruitment in the first place, and forward to address the needs of the small subgroup of child soldiers whose progressive maladaptation to the postconflict situation is tragic for their future prospects and poisonous for the society at large.

The Sierra Leone Special Court's model of hybrid collaboration between international and domestic experts provides a methodology for identifying and implementing policies for war-affected children and youth more generally. The limited and targeted provision of the DDR process, excluding as it did free schooling for many groups of child citizens, would need to be amended. Former child soldiers able to engage with the reconstruction process and take leadership roles in articulating their aspirations could be recruited as partners of other engaged stakeholders.[128] Traditional and customary healing practices, such as cleansing rituals, local mentoring initiatives, and other mechanisms used in the DDR process could be incorporated into a sustainable therapeutic model that would take seriously the long-term special needs of particular groups of children, needs that require investment of a hybrid package of local, traditional, national, and international resources similar to those of the justice initiatives. These interventions would include a combination of psychosocial strategies designed to restore the social and material environment drawing on local healing and psychiatric interventions adapted to the specific setting. "Although psychosocial and psychiatric approaches are driven by different philosophies and field practices, the greatest strength lies in using these two approaches in a complementary fashion."[129]

Conclusion

The Sierra Leone Special Court's conviction of war criminals for the recruitment of child soldiers is an important human rights milestone. It formed a critical component of the evidence that led to the conviction and sentencing of Charles Taylor. The court will continue to lay important groundwork for other pending child-soldier-based prosecutions elsewhere. More generally, the process of establishing the criminal accountability of high-ranking government officials engaged in brutal postcolonial wars contributes to the development of democratic regimes based on the rule of law.

These are significant achievements. But what of the child soldiers whose rights violations (as victims, witnesses, and even perpetrators) form the basis for the convictions? International human rights efforts have so far failed to contribute to a comparable improvement in their prospects. Perhaps without precedent, the massive recruitment, brutalization, and traumatization of children through the process of armed conflict in Sierra Leone has attracted widespread attention. The extraordinary commercial success of the Hollywood film *Blood Diamond* and the Starbucks-supported autobiography *A Long Way Gone* by Sierra Leonean former child soldier Ishmael Beah attest to this.[130] These cultural products might be ammunition for serious investment in economic development to benefit children just as Graça Machel's 1996 UN report on Children in Armed Conflict paved the way for dramatic developments in international criminal justice for children.

Local projects cannot substitute for a consistent state-driven program catering to the ongoing social and economic needs of the population. Attention targeted at children's needs has so far been confined to the immediate postconflict period, to the roll-out of DDR programs and the conviction of child recruiters. After those initiatives came to an end, international engagement with the issues moved elsewhere. Is there a vicious trade-off at work here? Does the finite route to justice compromise the pursuit of enduring social and economic solutions and long-term peace building? Does the focus on international treaty making, on individualized forms of formal justice, provide an achievable goal—a way of being seen to "do something"—that exonerates relevant actors from the obligation to pursue other rights-based strategies that are more costly politically and economically?[131] Or could the two processes be considered complementary and mutually reinforcing? Can the establishment of justice in one sphere generate a civic infrastructure that encourages self-reliance and the development of local claims-making, as well as the confidence of regional and international parties to engage in more long-term strategic investments? These are important questions that in future will need empirical answers as the political processes enabling the implementation of enduring justice for conflict-affected children and their societies take shape.

PART III
Demanding a Future: Child Migration for Survival

CHAPTER 6

David and Goliath: Children's Unequal Battle for Refugee Protection

> If you would deport children without knowing why they would make the journey to this country, you may be deporting them to death, when all they were looking for was life.[1]

Introduction and Background

Edgar Chocoy made two international journeys in his short life. He chose the first himself at the age of fourteen—an overland solo migration from Guatemala, via Mexico, to California. His purpose was to find what the UN Convention on the Rights of the Child mandates for each child—"a family environment . . . an atmosphere of happiness, love and understanding."[2] Edgar sought to leave behind the dangers and hardships of the street and gang life in Guatemala that he had been forced into after his mother abandoned him as an infant. Hoping to find her, Edgar made his way to Los Angeles and eventually reunited with his mother. At the age of sixteen, he applied for asylum on the basis of the persecution he feared from the street gang he had turned his back on.[3] The US government chose Edgar's second trip: a forced removal from Los Angeles back to Guatemala following denial of his asylum application. The US government had advance notice of the intensity of Edgar's fear of return and of the risks facing him in Guatemala: after being informed that his asylum claim had been refused and that he was going to be sent back, Edgar attempted to hang himself with his own shoelaces while in detention. Nevertheless he was returned to the place he fled and the people he feared. Seventeen days after his removal from the United States, members of Edgar's former gang murdered him.[4]

Edgar's first journey was prompted by his need for international refugee protection, and by considerations of his own "best interest." A fundamental tenet of international law is that the best interests of children be a primary consideration in all actions affecting them.[5] Normally, best-interest calculations (as indeed most plans affecting children's lives) are made by adults on the behalf of children. In this case the best-interest judgment was exercised by the child himself, without adult intervention or oversight. A "left-behind child" trying to make the best of his limited options, Edgar chose migration followed by an asylum application over continued danger and destitution at home. Edgar's second journey was decided by US government immigration officials and an immigration court judge, but with no regard for his "best interest." The child exercised his agency to secure protection and the possibility of a viable life; the "responsible" adults intervened and sent him to his death.

The circumstances of Edgar's case are tragic and increasingly familiar. Latin American children and adolescents continue to seek US asylum due to fears of gang violence and retaliation,[6] yet the overwhelming majority are rejected and returned to the danger they fled. Some die; many live in hiding.[7] This state-induced return migration prompts fundamental questions about state complicity in serious human-rights violations against children. These are the questions that first led me to investigate this area of law. I wondered why the simple expectation that vulnerable children would be more rather than less favored compared to more privileged or competent populations seeking state protection proved so flawed. In Edgar's case, how could the authorities have forced a suicidal child to return alone to the site of danger and to a society known to be rife with gang violence?

Children fleeing persecution would seem to have a peculiarly strong claim to protection, placed as they are at the intersection of two distinctly vulnerable populations, refugees and children, and faced with alternatives likely to irreparably harm their life prospects. Prevention of violence at a minimum would seem to mandate protective intervention. And yet, as this chapter will explain, a severely restrictive immigration climate propels states to impose exclusionary measures even where, as in Edgar's case, family networks and informal welfare arrangements in the destination state would serve the refugee child's needs adequately without generating any additional fiscal burden on that state. Because of this hostile climate, the application for refugee protection does not provide the panacea many children seeking asylum hope for. Instead it compounds the fear, suffering, and vulnerability that led to their forced migration in the first place. As in previous chapters, I ask why it is that children migrating away from severe adversity, in this case migrating for survival, encounter hostility and a climate of suspicion despite a broad international consensus supportive of their right to protection.

Recognition of refugee children's strong claim to international attention has a long history, dating back to the years when the system of international protection was in its infancy. It was concern over the special problems facing refugee children during and following war that led to the submission to the League of Nations[8] of the first draft of the 1924 Declaration of the Rights of the Child, the precursor to the 1989 Convention on the Rights of the Child. Early refugee law also reflected a particular concern for children: the first legal definition of a refugee, crafted to regularize the situation of World War II refugees and set out in the 1946 Constitution of the International Refugee Organization (the IRO), includes, among only four listed categories of refugees, "children who were war orphans or whose parents had disappeared."[9]

Today too one might expect that children caught up in the refugee process, particularly children traveling alone or separated from their families, would encounter an institutional environment that promoted their access to safety. But the uncomplicated concern for refugee children of the early and mid-twentieth century no longer exists. Recent official attention to the distinctive needs of child refugees and asylum seekers has been limited and inconsistent. For much of the 1980s and 1990s child asylum seekers and refugee children were in effect invisible to policy makers and enforcers, ignored in broader contemporary debates about migrant protection. The needs of accompanied children were subsumed under the general eligibilities of their families, so that children were formally acknowledged as refugees when their parents were, but were rejected and returned home when their parents were refused. Children traveling without an accompanying family member or caretaker were treated on an ad hoc basis, in a policy-free zone where discretion and arbitrary decision untrammeled by formal procedures drove outcomes. This approach governed the treatment of both groups of children traveling without family, *unaccompanied* children migrating completely alone (like Edgar Chocoy), and *separated* children traveling apart from their family but accompanied by someone other than a parent or habitual caregiver,[10] such as a family acquaintance, another child or relative, or a smuggler or trafficker (like Tara, the trafficked Indian six-year-old described in chapter 4).

Not considered "real" refugees in their own right, the best these unaccompanied or separated children could hope for was a compassionate or humanitarian status allowing them to remain on a discretionary basis (sometimes only until they reached the age of eighteen) outside the formal system of refugee adjudication. Policy makers, immigration judges, asylum officers, and refugee advocates were all responsible for this approach—no one pressed the case that children had an entitlement to refugee protection independent of related adults. Social workers, child-health officials, and school authorities also neglected the fiduciary duties they owed their young charges—ignoring the pressing legal issues facing the children as life or death alternatives. The immigration authorities, when minded to allow unaccompanied or separated child asylum seekers to remain, were content to get around the rules by creating one-off discretionary concessions for children's cases as they came up, insisting that no precedent could be created, but at the same time conceding that removal or deportation might not be appropriate while the children were minors. The child-welfare and education experts ignored a problem staring them in the face—the immigration uncertainties that would arise on majority—because of their lack of legal expertise and their interest in short-term fixes (the only solutions they often understood as available to them).

Over the last decade and a half, this situation has changed. Separated[11] child asylum seekers have been arriving in consistently significant numbers, with substantial increases in recent years.[12] This has forced the authorities in both fields—international migration, refugee and human-rights law on the one hand, and domestic child welfare, health, and education on the other—to take note.[13] As a result, invisibility is no longer the primary issue driving unsatisfactory protection outcomes. The cases of children present themselves with sustained regularity, and are therefore impossible to ignore. However, attitudes remain strangely polarized. Once again, as with the other types of child migration discussed in previous chapters, I suggest that instead of invisibility, it is more helpful to focus on *ambivalence* as the main issue complicating separated child asylum seekers' quests for refugee protection. All child asylum seekers, but especially those who are separated and therefore forced to apply for protection in their own right, encounter mixed messages from the authorities as they navigate the web of administrative procedures and legal requirements. They confront regimes that make important concessions to their age (for example, exonerating them unlike adults from return to transit countries to have their cases processed).[14] However, the same regimes refuse to accept responsibility for some of the most egregious harms the children face (for example, by refusing to grant gang-based claims).[15] So these unaccompanied and separated child asylum seekers navigate procedures that at times are strongly protective (for example, insisting that children not be placed in facilities side by side with unrelated adults)[16] but at other times are resolutely punitive (for example, by returning them to places they fear). As in Edgar Chocoy's case, adjudication procedures often undermine child asylum seekers' rights through punitive and exclusionary measures that ignore their views and underestimate the dangers they face.

Inconsistency is a major part of the problem (as it is with many large and underfunded public bureaucracies), but so too are some child-specific attitudes: suspicion, condescension, and a patriarchal perspective that denies the significance of children as political agents while highlighting their culpability as irresponsible and irregular migrants. The use of professional people movers is increasingly necessary for those seeking asylum, given heightened border security and the growth of obstacles to movement across borders described later in this chapter. But the involvement of smugglers in children's asylum-seeking voyages exacerbates the hostile suspicion of the immigration authorities and generates increasingly punitive practices that damage access to protection. At worst, children are removed without any legal redress, as are the majority of Mexican and some other Latin American child asylum seekers arriving in the United States.[17] A close second, child asylum seekers find themselves incarcerated—in state custody—either because their claim to be children is disputed and so they are held with adults pending verification of their age,[18] or because the authorities are unable or unwilling to find more suitable temporary accommodation for them.[19] This chapter explores why the commonsense expectation that child asylum seekers would be treated generously, indeed more generously than adults, does not materialize in practice. It questions prevailing explanations for the David and Goliath struggle that refugee children encounter—that children have been forgotten and are invisible, battling against a system that ignores their very existence.

Refugee Children in Camps

More than 4.5 million children worldwide are refugees or live in refugee-like situations (people with some form of temporary protection or humanitarian leave, but who have not been granted permanent refugee status).[20] These children constitute 44 percent of the world's 10.5 million refugee or refugee-like population. The majority of these children live with members of their families in refugee camps, improvised or temporary settlements right across the border from their home country. Unlike Edgar, they do not travel to distant countries or make individualized asylum applications. A significant minority live in this harsh environment alone, separated from immediate caregivers.

In their seminal 1988 work on unaccompanied children, Steinbock, Ressler, and Boothby[21] make the obvious point that wars, famines, and natural disasters have almost always resulted in the separation of children from their families. Nothing much has changed. According to UNICEF, by the end of the Rwandan genocide, over 100,000 children had been separated from their families; only 51,000 were eventually reunited.[22] The conflicts in countries such as Yugoslavia, Afghanistan, Sri Lanka, Liberia, Sierra Leone, the Democratic Republic of Congo, Iraq, Iran, Syria, Myanmar, Somalia, and Sudan have reproduced this tragic legacy. Like their adult counterparts, refugee children flee their homelands to escape war, persecution, and political upheaval. But, whereas in the past, children were bystanders to conflict, incidental victims of harms inflicted on others, now as the previous chapter describes, with the changing nature of modern warfare engulfing civilian populations, they themselves are frequently directly targeted both for inter- and intrastate violence. In her groundbreaking 1996 UN study of the effects of armed conflict on children,[23] Graça Machel documented this trend, examining the extent to which children are subjected to calculated genocide (Srebrenica is a case in point),[24] forced military conscription (Sierra Leone and Uganda are probably the most egregious examples), gender-based violence,[25] torture, and exploitation. The very long-term detention at Guantanamo of a Canadian child arrested at the age of fifteen in the theater of war in Afghanistan and accused of al Qaeda connections[26] is a reminder that these violations are not confined to developing countries.

Refugee children and their female caregivers are much *less* likely than adult men to reach a wealthy destination state where they can make an application for permanent refugee protection. Though, as I have just noted, children constitute almost half of the world's refugees, they amount to less than a third of asylum seekers in developed states.[27] Among the majority of children who do not make it to a developed state to claim asylum, some 1.4 million live in impoverished and overcrowded refugee camps and settlements.[28] Giorgio Agamben describes this lengthy warehousing characteristic of protracted refugee situations as a permanent "state of exception," a limit situation outside the boundaries of civil society.[29] Tragically, more than two-thirds[30] of today's refugees have spent five years or more "warehoused" in such camps where the average length of stay is close to twenty years.[31] These refugees include millions of children trapped in a limbo of *temporary permanence*, dependence, and despair, where only periodic aid handouts from international organizations or intracamp fights interrupt the endless flow of boredom and depression induced by the lack of prospects. The world's largest refugee complex, Dadaab in Kenya, hosts 463,000 refugees, including 10,000 third-generation refugees born to parents who were also born there.[32] More than half of all Dadaab residents are under eighteen.[33] To spend one's life in such a state of disenfranchised destitution is devastating for children. Epidemics abound, depression and violence are endemic, and a confident sense of future self-sufficiency and the well-being necessary for the development of a healthy growing child are impossible to achieve.[34] No wonder, then, that refugee camps are well-known recruiting grounds for child soldiers and for trafficked children—the lure of any exit option is powerful.

Child Asylum Seekers in Individualized Determination Systems

Children who manage to leave or avoid refugee camps to seek asylum in developed states also face a daunting set of obstacles and hardships, experiences that generate traumatic memories and exacerbate the problems provoked by forced migration in the first place. The migration-related situations in which serious human-rights violations arise can be grouped into three, temporally sequential, clusters. First in time, children experience rights violations in the course of their *migration journeys*, violations that may generate ongoing threats even once the journey is over. Once a child has managed to flee from danger and reach a country where it is possible to make an asylum claim, a second set of human-rights challenges presents itself. *The asylum application process* often generates insurmountable obstacles rendering elusive in practice the theoretical entitlement to asylum. These procedural impediments loom particularly large for separated child asylum seekers who have to turn to official agencies for the support normally provided by parents. Last in time, and most fundamental to the claim for international protection, is the challenge of proving that the home-country circumstances precipitating flight justify the grant of asylum. Here, the challenge is strictly legal. Child asylum seekers have to demonstrate that *the human rights violations they are fleeing amount to "persecution."* They have to rebut some frequently advanced counterarguments—the claim that "child persecution" is a contradiction in terms because children are too insignificant as political actors to be targets of persecution, or that child persecution is a domestic child-welfare rather than an international-protection issue. These three clusters of rights violations present formidable potential obstacles to protection. Why do these obstacles persist and what can be done about them?

Perilous Journeys to Safety

According to the Separated Children in Europe Program, in the early years of the twenty-first century, approximately 20,000 separated children arrived and made asylum applications in Europe every year.[35] Canada, Australia, and the United States also witnessed sizable arrivals[36] of child asylum seekers traveling alone. The average number of children caught by the US immigration authorities between 2004 and 2008 was 9,811.[37] The journey to safety can present daunting challenges to all forced migrants, despite the international acceptance in principle of the right to seek asylum. Tales of shipwrecks, cases of suffocation from prolonged concealment in car or lorry trunks and containers to avoid detection, stories of dehydration from scorching desert border crossings abound.[38] To the natural hazards of attempting clandestine entry to a safe country must be added the political hazards generated by the prevailing xenophobic climate. The increased policing of frontiers;[39] the implementation of stringent visa policies; the imposition of deterrent fines on commercial airlines, ships, or trains carrying unauthorized migrants; and the monitoring of the Mediterranean by FRONTEX, a European agency established in 2004 to survey the waters and intercept irregular migrants, make access to safety in "Fortress Europe" increasingly elusive. The same is true in North America, where militarization of the US/Mexico border and expedited removal and harsh detention to deter undocumented travel contribute to the creation of enormous obstacles for asylum seekers attempting to access a place of safety.

This militarized exclusion system generates a vigorous industry in smuggling people and produces the concept of a "bogus" asylum seeker or an "illegal immigrant." As the obstacles increase, so do the charges levied by border-crossing professionals for the technical assistance required to beat the system. Immigration-control complexity increases the risks of smuggling people and the infrastructure required to carry it out. The growing militarization of immigration control also increases the power imbalance between migrant and smuggler and the vulnerability of refugees to extortion and exploitation by migration professionals. Unaccompanied child asylum seekers are particularly at risk.

A down payment on the transportation fee (typically loaned by family members) is often made before departure, and the balance is paid from earnings after arrival. As a Chinese asylum-seeking girl—fleeing forced marriage and smuggled to the United States by snakeheads (professional Chinese people smugglers) whose fee was paid in advance—explained to a US Federal Appeals Court, "If I can come to the U.S . . . then I can earn money to repay my relative."[40] But these facilitated journeys can have terrifying consequences—dangerous itineraries to evade migration control, brutalizing encounters with those in charge of the journey, and always, the looming prospect of harsh punishment for failure to repay mounting travel debts once the journey is over. The story of a Salvadorian seventeen-year-old who walked north through El Salvador to Guatemala, catching rides on buses where he could, covering the rest of the distance on foot, conveys the extreme vulnerability of child asylum seekers. By the time he reached the Mexico/US border he was ill from hunger, and exhausted by having walked day and night, trekking though cities and swamps with no clear idea of where he was headed, worrying only about where his next meal and drink of water would come from. He had lost or sold all his belongings except for a backpack, a pair of pants, a shirt, and a prayer that his grandmother had given him "on a piece of paper":

> I left El Salvador because I was frightened by gangs threatening to kill me for refusing to join them. My brother paid for us to take a bus from El Salvador to Guatemala, and then we walked and hitchhiked to Mexico. . . . I waited in the small town near the Mexican border for a truck to take me further, but it never came. So, we walked through the mountains and at night we stopped and stayed at homes along the way. We were put into vehicles that transport goods . . . At the U.S.-Mexican border there were 180 people hidden inside buildings. We waited for 36 hours and all we had were 2 apples and an orange among us. Eventually a guide put us on a truck in the middle of the night and we proceeded into the desert. Then I was told to get out and find cover. We were in Phoenix, Arizona. There were trucks from Immigration waiting for us. My first impression when I ran into the officials was they thought I had robbed a bank or was a criminal. They yelled at me not to move and that made me very nervous. . . . After I was questioned, I was put in a truck and taken back to the border. No one asked if I was afraid to return to Mexico. The trucks just unloaded us and drove off. . . . I tried again. . . . I realized that [I]mmigration was rounding everyone up, so I hid behind a small plant. There was a snake near me and I couldn't move for 3 hours. . . . [E]ventually I was stopped by immigration again.[41]

Small wonder that this child was eventually diagnosed with posttraumatic stress disorder (PTSD).[42] Some children embark on perilously long journeys in unseaworthy vessels, from China to Canada, from Mali to Malta, from Indonesia to Australia. In the summer of 1999, 134 separated Chinese children arrived off Canada's west coast in precarious vessels. Others confront equally hazardous conditions over much shorter distances: Elian Gonzalez, a six-year-old Cuban boy, was rescued on Thanksgiving Day 2000 from the high seas between Cuba and Florida, where he'd been clinging to a raft for five days after his mother and all the other passengers on his shipwrecked vessel had drowned.[43] A month later, two Haitian children, ages eight and ten, were shipwrecked with their mother when their boat ran aground off the Florida shoreline. Across the world, ten years later, a nine-year-old Iranian boy was rescued by the Australian authorities after the boat he was on broke apart off the coast of Christmas Island near Australia, drowning both his parents and his brother.[44]

Natural dangers are stark enough. But young girls seeking asylum alone often report predatory sexual encounters en route to their asylum destination.[45] In some cases, the risk of rape and other forms of sexual assault is limited to the time the child is en route; on arrival immigration procedures take over, and, whatever their outcome, at least the child is not exposed to continuing assault. In other cases, however, as discussed in chapter 4, the sexual predation continues beyond arrival in the destination country, with an asylum application only a device to ensure that the child is released after arrival, so that the traffickers can put her to work as originally intended. For children exposed to these sorts of hardships, over and above those that precipitated the original decision to flee home, the challenge of recovering sufficiently to attempt integration into the host society and to pursue an asylum claim can be overwhelming.

Navigating the Labyrinth of State Asylum Procedures

The extreme dangers facing refugee children and adolescents as they flee from persecution and attempt to translate the abstraction of international protection into a lived reality give way to other serious human-rights challenges once the journey itself is over. In the United States, only a minority of children make their application for asylum immediately on arrival; most apply after they have already entered the country. But in other countries, such as Australia and many European states, most asylum-seeking children do make their application as soon as they arrive, at the seaport, the airport, or the land border.[46]

The optimal scenario for any unaccompanied or separated child making an asylum claim is to be promptly assigned a child-welfare professional independent of the immigration authorities—fluent in the child's language, and specially trained—responsible for arranging immediate care and setting in motion a procedure to secure a guardian. Once appointed, the guardian should without delay explore the child's needs and wishes from a holistic perspective, ensure appropriate medical or other urgent attention. He or she should also set in motion a process for exploring long-term-care arrangements, and should arrange free and high-quality legal representation for asylum proceedings that will be handled in an age- and gender-sensitive manner. The guardian should act in loco parentis attending to the best interests of the child in all relevant matters. The child should be fostered with relatives, or other suitable caregivers while long-term-care arrangements are being made. He or she should also be enrolled in school and have access to physical and mental health care as needed. If the child gives permission and there are no counterindications, vigorous attempts should be made to trace the child's parents or other habitual caregivers in the home country or elsewhere. The child should be allowed regular telephone contact with family far away. Eventually, once settled, the child should be allowed to apply for family reunification to bring relatives from abroad.

This scenario will appear fanciful and utterly extravagant to any seasoned asylum advocate given present procedures. A domestic child found unaccompanied after traumatic experiences would be expected to receive this sort of reception to ensure permanency and the long-term suitability of a caring regime. But this is not the case for asylum-seeking children. The contrast is sharp because the institutional approach to these children is ambivalent, torn between acknowledgment of protection duties and exclusionary suspicions and hostilities. Their needs as children are complicated by their status as migrants. In 2005, the UN Committee on the Rights of the Child, the treaty body that oversees implementation of the CRC, published a General Comment on unaccompanied and separated migrant children. General Comments are not binding law. They are "soft law," authoritative interpretations of prevailing obligations that establish a benchmark and guidance for the development of national policy. While acknowledging the "multifaceted challenges"[47] facing states, General Comment No. 6 emphasized host countries' obligation not to discriminate against separated migrant children, to vigorously apply the "best interests" principle in all decision making, and to make available to them the full range of protective services offered to vulnerable domestic children, including education, health care, and suitable accommodation.

Child asylum seekers rarely benefit from all or even most of these measures. Procedures vary considerably between different destination states. Separated child asylum seekers frequently encounter a confusing overlap of protective and punitive functions in the state officials they come into contact with. The General Comment notes that

> states parties must protect the confidentiality of information received in relation to an unaccompanied or separated child, consistent with the

> obligation to protect the child's rights, including the right to privacy. . . . Care must be taken that information sought and legitimately shared for one purpose is not inappropriately used for . . . another.[48]

But until recent reforms, countries as different as the United States, Australia, and Spain all had dangerously merged functions within their child migration offices. Welfare and nurturing responsibilities, including the obligation to accommodate, educate, and protect unaccompanied child asylum seekers, were held by the same government employees charged with ensuring compliance with immigration-control regulations, including eliciting evidence of border-control violations and ineligibility for asylum. Staff running child shelters where migrant children were held would on the one hand ask them about their histories, their needs, their family experiences, as mentors or counselors, and on the other hand make notes in the children's files that formed part of the government's record for assessing immigration status. These conflicts of interest have, for the three countries mentioned, been eliminated following advocacy pressure, by separating the respective governments' child-welfare responsibility from their asylum- or migration-investigation function.[49]

But several unsatisfactory features of the procedure for dealing with separated children's asylum claims remain pervasive. Appointment of a legal guardian charged with the duty of acting in loco parentis, is in many countries rare.[50] This is surprising from a child rights perspective. According to the General Comment, "appointment of a competent guardian as expeditiously as possible serves as a key procedural safeguard to ensure respect for the best interests of an unaccompanied or separated child. . . . [S]uch a child should only be referred to asylum or other procedures after the appointment of a guardian."[51] Given the complexities of a child asylum-seeker's life—including an insecure immigration situation and related apprehensions about the future, problematic personal facts and past separations and other traumas, as well as tenuous economic, social, and cultural connections to the host society likely leading to severely strained daily living conditions—the claim to consistent and continuing adult mentoring is overwhelmingly strong. No other group of children with comparable needs, except perhaps convicted juvenile offenders, is expected to fend for themselves in the face of such overwhelming legal and personal complexities. As one unaccompanied child asylum seeker commented: "The words for applying for asylum in my language are translated as 'giving up your hand' [surrendering]. The picture I had was that I would surrender to someone with guns."[52]

In contrast with the dearth of implementation of the guardianship provision, asylum countries are more likely to acknowledge a child's need for free legal representation, in line with the clear recommendation of the General Comment.[53] But not all countries do even this: to this day, the United States does not guarantee free legal representation to unaccompanied child asylum seekers.[54] The advocacy community, instead, has to scramble to identify pro bono representation, a critical necessity that is in short supply and sometimes staffed by attorneys lacking in experience.[55] As a result, many children find themselves navigating an inscrutable system alone, trying to claim potentially life-saving protection without the benefit of expert legal assistance. Some children in detention and under pressure from enforcement officers, make ill-informed decisions to withdraw their asylum applications in return for the "freedom" to be sent back home. As one child commented about her experience being interviewed in the Border Patrol office, "Lots of paper; I didn't know what the papers said, but I signed them."[56]

Given the known positive correlation between legal representation and successful outcome of an asylum application,[57] it is particularly concerning that children are deprived of this critically important support during the asylum application process. In Australia, between 1999 and 2005, for example, "virtually all unrepresented children appearing before the Refugee Review Tribunal 'without effective guardians' lost their appeals, withdrew their appeals or 'departed the country.'"[58] Even where children are represented, they may come up against zealous government officials intent on finding inconsistencies in their stories as a prelude to refusal of their asylum claims. Traumatic incidences that a child blocks out in order to recover some mental equanimity might lead to imprecise or incoherent narratives that engender suspicion or downright refusal of the child's asylum claim. Consider the nature of this asylum interview with an unaccompanied child:

> They asked me who my president was, what the flag of my country is, why I have problems and why my father was killed by the government. I felt very bad so I started crying. At that point, the . . . interviewer stopped the interview. I was afraid because I didn't understand what asylum and refugees were. . . . She kept asking me questions that I didn't understand.[59]

In another case, a child was asked to draw a map of his voyage. He told researchers that he just stared at the paper in front of him. He explained that he did not even know what a map was.[60] These techniques for eliciting testimony from child asylum seekers are inappropriate and ineffective. But they are pervasive.

Another common aspect of child-asylum cases is the use of mechanistic age-determination tests to ascertain whether an applicant's claim to be a minor is borne out by the physical evidence. Age is relevant to the treatment of the asylum applicant while his or her case is being decided: a minor should not be detained, except as a last resort, and if detained, should not be placed in the same facility as adult detainees. Erroneous age determination leads to incorrect placement decisions—the comingling of adults and minors—which can pose serious risks to the physical safety of child migrants. Experts have long questioned the validity of the widely used one-dimensional physical exams, such as dental, wrist, or clavicle X-rays to establish chronological age, particularly given the known variability between different racial and socioeconomic populations. As the UK Royal College of Pediatricians and Child Health stated: "[A]n age determination is extremely difficult to do with certainty, and no single approach to this can be relied on. Moreover, for young people aged 15–18, it is even less possible to be certain about age. . . . Age determination is an inexact science and the margin of error can sometimes be as much as 5 years either side."[61] Yet immigration authorities continue to rely on these tests.

According to the United Nations High Commissioner for Refugees, the UN body responsible for the protection and rights of refugees, the appropriate adjudicatory standard for processing and deciding children's asylum claims is the "liberal application of the benefit of the doubt,"[62] a standard that complements the more general "best interests of the child" principle. Together these rules support a flexible, open approach to age claims by young asylum seekers. In practice, however, many immigration officials interviewing young asylum seekers adopt a highly skeptical and suspicious stance, enacting an institutional ideology shaped by exclusionary goals rather than human-rights principles. The result is an overclassification of children as adults rather than the opposite. A UK study found that between 2001 and 2004, the numbers of unaccompanied or separated asylum-seeking children who had their age disputed and had to submit to physical examinations increased sharply, from approximately 11 percent of asylum-applicant children in 2001 to as many as 43 percent in 2004. The result is that many child applicants are wrongly treated as adults during the asylum process. According to one study, 50 percent of asylum applicants whose ages were disputed turned out to be minors. A child asylum seeker reported "becoming very upset when immigration staff were rude and kept laughing at him when he showed them his birth certificate and said he was 16."[63] A consequence is the pervasive use of detention for child asylum seekers, including incarceration in harsh and inappropriate facilities usually reserved for those charged with criminal offenses. In early 2012, the UK government acknowledged its erroneous classification of forty child asylum seekers and the damaging consequences of long incarceration by giving each child compensation of £2 million.[64]

Inaccurate age determination leads to incarceration of child asylum seekers in many destination states, including the United States.[65] The following first-person narrative illustrates the bewilderment this approach can cause:

> I lost my birth certificate in Puerto Rico when it fell in the water. . . . I was at Boystown [a children's detention facility in the U.S.] for one month when they brought me to the dentist. . . . They did not do wrist x-rays, just a dental exam. They said that I was 19 years old. I tell people [I am 17], but they don't listen. . . . I went from the doctor to Boystown just long enough to pack my clothes and things and then I was handcuffed and put in the van alone and driven to Krome [a notorious adult detention center in Florida]. I'm lost, a child, I was 17.

Eventually, after prolonged detention, a judge ordered this boy's relocation to a juvenile facility.[66] Regrettably it is not only wrong age determination that results in the imprisonment of asylum-seeking children.[67] As advocates have long pointed out, even where the authorities concede that the applicant is a child, immigration detention is still very widely used pending a decision on the child's asylum case.[68] Policy makers and judges have criticized these practices, more emphatically *after* egregious harm has occurred than *prospectively* to prevent detention occurring in the first place. As Lord Justice Brooke commented (in a case involving children detained with their parents): "If a court judges that in making his decision to detain, an immigration officer failed to take into account matters of material significance . . . including that the prospective detainee is a child . . . then he will have strayed outside his wide ranging powers."[69] Nevertheless such instances of straying are legion. The Children's Commissioner for England estimates that approximately two thousand children are placed in immigration detention each year.[70] The understatement in the description of the reality of detention provided by an asylum-seeking child detained in a "secure facility" in the United States is poignant:

> My first couple of days there, I didn't like it. I didn't like the food there. I couldn't sleep. At 5 a.m. when they opened the cells for us to take showers, there was a table with clothes assigned to us by name. It didn't take into account our size, so I got shoes that didn't even fit me. . . . I asked if I could call my family, but they told me not until I had been there for 25 days was I allowed to make a call.[71]

Some reported cases are particularly disturbing: a Human Rights Watch investigation some years ago into the detention circumstances of child asylum seekers in the United States unearthed the following case history:

> For six months, Xiao Ling lived in a concrete cell . . . completely bare except for bedding and a Bible in a language she could not read. Locked up in prison-like conditions with juveniles accused of murder, rape, and drug trafficking, Xiao Ling told Human Rights Watch . . . that she was kept under constant supervision, not allowed to speak her own language, told not to laugh, and even forced to ask permission to scratch her nose. Bewildered, miserable, and unable to communicate with anyone around her, she cried every day. Only fifteen years old at the time of her detention, Xiao Ling was never charged with any crime.[72]

She was one of the thousands of unaccompanied child asylum seekers apprehended by the US immigration authorities every year.

Other notorious examples of inappropriate detention of asylum-seeking children abound. One attracted considerable domestic and international censure—the open-ended placement of unaccompanied children until mid-2005 at the Woomera immigration detention center in Australia, a remote fortified site in the middle of the outback. The extraordinary suffering and desperation induced by this prison was translated into frequent acts of self-harm: "People sewing their lips together was common. That used to happen every day. . . . The thing is, you think what is your fault? Leaving your country because it was war-torn, people had been dying—what's your crime?" The isolation and despair of many of the detainees is captured by this fifteen-year-old Afghan boy's testimony: "I think I am totally broken and I'll be in this cage forever."[73]

Thankfully, this extreme detention situation no longer exists. A comprehensive and damning report by Australia's Human Rights and Equal Opportunities Commissioner accelerated the closing of Woomera and eventually the discontinuance of routine detention of child asylum seekers in

Australia. But egregious behavior still occurs, including in Australia. The nine-year-old Iranian orphan mentioned earlier, whose family drowned when their boat broke apart off the coast near Australia, was placed in immigration detention after being rescued by the Australian authorities, released to attend his father's funeral (the bodies of mother and brother were never found), and then detained once again until the threat of court action compelled his release.[74] Elsewhere, similar practices occur. Despite considerable public pressure and election promises,[75] the UK government continues to allow the detention of child asylum seekers in detention centers, including in one reported case, a Pakistani woman and her eight-month-old daughter.[76] The European Court of Human Rights has repeatedly criticized Belgium's policy of detaining child asylum seekers. In a December 2011 ruling, the Court found that the detention of a Sri Lankan woman and her three children violated the prohibition on inhuman and degrading treatments and on deprivation of liberty.[77] More recently the Court condemned Belgium's month-long detention in a closed camp of a Chechen woman and her four children ranging in age from seven months to seven years. The Court held that the children's detention constituted a violation of the prohibition on inhuman and degrading treatment and the right to liberty and security.[78] The family had fled the Russian bombing of Grozny and arrived in Belgium to seek asylum. Instead of assisting this highly vulnerable family with their asylum application and accommodating them in an appropriate setting pending a decision, the Belgian authorities placed the family "in a closed center designed for adults and ill-suited to [the children's] extreme vulnerability." Psychological evidence presented to the asylum court revealed serious psychotraumatic symptoms, particularly in the five-year-old girl. The family was eventually refused asylum and returned to a refugee camp in Poland.

While detention is the most serious human-rights violation affecting child asylum seekers, other procedural defects also have a negative impact on children's access to protection. They stem from a punitive migration-management system that prioritizes deterrence even for child migrants seeking asylum alone. Impediments to protection include the application of rigid time limitations on children appealing refusals of asylum, a particularly serious obstacle for unrepresented children; a pervasive culture of disbelief, often manifested as a refusal to listen carefully to the child's evidence; and stern insensitivity to the distress of asylum-seeking children ensnared in a labyrinthine process that at times re-evokes the terror they sought to flee in the first place. An example of this insensitivity was the announcement by the Australian government that it was considering returning unaccompanied asylum-seeking children to Malaysia without even investigating the merits of their cases so as to deter potential future arrivals and send a message to parents considering such migration options for their children. As the Australian immigration minister bluntly put it: "I don't want unaccompanied minors. I don't want children getting on boats to come to Australia thinking or knowing that there is some sort of exemption in place."[79] To nullify child-protective migration policies by threatening to close the door to child asylum altogether is to set the clock back to the era when children were not thought capable of being asylum claimants in their own right.

Even without such retrograde measures, however, separated children's access to an adequate asylum-determination system remains flawed. Many asylum-seeking children fail to secure the protection they need. Some are returned to the countries they fled, others muddle through parts of the asylum system, avoiding removal but without securing a permanent positive outcome. In some cases they receive a temporary status until they turn eighteen; in others they simply avoid contact with the authorities and subsist in the shadows of society as irregular migrants. Very few obtain the permanent refugee status that can herald a secure future. The following pages describe the legal process that produces this unsatisfactory result.

Child Persecution: Demonstrating It Exists and Defining Its Confines

Refugee children who travel with their families to a country where an asylum claim can be made are typically subsumed within the family's application—they needn't make a special case for themselves. Because of the principle of family unity,[80] it is widely accepted that refugee status accorded a head of household also covers the spouse and dependent children. But child asylum seekers fleeing without their families, about 4 percent of total annual asylum seekers,[81] have to prove their own cases. Given these sizeable applicant numbers, it is noteworthy just how limited the jurisprudence on child asylum seekers still is. In part this is not surprising: as already noted only a small proportion of unaccompanied or separated child asylum seekers manage to assemble the evidence they need to prove an asylum case, to secure competent and affordable legal representation, and to participate in an effective asylum adjudication process. No international body or senior official, no UN department, institute, or treaty body is charged with responsibility for migrant children per se. I have already discussed some of the procedural obstacles that flow from this vacuum. They are however only part of the story. Another part, to which I now turn, is the substantive legal challenge.

Attention to child-asylum claims and to a child-specific approach to persecution is relatively recent, following, with a gap of some years, the ratification of the 1989 Convention on the Rights of the Child in September 1990. The refugee definition, though age neutral, has yet to be consistently applied to the circumstances of child applicants[82] to definitively bring to a close the long period when it was not thought to be directly applicable to children at all. To this day, most child asylum seekers receive a humanitarian or discretionary status rather than full asylum, with deleterious consequences for their long-term security and prospects.[83] To qualify for political asylum, a child must, like any other applicant, establish that he or she meets the international definition of a refugee. This definition, incorporated into domestic law by a very large number of refugee receiving states, can be found in Article 1A(2) of the 1951 UN Convention on the Status of Refugees. It states that a refugee is a person who

> owing to well-founded fear of being persecuted for reasons of race, religion, nationality, membership of a particular social group or political opinion . . . is outside the country of his nationality and is unable or, owing to such fear, is unwilling to avail himself of the protection of that country; or who, not having a nationality and being outside the country of his former habitual residence . . . is unable or, owing to such fear, is unwilling to return to it.

Being a refugee, therefore, is a state that is independent of the official decision to accord refugee status. The decision merely confirms the state, rather like a doctor's diagnosis confirms but does not create the state of having influenza. To qualify for the grant of asylum, or to be accepted as a refugee (one and the same thing) the child, like the adult, has to prove that he or she was persecuted in the country of origin or has a well-founded fear of persecution in the future, and that the persecution is on account of one of the five grounds enumerated in the refugee convention definition just cited. In addition the child must show that the persecution feared is either at the hands of the government or of someone the government is unable or unwilling to control.

Several states have recognized the importance of general human-rights principles in construing the scope of asylum protection for children. They have done this in two ways; some have adopted child-specific asylum guidelines based on human-rights principles, while others have developed a body of case law that incorporates those principles.[84] The key/threshold legal concept in qualifying for asylum is "persecution," a term that is not defined in the 1951 UN Refugee Convention or elsewhere in international treaty law. This lack of definition is not an oversight: the term's open-endedness allows states to accommodate (or not) a wide range of situations and to encompass new human-rights challenges as they emerge. Certain principles have become clearly established and apply to asylum-seeking children just as they apply to adults. A threat to life or freedom caused by a failure of state protection and based on civil or political discrimination always constitutes persecution. Other serious though not life-threatening human rights violations also qualify—the threat of torture, for example—whether the state is directly responsible for the threat or indirectly responsible by failing to protect the child from it.

Over the years, there has been expansion in the application of the notion of persecution. For example, an accumulation of individual acts, none of them sufficient on their own to constitute persecution, may nevertheless, when taken as a whole, constitute persecution.[85] Thus one act of police brutality for sleeping rough as a street child in a city square may not amount to persecution, but repeated such acts may. On the other hand, lawful punishment cannot as a rule constitute persecution. As the UNHCR *Handbook* notes, "A refugee is a victim—or potential victim—of injustice, not a fugitive from justice."[86] Often, though, the distinction between punishment and persecution is not clear. Excessive punishment, particularly if discriminatorily applied (against some sections of the population, for some offenses) might in some contexts amount to persecution. Politically active adolescents engaged in peaceful protests or child beggars subjected to brutal police or military responses can with justification argue that these attacks constitute the basis for an asylum claim. By crafting an open-ended definition, the framers of the Refugee Convention wisely foresaw that new situations justifying refugee protection could emerge.[87] And certainly many common child-persecution situations were not explicitly envisaged when the refugee protection regime was established in the immediate aftermath of World War II. In practice however, adjudicators have not been expansive in their application of refugee jurisprudence to child-asylum applications. The David and Goliath paradigm applies here too. It is to this complex body of case law that I now turn.

The normative conflict between different approaches to separated children influences the chance of a successful asylum claim. It increases the unpredictability of the outcome and the broad range of arguments that decision makers rely on to justify their conclusions. On the one hand, reflecting a traditional child-welfare approach, children are viewed as passive victims of harms inflicted by others, and as individuals who need and deserve refugee protection because of their particular vulnerability. We might label this the "child as victim" approach. From this perspective, refugee status is a supplement to the protective obligations owed by the state, in its capacity as *parens patriae*, to children who find themselves outside a caring environment irrespective of their national origin or immigration status. On the other hand, by adopting a "child as juvenile" lens, decision makers reflect the disciplinary and punitive approach to nonconforming adolescents developed in the criminal justice system and link it to the exclusionary mandate of immigration control. From this vantage point, separated child asylum seekers are viewed as threats, insubordinates, knowing and even willing participants in illegal migration practices. As a result of these profoundly different stances toward separated migrant children, case law concerning their asylum applications is inconsistent.

"Child as Victim" Approach to Child Asylum Claims

The welfare-protection approach justifies grants of refugee status for apparently defenseless children provided they can prove they are victims of persecution. It can include children who flee their homelands for the same political, religious, or ethnic reasons as adults. In some cases, though the persecution alleged is not child-specific, the fact that the asylum applicant is a child is central to the court's reasoning. An example is the case of a seventeen-year-old Jewish Ethiopian girl who lost both her parents and her eldest brother during the 1974 Communist revolution because the government believed them to be Eritrean rebels. In reversing the refusal of asylum by the US Board of Immigration Appeals and remitting the case for reconsideration, the Ninth Circuit Court of Appeals emphasized the particular vulnerability of a child: "The fact that [the appellant] did not suffer physical harm is not determinative of her claim of persecution: there are other equally serious forms of injury that result from persecution. For example, when a young girl loses her father, mother and brother—sees her family effectively destroyed—she plainly suffers severe emotional and developmental injury."[88] Similar reasoning has been applied in cases where a child's family members are still alive, but the child faces the prospect of severe harm due to his or her dependent status: "[A] child's reaction to injuries to his family is different from an adult's. The child is part of the family, the wound to the family is personal, the trauma apt to be lasting."[89]

A child-welfare approach enables the grant of refugee status to children who flee child-specific persecution. Sometimes the child's persecution is related to both familial and societal circumstances. Two US cases exemplify this approach. In one an immigration judge granted asylum to a sixteen-year-old Chinese girl fleeing a forced marriage arranged by her parents "for money according to feudal practices."[90] The family's commodification of their daughter into a capital-generating asset was considered persecution justifying the grant of asylum. In another case, the BIA awarded asylum to a Honduran child who had been persistently tortured by his stepfather from the age of three, and risked returning to life on the streets if returned to Honduras; the decision cited U.S. State Department reports that "the police are responsible for torturing street children and a number of extra judicial killings."[91] The child's well-founded fear arose out of his abuse-induced homelessness and the endemic social dangers facing Honduran street children in his situation. While successful claims have been advanced by other street children from Honduras, Nicaragua, and Guatemala,[92] a recent Third Circuit decision represents a departure from the child-welfare approach. Rejecting "homeless Honduran street children" as a particular social group, the court held that "poverty, homelessness and youth" were too vague and too universal to qualify as protected grounds.[93] Nevertheless, other jurisdictions continue to recognize these characteristics as central to determinations of child-specific persecution.[94]

On occasion, courts have used international human-rights standards to assess child-rearing practice or family customs in a child's country of origin. A US court granted refugee status to a twelve-year-old Indian girl who was beaten by her parents and sold to traffickers for domestic service in the United States. The court argued that, though

> standards for child treatment vary among cultures and families, and . . . indeed, gradations of child treatment exist which reasonably include disciplining a child and requiring a child to work . . . the treatment suffered by the applicant is beyond the limits of acceptable rearing practices to such an extent that it rises to the level of persecution.

The court found that the child's persecution was on account of membership in the particular social group of "Indian children sold or abandoned by their parents."[95] Another example of this approach is a Canadian case concerning a thirteen-year-old Chinese boy who claimed asylum after being smuggled into Canada following arrangements made between his parents and smugglers. The asylum claim was based on the child's fear of persecution if returned to China. The fines the family would incur on account of the child's illegal exit and the onerous debts to the smugglers meant that the child had a well-founded fear of being trafficked in future to ensure he would be put to work to repay the migration-incurred debts. The government, adopting a "child as juvenile" lens, had opposed the asylum claim on the basis that the child, an adolescent and therefore "not of tender years," had consented to being smuggled in the hope of economic betterment. The court found that the child had only consented to being smuggled in the first place because of the Chinese "cultural phenomenon of filial piety." Granting refugee status, the court held that the child had a well-founded fear of future trafficking, and that as a minor he was incapable as a matter of law (as discussed in chapter 4) of "consenting" to being trafficked.[96]

International human-rights norms provide a baseline standard for evaluating the acceptability of forms of conduct. But cultural biases can compromise their social relevance to particular contexts. Advocates (following earlier strategies used for gender-based asylum claims)[97] have on occasion juxtaposed a Western, "civilized" standard with the applicant's "barbaric" or "primitive" culture of origin.[98] Judges have sometimes colluded with this essentializing and reductive appropriation of rights discourse—what Mutua has aptly termed the "savage, victim, savior" approach[99]—to denigrate whole cultures. The applicant then is rewarded with asylum for rejecting barbarism and seeking out civility. For example, a twelve-year-old Jordanian child applied for asylum with his mother on the basis of his acute trauma resulting from the father's long history of severe domestic violence against the mother. According to the judge, the mother was "targeted for abuse because she is a woman who seeks to have her own identity, who believes in the 'dangerous' Western values of integrity and worth of the individual. . . . [She] is not content to live in a harem completely 'protected' by her husband, his society, his government." The judge granted mother and child asylum because they had "remain[ed] unbowed. They now seek protection in this country for their political belief in the importance of individual freedom. Not just freedom for adult males, but freedom for women and children too."[100] Equating "foreign," non-Western cultures with acceptance of severe domestic violence is an effective but problematic strategy. It suggests that asylum in the West continues to be part of the civilizing mission of refugee protection launched in the Cold War period, with the protection of asylees fleeing the barbarism of Soviet Communism.[101] Some cases where children have received asylum because of the risk of female circumcision have also been presented in this way.[102]

"Child as Juvenile" Approach to Child Asylum Claims

Children who can present asylum claims based on their vulnerability and victim status thus have had some success in securing refugee status. These cases stand in contrast to cases where children's asylum claims are based on their political beliefs, their activist behavior, their role as agents and decision makers, their conscious choices about prospects. In this group of cases, minority is not an advantage; indeed it can act as a disqualification. One can identify two different strands in the rejection arguments. On the one hand, the claims of separated child asylum seekers are conflated with those of adults—they are not "really children," or they are not of tender years,[103] or no special considerations apply. This is the "child as juvenile" perspective, which tars unaccompanied migrant adolescents with suspicion regarding their motivation for travel, a perspective that complements the exclusionary goals of the immigration control system. The case of a fifteen-year-old Salvadorian wounded while fighting with guerilla forces, exemplifies this approach. The child testified that family members had been murdered by both the guerillas and the government army; he had eventually fled the guerillas and was forced into hiding from both guerillas and government soldiers whom he believed were seeking to arrest or kill him. The US Fourth

Circuit rejected his asylum application, holding him to the same objective standard as an adult—the child had failed to show "that a reasonable person in similar circumstances would fear persecution on account . . . [of one of the enumerated grounds in the Refugee Convention]."[104] A more appropriate description would have labeled him "a reasonable child."

Courts have repeatedly treated children's testimony, even in the case of young children, as if it were advanced by adults, assuming that inconsistencies or lapses in memory are evidence of deceit rather than mental immaturity. A Canadian federal judge criticized this approach when reversing a decision of the Canadian Refugee Determination Division, regarding two Sri Lankan Tamil children:

> I . . . find that the panel committed a patently unreasonable error of fact that influenced its final conclusions. The panel clearly did not take into consideration the fact that the applicants were ten and twelve years of age when they travelled to Canada and that the two children clearly did not have to keep a log through their travels. Furthermore, it was quite possible, and perhaps even likely realistic, that both of the applicants could not precisely remember all of the circumstances of the journey, which must certainly have been very stressful in the circumstances.[105]

The second rejection argument does not conflate child claimants with adults. Rather it uses their minority as a disqualification. Because they are children, the argument goes, they are not capable of political activism, or of being viewed as a political threat or, indeed, of providing reliable testimony about their political experiences. This disqualification process occurs in several ways: identical political acts carried out by adults and children are discounted in the case of children simply because of their minority—it is suggested, despite contrary evidence, that governments would not take actions by children seriously and therefore would not view them as a threat. In the case of a sixteen-year-old Salvadorian, the US Board of Immigration Appeals accepted "the immigration judge's finding that it was unlikely that the National Guard would seek out such a young person."[106] Ignorance about human-rights violations against children fuels this approach. Decision makers have also questioned the claim that children can achieve prominence or leadership positions in political organizations.[107] Second, political acts by children—such as stone throwing, tire burning, street protests, school strikes—are discounted as not being "really political," because prevailing judicial conceptions of political activism revolve around an adult norm.[108] This approach is reminiscent of decisions that dismissed women's distinctive form of political activism—providing shelter for guerillas, cooking, hiding ammunition—because they diverge from a norm of political activism that is male gendered, centered on activities such as leafleting, ambushing, shooting, demonstrating, being a combatant in a guerilla army. The concept of a "political act" in refugee law is still insufficiently gender- and age inclusive.[109]

The Three Different Forms of Child Persecution

One can analytically distinguish three different forms of child persecution. The first are *forms of persecution that are nonspecific to children*. Many child asylum seekers, like their adult counterparts, flee their homelands to escape politically or religiously motivated or ethnically based persecution that has no particular relationship to the fact that they are children. The case of two Tamil Sri Lankan brothers, eleven and thirteen years old, who obtained refugee status in Canada after being targeted as guerilla recruits[110] is an example. Over the course of the Arab Spring uprisings in Tunisia, Libya, Egypt, and Syria,[111] it has become apparent that active opponents of the regime risk persecution and murder whether they are fifteen or twenty. Even in such "mainstream" cases, however, there may be age-related aspects to the persecution that an adult-centered bias can lead decision makers to ignore. Children may be particularly targeted as a means of "getting at" activist parents. In one such case, a Romanian opposition political activist and her young son applied for asylum in Germany after the son had been pushed in front of a moving car to threaten his mother.[112] More recently, Syrian children have been a particular target of government forces intent on quashing public protest and terrorizing parents into placing their children under curfew.[113]

Some child-asylum applications fail because the decision maker disbelieves the claim that the child could be considered a serious political threat. A case in point is a US immigration judge's denial of asylum to a Haitian boy who was threatened and whose house was stoned and dog killed after he was overheard publicly supporting an opposition leader. The judge commented: "It is almost inconceivable to believe that the Ton Ton Macoutes (the government militia) could be fearful of the conversation of 15-year-old children."[114] Clearly this judge, perhaps generalizing an American view of adolescence,[115] did not appreciate the extent to which quite young children may be highly politicized in unstable and violent societies.[116]

Age bias is also apparent in cases where behavior is reinterpreted just because the applicant has reached majority, as happened to a young Salvadorian woman who had her asylum refusal reversed by a judge who pointed out that she was now no longer a teenager.[117] Sometimes the barrier to protection is an unproven assumption of unreliability based solely on age. In the case of the seventeen-year-old Ethiopian orphan discussed earlier, the appellate judge remanding her case for reconsideration commented: "Even at age three, one is likely to remember the traumatic loss of one's family."[118] Age bias in asylum adjudication is inconsistent, reflecting the tension between a view of children as vulnerable victims deserving of protection because of their minority, a view of children as treacherous juveniles, intent on border crossing by nefarious means, and a view of children as passive entities, incapable of posing political threats. The challenge for children and their advocates is to devise skillful strategies for resisting these simplistic stereotypes, and presenting child asylum seekers in all their complexity and variety.

In a second typology of child persecution situations, *child asylum claims are based on persecution that specifically applies to children*.[119] Cases in point include the threat of infanticide,[120] recruitment as a child soldier,[121] child abuse suffered at the hands of relatives,[122] mistreatment and neglect suffered by children without families,[123] incest,[124] female circumcision (in countries where this practice occurs before puberty),[125] bonded or hazardous child labor,[126] recruitment as a minor into the international sex trade,[127] and child marriage.[128]

Child applicants in these situations often face an uphill battle convincing courts or other decision makers that the behavior complained of constitutes "persecution" and that it justifies a grant of international protection. The following is a typical example. A fifteen-year-old child from Iran applied for asylum in the United Kingdom on the basis of child abuse from her father. The record suggests there was evidence of alcohol-related "extreme violence." Though the adolescent was accepted as a credible witness by a special adjudicator, the Immigration Appeal Tribunal rejected her application inter alia because it held she could have relied on the Iranian authorities for protection and "neither gender nor violence within a family is sufficient to create a social group." Nowhere in the record is there any mention of the fact that the applicant was a minor,[129] nor is there any discussion of whether being a victim of extreme child abuse could constitute persecution on the grounds of membership in the particular social group of children living with violent alcoholic fathers.

Despite the obstacles, however, some child-specific asylum applications have been successful, indicating expansion of the scope for child protection in this field. Applications based on child abuse, stigmatization of childhood autism,[130] and cerebral palsy[131] have been granted, as have cases arising out of forced marriage and slavery-like child labor. The overall picture here is one of inconsistency—a vacillation between protective outcomes and less generous findings rooted in a more traditional rejection of children as independent asylees.

Finally, a third group of child-asylum cases exist. These are cases where children have *a valid claim to asylum based on conduct that might not be sufficient to constitute persecution for an adult* but, because of the different sensibility and vulnerability of children, should be deemed to give rise to a well-founded fear of persecution in the case of children. This is the opposite strategy to the one just discussed where asylum was granted to a Salvadorian applicant after she became an adult on the basis that her claim of persecution had become more credible as her perceived threat to the authorities increased with the transition from childhood to adulthood. Scholars have demonstrated that for children witnessing violence, especially against a parent or other close relative, there can be profoundly long-lasting and traumatic impacts, rising to the level of persecution.[132] The harm alleged need not involve violence at all: in one striking case, the High Court of Ireland granted relief to a Roma boy on the grounds that racial discrimination in Serbia would almost certainly prevent him from accessing education, a fundamental human right.[133] As the US Seventh Circuit Court of Appeals has stated, "There may be situations where children should be considered victims of persecution though they have suffered *less harm* than would be required for an adult."[134] The Convention on the Rights of the Child is a good guide in these cases, because it highlights both the peculiar obligations inherent in application of the "best interest" principle and the particular needs of vulnerable children.

Situations that fall under this heading include family separation following war; civil upheaval or forced displacement; trafficking; gang violence; and homelessness. Often the facts in these cases are compelling. Consider the asylum application of a nineteen-year-old Guatemalan girl and her eighteen-month-old daughter; a victim of physical, psychological, and sexual abuse by her parents, the former had become a street child and been recruited by the notorious 18th Street gang. Only when she was targeted with a death threat did she decide to flee with her baby to the United States. This young asylum applicant was awarded asylum given the severity of her suffering.[135] At other times, the first-instance decision maker's failure to adequately consider the "age, maturity and particular circumstances" of a child claimant has been central to a court's decision to review an asylum refusal. In one case, an unaccompanied minor fleeing recruitment by the Taliban and threats from the Afghan government was denied asylum in Ireland. The High Court remanded the case for another hearing, noting the failure to "liberally apply" the benefit of the doubt with regard to the claimant's age and immaturity, particularly in light of his risk of "being press-ganged as a child soldier" or "forced to undertake a suicide bombing" by the Taliban.[136] In another case, the UK High Court held that the government erred in denying relief to a sixteen-year-old boy from Afghanistan who had killed a family member in self-defense. The court noted that when dealing with child claimants, even those accused of committing serious crimes, "the primacy of welfare considerations should be manifest. . . . What might be regarded as the right approach for an adult is not always the right approach for a child or young person."[137] A US judge cited similar reasons for remanding the case of two young brothers fleeing guerilla violence in Guatemala, stating that the immigration judge "did not look at the events from their perspective, nor measure the degree of their injuries by their impact on children of their ages."[138]

In general, however, asylum claims that rely on establishing this form of child-specific persecution have been difficult to win. They depend on judicial acceptance of the subjective component inherent in the concept of a "well-founded fear of persecution" and the acknowledgment that children are likely to have a lower threshold for experiencing "fear," and that this experience is " well founded" because of their heightened sensitivity when confronted by extreme stressors. Success in these cases depends on official acknowledgment of children's distinctive dependence on adult protection, a dependence that lays them open to more extreme fear, panic, or despair in the face of loss or separation or abandonment. As one child asylum seeker put it: "I didn't really think about getting to the U.S. or what would happen to me there because I was so worried about what I would eat and about not arriving at all."[139] In practice asylum adjudicators regularly apply a purely adult standard in their decision making, rather than a child-centered perspective. In a Canadian case, for example, a sixteen-year-old Sikh child fleeing heightened unrest in northern India was refused protection on the basis that he could avail himself of an "internal flight alternative"—that is, find an entirely new place to live away from his home area. Many more recent cases follow this bleak approach. Fortunately for the Sikh boy, the judge hearing this case on appeal remanded it for rehearing on the basis that forcing a sixteen-year-old back alone to find a safe haven might be unreasonable.[140]

Child-specific Persecution and Gangs

The clearest example of obstacles to asylum for children, and one that deeply occupies child-asylum advocates in the United States, is gang-related litigation. This is not surprising. The sheer scope of gang activity in Central America, much of it fueled by deportees trained on the violent streets of US inner cities and by US drug consumption, is staggering. In Guatemala alone, a small country with a population of only fourteen million people, there are estimated to be 434 gang cells with at least eighty thousand gang members. Gangs also proliferate in Mexico, El Salvador, and Honduras.[141] Several gangs are particularly infamous, including the two best known, Mara 18 and Mara Salvatrucha, or MS-13. Members are easily identifiable by prominent, distinctive tattoo markings all over their bodies, including on their faces. Once someone is thus marked, avoiding gang attention is next to impossible, so that refugee flight and plastic surgery may be the only survival options.

Gang activity presents an acute danger to Central American children, particularly the most vulnerable among them—those abandoned or forced out by their families, and who live alone on the streets of big cities. Gangs may target not only individuals they want to recruit, but their family members as well, to put pressure on the individuals concerned. The recruitment dynamic has close parallels to the forced conscription of child soldiers discussed in chapter 5. In both cases, the target children—often casualties of prolonged civil war and weak social infrastructure—experience a dramatic protection vacuum and dire social and economic need. The void is filled by powerful criminal organizations headed by leaders equipped with significant material resources who control young recruits through a mixture of coercion and enticement, exploiting the absence of robust positive alternatives.[142]

There is overwhelming evidence of extreme brutality and persecution within gangs, particularly against those who decide to leave them or reject membership in the first place. There is also a considerable empirical basis for claiming that children and youth are at particular risk of recruitment.[143] And yet, the prospects of success for such individuals in an asylum application are minimal. The positive outcome of an early case involving a visibly scarred Honduran street child constitutes a rare exception: the immigration court held that as a former gang member who had fled the gang, he would be liable to the infliction of harm were he to be returned to Honduras.[144] More recent cases[145] have increasingly demonstrated the authorities' determination to resolve the tension between protection of child asylum seekers and the enforcement of stringent migration control by opting for child expulsion.

Two key US cases illustrate the problem. In one case called *Matter of S-E-G-*, two sixteen-year-old Salvadoran brothers who sought asylum (with their nineteen-year-old sister) on the basis that they had resisted recruitment by the MS-13—"because of their personal, moral and religious opposition to the gang's values and activities"—had their cases rejected. The children testified that MS-13 had stolen money from them, harassed and beaten them, and threatened to rape their sister. When they refused to be recruited, the gang members returned to warn them that if they did not change their minds, their bodies "might end up in a dumpster or in the street someday." To rebut the suggestion that the children should have relied on the Salvadorian government to deal with the gang threat, an expert witness on Central American gangs testified that MS-13 had become quite invincible in El Salvador over the years, despite the Salvadorian government's "Mano Dura" policy, because of its growing influence within the government and the police force. The boys' asylum claims were rejected. The BIA held that the boys had not demonstrated that they were being singled out for persecution, or that they were "in a substantially different situation from anyone who has crossed the gang, or who is perceived to be a threat to the gang's interests."[146] The BIA also found that the boys had failed to demonstrate that a political opinion motivated their refusal to join the gang. They cited the lack of evidence of political activism, or public anti-gang statements by the boys, or any indication that the "MS-13 gang in El Salvador imputed, or would impute to them, an anti-gang political opinion." But requiring children fleeing gang recruitment to be outspoken public critics or otherwise socially visible opponents seems tantamount to setting death as the bar for qualifying for asylum—a completely unrealistic and decontextualized threshold. Given this precedent, it is hard to imagine when a child might succeed in proving their opinions led to the threat of persecution.

A second gang-based asylum case called *Matter of E-A-G-* is also troubling. A young Honduran boy, two of whose brothers had been killed by gangs, had resisted repeated pressure to join the Mara Salvatrucha (MS) gang and eventually fled to the United States to avoid gang recruitment altogether. Though the immigration judge at first instance granted the boy asylum, finding that he had been targeted by gang members because of his "youth and affiliation or perceived affiliation with gangs,"[147] and because of his political opinion, the Board of Immigration Appeals reversed on both counts. They held that no visible social group to which the boy could be held to belong existed, so he could not be considered a target for persecution under the terms of the Refugee Convention definition. The BIA also held that resisting gang recruitment did not constitute a political opinion.

These disappointing decisions have been further entrenched by higher-court decisions rejecting the claim that child gang resisters constitute a *visible social group* for purposes of refugee protection.[148] This insistence on the "visibility" of a social group as a necessary precondition for asylum grants has attracted criticism because it introduces a new barrier to protection that predicates access to asylum on social acknowledgment of the harm in the home country.[149] Asylum protection was not intended to be a lowest common denominator reflecting concerns already established domestically, but rather an international remedy that advanced human-rights protections for populations with no access to them. Certainly it makes sense to construe membership of a particular social group to require identifiable characteristics that link group members to one another in some way independent of the threat of persecution itself: targets for oppression have to be nonrandomly selected. If gang recruitment took place by enlisting each twentieth person encountered in a street roundup irrespective of age, gender, or other demographic characteristics, those selected would not constitute a particular social group. But this should not mean that, like the Jews forced to wear yellow stars or the homosexuals forced to wear pink triangles in Nazi Germany, persecutees have to exhibit visible markers identifying them as targets. If there is a reasonable chance they will be targeted, given their demographic, familial, and residential characteristics, then they should succeed in their social-group membership claim. For young boys and girls residing in known neighborhoods in some of the impoverished slums of Tegucigalpa, Mexico City, and San Salvador, this is easy to demonstrate.

Recently, the Third Circuit remanded the case of a twenty-one-year-old Honduran applicant beaten for resisting recruitment by MS-13 gang members. The court rejected the "social visibility" and "particularity" requirements as unreasonable and directed the BIA to reconcile the different approaches followed in preceding case law. Alternatively, the court argued, the Board of Immigration Appeals should articulate a new approach justifying deviation from the long-standing "immutability" standard that required a successful asylum applicant to show he or she could not change the characteristic eliciting persecution.[150] The impact of this shift remains to be seen. The prospects of refugee protection for children fleeing gang recruitment remain close to nil. The publicized cases of Benito Zaldivar, returned to the clutches of the gang he fled in El Salvador following an unsuccessful asylum application and then killed, and of Nelson Benito Ramos, in hiding from his former gang to avoid a similar fate, may have increased political pressure on the administration and the courts to expand the protective scope of the law.[151] But skepticism about the justification for protecting these young people and an overall political mandate to reduce migration contribute to an adverse adjudicatory climate that frequently resolves itself in decisions that go against these imperiled child asylum seekers.

Conclusion

The challenge of including separated children and adolescents within the protective scope of refugee law is significant, particularly at a time when refugee protection as a whole is under threat by restrictive border control and migration-management policies. However, some hopeful developments exist. Several countries, including Canada, the United States, and the United Kingdom have promulgated Guidelines for Child Asylum claims,[152] growing numbers of dedicated advocates and a few child-rights-oriented adjudicators are challenging the adult-centric asylum adjudication norms of the past, and most important of all, children themselves are demonstrating by their actions and affiliations that they belong within the protective embrace of international refugee law. In 2010, UNHCR published a *Guidance Note on Refugee Claims Relating to Victims of Organized Gangs* that drew special attention to the need for "proper consideration of the age and gender aspects of a claim . . . in applications made by children."[153]

Whether through the creative use of social media or the time-worn strategies of resolute political organizing, young freedom fighters and survivors of familial or communal brutality are increasingly asserting their justified claim to equal protection by the international community, and bringing egregious cases to public attention. At the same time, in some jurisdictions, acknowledgment of the need for improvements in the treatment of separated child asylum seekers is growing. The European Council Directive on minimum standards for the reception of asylum seekers defines unaccompanied minors as *persons with special needs* and requires that their best interests be the primary consideration for member states receiving them. Some of the elements for implementing this approach, specifically enumerated in the Directive, include access to rehabilitation and mental-health care as well as expert counseling for victims of abuse or rape or for those who are war affected. The EC Directive requires a representative to be appointed for unaccompanied minors and stipulates they be placed with adult relatives, a foster family, or in other accommodation suitable for minors. A robust policy is being promoted even as ambivalence toward unskilled youth migration and suspicion of the legitimacy of child-asylum applications persist at Europe's borders and among its immigration enforcers. As a recent report on child asylum seekers in Finland noted: "A strong climate of suspicion prevails in society, in which children are stigmatized and their stories questioned for the simple reason that they are asylum-seekers."[154] This is regrettable. It is time for the adults with power and authority to reexamine their fears, to analyze their inconsistent responses and to parse the complexities of childhood and adolescence with more sophistication. Only then can the thousands of would-be young Davids prevail without having to slay too many Goliaths and tragic cases similar to Edgar Chocoy's cease to occur.

CHAPTER 7
Demanding Rights and a Future: Adolescents on the Move for a Better Life

> It turned out that the moment human beings lacked their own government and had to fall back upon their minimum rights, no authority was left to protect them and no institution was willing to guarantee them. . . . [What was] supposedly *inalienable*, proved to be *unenforceable*.[1]

Introduction

The first four months of 2011 will go down in history as "the Arab Spring," a moment when the unmet aspirations of the next generation in several Middle Eastern countries hit global headlines. Alongside the inspiring images of young people taking to the streets to demand freedom in Tunis, Cairo, Benghazi, Tripoli, and Homs,[2] reports noted the region's unique demographic gift (60 percent are under thirty) and simultaneous risk (25 percent of those under thirty-five are unemployed).[3] Complementing both were disturbing news stories of children and adolescents[4] squeezed with adults into precarious boats, fleeing violence, chaos, and unemployment at home to search for a future across the Mediterranean Sea. Young people were on the move, taking their life into their own hands at whatever cost.

For many involved in the Arab exodus, their courageous journey ended badly.[5] Disturbing stories abound. On August 1, 2011, "[t]he Italian Coast Guard found the bodies of 25 young men in the hold of a boat crowded with migrants that was intercepted . . . en route from Libya." Among the survivors were twenty-one children.[6] Sympathy with liberation movements and concern with youth unemployment abroad do not translate into a hero's welcome for brave young migrants. On June 22, 2011, an Egyptian adolescent drowned trying to swim to the Sicilian shore as the boat's propeller hit him; on the same day, the humanitarian organization Terre des Hommes reported that 260 migrant children had been detained for over a month on the southern Italian island of Lampedusa at a former NATO base with a maximum capacity of 180.[7] Just months before, at the same base, Amnesty International complained of inadequate child supervision, bullying, severe anxiety, and other indications of distress from the minors.[8] Children fleeing conflict and destitution in North Africa and hoping for a better life had ended up in painful detention in Europe.

The Arab exodus illustrates the reality of youthful mixed migration today,[9] a flow that includes asylum seekers, exploited unaccompanied children, job seekers, education or opportunity seekers, adolescents seeking family reunion with previously migrated parents. All of them, in one way or another, are young people on the move for a better life. The exodus also spotlights a growing phenomenon—the presence of children and adolescents in contemporary migration. Worldwide, 13 percent of today's mixed migration flow consists of children, adolescents, and youth under twenty,[10] many of whom travel alone to advance their generational interests, despite the sizable institutional challenges and ambivalent political responses discussed in earlier chapters of this book.[11] The Middle East and North Africa region does not have a monopoly on such migrations. Tens of thousands of child migrants have crossed the US-Mexico border for decades in search of better opportunities—between 2011 and 2012 alone, US Customs and

Border Protection authorities apprehended 18,000 children, while the Division of Child Services placed 10,005 unaccompanied children in care.[12] Europe has also witnessed a huge movement of child migrants traveling from Third countries into the European Union;[13] and in Africa, Latin America, and Australia, too, many thousands of adolescents are on the move each year.

Around the time that the North African migrant adolescents just described were leaving home to seek opportunities across the Mediterranean, the UN General Assembly held its first discussion on international migration and development. On May 19, 2011, Secretary-General Ban Ki-moon called on member states to "harness the unstoppable force of migration for the greater good," citing statistics showing "that the economic contribution of migrant workers far outweighs any costs."[14] The secretary-general's key points were not new. Despite enormous investments in policing, effective border control continues to elude target destination states.[15] As former US Secretary for Homeland Security Michael Chertoff acknowledged: "Enforcement alone is not enough to address our immigration challenges. . . . [As long as the] opportunity for higher wages and a better life draws people across the border illegally or encourages them to remain here illegally [preventing migration will be difficult]."[16] This is not surprising, given the lack of robust engagement with policies to address rights and needs in the countries of origin of young migrants, an essential complementary development.

Ban's call for positive approaches to migration is welcome. States have generally failed to demonstrate their intention or ability to harness the force of migration for the greater good—despite ample evidence that migrant workers, especially young, unattached, and healthy ones, are likelier to add far more to their economies than they cost.[17] With ambition, energy, and years ahead of them, this cohort has an untapped capacity for contributing to rapidly aging societies. Yet EU member states have turned their back on countries with which they have had long-standing historical links and instituted blanket return policies: for example, in 2009, Italy adopted a policy of returning migrants in international waters to Libya, a former colony and close trading partner, without any prior evaluation of their protection needs. Nowhere is the impact of this failure to harness migration flows for positive outcomes clearer than in the case of young migrants on the move to secure a better future for themselves and their families.

A global commitment to protect children from adversity shares the policy agenda with an international determination to punish and deter irregular migration. Young migrants are high priorities for both. Whether they are asylum seekers, independent migrants, trafficked youth, or children smuggled for family reunion purposes, or whether their status is unclear (between categories or within several), all young migrants need protection and assistance—safe accommodation and protection from exploitation, from the risks of criminalization, from deprivation of food and medical care at a minimum. Indeed, as Save the Children Brussels has noted, "The rights and needs of these children to assistance arise often before the appropriate protection route or long-term solution options are known." Devising mechanisms to satisfactorily engage this need for a "horizontal" approach[18] to adolescent migrant protection, independent of the particular categorical silo that encompasses the child's legal status, is an unfinished task. In this final chapter, I address the entitlements this population of young people has as a matter of international and domestic law, and the reality behind these entitlements.

The Right to Have Rights

With characteristic foresight, Hannah Arendt recognized the fundamental human-rights challenge of our age: supposedly "inalienable rights are unenforceable for individuals who "lack . . . their own government."[19] The international community acknowledged Arendt's insight about the perils of this situation by enshrining a comprehensive body of principles—human-rights norms—designed to reduce individuals' dependence on "their own government" for protection of their basic rights. Migrant adolescents, like everyone else, are covered by these generic principles first articulated in the 1948 Universal Declaration of Human Rights and subsequently consolidated into binding international treaties that include both civil and political rights[20] and economic, social, and cultural rights.[21] They are also the beneficiaries of specific measures designed to protect them in light of their particular vulnerabilities.[22]

The hazardous journeys and miserable detention experiences of adolescents described above suggest that, over half a century after Arendt's pessimistic pronouncement, the access to fundamental rights protection for young people without a government remains elusive. Many young people embark on international travel to secure rights they lack at home, rights to adequate shelter, health care and food, an education, the means to earn a living. Some do manage to secure these rights—previous chapters have described family reunion, asylum, and other mechanisms for migrating legally. In addition to these legal child migrants, there are children who start their journeys irregularly, using smugglers or false documents or surreptitious means of border crossing, but who then acquire lawful status during the period after migration, through changes in domestic law (e.g., amnesty), changes in their personal situation (e.g., marriage), changes in their legal position (e.g., compassionate or humanitarian leave), or changes in their nationality through international treaties (e.g., the redrawing of state boundaries)—the process of joining the "state people" that Arendt described.[23]

A significant proportion of children on the move are not so fortunate. Their access to a legal status during and postmigration is at best uncertain. Many fall into the precarious position of being unprotected for varying lengths of time, moving in and out of legal status depending on their circumstances. Sizable numbers are unable to switch from irregular to legal status, for lack of opportunity, know-how, or both. Others may begin their journeys or residences with a legal status, but lose that status over time. A teenager entering as a lawful visitor invited by relatives abroad may end up as an overstaying unpaid domestic worker; a young asylum seeker may be unable to provide adequate evidence to support the claim for refugee status but elect to stay on rather than risk persecution by returning; a student may lose legal status by working without employment authorization.

Irregular or undocumented status, then, may not be a fixed category defining a migrant's interactions with the state for all time, but rather a varying condition through which a migrant moves at different stages of his or her personal journey. It follows, as Sigona and Hughes note, that:

> Contrary to popular perception, the definition of who is an irregular migrant is . . . only apparently unproblematic. There is no single category of irregular migrant but differing modes of irregular status resulting from the increasing scope and complexity of international migration. . . . [T]he partition of migrants into two mutually exclusive and jointly exhaustive parts—either "legal" or "illegal"—dominant in political and public

discourse is neither clear in practice, nor conforms to migrants' own experiences and conceptions of their status.[24]

Irregular migration status brings with it a serious risk of rightlessness for children despite their entitlement to extensive human-rights protections by virtue of their status as minors. As I have already noted, adequate mechanisms for supervision, accountability, and the ability to insist on appropriate treatment, even for the most basic human needs, do not exist. The Women's Refugee Commission report on migrant children in US detention illustrates the risks involved:

> Nutrition provided to children during their time in border patrol stations is not appropriate for children's physical condition or cultural norms. . . . One 17-year-old girl reported being held in a Border Patrol station for an entire day with no food. Another child reported being held for an entire day with no water. A 17-year-old boy said he was held for three days and only received juice and one apple.[25]

The next section explores how rightlessness impinges on the material and psychological well-being of adolescent migrants.

Adolescent Migrants and Liminal Living

Despite their demographic and cultural differences, many adolescent migrants share key risk factors. Minority, alienage, separation from caregivers, and some form of irregular status contribute to a common experience of marginalization and psychological insecurity—"a dynamic constellation" of vulnerabilities vis-à-vis the state[26]—with far-reaching consequences. Most fundamental, perhaps, is the absence of a regular immigration status, which generates vulnerabilities that compound or exacerbate preexisting rights deficits. Addressing this central risk factor is critical to securing a stable rights-based environment.

Many thousands of adolescents have been raised as irregular migrants in states they consider home. The experience of what some have termed "legal liminality"[27] can be all-pervasive. As a seventeen-year-old Afghan boy living in England reflected, "Only when I have documents can I say that I will be complete."[28] A similar sentiment was expressed by an undocumented young Brazilian in the United States: "You're a nobody in society."[29] Like him, there are approximately 1.1 million unauthorized[30] minors currently in the United States.[31] Many have lived for years with the daily threat of deportation,[32] and all experience insecurity vis-à-vis their future. A radical improvement in status may be forthcoming for some. On June 15, 2012, Janet Napolitano, the secretary for Homeland Security, announced that undocumented migrants under thirty who were brought to the United States before they were sixteen, with at least five years continuous residence, no significant criminal convictions, and good school-attendance records would be protected from deportation and become eligible to apply for renewable two-year visas.[33] For many so-called DREAMers, young people covered by the draft DREAM Act,[34] this change in policy presents an exceedingly welcome and long-awaited concession. But for those with disqualifying factors, the insecurity of irregular status will continue.

Given the importance of the peer group during adolescence, considerable effort goes into avoiding the loss of status that "being illegal" is thought to entail. For example, a classmate's invitation to join driving lessons can precipitate complicated justifications to conceal one's inability to register as a learner driver. This is how one undocumented boy described the conundrum: "And it's kind of annoying not for anybody to know. . . . [T]hey're [his friends] always like 'Dude, get your license!' So I kind of make up this whole—like—you know—like image of me like 'I don't want to. My parents will drive me.' You know, kind of lazy." A school trip to Canada can pose an insurmountable problem and reveal the guilty secret of "illegality" to one's classmates. As one young Brazilian woman reflected: "You are already a minority, and already treated differently. Imagine people finding out you were an *illegal* minority? None of my friends ever knew. I probably wouldn't have had the ones I had if they had known."[35]

Unlike other young people their age, this population fears all contacts with state authorities, not just with the law-enforcement branches. An illness can precipitate a crisis about access to public services and the risks of being discovered. Academic success can generate dilemmas about financing college education without eligibility for public support, and about the need to curtail unrealistic hopes of career opportunities.[36] Undocumented status depresses aspirations as young people emerging from school discover the reality of transitioning to illegality.[37] For many irregular adolescents who have grown up in the United States, public services established to protect fundamental rights to health and education are instead perceived as potentially dangerous enforcement agencies capable of precipitating unwanted inquiries into a family's immigration status.[38]

The precarious situation of adolescents in the United States occurs, mutatis mutandis, in many other destination countries. In the United Kingdom, there were 155,000 irregular migrant children at the end of 2007; over half (85,000) were estimated to have been born and to have lived their entire life there.[39] Unlike US-born children, those born in the United Kingdom to parents without a permanent immigration status or British citizenship do not themselves acquire British citizenship automatically, even if the parents' immigration status is legal. If their parents are undocumented or irregular migrants, frightened to approach the authorities for regularization of their newborns' status, then these children become irregular migrants themselves. For this reason, among others, young migrants feature significantly in populations that are regularized as a result of amnesties or other government regularization programs. And yet they have received little policy attention so far. Sigona and Hughes draw attention to this policy gap. They estimate that in the United Kingdom,

> of 50,000 regularized dependents a large majority are minors as the presence of dependent children was one of the key criteria for assessing an application positively. . . . [T]he distance between a political debate almost exclusively focused on trafficked children, unaccompanied asylum-seeking minors and on specific issues such as child detention on the one hand, and on the other a far larger group of child migrants without legal status who stay invisible, uncounted and largely outside the policy agenda and public debate, is striking.[40]

The absence of legal status time and again trumps the nondiscrimination injunction to protect basic human rights. According to PICUM, the Brussels-based Platform for International Cooperation on Undocumented Migrants, "[c]hildren in an irregular migration situation face numerous barriers to realizing their rights in most European countries. They face high risks of poverty, exploitation, social exclusion, and violence."[41] The same is true in other migration destinations. The contradiction between international constitutional obligations to protect vulnerable children (described in the following section) and domestic pressures to disqualify all undocumented populations from access to state services manifests itself in different ways. In France, the central government has refused to provide resources to local councils charged with implementing child-protection services for unaccompanied migrant children, forcing affected municipalities to initiate legal proceedings to recover costs incurred in fulfilling their statutory responsibilities.[42] In Germany, the opposite process has taken place: although all children, including undocumented children, have a constitutional right to education, until recently,[43] this right has been nullified by public officials' duty to report the presence of all undocumented individuals (including children) to the immigration authorities.[44] In France, local authorities have been the protectors of undocumented children's basic rights; in Germany they have spearheaded threats to those rights.

In the Netherlands, challenges have also been mounted in response to child-protection violations by the state: officials refused child support to undocumented parents until an appeals tribunal ruled that this violated the local authority's duty of care toward the children.[45] UNICEF has expressed concern about unaccompanied migrant adolescents in the United Kingdom living outside any system of care or protection: "the numbers of unaccompanied or separated migrant children who are not known to the authorities could be in the thousands . . . likely . . . more numerous than those . . . known to the authorities and . . . seeking asylum." An NGO worker reported the following case to the agency:

> We had a child who ended up becoming completely destitute at one of our projects. He had been living with a guy who he said was his uncle, who had then gone off to Pakistan for six months and left him in the house on his own. He had no food, no money, he didn't even have a coat, actually, and it was the middle of winter.[46]

Applying the Best Interest Principle to Migrant Children and Adolescents

Sixty years after the Universal Declaration of Human Rights was signed, nearly twenty years after ratification of the UN Convention on the Rights of the Child, and several generations into what Louis Henkin memorably called an "age of rights,"[47] there appears to be no clear consensus on the rights to which migrant children and adolescents are entitled. Though the centrality of the CRC's "best interests of the child" principle is undisputed, its application to migrant adolescents is contested. Two issues in particular complicate the enforcement of adolescent migrant rights: the relative importance of family unity as a factor in assessing the child's best interests, and the relevance of socioeconomic rights, including access to employment opportunities, in assessing an adolescent's best interests.

The right to respect for family and private life, enshrined in many human rights conventions,[48] is critical for children, a point repeatedly emphasized in earlier chapters in this book. Not only is the family widely considered the fundamental unit for rearing and nurturing minors, but its absence is a known risk factor precipitating a range of physical, psychological, and social vulnerabilities.[49] However, the role that families play changes as children mature: infants, toddlers, and young children depend on their parents for basic survival, nurturing, and a sense of well-being and self-confidence. For older children, the balance of dependence changes, particularly in families facing severe hardships—HIV/AIDS, conflict-induced displacement, economic destitution, unemployment, illness, or familial conflict. These are the sorts of families from which many independent adolescent migrants come, families fractured by crisis or calamity, by unmet need and other forms of acute distress.[50] What role should the possibility of reestablishing family unity play in the assessment of migrant adolescents' best interests? While government decision makers regularly assume it should be a central consideration in arriving at future plans for all child migrants, many young migrants and their representatives disagree. Not only are families on occasion sources of oppression and abuse from which children flee; but older children sometimes diverge from their parents in calibrating the place of family unity among key elements of a best-interest decision. These points are explored in more detail below.

The second issue differentiating the assessment of adolescents' best interests from those of younger children is the relative importance of various social and economic factors, including income-generating opportunities. While human-rights instruments and discourse emphasize the importance of educational goals—not only the non-negotiability of the right to primary education but also the centrality of secondary and tertiary education to the realization of rights[51]—most migrant adolescents aspire to employment opportunities as a precondition not a sequel to postprimary education. Official government decision-making bodies do not take this approach. Rather, migrant adolescent employment, invariably unauthorized and typically "informal,"[52] is considered a factor justifying exclusion rather than an element relevant to a best-interest assessment. In the United States, adolescents without a secure immigration status who abscond from government shelter facilities to find work while their immigration cases are being decided are considered security threats rather than responsible, self-reliant young people exercising independent agency.[53]

These two issues are often intertwined in the life of adolescent migrants. Family pressures induce urgent income needs, whether because relatives have failed to support the adolescent or because the adolescent is relied on to generate resources for the family. In either case, an assessment of the best interests of the minor that prioritizes, as official approaches have tended to, family unity and educational access over the considerations just outlined may be flawed.[54] In the words of seventeen-year-old Omar, an unaccompanied Moroccan child migrant in Italy: "Your mother doesn't need to say: 'Send the money.' You know from the beginning that they need it. When you call them, and they tell you about their troubles, the loans, the lack of this and that . . . you know perfectly well what you have to do."[55] The luxury of a carefree adolescence is not available to most unaccompanied young migrants. Irregular migration status and the difficulty of accessing appropriate state services compound their vulnerability.[56]

Competing desires of adolescent migrants complicate the process of determining what is in their best interest. Unlike younger children, whose needs and best interests can be determined by competent (even if unfamiliar) adults, adolescents' own critical insights need to be factored into the decision-making process. Co-production of decisions engaging adolescent participation is a more effective strategy[57] than the automatic prioritization of one-dimensional "family unity." This more complex and time-consuming decision-making strategy is rare in practice. Instead institutionalization and other unacceptable forms of "secure accommodation" amounting to detention continue to be pervasive responses to the presence of independent adolescent migrants. In the United Kingdom, for example, unaccompanied or separated asylum-seeking children "are now thought to represent around 10 per cent of all children in care."[58] In the United States, 7,211 migrant adolescents are placed in secure facilities annually.[59]

Neither of these responses to the presence of unaccompanied migrant adolescents—infantilizing foster care or punitive detention—are responsive to the search for the self-realization that often drives the migration project in the first place. This search frequently includes risk-taking behavior, driven by the dual imperatives of "having fun" and "earning money."[60] Mainstream opportunities in the formal economy, in higher education, in salubrious neighborhoods are generally closed off by discrimination, irregular status, and lack of necessary skill sets.[61] So the avenues available are predominantly antisocial, sometimes[62] self-harming: begging, stealing, drug selling, and prostitution. Nicola Mai describes the complexity of youth migration, based on his research with North African and East European unaccompanied minor migrants in EU countries. He links the development of a very utopian migratory project, often based on an idealization of the West as a place where "everything is possible" to the consumption of Western television depicting an Eldorado of plenty and permissiveness. "The clash between the adolescent utopian fantasy and the dynamics of social exclusion faced at home and after arrival" in the destination state generates, in Mai's view, "the search for new rituals accommodating the passage between adolescence and adulthood"; . . . in this context, "'making money' emerges as a key discourse and priority for independent young migrants."[63] State responses to these complex choices reflect how they "see" this elusive population[64] and interpret its entitlements to a range of state services.

The Rights of Undocumented Migrant Adolescents: Political Pronouncements and Practical Realities

In the political domain, there is no consensus on the scope of undocumented children's rights, even at the level of abstract entitlement. Progressives tend to agree with the European Commission's statement that "children are vested with the full range of human rights" and that states are obliged to "[give] all children equal opportunities, regardless of their social background."[65] They also concur with the famous 1982 US Supreme Court ruling in *Plyler v. Doe* that unauthorized migrant children are people "in any ordinary sense of the term" and are therefore entitled to free, state-funded education.[66] But many commentators have challenged this liberal assumption of social inclusiveness, arguing against automatic access to welfare benefits and basic public goods. According to a senior US juvenile immigration officer, unaccompanied child asylum seekers are "runaways or throwaways," petty criminals in the making.[67] Because of their harsh backgrounds, these young migrants are considered to be threatening adults more than children "like our own." In the words of a former Republican congressman, "Denying social services to *them* is something you have to do to stop the magnet effect that all of these combined things have, the health care, free schooling. This is all a magnet that draws people into this country and I'm trying to demagnetize it."[68] In the United States today, there is an audible and persistent grumble among anti-immigration hawks questioning the legitimacy of the social membership of indigent migrants, including, as chapter 2 discusses, child citizens born to unauthorized migrants.[69]

This perspective is not the preserve of US nativism. Many leaders of countries experiencing high levels of irregular migration openly voice their opposition to protections for young migrants, even if unaccompanied and unprotected. According to the former premier of the Canary Islands, Adan Martin Menis, Moroccan migrant children arriving alone on Spanish territory should be treated like adults, detained or returned to their country of origin.[70] In nearby Italy, the authorities have adopted the same approach. On the island of Lampedusa, a destination of much cross-Mediterranean migration referred to earlier in this chapter, rights protection for unaccompanied adolescent migrants is minimal: "Hundreds of children of all ages are detained in inadequate and overcrowded infrastructures in breach of national and international law. They lack medicines, children products and care. Some have already been victims of violence during the increasingly frequent riots between newly arrived migrants and police in the centres."[71] Greece, Hungary, Slovakia—as one moves east through contemporary Europe, the drumbeat of anti-immigrant sentiment increases, magnified by domestic unemployment and economic stringency.[72]

The daily encounter with sizable numbers of would-be entrants combined with an institutional ideology that promotes border security and firm immigration control generate a skeptical, even hostile attitude. The practice of UK border officials toward adolescent migrants illustrates the serious consequences of this stance. In 2004, as many as 43 percent of those applying for asylum as unaccompanied or separated children had their cases "age-disputed"—far from being accorded the benefit of the doubt as international agencies recommend,[73] they were disbelieved when they claimed to be minors. While forensic age evidence was examined, they were treated as adults, detained in harsh conditions so unsuitable for minors that in January 2007, British Home Secretary Jack Reid admitted publicly that the government had been operating an unlawful policy.[74] In this light, the European commissioner for Human Rights was perhaps too generous two months later when he said:

> [D]ecision-making politicians appear sometimes to be *confused* about how to treat migrant children. On the one hand, they state their full support of the idea that children do have rights and also recognize that our aging continent will need migration, not least young migrants. On the other hand a number of them appear not to be able to draw the *necessary conclusions* [about the rights of migrant children] [italics added].[75]

A year and a half after the British home secretary criticized his government's child migrant detention practices, the children's commissioner for England visited Yarl's Wood Immigration Removal Centre, a notorious detention center at the heart of much public criticism of government policy. Equipped with family accommodation facilities, it has detained up to two thousand migrant children a year pending their removal from the United Kingdom. The visit confirmed that, contrary to government policy and the requirements of the Convention on the Rights of the Child, detention was not being used as a ."last-resort measure" or for the "shortest length of time possible." Children who required hospitalization during their detention had twenty-four-hour police surveillance in the hospital. The children's commissioner reported that this intrusive presence had led to a suicide attempt by one teenager; in another case, he observed "4 officers around the bedside of a 13 year-old girl."[76] In May 2010, the UK government announced that Yarl's Wood would no longer be used to detain children.[77] As noted in chapter 6, in February 2012, the UK government paid £2 million to child asylum seekers wrongly placed in detention.[78]

The treatment of migrant children at the US border is, if anything, even more abusive. The Women's Refugee Commission interviewed children held in custody at the US border for periods of up to two weeks.

> The vast majority reported receiving inadequate food and water, being denied blankets despite holding rooms being kept at frigid temperatures and having no access to bathing facilities. Many . . . could not accurately say how long they were in holding cells as the lights were constantly on and there were no windows to the outside. . . . One child described how

the children organized themselves to sleep in shifts because there was not enough room in the holding cell for all of them to lie down. Pregnant girls reported that they did not receive adequate medical attention or food.[79]

Postborder Child-rights Violations by State Officials

Some public employees working away from the border reveal similar attitudes and an inability to draw "the necessary conclusions" about what children need. French police violence against migrants,[80] including children, is widespread. In the words of an unauthorized Romanian fifteen-year-old living rough in Paris: "It was eleven at night. Four police cars came after us. I did eighteen hours of detention. They don't touch your face, they beat you in the ribs, on the legs, the feet, everywhere."[81] Dutch officials have been criticized for evicting undocumented children from reception centers once their residence applications failed, thus putting them "in a situation of outright helplessness and living on the street, according to the European Committee of Social Rights."[82] Even officials working away from immigration and law enforcement, in the welfare departments, may be unsympathetic to migrant children's basic rights claims. An investigation into the circumstances of asylum-seeking children in the United Kingdom produced the following case study:

> "Y" was a 16-year-old boy from Chad. He claimed asylum on a Friday and the Asylum Screening Unit in Croydon told him that they did not believe that he was a child. It referred him to the Refugee Council's Children's Panel in Brixton. The Panel referred him on to the local social services department, who had closed their offices by the time he arrived there. He returned to the Refugee Council to discover that it too was closed. He spent the weekend living on the street.[83]

Access to basic shelter, to subsistence-level welfare payments and in-kind benefits is as fundamental to modern conceptions of rights in general, and children's rights in particular, as protection from physical violence.[84] The same is true for access to such social and economic rights as education and health care, as the Committee on the Rights of the Child has frequently noted.[85] Yet here, too, public officials operate with personal codes of conduct that deny adolescents their basic rights as part of a broader strategy: "Curtailments of social rights . . . have become essential components of restrictive immigration policies. . . . The threat of destitution as a deterrent against irregular migration generates acute tensions within host states between immigration laws and human rights protections."[86] Consider the following Spanish case:

> Sixteen-year-old `Abd al Samad R. has been in Ceuta [an autonomous Spanish city located on the Moroccan coast] for about five years, including two and a half years living at the San Antonio Center. While at San Antonio he was diagnosed as suffering from renal disease, a potentially life-threatening medical condition, and he received medical treatment. Then, in October 2001 he was told to leave San Antonio, apparently for disciplinary infractions. When we interviewed `Abd al Samad on November 8, 2001, he was living with a group of other children and youth in makeshift hovels squeezed between a breakwater and piles of ceramic tiles and other building supplies. He had received no medical treatment since leaving San Antonio, although he was frequently in severe pain. "The pain comes often, when it is cold, or when someone hits me," he said. "I tried to go to the hospital when I was in pain but they wouldn't admit me. *They won't accept you at the hospital unless someone from San Antonio comes with you*. When the pain comes I can't move so who will come to take me to the hospital?"[87]

Without official confirmation of the child's social entitlements, he was excluded from the protections he was entitled to. The acute risks to which this willful, official turning away, combined with the fear of detection as an irregular migrant by state officials, can give rise were noted by the European Court of Human Rights in the case of *Siliadin v. France*. In this case, an unaccompanied child from Togo "unlawfully present in [France] and afraid of being arrested by the police . . . was subjected to forced labour . . . and held in servitude," compelled to carry out housework and child care for fifteen hours a day without holidays; the Court commented: "The applicant was entirely at [her employers'] mercy, since her papers had been confiscated; [she had no freedom of movement or free time. In addition, as she had not been sent to school] . . . the applicant could not hope that her situation would improve." Irregular migration status increases the risk of being discounted as a person with basic rights entitlements. As the Court pointed out, state parties must recognize this serious risk and act "with greater firmness . . . in assessing the infringements of the fundamental values of democratic societies."[88] The challenge is to devise mechanisms for improving a state's firmness in acting in the face of widespread official hostility to the migrants-rights agenda.

A Right to Have Rights: Making Laws versus Making a Difference

If practical approaches to the rights claims of migrant adolescents differ, is there a clearer answer in the law? What does it mean for a rights claim to be asserted by or on behalf of an irregular adolescent migrant?

In a straightforward sense, of course, migrant adolescents irrespective of legal status have human rights: positive international human-rights law encompasses all children within its normative framework. The 1948 Universal Declaration of Human Rights, the founding document of modern international human rights, says as much. "Everyone is entitled to all the rights and freedoms set forth in the Declaration, without distinction of any kind such as . . . social origin . . . birth or other status." And indeed all but one of the thirty articles in the UDHR—Article 16, which articulates the right to marry and found a family—are age neutral. They are addressed to "everyone" (e.g., "Everyone has the right to life, liberty and security of person") or "no one" (e.g., "No one shall be subjected to torture or to cruel, inhuman or degrading treatment or punishment").[89] There is no minimum age requirement, no developmental maturity criterion, no citizenship or even "legality" requirement. Undocumented and noncitizen minors seem to clearly fall within the scope of universal protection as do children of undocumented parents.

However, apart from a single reference in the UDHR to children's special needs for protection within the article on the right to health,[90] there is no acknowledgment of children's distinctive status. The approach of the Universal Declaration is to mandate nondiscrimination, rather than to directly promote substantive equality. Because of this, as with women's rights, societal pressure to promote children's rights led to the formulation of a subject-specific convention. If the UDHR signaled a general though implicit acknowledgment that children's rights were human rights because all children were part of the "human family,"[91] the Convention on the Rights of the Child expanded the normative perspective to promote awareness of children's agency and individuality. If the UDHR laid the foundation for acceptance of all children's human rights vis-à-vis the state, the CRC, albeit cautiously, added to that the scope for the assertion by these children of their human rights in relation to their families,[92] their teachers,[93] their communities.[94]

Formally, this exercise in international norm building and standard setting was spectacularly successful, apparently proving that children's rights, even detailed and expansive articulations of them, were acceptable across continents, cultures, and religions. Indeed, as the Child Rights Information Network notes:

> Since its adoption in 1989 after more than 60 years of advocacy, the United Nations Convention on the Rights of the Child has been ratified more quickly and by more governments [all except Somalia and the United States][95] than any other human rights instrument. . . . This Convention is also the only international human rights treaty that expressly gives non-governmental organisations (NGOs) a role in monitoring its implementation (under Article 45a). . . . The basic premise of the Convention is that children (all human beings below the age of 18) are born with fundamental freedoms and the inherent rights of all human beings.[96]

Even those who are critical of aspects of the twentieth-century children's-rights movement, particularly as a framework for dealing with dispute resolution within families, concede that for relations between minors on the one hand and states on the other, this rights-based approach provides a crucial baseline.[97] International moves have been followed by regional adoption of similar principles, most vigorously in Europe, where children's rights were not only recognized in the European Charter of Fundamental Rights[98] but were identified by the European Commission as one of its main strategic objectives between 2005 and 2009.[99]

Formally, then, there could be no clearer affirmative answer. Children's rights, including those of migrant adolescents, feature centrally in international human-rights law. This leads to other aspects of the international human-rights machinery—regular reports by state parties to the UN Committee on the Rights of the Child; investigations of child-specific human-rights violations by UN special rapporteurs,[100] other internationally appointed experts,[101] and national human rights institutions;[102] the development of regional standards for protecting children;[103] recitation of children's international legal rights in both domestic and international migration and social-welfare policy; the preparation of general comments on detailed aspects of migrant children's rights by the CRC Committee;[104] and the opportunity to challenge state practice through litigation.[105] A 2011 Hungarian Helsinki Committee report demonstrates the use of a clear international standard establishing a minimum acceptable quality of behavior. It documents Hungarian immigration-detention practices—including the detention of two unaccompanied children in clearly inappropriate facilities, despite explicit prohibition by the Aliens Act.[106] The Committee urges the Hungarian government to desist from ever detaining children merely because of their irregular migration status.

But near-universal ratification of the CRC and the invocation of international standards by specially appointed international and regional child-rights officials does not, in and of itself, ensure the treaty's efficacy in protecting children's rights. For one thing, there is a major gap in the pattern of ratification of the Convention: the United States has not ratified it despite having signed it, so the obligation to bring its domestic law into conformity is limited. Moreover, even in states that have ratified it, the situation is less than encouraging. So far, no mechanism has existed for bringing an individual complaint under the Convention against a state.[107] Several states have entered broad reservations exonerating them from applying many of the Convention's articles to noncitizen children.[108] Deficiencies in political will and societal mobilization exacerbate the difficulties facing adolescent migrants. Formulating and passing laws, especially international laws, for all the complications and frustrations inherent in the process, is probably the easiest step in the journey from aspirational principle to practical realization. Indeed some argue that states knowingly sign on to human-rights instruments without serious political commitment to changing their practice, precisely because they realize there is so little accountability and the diplomatic kudos of signing is not offset by corresponding costs for non-enforcement.[109]

Domestic political vicissitudes—headlines about teens drowning as they flee forced recruitment at home or animosity generated by undocumented youth gang-related crime—can turn adolescent migrants into policy footballs, kicked in different directions depending on the prevailing climate. Two aspects of public policy toward adolescent migrants—the use of immigration detention, and the appointment of guardians—illustrate the looming protection gaps that persist and the absence of a consistent understanding of adolescence underpinning implementation of the current legal framework. On both issues, policy makers and enforcement agencies adopt an inconsistent and ambivalent approach, one that undermines human-rights protection and the opportunities adolescent migrants have for moving forward constructively with their lives.

The Enforcement Gap: Detention

The strategic use of detention to deter and manage migrant adolescents illustrates the contradictory approach to adolescence that underpins current migration policy in a majority of destination states. There is no dispute that, as a matter of law, detention of children is to be a last resort, an option used as sparingly and humanely as possible.[110] In practice however this is frequently not the case. Reference has already been made to the use of detention in the United Kingdom for age-disputed migrants resulting in significant rates of adolescent migrant incarceration. Elsewhere, too, measures leading to the detention of young migrants persist, or are reinstated in response to political pressures for immigration enforcement. Consider the Belgian situation. Some years ago, in response to popular criticism, a Belgian minister prohibited the incarceration of undocumented families with children, establishing instead open facilities for holding these families prior to their repatriation. But in May 2011, in a different political climate, this approach was turned on its head and permission to detain undocumented families, including children (in the same closed detention facilities that had been criticized earlier) was reinstated.[111] The UN Special Rapporteur on the Human Rights of Migrants has complained that

> accompanied and unaccompanied children are often detained in punitive conditions, deprived of the care, protection and rights to which they are entitled under the CRC and other international human rights norms, including the right to education, physical and mental health, privacy, information, and rest and leisure, among others.[112]

But governments battling xenophobic political pressures, regularly resort to established detention facilities to deter and contain migrants lacking legal status, including children.

The Enforcement Gap: Guardianship

The failure to promptly appoint guardians or legal representatives for unaccompanied minors also exemplifies the absence of a coherent approach to adolescent migrants. The crucial role of a guardian for unaccompanied minors was first noted in chapter 4, in relation to Tara, the pencil-thin six-year-old from India sold into domestic servitude by her parents. But it is also relevant to the discussion of incarceration since the absence of vigorous legal advocacy contributes in large part to the persistence of detention as a viable government strategy for the containment of adolescent migrants. As I noted in chapter 6, when discussing the circumstances of asylum-seeking children, the Committee on the Rights of the Child has unambiguously urged states to provide comprehensive guardianship and effective legal representation to unaccompanied or separated child migrants.[113] The EU Resolution on unaccompanied child migrants also requires member states to provide them with necessary representation as soon as possible.[114] The reality, however, does not match these standards.

In the United States, where the CRC treaty has not been ratified, neither publicly funded legal representation nor access to guardianship or any form of individualized and consistent mentorship exists as a matter of entitlement.[115] The celebrated and photogenic six-year-old Cuban survivor Elian Gonzalez lacked his own legal representation or guardianship,[116] despite the evident need for an independent, child-focused approach given the vigorous and politically partisan legal sparring occurring between interested adult parties with divergent views of his best interests. In the United Kingdom, where the CRC has been ratified and a broad reservation to curtail the rights of migrant children was recently withdrawn,[117] the situation is somewhat better: unprotected adolescents are entitled to publicly funded legal representation. But no system of guardianship exists in the United Kingdom, and, as the following vignette illustrates, access to representation is neither prompt nor guaranteed:

A young age-disputed girl from Guinea interviewed in 2005 found herself alone and unaccompanied in the United Kingdom. Her local authority refused to provide her with welfare support until she produced medical confirmation of her age to convince the immigration authorities that she was a minor. She reflected: "Social services treated me like a dog . . . because the Home Office said I was not under 18. They just told me to go away. I was so sad. *They need to treat people as humans* and give them food and shelter."[118] This girl was one of an estimated 100,000 unprotected migrant children living in Europe[119] facing daily hardships in the struggle to survive. Her problems are shared across the continent, as the following excerpt illustrates:

> Amnesty International spoke to "John" who arrived in Italy as an unaccompanied minor fleeing a life as a child soldier. . . . After arriving on

> Lampedusa, he was taken to an adult detention centre and ordered to get undressed for a body check. He told them that he was only 16 years old, yet he was detained at the Lampedusa centre for 2 days where he slept in a room with 6 adult men. He was later transferred to another centre in southern Italy where he had to share a room with 12 adults for a month. "John" eventually found accommodation in a reception centre for minors. However, *5 months after his arrival in Italy*, a guardian had still not been appointed to represent him.[120]

The absence of automatic access to effective guardianship and legal representation for unaccompanied young migrants neutralizes their legal entitlement to special treatment and effectively obliterates social acknowledgment of their rights. The absence of support fixes these minors in a position of radical "otherness," a deracination from the "normal" structures of a society designed to care for and protect vulnerable children. The absence of a mechanism for accessing legal protection can even threaten one's basic claim to humanity and return one to the "nakedness of being human," a nakedness no longer abstract but frighteningly concrete. We are sadly familiar with this scenario in the refugee camps in Kenya, the internal displaced-persons camps in Darfur, the HIV/AIDS orphanages in Ethiopia. But the anecdotes just cited took place in the heart of Europe. Earlier chapters have noted similar incidents facing unaccompanied asylum-seeking children in the United States. The enforced social nakedness of migrant children in advanced democracies reveals the deep fissures in "the right to have rights."

The Impact of Human Rights Treaties on Enforcement of Rights

Global mobility and desperation are removing the comfortable distance of geographical separation, leaving the First World with the challenge of translating adolescents' rights into human rights on our own doorsteps.[121] Paraphrasing Arendt, we might want to argue that the "heart of darkness" representing Europe's imperial plunder of Africa has now struck home, revealing the brutal hand of the imperial state toward noncitizens within its own borders.[122] For migrant adolescents, the right to rights has frayed at the margins. Was Hannah Arendt right to be deeply pessimistic about the possibility of international protection (despite her moral cosmopolitanism)?[123] What is the point of international rights treaties for migrant adolescents if translation into practice is so flawed?

Proving the impact of treaty making and monitoring on rights enforcement is not easy. Nor is it as clear as sometimes assumed that this international legislative exercise is unquestionably a good mechanism for increasing the political will to secure change. As a scholar pertinently reflected: "What if claims made in the name of universal rights are not the best way to protect people?"[124] The amount of time spent on treaty ratification and legal strategies might be a diversion from more concrete and specific approaches to rights enforcement. Assessing the relative impact of such strategies is a complex matter. Expert opinion on the topic is divided between the radical skeptics who argue that "the costs and benefits of [treaty ratification] are very small,"[125] and the human-rights triumphalists who see treaty ratification as a crucial piece of rights enforcement. Often the different assessments reflect divergent analytic methodologies, with qualitative studies portraying a more optimistic account of the impact of human rights advocacy than quantitative measures.[126] A systematic survey of the ratification of human-rights conventions and state practice following it, including the CRC, concludes that "once made, formal commitments to treaties can have *noticeably positive consequences*. . . . Treaties signal a seriousness of intent that is difficult to replicate in other ways. They reflect politics, but they also shape political behavior, setting the stage for new political alliances, empowering new political actors, and heightening public scrutiny."[127]

What are the "noticeably positive consequences" for migrant adolescents? A detailed look at several critical policies, procedures, and practices affecting the basic rights of these young people, reveals inconsistencies and differences between jurisdictions. Treaty compliance varies widely across different political and legal systems in relation to cardinal human-rights principles such as the primacy of the adolescent's "best interests"[128] and the obligation to accord children the benefit of the doubt.[129] Apart from the use of detention and the appointment of guardians, two other areas of policy that impinge on decision making regarding migrant adolescents—age determination and the immigration interviewing procedure—reflect this divergent state practice. They also signal lack of consistency in views about the nature of adolescence itself.

Treaty Impact: Age Determination and the Rights of the Child

An effective, reliable, and consistent mechanism for ascertaining the age of an applicant is clearly a necessary precedent for protecting the rights of children, including minor adolescents; without it minority-specific protections will not reach their intended recipients. Yet despite years of advocacy, no such mechanism is uniformly in place. Previous chapters have discussed this issue as it relates to children seeking to exercise rights to family reunification and children applying for asylum. But the procedure for determining age has a broader relevance to the way in which a child is processed at the port of entry or thereafter. In the United States, the Netherlands, and Australia, for example, determining whether a migrant applicant is under eighteen, and therefore entitled to child-specific procedures, is conducted by reliance on mechanistically implemented physical tests—dental, wrist, or clavicle X-rays or rule-of-thumb personal assessments. Generally, these tests yield results that ignore the physical variability of children from different social, economic, and ethnic backgrounds.[130] By contrast, in the United Kingdom, where the use of age assessment is widespread (1,400 individuals were "age-disputed" in 2008),[131] a holistic test has been developed (though not yet implemented), as a result of persistent advocacy on the topic.[132] This is an example of a rights-respecting approach, approved by the courts,[133] which takes the "best interests" of the minor and his or her own views into account.[134] The holistic test creates a psychologically and socially nuanced tool for assessing age to complement the raw indicators of physical development.

Decision makers of necessity function in relation to the social constructs embedded in their society. Since childhood is one such construct, decision makers must unpack such societal elements to effectively map the category and its relationship to chronological age onto subjects with a wide range of nutritional and cultural backgrounds, appearances and styles of behavior. The previous chapter made reference to the statement by the UK Royal College of Paediatricians and Child Health that "age determination is extremely difficult to do with certainty . . . [It] is an inexact science and the margin of error can sometimes be a much as 5 years either side; . . . estimates of a child's physical age from his or her dental development are [only] accurate to within + or –2 years for 95% of the population."[135] As just noted, a climate of disbelief toward the claims of adolescents and a parochial conception of adolescence as late childhood have resulted in significant numbers of migrant adolescents being exposed to prolonged periods in detention while their age claims are validated. Age disputes do not only have an impact on practical case outcomes, they can affect the adolescent's education placement, the type of accommodation provided, and more generally the whole way in which a young migrant experiences the official immigration process.

Disbelieving an adolescent's description of age can negatively impact his or her emotional well-being overall quite significantly.[136]

Treaty Impact: Child-friendly Enforcement Procedures

A second set of procedures confirms the claim that treaty obligations toward adolescent minors are not consistently upheld and that widespread CRC ratification has not generated, in this policy area, "noticeably positive consequences." The merits of different strategies for eliciting information from migrant adolescents regarding their claims for regularization of their status are sharply contested. As a legal advisory-services representative in the United Kingdom said: "Migrant children who aren't claiming asylum, I find much more confusing and you've obviously got to address the immigration issue but it's harder to work out on what basis you can regularize their status."[137] It is clear that adversarial interrogations, such as those currently conducted in the United States and Australia for undocumented children, run counter to the child's best interests, particularly where these interrogations take place in alienating settings such as formal courtrooms or detention centers. But the converse—the elimination of direct questioning of the adolescent—is not self-evidently more rights-protective. States such as Canada and the United Kingdom refrain from any direct questioning of children by immigration authorities. Instead they rely on written submissions by legal representatives, at best the product of multiple encounters and child-friendly interviews between the adolescent and his or her legal representative. This procedure may protect children from the adversarial and inappropriate cross-examination so frequently used in the United States. But it may compromise children's ability to convey their view of relevant circumstances, and they may interfere with the CRC principle that "the child . . . capable of forming his or her own views [should have] the right to express those views freely in all matters affecting the child."[138]

In the migration context, how should this principle be construed? Recent developments in participatory child rights, which emphasize the importance of adolescent agency and the positive impact on outcomes of direct child engagement,[139] may lead to different conclusions from the more protective approach, which relies on the substitution of a professional adult's voice for that of the minor. The dramatic effect of first-person narratives by some adolescents illustrates the danger of eliminating direct oral testimony.[140] A compromise suggested by some is the institution of child-friendly courts, where direct testimony is presented but some of the negative impacts of the adversarial procedure are tempered. However, attempts to sustain a non-threatening court environment would be difficult in the face of prevailing hostility toward adolescent migrants.[141] No sustained debate on the merits of these differing approaches has taken place within the advocacy or policy community. Translating the human rights of a hugely diverse and complex cohort of adolescents into policy requires not a mechanistic rolling out of pre-established entitlements but an evolving tool kit of options and specifically tailored strategies for change. Engagement with these rights challenges is in its infancy.

Challenging Rightlessness: Migrant Adolescents and the Space of Exception

Principles of international human-rights law have been incorporated into policies regarding migrant adolescents—the elaboration of holistic age-determination procedures or the principle that unaccompanied child migrants need appointed guardians—but as we have seen, predictable and uniform implementation has not followed. The weakness of a human-rights regime in the absence of well-resourced legal advocacy and vigilant and proactive civil society is particularly apparent when the target of that regime is a constituency that has little access to political leverage or public visibility.

> North African children trying to escape from the child immigration detention in Spain report being hit by the staff when caught: A thirteen-year-old Moroccan boy told Human Rights Watch: "One time we escaped, three of us, when a boy took a piece of metal and broke the door of the punishment room. One of the older boys caught us and hit us. They took us and put us in another room and locked the door and then one of the educators came and hit us with a baton like the police use. He hit me on the head and the face and leg."[142]

These arbitrary and punitive processes are, apparently, beyond the reach of domestic structures of accountability or the international oversight of monitoring bodies such as the UN Committee on the Rights of the Child. The situation recalls Giorgio Agamben's provocative analogy between the treatment of refugees in camps and the archetypal experience of encampment, the concentration camp:

> The paradoxical status of the camp as a space of exception must be considered. The camp is a piece of land placed outside the normal juridical order but it is nevertheless not simply an external space. . . . The camp is . . . the structure in which the state of exception—the possibility of deciding on which founds sovereign power—is realized normally.[143]

This is the extreme situation of rightlessness—the normalizing of an exceptional state. Without a state to call their own or advocates watching out for them, detained adolescent migrants can come to occupy such a liminal space at once inside and outside the state.

Rights Enforcement through Litigation

If human rights in general, and children's rights in particular, are essentially about redistributing political justice and socioeconomic resources in favor of the disadvantaged, then the most effective and visible positive outcome is that in which a treaty gives individuals or their representatives the right to challenge state failure to implement the right by bringing a case before a court. The CRC does not yet afford this opportunity,[144] but other human rights treaties do, and in the process of using them, advocates can and do make reference to the children's-rights principles of the CRC. The vast majority of migrant adolescents have no access to effective legal representation. That is what the "normalized state of exception" is—a space routinely outside the reach of the law. However, human-rights instruments wielded effectively in the courts have benefited some minors, but not, so far, adolescents. As chapter 6 noted, court challenges on behalf of youth fleeing gang recruitment or violence have been unsuccessful. Young children, however, have in some cases succeeded in asserting, if only retrospectively, their right to have rights. The following two cases, both concerning children under ten, illustrate this point.

The much-discussed case of *Tabitha Kaniki Mitunga*, a citizen of the Democratic Republic of Congo (DRC), who found herself alone in Belgium, is emblematic. One of the many thousands of "left-behind" children[145]—her mother fled as a refugee after Tabitha's father had been killed—Tabitha's ordeal illustrates the effect of rightlessness on migrant children in the absence of a safety net of rights-respecting state procedures. Without the automatic appointment of a guardian to represent Tabitha's legal rights, Belgium, the seat of the capital of the European Union, functioned as a state of exception, beyond the pale of the law. Since there are approximately 100,000 such unprotected migrant children in Europe at present, the likelihood that others are exposed to comparable treatment is high. Because Tabitha had a competent and vigilant mother, her case came to light and eventually found its way to Europe's highest human-rights court. In October 2006, the European Court of Human Rights ruled that Tabitha's experience at the hands of the Belgian authorities amounted to "inhuman treatment," a violation of Article 3 of the European Convention on Human Rights.[146] Breaking with the European Court of Human Rights' customary allocation of low financial awards, the court awarded Tabitha and her mother a total of €35,000 ($44,905) beyond reimbursement of their significant legal costs.

Tabitha was five at the time of the incidents described. Like about eight thousand other undocumented migrants per year, she was detained in Belgium's notorious no-man's-land detention facilities for several months. Belgian law allows undocumented migrants to be detained for five months without charge or other legal procedures, and each time the migrant resists removal or deportation, the clock is reset. As a result, many migrants face long periods in this legal state of exception. Among them are a growing number of children, including unaccompanied minors, of whom 1,800 or more arrive in Belgium each year.[147] The facts in Tabitha's case were straightforward. She had been living in the DRC with relatives while her mother sought asylum in Canada. Once her mother was able to legally bring Tabitha to join her, she asked her brother, a Dutch national living in the Netherlands, to collect the child. However, at Brussels airport, despite her age, Tabitha was separated from her Dutch uncle. The five-year-old was detained for two months without any known caregiver in the remand center near the airport, while her frantic mother tried to secure her release and lawyers applied (without receiving any response from the authorities) for her to be placed in the care of foster parents. The child was deported and flown back to the DRC, without any investigation into the suitability of arrangements for receiving her. No guardian was appointed but instead a flight attendant was assigned to look after her. A DRC official took charge of the child after she had waited for six hours at the Kinshasa airport following her long flight from Amsterdam.

Eventually the case was heard by the European Court of Human Rights. The justices commented on the "*vide juridique*" or legal vacuum in which the Belgian authorities' action had placed Tabitha. They criticized the prolonged and abusive detention and found Belgium in violation of several articles of the European Convention on Human Rights.[148] As a result of this case, changes have been made to Belgian law prohibiting the detention of unaccompanied child migrants and requiring the appointment of a guardian in each case.[149] Tabitha's experience propelled Belgium from one of the least to one of the most rights-respecting EU states for migrant children.

The case illustrates the powerful reach of the arm of the law, while at the same time highlighting its partial impact. Once the state of exception was subjected to the full scrutiny of the legal mainstream, previously binding obligations were translated into new legal provisions to guarantee their implementation. The obligations on their own had proved toothless. Many children and adolescents detained in harsh and punitive conditions on the Canary Islands,[150] on the island of Lampedusa,[151] in Malta and Cyprus, and summarily returned to their home countries without any "best interest" assessment, would benefit from the implementation of this judgment on their behalf. There are other court decisions relevant to their circumstances too. For example, in a 2002 judgment, the European Court of Human Rights held:

> Where treatment humiliates or debases an individual showing lack of respect for, or diminishing, his or her human dignity or arouses feelings of fear, anguish or inferiority capable of breaking an individual's moral and physical resistance, it may be characterised as degrading and may fall within the prohibition of Article 3. The suffering which flows from naturally occurring illness, physical or mental, may be covered by Article 3, where it is, or risks being, exacerbated by treatment, whether from conditions of detention, expulsion or other measures, for which the authorities can be held responsible.[152]

This case law provides powerful, as yet underutilized, tools to the human-rights-advocacy community.

Social and Economic Rights: To Have and Not to Have

International and widely enacted domestic laws entitle migrant adolescents to protection from torture and from cruel, inhuman, or degrading treatment or punishment, along with a series of other civil and political harms. The preceding sections have, however, demonstrated that these protections are often not enforceable in practice. Adolescents, including undocumented migrant adolescents, are also entitled to several fundamental economic and social rights, again both as a matter of international and domestic law.[153]

The distribution of entitlements and implementation of these rights is still more uneven than for civil and political rights. There are two reasons for this. First, there is extensive divergence in state policy—as we will see, the apparently simple mandates of international human-rights law have been translated differently across states, even within the relatively homogenous European Union. Second, attention to the social and economic lacunae in support of unaccompanied migrant children and adolescents is relatively recent. As the numbers of moving children have grown, their length of residence as independent or unaccompanied child migrants has increased and the removal pressures from destination states have escalated, so their access to effective social and economic protection has started to become a central concern. The possibility of survival, and the minimum threshold considered acceptable for that survival, is gradually becoming an object of public discussion and scrutiny.

Discriminatory attitudes map onto political pressures to reduce migrant adolescents' access to basic protections in different ways—earlier in this chapter, I contrasted the conduct of France and Germany toward access to health care for adolescent migrants. This point can be expanded. In some countries, such as Denmark, legislators have restricted migrant children's legal entitlement to health care, but in practice, health-care providers have ignored these obstacles and granted the treatment required.[154] More common is the converse situation, where relatively generous legal entitlements are whittled away by practical requirements and budget shortfalls. In December 2007, the UK government announced plans to pilot a new scheme for adolescents in state custody allowing them to remain in foster care until twenty-one. At the same time, however, the government introduced measures to place unaccompanied minors in more independent-living arrangements from the age of sixteen. As a (then) House of Lords member remarked: "Sadly, the proposition appears to have more to do with preparing the child for removal than with meeting the young person's needs."[155] A UNICEF study confirmed that social-services departments frequently fail to meet these young people's needs: "Evidence suggested . . . children being looked after by [social services] . . . may . . . miss out on the specialist care and immigration advice they require."[156]

As a result of the failure of state services, there is growing and alarming evidence, referred to in chapter 4, of adolescents trafficked to work under exploitative conditions[157] and who have no alternative but to continue begging or prostituting themselves on the streets of Western cities and sleeping rough, without access to education, shelter, or adequate health care.[158] One response to this has been to call for vigorous removal programs, to ensure that these unprotected adolescents are promptly returned to their "homes." An immigration-control agenda dovetails with a child-protection concern—as pointed out earlier in this chapter, removing undocumented young migrants, it is claimed, furthers the adolescents' best interests by reuniting them with their families and familiar communities. But the desperation of many of these young people to leave their home countries and indigent families, and to try for a better life with the possibility of education or employment elsewhere, complicates the plausibility of this convenient official policy. Growing evidence of the crisis in skill training and employment opportunity for youths should lead immigration and welfare officials repatriating adolescent migrants to question their assumptions and engage in individualized, evidence-based assessments of best interest. As Arendt remarked with prescience half a century ago: "Nonrecognition of statelessness always means repatriation, i.e. deportation to a country of origin."[159] But what options for realizing "best interests" exist in the country of origin? A first-person account of the serious push factors driving a fifteen-year-old Romanian to leave home answers this question:

> I was the youngest of all my brothers. I did nothing there. . . . At ten, I was all alone. My brothers, they had all left, traveled to Germany, Austria, Italy. . . . I was all alone. I did nothing. So I said: "I have nothing here. . . ." My father and mother, what could they say to me? My father, he has a farm. I had to work with him. Are you mad? . . . My father came to me from time to time, slapped me around the head. "Wait. Leave me alone! I'm going." That's how it started. "I'm leaving home."[160]

The reality of poverty, child abuse, and lack of opportunities reinforces the determination to exit, to make a bid for adventure, to "put some air in your head,"[161] even if the journey is known to be arduous, the risks great, and the guarantees of success minimal.

> Every day in the port of Tangiers, at any time of the day or night, a fierce battle takes place; like a flock of birds, dozens of children try to squeeze into a trailer, a container or some other vehicle, with the sole objective of reaching Europe. The police pursue them relentlessly, and beat them up if they catch them. . . . They persist, constant, another time. . . . Some have made the return journey several times.[162]

Some have called this growing flow of child and teenage exiles, this flight from hopelessness on the part of *ados*,[163] a "third wave" of contemporary migration, following the mid-twentieth-century migration led by single men and the later pattern of migration driven in part by the mass movement of single female workers.[164]

The decision to leave home in search of opportunity and livelihood complicates the child-protection challenge facing law enforcement and welfare agencies. As noted at the start of this chapter, there is no satisfactory consensus on the appropriate balance between a welfare-driven notion of "the best interests of the child" and an adolescent agency-driven notion of "autonomy and independence." Indeed, as Sigona and Hughes point out, undocumented child migrants often do not exist as bureaucratic subjects of concern to state entities in their own right. Rather they encounter public services, haphazardly, through a range of "proxy routes," as children of domestic-violence victims or failed asylum seekers, or because of "policy rationales" that relate to their circumstances (addressing poverty among street children, reducing infant mortality).[165]

Because their migration is fueled by a desire to work, large numbers of adolescents placed in open child-welfare shelters or institutions leave shortly after their placement. Containment in a children's home or a protection facility is not part of the navigational strategy[166] the adolescent envisages to realize his or her goals. The Caritas reception center for migrant youth in Rome, for example, reported in 2005 that about 80 percent of accommodated minors left without authorization.[167] This suggests that the "protection" being offered does not cater to the adolescents' needs and wishes, perhaps because it is infantilizing, non-income-generating, patronizing, and often punitive. Some state authorities, in the United States and Belgium,[168] for example, have resorted to locked shelters to prevent the escape of unauthorized young migrants. This detention is also justified by a concern to protect the minors from traffickers or other sources of exploitation. However, detention for protection is a suspect approach, discredited in most situations: victims of domestic abuse are not incarcerated for their protection, nor are children at risk of abduction. On the other hand, those such as the Italian and Spanish authorities, who do not detain unauthorized child migrants, acknowledge that a best-interest calculation might justify more stringent supervision measures as large proportions of at-risk children, many suspected to have been trafficked, disappear from state provision within days of being placed.[169]

Mai argues that standard approaches to adolescent migrants, which highlight the fact of separation from parents and deviance ("errance") unhelpfully pathologize the adolescents' behavior rather than supporting and strengthening their capacity for independent agency. As a result of this failure to provide effective support, these young people frequently end up in the most exploited occupations, as agricultural laborers, factory hands, or, when other options are not available, prostitutes or petty criminals. To use Mae Ngai's phrase, they constitute an imported "proletariat outside the polity."[170] Save the Children Italy describe the recruitment conditions of some of these adolescents:

> Adolescent and post-adolescent males of Maghreb and sub-Saharan origin employed in the agricultural sector for primarily seasonal work, particularly in Puglia, Calabria and Sicily. Normally the employer uses recruiters (called corporals) to make daily contact with the workers (including the minors) for work in the black economy at wages far below union rates and without required security guarantees. In addition, the "corporal" normally supervises the conduct of work, using extreme verbal insults which undermine the workers' dignity to accelerate the pace of work as much as possible (preventing breaks or pauses, even in very adverse weather conditions) and demands from each worker a percentage of daily earnings. The contact between the recruiter and the minor takes place in public places where the workers gather every morning waiting for the "corporal," who only offers work on a daily basis.[171]

The assessment of "best interest" raises a range of considerations, into which the views of the adolescent him- or herself need to be factored. Skill development and rights-protective work opportunities are appropriate strategies for some; supervised return home opportunities for others; and social welfare, educational, and counseling support services for yet others. Blanket policies prescribing a one-size-fits all solution are not more appropriate for this population than they would be for any diverse and complex group of nonmigrant children and young people. Critical variables may not be susceptible to regulation. For example, even if it were possible for destination states to establish that repatriation of an adolescent would be in his or her best interests, the country of origin may pose obstacles to this course of action. Senegal, for example, has recently refused to accept the return of some of its irregular minor migrants because lack of birth registration and adequate documentation make it impossible for the Senegalese authorities to confidently reinsert them with their families.[172]

It is indisputable that all children and young people require access to some fundamental economic and social rights. Among these obligatory rights, two are key for migrant adolescents, already touched on earlier in this chapter: nondiscriminatory access to education, and recognition of everyone's right to "the enjoyment of the highest attainable standard of physical and mental health."[173] I conclude with a closer look at the way in which some states have interpreted their obligations to realize these two critical sets of human rights.

A Comparative Education Snapshot

As a matter of widely respected international law, primary education is required to be compulsory and freely available to all children irrespective of status, and states are encouraged to make secondary education accessible to all too.[174] Most states have established comprehensive entitlements for migrant children and adolescents that match those of the domestic child population and mirror the obligations set out in international law.[175] This is certainly true in the European Union, where member states are signatories to the CRC. In Italy, for example, all migrant minors, whether unauthorized or not, enjoy the same legal right/obligation to attend compulsory education as the domestic population.[176] Indeed regular school attendance is one of the requirements undocumented children have to comply with to regularize their status.[177] This is also the case in Spain, France, the United Kingdom, Belgium, and Germany. A PICUM survey of nine EU member states found that some of the states (Belgium, Italy, the Netherlands) had explicit constitutional protection for the right to education all children, irrespective of their status, whereas other states (France, Spain, Poland, United

Kingdom) had an implicit protection of this right for all; a third group (Hungary and Malta) guaranteed the right to education only for migrant children with a regular resident permit.[178]

The theory however is not always mirrored by the reality on the ground. In practice, migrant adolescents' liminal legal status trumps the universality of the right to education in ways that may be subtle and inconspicuous. Whereas many undocumented children do attend state schools and report a sense of well-being and security that comes from the opportunity to enjoy a "normal" child-centered environment, distinctions based on their irregular migration status impinge with depressing regularity. Lack of eligibility for free school meals or for facilities made available to other children outside of the compulsory school-day schedule can painfully mark a sense of otherness, despite the satisfaction of being part of the school system.[179] The absence of identification documents, particularly proof of residence in the school district, presents a considerable hurdle for many, at times compounded by hostile local officials exploiting their discretion to exclude insufficiently documented applicants from the classroom. I have already remarked on the anxiety experienced by irregular adolescents concerned about the risks of deportation that might arise from contact with government bodies. Parents of course feel this at least as powerfully. Many prefer to keep their children out of school than risk interactions with officialdom that can result in detection and deportation of the family as a whole.

Consider the situation that arose during 2006 in France. Then–Interior Minister Sarkozy, intent on keeping his promise to deport 25,000 migrants a year, sent police into French schools to pick up undocumented parents collecting their children. Some particularly egregious reported incidents included virtual hostage-taking of children straight from school: "The police arrived in schools, saying your parents are looking for you, they are at the police station. So, even though this wasn't true . . . they took away the children" holding then hostage to lure the parents. This practice recalls the similar tactic described in chapter 1, where US authorities holding undocumented children in detention facilities, refuse to release them into the custody of legally resident relatives if undocumented parents are known to be in the country, in order to use the children as bait for arresting the adults.[180] In France, eventually, societal protests and a vibrant advocacy movement, Education Without Borders (Réseau Éducation Sans

Frontières) led to discontinuance of this harassment, but fears of detection linked to sending children to school persisted.[181] For those undocumented adolescents who do make it through the school system, lack of identification documents can prevent them from securing a diploma or other proof of scholastic achievement at the end of their course of study.[182]

Precarious living and economic situations also disproportionately impact undocumented or irregular migrant children and adolescents, in some cases making it impossible for families to buy necessary materials and textbooks. As a researcher with Save the Children Italy noted: "Undocumented children can attend school, but they have no right to transportation, books, or lunch, which are all a series of measures that make access to education difficult for those who are already poor." In other cases, students are excluded from school because their parents are not available to register them: "The objection is that you cannot register the child because you are not the parent. There are many children who are perfectly legally in the care of their uncles or aunts; as the law states, it is the adult responsible for the child, whether they are the child's parent or not, who must take responsibility for their school registration."[183]

Exclusion from school produces hazards over and beyond a deficient education. As shown in chapter 4, many of these young migrants become victims of trafficking, some in conditions of absolute servitude, where their movements are closely monitored and controlled by their exploiters. Yet others, destitute and living on the streets, have little access to mainstream structures. A young Albanian undocumented migrant in France describes how this happens:

> The best thing is school. Yes, school. In Tirana, I did well in school, I spoke Italian, English, Albanian. I also speak a bit of Turkish. I had good grades. Then, because of my family problems—I am a bit sensitive, I can't stand misery—I was forced to leave home. I never imagined I'd end up in France, because already in school French was difficult and I didn't like it. . . . Then I said to myself, this is my fate, you've got to make the best of it and move on. When my family problems started—my mother had problems with my father—I couldn't go to school. I was good but I just couldn't go to school at all. If you don't go to school, you just hang around in the street; if you hang around without money, you end up stealing, and you'll be picked up and land in trouble. No one wants to steal, I just

> decided to leave. I didn't speak a word of French when I arrived . . . no papers; it'll be a stroke of luck if I am allowed to stay.[184]

So, despite the universal right to education, many adolescents are excluded from its benefits because of familial, social, and economic factors.[185] The situation in Poland is illustrative. Though noncitizen children have the right to education, and schooling is compulsory until eighteen, children of asylum seekers have to pass Polish language tests, and undocumented children have to pay fees before being enrolled in school.[186] In the United Kingdom, undocumented adolescents find themselves excluded for other reasons. According to one NGO worker, about two thousand children in London did not have a school placement. "Schools were avoiding them, because they didn't want to admit students who might have a negative impact on their test-score statistics."[187] Official skepticism about the ages of undocumented children and unsatisfactory procedures for age determination also complicate access to school: "Those who are assessed as being under 16 can usually access school education, while those who are over 16 will only be able to access English for speakers of other languages classes."[188]

Because the United States has not ratified the International Covenant on Economic, Social and Cultural Rights (ICESCR) or the CRC, international law does not impose obligations on the US government as it does on European and other developed states regarding core social and economic rights. Nevertheless, as a result of the 1982 *Plyler* case referenced above,[189] all children in the United States, whatever their immigration status, are entitled to state-funded public education for primary and secondary schooling. In a judgment with considerable contemporary relevance, Justice Brennan of the US Supreme Court commented:

> It is difficult to understand precisely what the State hopes to achieve by promoting the creation of a perpetuation of a subclass of illiterates within our boundaries, surely adding to the problems and costs of unemployment, welfare, and crime. It is thus clear that whatever savings might be achieved by denying these children an education, they are wholly insubstantial in light of the costs involved to these children, the State, and the Nation.[190]

Interestingly the court also argued that "charging tuition to undocumented children constitutes a ludicrously ineffectual attempt to stem the tide of illegal immigration."[191] Despite a virulent resurgence of nativism in the United States, and a dramatic increase in the population of undocumented migrants (over 11 million[192] of which over 1 million are under eighteen,[193] with approximately 6,000 unaccompanied migrant children apprehended while entering the United States each year[194]), it appears that a majority of the US population still support inclusive education policies.[195]

However, as in Europe, the legal right to participate in school can come under practical threat when immigration-enforcement measures undermine the undocumented community's confidence that their children really will be safe in school. During the administration of President George W. Bush, an escalation of workplace raids and arrests (rising to over 5,000 in 2007)[196] was reported to have led to declining school attendance in several school districts in North Carolina and Ohio.[197] Documentary requirements can also complicate access to school for migrant populations who cannot satisfactorily prove residence within the school district. Following reports that schools were checking children's immigration status before enrolling them, the New York Civil Liberties Union conducted a survey in May 2011 and found that 139 New York districts (20 percent) were "requiring children's immigration papers as a prerequisite to enrollment, or asking parents for information that only lawful immigrants could provide."[198] Communities close to the border are particularly affected. Carla Gomez, a woman with three children living with her sister-in-law in a Texas school district after her husband was deported, was notified that "her children would be dropped from enrollments if she couldn't provide proof of residency." Since all the acceptable official documents, such as utility bills or rent receipts were in her sister's name, Gomez concluded that she might be forced to homeschool her children.[199] Yet educational access is critical for adolescents living in a state of "suspended illegality, not only as a pedagogic resource, but as . . . an experience of inclusion atypical of undocumented . . . life."[200]

The Challenge of Securing Health Care

All adolescents irrespective of immigration status are entitled to health care on a par with the domestic population, just as they are to primary education.[201] In practice, irregular migrants experience acute difficulties in accessing these basic rights, difficulties that exacerbate what is often a precarious health picture. The ICESCR notes that everyone has a right to enjoy "the highest attainable standard of physical and mental health,"[202] though the Covenant only *obligates* states to provide *emergency* health care to all. Many now interpret the Covenant's provisions more broadly to include health obligations that go beyond emergency care. Some migration-destination states provide not only emergency, but also *necessary* and in some cases even *comprehensive* health care to child migrants irrespective of status. Within Europe are a spectrum of approaches. Spain and Italy, as a matter of law, provide free health care for all within the same comprehensive health care system; France, Belgium, and the Netherlands administer separate systems for migrants, but envisage free access for some types of health-care needs; the United Kingdom and Portugal have more restrictive systems: undocumented children's right to health care depends on a decision about whether the care is "essential," which is at the discretion of the general practitioner. Hungary and Germany allow free health care only in limited cases and, as mentioned earlier in this chapter, until recently have required health-care providers to inform on users if they have an irregular migration status.

Despite this generally enabling normative framework, and as described in the previous paragraph, even in countries where access to health care is protected by law, adolescent migrants encounter severe obstacles to medical treatment. Sometimes the problem arises from the way in which official discretion is exercised. There are reports, for example, of adolescents living outside shelters or reception centers in Spain who have been denied treatment because they are not in possession of documents and are not accompanied by official caretakers.[203] In Italy, children over six without a residence permit are not entitled to anything except emergency health care and in-patient care for contagious diseases. According to Médecins du Monde: "In some regions like Lombardia, children have to pay . . . because pediatricians are wrongly categorized as secondary health care."[204] In the United Kingdom, secondary health care is only available to migrants, including child and adolescent migrants, who can demonstrate that they have lived in the country lawfully for a year.[205] In the United States, too, undocumented child and adolescent migrants are eligible for emergency care but they are not otherwise eligible for publicly funded health services. In the state of California alone, there were an estimated 136,000 undocumented minors without health insurance prior to the introduction of compulsory health insurance following passage of the Obama administration's

Affordable Health Care Act.[206] In the Netherlands, restrictive interpretations of what constitutes the "necessary care" that is guaranteed by law have prevented access for some adolescent migrants. In other cases, proof of legal identity is the hurdle. In France, even emergency medical access depends on documentary proof of eligibility. Moreover, NGOs report significant regional disparities in the provision of health care; in the major cities and where NGO organization is strong, access is easier and standards are higher than in more rural areas.

Egregious cases occasionally hit the headlines. The British government shocked observers by ordering the removal of an unaccompanied three-year-old child with a serious kidney disorder while her mother was in immigration detention, a case reminiscent of the much criticized Tabitha episode discussed earlier. The child in question, a US citizen, was informed that as an alien she was ineligible for non-emergency medical treatment. Only after an injunction prohibiting removal was secured from the European Court of Human Rights was the child's removal put on hold, pending an investigation of the case.[207] This child was lucky; competent and vigorous lawyers took her case to the highest European human-rights tribunal to stay the government's hand. Other migrant children with serious health needs and risks are less fortunate. As the above examples demonstrate, many countries limit health-care provision for irregular child and adolescent migrants to emergency or urgent care. And yet irregular migrants, including adolescents, are likely to encounter significant physical and mental-health stressors in the course of their complex life journeys, stressors that result in higher than average incidences of anxiety, depression, infectious and respiratory diseases.

Supervisory bodies, fueled by vigilant societal groups and advocates, have attempted to temper the fallout from the inconsistent interpretations of terms such as "emergency medical care" or "urgent care." The European Committee of Social Rights, the body responsible for monitoring the application of the European Social Charter, has criticized the French government's use of the term "emergencies and life-threatening conditions" as applied to undocumented migrants' rights to health care, especially children with irregular status:[208] "Legislation or practice that denies entitlement to medical assistance to foreign nationals, within the territory of a State Party, even if they are there illegally, is contrary to the Charter." [209] But discriminatory exclusions from health care continue. No systematic study has documented this, but anecdotal evidence abounds. An NGO worker in the Netherlands complained strongly about the extent of discretionary power: "A lot of things depend too much on the goodwill of people, if they are willing or not willing to help. . . . [D]octors sometimes do not want to help migrants while others are willing to help them." A UK-based worker reported a case where local medical care was refused to a four-month-old baby because the mother was undocumented; the only alternative to no care was a long bus journey from a suburb into central London. An Italian representative for Save the Children noted the anxiety about health-care availability expressed by irregular migrant street children.[210] As with education, fear of being detected keeps many undocumented adolescents and their families away from health services; lack of knowledge of their rights, and language and cultural barriers also make access to critical health care elusive. Clearly, despite formal support on the part of the international community for access to education and health care, the reality on the ground often vitiates realization of these very rights.

Conclusion

Tabitha's abusive and traumatic separation from her family by the Belgian authorities, the Albanian boy's lack of access to schooling in France, the unaffordable charges for health care imposed on migrant adolescents in northern Italy—all these cases and many more illustrate the multiple obstacles to rights enforcement that confront migrant children and adolescents. In Tabitha's case, the absence of a responsible adult compounded the disadvantages she faced as a noncitizen, with no country to call her own. The Albanian child could not reinsert himself in school once he left Tirana; migrant adolescents in Italy have no right to register for the National Italian Health Service and are therefore dependent on NGO providers if their cases fall outside the limited health-care cover provided by domestic law. None of these problems would have arisen had these children been citizens. Universal rights turn out not to be enforceable where a child or adolescent does not have a state he or she can turn to.

These problems would also not have arisen had policy makers and administrators adopted the child-centered approach of the UK Supreme Court in the case of *ZH (Tanzania) (FC) v. Secretary of State for the Home*

Department,[211] or the approach of the European Court of Justice in the cases on caregivers of child migrants engaged in education that were referred to in chapter 2. In the UK Supreme Court case, the child's best interests were prioritized as an important consideration capable of limiting the impact of other state obligations, such as immigration enforcement. In the latter cases, *London Borough of Harrow v. Nimco Hassan Ibrahim* and *Maria Teixeira v. London Borough of Lambeth*,[212] the European Court of Justice confirmed the migrant child's right to have his or her primary caregiver stay with the child during the education process, even if the primary caregiver was dependent on social-security benefits or was looking after a child who was no longer a minor. The primary goal driving the court's reasoning was to enforce the applicable EU law supporting free movement of workers within the European Union by removing obstacles to such movement, including possible educational disadvantages for migrant workers' children (such as having their primary caregiver refused permission to remain with them to look after them during their course of study). Subsidiary state interests, such as immigration control or social-security savings, were not allowed to trump the primary concern. Universal access to basic education and health care are also cardinal state goals that promote long-term state interests such as stability, productivity, harmony, and justice. But these economic and social rights of migrant children have not yet been protected by domestic and EU courts as have family-unity rights. As a result young migrants continue to find their rights trumped by local xenophobia, bureaucratic discretion, or other forms of political expediency.

On an alarming scale, unprotected migrant adolescents regularly live out their lives in what Agamben has termed the zone of exception. Where political will is absent, advocacy weak, and the rights-holder weaker still, de facto rightlessness is the norm. Human-rights instruments have provided a framework for advancing claims for conceptualizing the entitlements of these children and for measuring the failure of current administrative practice. The instruments have on occasion fueled redistribution of resources and protections, as in the case of Tabitha's claim to family reunion in Canada analyzed earlier in this chapter, Catherine Zhu's claim to continued care from her mother in Ireland discussed in chapter 2,[213] expansions of the notion of persecution in refugee law to include child-specific persecution in some US jurisdictions, and European advances in children's asylum processing, discussed in chapter 6. More often the rights enumerated are imperfect or inchoate and awaiting realization. Child and adolescent rights are human rights that need much more thought, effort, and political will to become the reality they were designed to be. As the discussion on the merits of requiring direct interviews of child asylum seekers by state officials demonstrates, the correspondence between human-rights provisions and rights-respecting policies in practice has to be crafted, not assumed. Those who have developed parts of the initial tool kit by enacting international human-rights norms have left it for children—migrant children, stateless children, unprotected children—to prove that their undocumented status does not render them officially rightless.[214] Yet when these children navigate the routes they have available, exercise agency, and choose to further their chances of effectively shoring up their abstract claims to rights—whether by migrating across borders *sua sponte* or escaping from punitive detention "shelters" to create an independent living situation—they are more likely to be punished than rewarded. Many are detained and then forcibly returned "home" to their country of origin, or consigned to a life of limbo in which they are denied access to basic public services. The state still retains the monopoly on determining eligibility for meaningful access to rights, despite the universalist aspirations of the human-rights tradition. A final vignette synthesizes points made throughout this chapter:

Undocumented adolescents in the minors' facility in the Spanish enclave of Ceuta, on the Moroccan coast, are entitled to health care on production of a government-issued health card. But the identification data on the health card has to be verified by social-service officials before the document can be issued. According to a Human Rights Watch (HRW) report:

> Ala gives his age as thirteen but he looks younger. When he arrived in Ceuta in the last quarter of 2000, police took him to the Mediterraneo Center, a residential center for children age ten and younger. Though he spent three months at the center before running away he was never issued with a health card. Staff refused to readmit him to the center and he lived on the streets, sniffing solvents and developing several serious health problems. Doctors in the health clinic refused to treat him because he lacked a health card. When HRW interviewed the child a year after he arrived in Ceuta, "he was not receiving medical care and was visibly ill.[215]

These adolescents are not rightless because they are disqualified by their age as is the case for citizen children seeking to exercise family-reunion rights that adults in their circumstances would have, as chapter 2 points out. Nor are they rightless because they are not recognized as persons before the law, as is the case for children whose birth is not registered. Rather they are rightless because the structures of inequality embedded in the society are not adequately corrected by the resources that are made available. This disempowered situation is not going to be rectified by the denigration of human-rights claims-making favored by some radical skeptics[216] any more than it is by gratuitous recitation of human-rights treaty provisions. Clearly, migrant adolescents are more dependent on naming, shaming, and aggressive mobilization of advocacy strategies than the general population of children who have parents or fellow citizens watching out for them. Bottom-up mobilization is essential for the success of top-down litigation because without the former the latter is trumped by immigration control and national security-driven sentiments, particularly in the post-9/11 climate of suspicion. Thus, rights believers, so to speak, have their work cut out for them as opinion formers, as whistle-blowers, as supporters of adolescent agency and concerned members of civil society. Most of all, they have an obligation to raise and stimulate discussion of the difficult and contentious issues that arise in actualizing migrant children and adolescents' rights to have rights. The ambivalence that policy makers feel, torn between sympathy and hostility, between a concern to protect and a pressure to punish, needs to be addressed head on rather than minimized or ignored. Human-rights instruments can never deliver on their aspirations without the political honesty and the mobilizing muscle that transforms them into live demands. There are, alas, no shortcuts to justice.

Notes

Introduction

1. United Nations Department of Economic and Social Affairs (UN DESA), *Trends in International Migrant Stock: The 2008 Revision*.

2. UNICEF, *Children, Adolescents and Migration: Filling the Evidence Gap* (2010), 2.

3. Barbara Bennett Woodhouse, "The Constitutionalization of Children's Rights: Incorporating Emerging Human Rights into Constitutional Doctrine," *Journal of Constitutional Law* 2, no. 1 (1999): 1–52, 4.

4. This book generally avoids technical language to capture the interest of the non-specialist reader. However, in this chapter I have decided to follow the recommendation of one of the anonymous reviewers and adopt the preferred UN terminology of "intercountry" adoption over the more colloquial "international adoption." I do this because the former denotes a permanent change in the adoptee's country of residence whereas the latter simply describes a difference in the nationality of the adopter and the adoptee, which is compatible with in-country or domestic adoption too. For definitions, see http://www.un.org/esa/population/publications/adoption2010/child_adoption.pdf, 150.

5. David Martin, "The New Asylum Seekers," in David Martin, ed., *The New Asylum Seekers: Refugee Law in the 1980s* (Dordrecht, the Netherlands: Martinus Nijhoff Publishers, 1986).

6. The UN High Commissioner for Refugees began to publish disaggregated data on child asylum seekers and refugees in 1994, and on unaccompanied and separated children in 2001.

7. UNHCR, *Guidelines on Policies and Procedures in Dealing with Unaccompanied Children Seeking Asylum* (1997).

8. While the UNHCR, the United Kingdom, and Canada issued guidelines on refugee children prior to 1997, including unaccompanied children, they did so in the limited contexts of refugee camps, social services, and adjudication. See UNHCR, *Refugee Children: Guidelines on Protection and Care* (1994); UK Department of Health, Social Services Inspectorate, *Unaccompanied Asylum-Seeking Children: A Practice Guide and Training Pack* (1995); Immigration and Refugee Board of Canada, *Guideline 3: Child Refugee Claimants: Procedural and Evidentiary Issues* (1996).

9. Jacqueline Bhabha and Mary Crock, *Seeking Asylum Alone: Unaccompanied and Separated Children and Refugee Protection in Australia, the U.K., and the U.S.* (Sydney: Themis Press, 2006), 57–69.

10. European Union, Council Resolution 97/C 221/03 of 26 June 1997 on Unaccompanied Minors Who Are Nationals of Third Countries, *Official Journal* C 221, 19/07/97 [1997 Council Resolution on Unaccompanied Minors].

11. USCIS, *Guidelines For Children's Asylum Claims* (1998); UK Home Office Border & Immigration Agency, "Processing Asylum Applications from a Child," *Special Cases: Guidance* (2005). To date, Australia has not promulgated any child-specific asylum guidelines. Jacqueline Bhabha, "Too Much Disappointing: The Quest for Protection by Unaccompanied Migrant Children Outside Europe," in Jyothi Kanics, Daniel Senovilla Hernández and Kristina Touzenis, eds., *Migrating Alone: Unaccompanied and Separated Children's Migration to Europe* (UNESCO, 2010).

12. Council of Europe, Parliamentary Assembly, *Undocumented Migrant Children in an Irregular Situation: A Real Cause for Concern*, Doc. 12718, Sep. 16, 2011, 4; Jacqueline Bhabha and Susan Schmidt, *Seeking Asylum Alone: Unaccompanied and Separated Children and Refugee Protection in the US* (Cambridge, MA: President and Fellows of Harvard College, 2006) [*SAA (US)*].

13. Mae Ngai, *Impossible Subjects: Illegal Aliens and the Making of Modern America* (Princeton: Princeton University Press, 2004).

14. Convention on the Rights of the Child, 1577 UNTS 3, Nov. 20, 1989, entered into force Sep. 2, 1990, Art. 1 [CRC].

15. Tamar Ezer, "A Positive Right to Protection for Children," *Yale Human Rights and Development Law Journal* 7 (2004): 1–50.

16. See, respectively, CRC, Arts. 3, 9, 22.

17. UN Committee on the Rights of the Child (CRC Committee), *General Comment No. 6: Treatment of Unaccompanied and Separated Children outside their country of origin*, CRC/GC/2005/6, Sep. 1, 2005.

18. *Mubilanzila Mayeka and Kaniki Mitunga v. Belgium*, no. 13178/03, ECHR (2006).

19. Hannah Arendt, *The Life of the Mind. Volume One: Thinking* (New York: Harcourt Brace & Company, 1978), 183.

20. Giorgio Agamben, *Homo Sacer: Sovereign Power and Bare Life* (Stanford University Press, 1998), pp. 22–22.

21. Linda Bosniak, *The Citizen and the Alien: Dilemmas of Contemporary Membership* (Princeton, NJ: Princeton University Press), 140; Homi K. Bhabha, "Notes on Globalisation and Ambivalence," in David Held, Henrietta L. Moore, and Kevin Young, eds., *Cultural Politics in a Global Age: Uncertainty, Solidarity and Innovation* (Oxford: Oneworld Publications, 2008), 36–47.

Chapter 1. Looking for Home: The Elusive Right to Family Life

1. *Ahmut v. the Netherlands*, no. 21702/93, ECHR (1996), Dissenting Opinion of Judge Valticos.

2. Catherine Elton, "El Salvador Targets Smugglers Who Transport Children," *Christian Science Monitor*, Jan. 7, 2003.

3. Some international instruments consider family reunification one aspect of the right to respect for family life; others consider it a free-standing right, critical to realization of the best interests of the child. International Commission of Jurists, *Green Paper on the Right to Family Reunification of Third-country Nationals Living in the European Union (Directive 2003/86/EC): Response by the International Commission of Jurists* (2012), 2.

4. Jean Piaget, *The Moral Judgment of the Child* (London: Routledge and Kegan Paul, 1932).

5. However, the "ambiguous loss" of one or both parents may lead to situations where "the child's loss may thus go unrecognized and lead to disenfranchized grief, whereby silence surrounds the loss." Carola Suárez-Orozco, Irina L. G. Todorava, and Josephine Louie, "Making Up for Lost Time: The Experience of Separation and Reunification among Immigrant Families," *Family Process* 41, no. 4 (2002): 625–43, 628. 635.

6. But note that financial support may be inadequate to offset the value of lost labor. Rodolfo de la Garza, *Migration, Development and Children Left Behind: A Multidimensional Approach* (UNICEF, 2010), 9–14, 20.

7. See T. H. Gindling and Sara Poggio, "Family Separation and Reunification as a Factor in the Educational Success of Immigrant Children," *Journal of Ethnic and Migration Studies* 38, no. 7 (2012): 1–19, and Claudia Lahaie et al., "Work and Family Divided Across Borders: The Impact of Parental Migration on Mexican Children in Transnational Families," *Community, Work and Family* 12, no. 3 (2009): 299–312.

8. See, e.g., John Gibson, David McKenzie, and Steven Stillman, "What Happens to Diet and Child Health When Migration Splits Households? Evidence from a Migration Lottery Program," *Food Policy* 36, no. 1 (2011): 7–15.

9. Ernesto Castañeda and Lesley Buck, "Remittances, Transnational Parenting, and the Children Left Behind: Economic and Psychological Implications," *The Latin Americanist* 55 (2011): 85–110.

10. Stephen H. Legomsky, "Rationing Family Values in Europe and America: An Immigration Tug of War between States and Their Supra-National Associations," *Georgetown Immigration Law Journal* 25, no. 4 (2011).

11. "[T]he Migration of Mothers Is Likely to Be Particularly Disruptive to Child Development and Care Arrangements in The Household." Kristina A. Schapiro, *Migration and Educational Outcomes of Children*, HDRP 2009/57 (UNDP, 2009), 19. See also Jack Shonkoff and Deborah A. Phillips, eds., *From Neurons to Neighborhoods: The Science of Early Childhood Development* (Washington, DC: The National Academy Press, 2000), 5, 238.

12. The impact of deportation on long-settled migrants who moved when they were young can be devastating. See Daniel Kanstroom, *Deportation Nation: Outsiders In American History* (Cambridge, MA: Harvard University Press, 2008). Despite this, some jurisdictions afford little discretion to decision makers adjudicating deportation proceedings of "criminal aliens."

13. Suárez-Orozco et al., "Lost Time," 626, 637.

14. Leisy Abrego, "Parents and Children Across Borders: Legal Instability and Intergenerational Relations in Guatemalan and Salvadoran Families," in Nancy Foner, ed., *Across Generations: Immigrant Families in America* (New York: New York University Press, 2009), 174.

15. Suárez-Orozco et al., "Lost Time," 634.

16. Human Rights Council, Jorge Bustamante, Special Rapporteur on the Human Rights of Migrants, *Promotion and Protection of All Human Rights, Civil, Political, Economic,*

Social and Cultural Rights, Including the Right to Development, A/HRC/11/7 (May 14, 2009), para. 47; Lahaie et al., 91–103.

17. *Moore v. City of East Cleveland*, 431 US 494, 503–504 (1977), cited in David B. Thronson, "You Can't Get Here from Here: Toward a More Child-Centered Immigration Law," *Virginia Journal of Social Policy and the Law* 14 (2006): 58 at note 5.

18. Convention for the Protection of Human Rights and Fundamental Freedoms, 213 UNTS 22, Nov. 4, 1950, Art. 8 [European Convention on Human Rights or ECHR].

19. European Social Charter, 25 UNTS 89, ETS 35, Oct. 18, 1961, Art. 19(6).

20. The right to family life is protected in other regional human rights treaties as well: American Convention on Human Rights, 1144 UNTS 123, Nov. 22, 1969, Art. 17 [ACHR]; African Charter on Human and Peoples' Rights, 1520 UNTS 217, June 27, 1981, Art. 18; and African Charter on the Rights and Welfare of the Child, OAU Doc. CAB/LEG/24.9/49, July 11, 1990, Art. 18.

21. Universal Declaration of Human Rights, GA Res. 217A (III), A/810 at 71, Dec. 10, 1948, Art. 16(3) [UDHR].

22. CRC, Preamble, para. 5.

23. Thronson, "You Can't Get", 60.

24. Canadian Council for Refugees, *More than a Nightmare: Delays in Refugee Family Reunification* (2004), 18.

25. International Commission of Jurists, 14.

26. Ginger Thompson, "Guatemala Intercepts 49 Children Illegally Bound for U.S.," *New York Times*, Apr. 8, 2002.

27. Nearly one in five minors returned were not Mexican. "U.S. Hands Over 14,237 Unaccompanied Minors to Mexico in '11," *Latin American Herald Tribune*, Feb. 13, 2012.

28. Valeria Perasso, "Young Migrants Make Perilous US-Mexico Journey," *BBC News*, June 12, 2012.

29. There are no reliable estimates of the number of migrant children separated from their families. According to the UN, 15 percent of the 214 million international migrants (33 million) are under twenty. UN DESA, *International Migrants by Age*, Population Facts No. 2010/6 (2010), 2. A substantial majority likely experience separation from one or both parents during the migration process: this was the case for 85 percent of youth in a 2002 study of immigrant children in the United States. See Suárez-Orozco et al., "Lost Time," 631. Similarly, it is difficult to estimate how many children have been left behind, though the impact of parental migration on children is extensive. A 2005 study estimated "that roughly 10–20 percent of Filipino, and 2–3 percent of Indonesian and Thai children, have a parent overseas." Victor Abramovich, Pablo Ceriani Cernadas, and Alejandro Morlachetti, *The Rights of Children, Youth and Women in the Context of Migration* (UNICEF, 2011).

30. Francisca M. Antman, *The Impact of Migration on Family Left Behind*, IZA Discussion Paper No. 6374, Feb. 2012, 7–10.

31. Carola Suárez-Orozco, Hee Jin Bang, and Ha Yeon Kim, "I Felt Like My Heart Was Staying Behind: Psychological Implications of Family Separations & Reunifications for Immigrant Youth," *Journal of Adolescent Research* 26, no. 2 (2011): 222–57, 240.

32. Antman, 7–10.

33. Martha Gardner, *The Qualities of a Citizen* (Princeton: Princeton University Press, 2005), 224.

34. John Berger, *A Seventh Man: Migrant Workers in Europe* (New York: The Viking Press, 1975).

35. Report by President's Commission on Migratory Labor, quoted by Gardner, *Qualities*, 209.

36. Jacqueline Bhabha, Francesca Klug, and Sue Shutter, eds., *Worlds Apart: Women, Immigration and Nationality Law* (London: Pluto Press, 1984).

37. Jane Freedman, "The French 'Sans-Papiers' Movement: An Unfinished Struggle," in Wendy Pojman, ed., *Migration and Activism in Europe since 1945* (New York: Palgrave Macmillan, 2008).

38. David Kelly, "Taking Border Patrol into Their Own Hands," *Los Angeles Times*, Feb. 2, 2005.

39. Rick Bragg, "Elian Waits Inside as Tension Grows Outside," *New York Times*, Apr. 5, 2000.

40. See Tom Gibb and Ed Vulliamy, "Millions Join Tug of War Over Cuban Refugee Boy," *Guardian*, Dec. 11, 1999. See chapter 7, note 116.

41. UNHCR, *Statistical Yearbook 2010: Trends in Displacement, Protection and Solutions* (2011), 24. This figure does not include 4.8 million Palestinians or 27 million internally displaced persons. See James Milner and Gil Loescher, *Responding to Protracted Refugee Situations: Lessons from a Decade of Discussion*, Forced Migration Policy Briefing 6, Refugee Studies Centre (2011), 3.

42. Milner and Loescher, 3.

43. UNHCR, *Integration of Beneficiaries of International Protection in the European Union: Observations and Recommendations to the European Commission in Its Consultation on the Upcoming Second European Union Agenda for Integration* (2011), para. 5.

44. International Commission of Jurists, 8.

45. Convention Relating to the Status of Refugees, 189 UNTS 150, July 28, 1951 [Refugee Convention] as amended by the Protocol Relating to the Status of Refugees, 606 UNTS 267, Jan. 31, 1967.

46. UNHCR, *Handbook on Procedures and Criteria for Determining Refugee Status under the 1951 Convention and the 1967 Protocol Relating to the Status of Refugees,* 1979, HCR/IP/4?Eng/REV.1 (reissued Jan. 1992).

47. James C. Hathaway, *The Rights of Refugees under International Law* (Cambridge: Cambridge University Press, 2005), 545.

48. Thomas Hammarberg, Commissioner for Human Rights, Council of Europe, "Refugees Must Be Able to Reunite with Their Family Members," Aug. 4, 2008.

49. The Human Rights Committee, the treaty body overseeing implementation of the ICCPR, has criticized a narrow construction: "[T]he term family . . . must be understood broadly to include all those comprising a family as understood in the society concerned." *Ngambi and Nébol v. France*, CCPR, Comm. No. 1179/2003, 16 July 2004, para. 6.4.

50. *AS (Somalia) and Anor v. (1) Entry Clearance Officer (2) Secretary of State for the Home Department* [2008] EWCA Civ 149, para. 8. A subsequent appeal of the judgment was dismissed.

51. Ibid., para. 27.

52. The Parliamentary Committee of the Council of Europe has criticized these delays and stressed the importance "to facilitate family reunion . . . before the completion of the sometimes very lengthy procedure for determining refugee status, in exceptional cases and for humanitarian reasons." *Recommendation 1686 (2004) on human mobility and the right to family reunion*, cited in International Commission of Jurists, 17 at note 60.

53. In some countries, such as the United States, there are annual public quotas for refugee admissions. In others, such as the United Kingdom, there are no formal or publicly stated limits, but staff shortages and bureaucratic intransigence ensure a restricted flow of entrants.

54. "More than a Systems Failure," *Irish Times*, July 26, 2008. Opinion, 15.

55. Ruadhán Mac Cormaic, "Refugee Group Says Visa Errors Common," *Irish Times*, July 28, 2008.

56. UNDP, *Human Development Report 2009: Overcoming Barriers: Human Mobility and Development*, 40 [*Human Development Report 2009*].

57. Val Aldridge, "Alone in a Strange Country," *Dominion Post*, June 20, 2001.

58. See CRC, Art. 19(1).

59. Alice Tay and Sev Ozdowski, Australian Human Rights and Equal Opportunity Commission, *Woomera Immigration Detention Centre–Report of Visit by Human Rights and Equal Opportunity Commission Officers*, Feb. 6, 2002.

60. *Muskhadzhiyeva and Others v. Belgium*, no. 41442/07, ECHR (2010), para. 31, 32.

61. Ibid., paras. 60, 103.

62. Integrated Regional Information Networks (IRIN), *A Gap in Their Hearts: The Experiences of Separated Somali Children* (2003), 20.

63. International Organization of Migration (IOM), *World Migration 2010: The Future of Migration: Building Capacities for Change*, 115.

64. Richard Freeman, "People Flows in Globalization," *Journal of Economic Perspectives* 20, no. 2 (2006): 145–70.

65. Frances Cairncross, "The Longest Journey: A Survey of Migration," *Economist*, Nov. 2, 2002, 4. For further analysis, see New Immigrant Survey, http://nis.princeton.edu/index.html.

66. *Human Development Report 2009*, 50, 24.

67. See Ngai, 127–35 and Stephen Castles, "The Guest-worker in Western Europe: An Obituary," *International Migration Review* 20, no. 4 (1986): 761–78.

68. Gardner, *Qualities*, 208.

69. Alexandra Filindra, "The Emergence of the 'Temporary Mexican': American Agriculture, the U.S. Congress and the 1920 Debate over the Temporary Admission of Illiterate Mexican Laborers" (paper on file with author), 12.

70. *Human Development Report 2009*, 46.

71. Gardner, *Qualities*, 209.

72. *Human Development Report 2009*, 31, 83, 95, 36.

73. Ibid., 16–17.

74. Peter Orner, *Underground America: Narratives of Undocumented Lives* (San Francisco: McSweeney's Books, 2008), 141.

75. Bhabha et al., *Worlds Apart*, 130–31.

76. Some 48 million children lack birth certificates—documentary proof of their legal identity. Jacqueline Bhabha, "From Citizen to Migrant: The Scope of Child Statelessness in the Twenty-first Century," in Jacqueline Bhabha, ed., *Children Without a State: A Global Human Rights Challenge* (Cambridge, MA: MIT Press, 2011), 7.

77. Bhabha et al., *Worlds Apart*, 161–62.

78. For accounts of US–Mexico migration, see George Borjas (ed.), *Mexican Immigration to the United States: National Bureau of Economic Research Conference Report* (Chicago: University of Chicago Press, 2007) and Douglas Massey, Jorge Durand, and Nolan J. Malone, *Beyond Smoke and Mirrors: Mexican Immigration in an Era of Economic Integration* (New York: Russell Sage Foundation, 2002).

79. Ngai, 131–66.

80. Bob McEwen, "Thousands, Including Oregonians, Are Stuck in Passport Limbo," *Oregonian*, Oct. 5, 2008.

81. Physicians for Human Rights (PHR) and The Bellevue/NYU Program for Survivors and Torture, *From Persecution to Prison: The Health Consequences of Detention for Asylum Seekers* (2003).

82. Thomas Hammarberg, Commissioner for Human Rights, Council of Europe, "Methods for Assessing the Age of Migrant Children Must Be Improved," CommDH018 (2011), Aug. 9, 2011.

83. Nalton F. Ferraro, "Dr. Ferraro's Comment to the INS Regarding Determination of Chronological Age Using Bone Age and Dental Age Standards," Appendix A in PHR et al., *From Persecution*, 199–200.

84. *NA (Bangladesh) and Others v. Secretary of State for the Home Department* [2007] EWCA Civ 128.

85. For a sole responsibility case concerning a Jamaican mother seeking reunification with her child, see *T (s.55 BCIA 2009—entry clearance) Jamaica* [2011] UKUT 483 (IAC), cited in Asylum Aid, *Women's Asylum News*, Issue 107, Dec. 2011–Jan. 2012, 9.

86. *G.R. v. the Netherlands*, no. 22251/07, ECHR (2012).

87. *Regina v. Secretary of State for the Home Department, ex parte* Arman Ali [*2000*] Imm AR (28 Oct. 1999).

88. Migrants' Rights Network, *Keeping Families Apart: The Impact of a New Income Threshold for Family Migration* (2012). The United States, Belgium, Spain, Norway, and the Netherlands require applicants to meet income thresholds of at least 120 percent of the national minimum wage to sponsor a foreign relative. In the United Kingdom, a pending proposal would prevent as many as 60 percent of applicants from sponsoring foreign spouses. Arjen Leerkes and Isik Kulu-Glasgow, "Playing Hard(er) to Get: The State, International Couples, and the Income Requirement," *European Journal of Migration and Law* 13, no. 1 (2011): 95–121.

89. For a forceful argument that failure to do this amounts to a human-rights violation, see Shani M. King, "U.S. Immigration Law and the Traditional Nuclear Conception of Family: Toward a Functional Definition of Family that Protects Children's Fundamental Human Rights," *Columbia Human Rights Law Review* 41, 509 (2010).

90. Several scholars have noted a trend in ECHR jurisprudence to limit the definition of family to the nuclear unit. See, e.g., Dallal Stevens, "Asylum-seeking Families in Current Legal Discourse: A UK Perspective," *Journal of Social Welfare and Family Law* 32, no. 1 (2010): 5–22. In November 2011, the European Commission launched a public consultation asking whether "the rules on eligible family members [are] adequate and broad enough to take into account the different definitions of family existing other than that of the nuclear family." European Commission, *Green Paper on the Right to Family Reunification of Third Country Nationals Living in the European Union (Directive 2003/86/EC)*, COM(2011) 735 final, Nov. 15, 2011, 4.

91. See European Union, Council Directive 2003/86/EC of 22 September 2003 on the right to family reunification, EU, OJ L 251, 3.10.2003, Art. 4.1 [EU Family Reunification Directive].

92. *Tuquabo-Tekle and Others v. the Netherlands*, no. 60665/00 (unpublished), ECHR (2005).

93. Legomsky, "Rationing Family Values," 29–30.

94. Liav Orgad, "Illiberal Liberalism: Cultural Restrictions on Migration and Access to Citizenship in Europe," *American Journal of Comparative Law* 58, no. 1 (2010): 53–105, 72.

95. One Amsterdam district court ruled that the policy was illegal when applied to exclude the illiterate wife of a Dutch citizen, but the policy is still in force. LJN BD7189, Rechtbank's-Gravenhage, zittingsplaats Amsterdam, AWB 07/18932, cited in Orgad, 73, 19.

96. Lori A. Nessel, "Families at Risk: How Errant Enforcement and Restrictionist Integration Policies Threaten the Immigrant Family in the European Union and the United States," *Hofstra Law Review* 36 (2008), 1273.

97. Orgad, 36.

98. EU Family Reunification Directive, Art. 6.

99. *Gul v. Switzerland*, no. 53/1995/559/645, ECHR (1996), paras. 16, 15.

100. For another ECHR decision denying family reunification to children of an Afghan refugee, see *Haydarie and Others v. the Netherlands*, no. 8876/04, ECHR (2005).

101. Commission of Inquiry into the Actions of Canadian Officials in Relation to Maher Arar, *Report of Events Relating to Maher Arar: Analysis and Recommendations*, Sep. 18, 2006.

102. *Ahmut v. the Netherlands*, supra note 1.

103. Randall Monger and James Yankay, *U.S. Legal Permanent Residents: 2011*, US Department of Homeland Security (2012), 1.

104. "'[I]mmediate relatives' means the children, spouses, and parents of a citizen of the United States, except that, in the case of parents, such citizens shall be at least 21 years of age." Immigration and Nationality Act (INA) § 201(b)(2)(A)(i), 8 USC § 1151(b)(2)(A)(i) (2006). On January 3, 2013, the Department of Homeland Security published a new rule change allowing undocumented "immediate" relatives to remain in the United States while awaiting lawful status. US Dept. of Homeland Security, *Provisional Unlawful Presence Waivers of Inadmissibility for Certain Immediate Relatives*, 8 CFR Parts 103 and 212. However these waivers would not apply to parents of US citizen *children*. See David B. Thronson, "Entering the Mainstream: Making Children Matter in Immigration Law," *Fordham Urban Law Journal* 38, (2010): 393–413, 405 at note 58.

105. See US Department of State, *Visa Bulletin for June 2012* [*Visa Bulletin June 2012*].

106. US Department of State, *Annual Report of Immigrant Visa Applicants in the Family-sponsored and Employment-based Preferences Registered at the National Visa Center as of November 1, 2011*, and USCIS, *Adjustment of Status Form I-485 Performance Data (FY2009–Dec. FY2012)*.

107. Edward Hegstrom, "A Risky Border Business: INS Reports a Growing Number of Illegal Workers Are Paying Smugglers to Bring Their Families to U.S.," *Houston Chronicle*, Aug. 19, 2002.

108. Elton, "El Salvador Targets Smugglers."

109. "Immigrants Fight to Bring Adult Children to U.S.," *Associated Press*, Aug. 25, 2009.

110. H.R. 1209, "Child Status Protection Act," 107th Congress, signed into law Aug. 6, 2002.

111. *Matter of Wang*, 25 I&N Dec. 28 (BIA 2009).

112. Ibid., 34.

113. See David B. Thronson, "Thinking Small: The Need for Big Changes in Immigration Law's Treatment of Children," *U.C. Davis Journal of Juvenile Law and Policy* 14, no. 239 (2010): 240–62.

114. Bill Ong Hing, "The Dark Side of Operation Gatekeeper," *U.C. Davis Journal of International Law and Policy* 7, no. 2 (2001): 121 at 123.

115. This chapter concerns only documented migrants seeking to exercise their legal rights to family reunion. But it bears noting that the very status of "undocumented" or "illegal" migrant is socially constructed, and that the escalating numbers reflect the increasing inaccessibility of legal status. See Ngai, 4.

116. In 2011, there were at least 16,788 pending visa applications for unskilled workers, capped annually at 10,000. *Visa Bulletin June 2012* and USCIS, "Questions & Answers: Pending Employment-Based Form I-485 Inventory," July 1, 2011.

117. Thirty percent of US immigrants today are Mexican-born and over half are undocumented. Jeffrey S. Passel, D'Vera Cohn, and Ana Gonzalez-Barrera, *Net Migration from Mexico Falls to Zero—and Perhaps Less* (Pew Hispanic Center, 2012).

118. Luis Alberto Urrea, *The Devil's Highway: A True Story* (New York: Little, Brown and Company, 2005).

119. Thompson, "Guatemala Intercepts."

120. Barbara J. Fraser, "Left Behind: Amid Immigration Debate, Children Often Are Forgotten," *Catholic News Service*, Dec. 28, 2007.

121. Hegstrom.

122. Sonia Nazario, *Enrique's Journey: The Story of a Boy's Dangerous Odyssey to Reunite with His Mother* (New York: Random House, 2006), 21.

123. Hegstrom.

124. This figure is based on 2001 estimates: 14,420 unaccompanied children detained and 33,600 never apprehended. Nazario, 265. In 2011, US border authorities detained 15,949 unaccompanied children and it is reasonable to assume that tens of thousands escaped detection. US Customs and Border Protection (CBP), *US Border Patrol Fiscal Year 2011 Profile*, 4. Moreover, the number may only be increasing. See Nathan Koppel, "Child Immigration Is Rising," *Wall Street Journal*, May 7, 2012.

125. Amnesty International estimates that as many as six in ten migrant women and girls are raped. *Invisible Victims: Migrants on the Move in Mexico* (2010), 15–18.

126. Nazario, 2.

127. Thompson, "Guatemala Intercepts."

128. Nazario, 281, citing 1997 University of Houston study, "Potentially Traumatic Events among Unaccompanied Migrant Children from Central America."

129. Patricia Giovine, "Minors Are the Most Tragic Victims of Immigration," *Que Pasa*, July 7, 2003.

130. Elton, "El Salvador Targets Smugglers."

131. Hegstrom.

132. There are even cases where the "value" of a child to parents becomes part of the immigration bargain: a two-year-old Brazilian girl was held in Mexico "as collateral by immigrant smugglers who helped her mother illegally cross into the United States" until the $4,000 balance on the mother's smuggling fee was paid. Ben Fox, "Authorities Free Brazilian Girl Being Held Captive in Mexico," *Associated Press*, May 3, 2002.

133. Michael Marizco, "Smuggling Children, Part 1: Young Immigrants Become Human Cargo," *Arizona Daily Star*, Nov. 21, 2004.

134. Thompson, "Guatemala Intercepts."

135. Center for Public Policy Priorities (CPPP), *A Child Alone and Without Papers: A Report on the Return and Repatriation of Unaccompanied Undocumented Children by the United States* (2008), 7.

136. Mary Delorey of Catholic Relief Services, quoted in Fraser.

137. CPPP, *A Child Alone.*

138. Bhabha and Schmidt, *SAA (US).*

139. Julia Malone, "Security Bill May Help Undocumented Children," *Austin American-Statesman*, Sep. 28, 2002.

140. Fraser.

141. CRC, Art. 9.

142. Nazario, 46.

Chapter 2. Staying Home: The Elusive Benefits of Child Citizenship

1. I use the term "children" to refer to persons under eighteen, following the definition in CRC, Art. 1.

2. Toby Harnden, "Twin Towers Widow Wins Fight to Stay in US," *Daily Telegraph*, July 27, 2002.

3. Anastasia Hendrix, "An INS Mistake, a Mother Deported," *San Francisco Chronicle*, July 27, 2002.

4. UDHR. Art. 16(3) states: "The family is the natural and fundamental group unit of society and is entitled to protection by society and the State." Similar sentiments are expressed in CRC, Art. 9 and the International Covenant on Civil and Political Rights, 993 UNTS 3, Dec. 16, 1966, Art. 23(1) [ICCPR].

5. Jack Pugh, "Immigration: Part One, Erica Delgado and Miriam Ortiz," *Wyoming Eagle-Tribune*, Mar. 1, 2012.

6. Ibid., "Immigration, Part Two, Irma Mejia and Irma Avina," *Wyoming Eagle-Tribune*, Mar. 1, 2012.

7. Kanstroom, *Deportation Nation*, 8–11.

8. Judith Butler and Gayatri Chakravorty Spivak, *Who Sings the Nation State?* (London: Seagull Books, 2007), 102.

9. The removable alien must establish that "removal would result in exceptional and extremely unusual hardship to the alien's spouse, parent, child, who is a citizen of the United States or an alien lawfully admitted for permanent residence." INA § 240A(b)(1)(D), 8 USC § 1229b(b)(1)(D) (2006).

10. US Department of Homeland Security, Office of Inspector General, *Removals Involving Illegal Alien Parents of United States Citizen Children*, OIG-09–15, Jan. 2009, 5.

11. US Immigration and Customs Enforcement Agency (ICE), *Deportation of Parents of U.S.-Born Citizens Fiscal Year 2011: Report to Congress*, Mar. 26, 2012, 4.

12. Four and a half million American citizen children have an unauthorized parent. Paul Taylor et al., *Unauthorized Immigrants: Length of Residency, Patterns of Parenthood* (Pew Hispanic Center, 2011), 6.

13. See James D. Kremer, Kathleen A. Moccio, and Joseph W. Hammell, *Severing a Lifeline: The Neglect of Citizen Children in America's Immigration Enforcement Policy*, Report by Dorsey & Whitney LLP to The Urban Institute (2009), 74–79.

14. John Morton, Assistant Secretary, ICE, *Memorandum on Exercising Prosecutorial Discretion Consistent with the Civil Immigration Enforcement Priorities of the Agency for the Apprehension, Detention, and Removal of Aliens*, Policy no. 10075.1 (June 17, 2011), 4.

15. Applied Research Center, *Shattered Families: The Perilous Intersection of Immigration Enforcement and the Child Welfare System* (Nov. 2011), 29–30.

16. The US government does not track the number of cases where both parents and children are removed, or where deported parents leave US citizen children behind. US Department of Homeland Security, *Illegal Alien Parents*, 1.

17. *Delgado v. Holder*, no. 11–2648 (7th Cir., Mar. 22, 2012).

18. Mark Krikorian, director of the Center for Immigration Studies, quoted in Kristin Collins, "Deported Parents Leaving Children Born in U.S.," *News & Observer*, Dec. 20, 2009.

19. American Psychological Association, Presidential Task Force on Immigration, *Crossroads: The Psychology of Immigration in the New Century* (2012).

20. Collins. See also Kremer, Moccio, and Hammell, *Severing a Lifeline*, 65–71; and Ajay Chaudry et al., *Facing Our Future: Children in the Aftermath of Immigration Enforcement* (Urban Institute, 2010), 24, 27–54.

21. See Chaudry et al., ibid.; Seth Freed Wessler, "Thousands of Kids Lost from Parents in U.S. Deportation System," *Color Lines*, June 8, 2012; and Elise Foley, "What Happens to Children When Their Parents Are Detained or Deported?," *Washington Independent*, Nov. 16, 2010.

22. Applied Research Center, 15., 6.

23. One clinical psychologist who met with families affected by workplace immigration raids "concluded that the level of posttraumatic stress disorder and anxiety rivaled that seen in war-torn countries like Bosnia." Kremer, Moccio, and Hammell, *Severing a Lifetime*, 70.

24. H.R. 1176 was referred to the House Committee on the Judiciary in February 2009.

25. "Report: Over 100,000 Deportees Had Children in U.S.," *Oregonian*, Feb. 13, 2009.

26. Cohen describes children as semi-citizens, excluded from full citizenship because of their emotional and intellectual immaturity, but partially included because of their need for protection. Elizabeth F. Cohen, *Semi-Citizenship in Democratic Politics* (Cambridge: Cambridge University Press, 2009), 183.

27. Children's Charter, distilling recommendations of President Hoover's White House Conference on Child Health and Protection in 1930, cited in Beverly C. Edmonds and William R. Fernekes, *Children's Rights: A Reference Handbook* (Santa Barbara: ABC-CLIO, 1996), 182–85.

28. Bill Bell, "Are Children Citizens?," in J. P. Gardner, ed., *Citizenship: The White Paper* (London: British Institute of International and Comparative Law, 1996), 214–22, 215.

29. Charles Rabin and Alfonso Chardy, "Immigration Dragnets Target Ex-cons," *Miami Herald*, Mar. 4, 2003.

30. The US rule's disjunction from other established norms regarding the protection of family life prompts quixotic judicial reasoning. Unlike the *Andazola-Rivas* case, 23 I&N Dec. 319 (BIA 2002), the BIA found "exceptional and extremely unusual hardship" in *Matter of Gonzalez Recinas*, 23 I&N Dec. 467 (BIA 2002). How do the cases differ? Both concerned a single parent with English-speaking children and no family in Mexico: but instead of two children, the mother in *Recinas* had six children, and instead of a father who "could" (but did not) provide support as in *Andazola-Rivas*, the Recinas children had had no contact with their father. An assessment of relative hardships facing the mothers, not the children, seems to have driven the BIA's contrasting findings.

31. Taylor et al., 6.

32. ICE, *Deportation of Parents*, 4.

33. Several academic inquiries probe the consequences of this lacuna in public deliberation and social policy, exploring voting rights, child labor, juvenile justice, school schedules, nutritional policy, and questions of custody as examples of public practices with profoundly undemocratic impacts on children. See, e.g., Gerison Lansdown, "Children's Welfare and Children's Rights," in Pam Foley, Jeremy Roche, and Stan Tucker, eds., *Children in Society: Contemporary Theory, Policy and Practice* (New York: Palgrave Macmillan, 2001); Onora O'Neill, "Children's Rights and Children's Lives," *Ethics* 98, no. 3 (1988); Elizabeth F. Cohen, "Neither Seen nor Heard: Children's Citizenship in Contemporary Democracies," *Citizenship Studies* 9, no. 2 (2005).

34. Fran Abrams, *Freedom's Cause: The Lives of the Suffragettes* (London: Profile Books, 2003).

35. Norani Othman, *Muslim Women and the Challenge of Islamic Extremism* (Malaysia: Sisters in Islam, 2005).

36. Nottebohm Case (*Liechtenstein v. Guatemala*), 1955 ICJ 4, 6 April 1955, 23. While "citizenship" and "nationality" have different histories and scholarly literatures, the analytic distinctions have little practical consequence for the discussion that follows.

37. The Fourteenth Amendment to the US Constitution, ratified in 1868.

38. In practice, stringent language and general knowledge tests may operate to exclude disadvantaged groups from access to citizenship. Moreover, despite prohibitions against

racial and ethnic discrimination, there is a remarkable permissiveness in relation to them in international (and some domestic) citizenship law. See Joanne Mariner, "Racism, Citizenship and National Identity," *Development* 46, no. 3 (2003): 64–70.

39. See CRC, Art. 38, as amended by the 2000 Optional Protocol to the Convention on the Rights of the Child on the Involvement of Children in Armed Conflicts, GA Res. 263, Annex I, 54 UN GAOR Supp. (No. 49), 7, A/RES/54/263, Vol. III (2000), May 25, 2000 [Child Soldiers Protocol].

40. In the United States, family reunification accounts for two-thirds of lawful immigration each year. See Ruth Ellen Wasem, *US Immigration Policy on Permanent Admissions* (CRS, Mar. 13, 2012), 9.

41. Ruth Eglash, "Yishai Refuses to Meet Children of Foreign Workers," *Jerusalem Post*, Oct. 21, 2009.

42. This is the situation in the United Kingdom. See British Nationality Act 1981, Chapter 61, Section 1(3). In Canada, at least one parent must be a citizen or applying to become a citizen. Canadian Citizenship Act, RSC 1985, Chapter C-29 (Section 5).

43. Some exceptions have emerged in recent case law, including the UK Supreme Court case of *ZH (Tanzania) (FC) v. Secretary of State for the Home Department* [2011] UKSC, and the European Court of Justice cases of *Chen* and *Zambrano* discussed at notes 94–101 below.

44. Collins.

45. Engaging in citizenly acts does not of itself generate citizenship: "Citizenship cannot be earned simply by acting as a citizen ought to, or as most citizens seem to"; rather political institutions dictate the circumstances governing individuals' access to citizenship. Cohen, *Semi-Citizenship*, 21.

46. Women's Refugee Commission, *Halfway Home: Unaccompanied Children in Immigration Custody* (2009), 9.

47. Ginger Thompson, "After Losing Freedom, Some Immigrants Face Loss of Custody of Their Children," *New York Times*, Apr. 23, 2009.

48. Jeffrey S. Passel and D'Vera Cohn, *A Portrait of Unauthorized Immigrants in the United States* (Pew Hispanic Center, 2009), 17.

49. See *Garcia v. Hernandez*, 947 So.2d 657, 660 (Fla. 3d DCA 2007): "[A]bsent special circumstances, the primary residential parent should be awarded exclusive use and possession of the marital home until the youngest child reaches majority." A similar principle guides divorces in Italy, Spain, and England.

50. Indeed many industrial countries do not (or no longer) afford automatic birthright citizenship. In Japan, citizenship has always been based on ancestry rather than place of birth. Hundreds of children born and raised in Japan by irregular migrants have no legal basis for resisting their own deportation, let alone that of their parents. Blaine Harden, "Born in Japan, but Ordered Out," *Washington Post*, Jan. 17, 2010. In rare cases, the Japanese government gives the children the option to stay behind in Japan without their parents. Kyung Lah, "Schoolgirl Told to Choose: Country or Parents," *CNN*, Apr. 13, 2009.

51. Margaret Stock, "American Birthright Citizenship Rules and the Exclusion of Outsiders" (unpublished draft on file with author).

52. *Acosta v. Gaffney*, 558 F.2d 1153, 1157 (3d Cir. 1977) (emphasis added), citing *Perdido v. INS*, 420 F.2d 1179, 1181 (5th Cir. 1969).

53. *Nguyen v. INS*, 533 US 53 (2001).

54. Janice Tibbetts, "Federal Rulings Make Deportations More Likely: Canadian-born Children Now a Less-Important Factor," *Southam News*, Feb. 10, 2003. Since 2009, children born in Canada experience a form of semi-citizenship unless they have a citizen or permanent-resident parent through whom they qualify for Canadian citizenship. See Canadian Citizenship Act, RSC 1985, Chapter C-29 (Section 5).

55. *L. & O. v. Minister for Justice, Equality and Law Reform* [2003] 1 I.R. 1.

56. This principle applies to all children born in the United States, irrespective of the legality of their parents' status. *United States v. Wong Kim Ark*, 169 US 649 (1898).

57. Gardner, *Qualities*, 159–60, 161, citing *Lee Sing Far v. United States*, 94 F. 834 (9th Cir. 1899), 164–165.

58. Ibid., 165.

59. McEwen.

60. Peter Schuck, *Citizens, Strangers and In-betweens: Essays on Immigration and Citizenship* (Boulder: Westview Press, 1998), 213, 212.

61. Bonnie Honig, *Democracy and the Foreigner* (Princeton: Princeton University Press, 2001), 102.

62. See W. D. Reasoner, "Birthright Citizenship: A National Security Problem in the Making?" Center for Immigration Studies, Mar. 2011.

63. U.S. Rep. Hansen Clarke (D-Detroit) is one of the few politicians to acknowledge being the child of undocumented immigrants. Noncitizens accounted for 4 percent of all US military recruits between 1999 and 2008 and were less likely to drop out of service than citizens. Molly F. McIntosh, Seema Sayala, and David Gregory, *Noncitizens in the Enlisted US Military*, CNA Research Memorandum D0025768.A2/Final, Nov. 2011, 1, 26.

64. Lino Graglia, "Birthright Citizenship for Children of Illegal Aliens: An Irrational Public Policy," *Texas Review of Law and Politics* 14, no. 1 (2009).

65. Gerald L. Neuman, *Strangers to the Constitution: Immigrants, Borders, and Fundamental Law* (Princeton: Princeton University Press, 1996), 62–63.

66. Review of Peter H. Schuck and Rogers M. Smith, *Citizenship Without Consent: Illegal Aliens in the American Polity* (New Haven: Yale University Press, 1985) in Gerald L. Neuman, "Back to Dred Scott," 24 *San Diego Law Review* 485, 490 (1987).

67. Cited in Stephen Wall, "GOP Aims to Retool Immigrant Birthright Citizenship," *Inland Valley Daily Bulletin*, Feb. 14, 2010.

68. *Human Development Report 2009*, 35.

69. *Oforji v. Ashcroft*, 354 F.3d 609, 620–21 (7th Cir. 2003).

70. Federation for American Immigration Reform estimates that 165,000 babies are born each year in the United States to illegal immigrants and others who come here to give birth. Kelley Bouchard, "An Open Door Refugee Policy Has Its Critics," *Maine Sunday Telegram*, June 30, 2002, 11A.

71. Jacqueline Bhabha and Sue Shutter, *Women's Movement: Women under Immigration, Nationality and Refugee Law* (Stoke-on-Trent: Trentham Books, 1994), 76–86, 83.

72. Ibid., 84.

73. Schuck, 214.

74. Seyla Benhabib, *The Rights of Others: Aliens, Residents, and Citizens* (Cambridge: Cambridge University Press, 2004), 5, 73.

75. Ayelet Shachar, *The Birthright Lottery: Citizenship and Global Inequality* (Cambridge, MA: Harvard University Press, 2009), 12.

76. Bhabha and Shutter, *Women's Movement*, 16–17.

77. Ibid., 18.

78. For example, a child born in France to a Moroccan father and a French mother is eligible for French citizenship by descent (*ius sanguinis*). Code Civil, Art. 18 (Fr.). A child born in the United Kingdom to undocumented parents is eligible for British citizenship after spending ten years continuously in the United Kingdom. British Nationality Act 1981 Chapter 61, Section 1(4).

79. Linda Kerber, "Birthright Citizenship: The Vulnerability and Resilience of an American Constitutional Principle," in Bhabha, *Children Without a State*, 255–76; Karen Knop, "Relational Nationality: On Gender and Nationality in International Law," in T. Alexander Aleinikoff and Douglas Klusmeyer, eds., *Citizenship Today: Global Perspectives and Practices* (Brookings Institution Press, 2001), 89–119.

80. Stephen Macedo and Iris Marion Young, eds., *Children, Family, and State (Nomos XLIV)* (New York: New York University Press, 2003), 1.

81. "[T]he family [is] the fundamental group of society and the natural environment for the growth and well-being of all its members *and particularly children*." CRC, Preamble (emphasis added).

82. This right is by no means unqualified or absolute, see Sarah van Walsum, "Transnational Mothering, National Immigration Policy, and European Law," in Seyla Benhabib and Judith Resnik, eds., *Migrations and Mobilities: Gender, Citizenship, Borders* (New York: New York University Press, 2009), 229–44.

83. Schuck, 166–67.

84. The Commission was the court of first instance within the Council of Europe system until it was abolished in 1998. Now all cases brought under the ECHR go straight to the European Court of Human Rights.

85. See, e.g., *Moustaquim v. Belgium*, no. 12313/86, ECHR (1991); *Boughanemi v. France*, no. 22070/93, 22 EHRR 228 (1996); and *A.W. Khan v. United Kingdom*, no. 47486/06, ECHR (2010).

86. The lack of primacy given to the child is reflected in the procedural posture of the reported cases before the Court: with one exception, the citizen child is not a co-applicant, and therefore not the prime focus of the balancing exercise between state and individual. See *Fadele v. United Kingdom*, no. 13078/87, 12 Feb. 1990.

87. *Berrehab v. the Netherlands*, no. 10730/84, 11 EHRR 322 (1988).

88. *Yousef v. United Kingdom*, no. 14830/89, ECHR (1992), and paras. 22, 43.

89. *Ciliz v. the Netherlands*, no. 29192/95, ECHR (2000), and para. 55.

90. In a case concerning three children of a drug-addicted and multiply convicted father threatened with removal, the court has held that "the removal of a person from the country

where close members of his family are living may amount to an infringement of the right to respect for family life . . . which is among the fundamental rights . . . protected in Community law." *Georgios Orfanopoulos and Others* and *Raffaele Oliveri v. Land Baden-Württemberg* [2004] ECR I-5257, Cases C-482/01 and C-493/01, at 98. The court has even looked beyond biological parents to uphold the interests of children to the enjoyment of family life: "Besides the interests of Mrs. Carpenter as a spouse, there are also the interests of the step-children. . . . The intensity of the relationship between Mrs Carpenter and her stepchildren and the ages of the children are relevant." *Mary Carpenter v. Secretary of State for the Home Department* [2002] ECR I-6279, Case C-60/00, at 94.

91. *Zhu and Chen v. Secretary of State for the Home Department* [2004] ECR I-9925, Case C-200/02.

92. Ibid., para. 10, citing British Nationality Act 1981.

93. For more discussion of the Irish situation, see Siobhan Mullally, "Crossing Borders: Gender, Citizenship, and Reproductive Autonomy in Ireland," in Sarah van Walsum and Thomas Spijkerboer, eds., *Women and Immigration Law: New Variations on Classical Feminist Themes* (London: Routledge-Cavendish, 2007), 223–40.

94. *Zhu and Chen*, Written Observations of Ireland, para. 4.4, Sep. 17, 2002 (on file with author).

95. Ibid., supra note 91, para 45. The ECJ delivered its judgment in May 2004; by June 2004, Ireland had passed a constitutional amendment withdrawing citizenship rights from children born in Ireland without an Irish parent; see discussion below.

96. *Gerardo Ruiz Zambrano v. Office national de l'emploi (ONEm)*, ECJ 8 Mar. 2011, Case C-34/09.

97. "[T]he longer term consequences for Diego and Jessica of *not* recognising a derivative right of residence for Mr Ruiz Zambrano are stark. They cannot exercise their right to reside as Union citizens effectively without the help and support of their parents. Their residence right will therefore—until they are old enough to exercise it on their own—be almost completely devoid of content." Ibid., para. 117.

98. Ibid., para. 63.

99. Ibid., paras. 96, 95.

100. "They have not yet moved outside their own Member State. . . . If the parents do not have a derivative right of residence and are required to leave Belgium, the children will, in all probability, have to leave with them. That would, in practical terms, place Diego and Jessica in a 'position capable of causing them to lose the status conferred [by their citizenship of the Union] and the rights attaching thereto.'" Ibid.

101. Ibid., paras. 118–21.

102. Subsequent European Court of Justice jurisprudence suggests some retrenchment from the position adopted in *Zambrano*. In *McCarthy v. Secretary of State for the Home Department* [2008] EWCA Civ 641, the ECJ held that a dual national who had never exercised her rights to freedom of movement could not rely on her EU citizenship to secure residence for her spouse, since refusal violated no fundamental rights protected by her citizenship. Since this case did not concern a citizen child, *Zambrano*'s embrace of prospective considerations linked to EU citizenship for child citizens appears to be unaffected.

103. Gardner, *Qualities*, 190.

104. Kanstroom, *Deportation Nation*, 3.

105. *INS v. Jong Ha Wang*, 450 U.S. 139, 145 (1981).

106. Edith Z. Friedler, "From Extreme Hardship to Extreme Deference: United States Deportation of Its Own Children," *Hastings Constitutional Law Quarterly* 22 (1995): 491. The cases cited in the previous three notes are described in detail in this article.

107. *Villena v. INS*, 622 F.2d 1352, 1359 (9th Cir. 1980) (emphasis added).

108. Constructive in this context is a legal term of art. It means that though the US government did not actually initiate legal proceedings against the children, the impact of the government's action amounted to de facto deportation of the children.

109. *Hernandez-Cordero v. INS*, 819 F.2d 558, 563 (5th Cir. 1987) (en banc).

110. *Inre Bing Chih Kao, In re Mei Tsui Lin*, 23 I&N Dec. 45 (BIA 2001).

111. *In re Francisco Javier Monreal*, 23 I&N Dec. 56 (BIA 2001), 65.

112. Ibid.

113. National Immigration Law Center, *Immigrants' Rights Update*, vol. 15, no. 4 (2001).

114. *Barco-Sandoval v. Gonzales*, 516 F.3d 35 (2d Cir.2008).

115. *Mendez-Castro v. Mukasey, 552 F.3d 975, 979 (9th Cir. 2009).*

116. The BIA publishes "precedent decisions," which are binding on all immigration officers and judges but can be modified or overruled by a federal court. Where the Board determines that the draconian "hardship" standard has not been met, there is no possibility of review by a higher court, nor appeal for the exercise of discretion; see *Romero-Torres v. Ashcroft*, 327 F.3d 887 (9th Cir. 2003); *Martinez-Maldonado v. Gonzalez*, 437 F.3d 679 (9th Cir. 2006).

117. *Acosta v. Gaffney*, 558 F.2d 1153, 1155 (3d Cir. 1977).

118. *Lopez v. Franklin*, 427 F. Supp. 345 (E.D. Mich. 1977).

119. The leading precedent, *Perdido v. INS*, 420 F.2d 1179 (5th Cir. 1969), widely cited to support the proposition that constructive deportation does not violate US children's constitutional rights, may be ripe for reconsideration. See Christina Coll, "U.S. Citizens Deported: The Rejection of American Children Born to Immigrant Parents" (unpublished manuscript, Jan. 8, 2007) (on file with author).

120. *Beharry v. Reno*, 183 F. Supp. 2d 584, 588 (E.D.N.Y. 2002), overruled by *Beharry v. Ashcroft*, 329 F.3d 51 (2d Cir. 2003).

121. *Beharry*, 329 F.3d 51.

122. *Nwaokolo v. INS*, 314 F.3d 303, 308 (7th Cir. 2002), and 310.

123. *Oforji*, 354 F.3d at 609.

124. Ibid., 617–18 (emphasis added).

125. *ZH (Tanzania) (FC) v. Secretary for the Home Department* [2011] UKSC.

126. See Ezer, 1.

127. Karl Eric Knutson, "A New Vision of Childhood," in Parliamentary Assembly, Council of Europe, ed., *The Child as Citizen* (Strasbourg: Council of Europe Publishing, 1996), 17–18.

128. Honig, *Democracy and the Foreigner*, 102, quoting Michael Walzer.

129. See chapter 1, note 38.

130. Migration Policy Group, "Migration News Sheet, Aug. 2003," 3.

131. Johanna Simeant, *La Cause des Sans-Papiers* (Paris: Presses de Sciences Po., 1998), 137.

132. Law No. 2003–1119 of 26 November 2003 on immigration control, foreigners' residence in France, and nationality.

133. Migration Policy Group, "Migration News Sheet, Aug. 2003," 3.

134. Order No. 2004–1248 of 24 November 2004 regarding the legislative section of the Code for the entry and residence of foreigners and the right of asylum.

Chapter 3. Family Ambivalence: The Contested Terrain of Intercountry Adoption

1. Chris Hammond, director of a British association of government and nonprofit adoption agencies, quoted in Jordana P. Simov, "The Effects of Intercountry Adoptions on Biological Parents' Rights," *Loyola of Los Angeles International and Comparative Law Review* 22, no. 2 (1999): note 42 at 251.

2. Sarah Jacobs, "Head to Head: Madonna Adoption," *BBC News*, Apr. 1, 2009.

3. Adoption Cause No. 1 of 2009, *In the Matter of the Adoption of Children Act (Cap 26:01) and In the Matter of CJ (A female infant)*, 2.

4. Ibid., 3, 4.

5. Ibid., 23, 26.

6. Adoption Cause No 2 of 2006 *In the Matter of the Adoption of Children Act (Cap 26:01) and In the Matter of David Banda (A Male Infant)*, 3, 12.

7. Diana Marre and Laura Briggs, "Experiences in Receiving Countries," in Diana Marre and Laura Briggs, eds., *International Adoption: Global Inequalities and the Circulation of Children* (New York: New York University Press, 2009), 223.

8. Domingos Abreu, "Baby-Bearing Storks: Brazilian Intermediaries in the Adoption Process," in Marre and Briggs, 148, 138.

9. Peter Selman, "The Movement of Children for International Adoption: Developments and Trends in Receiving States and States of Origin, 1998–2004," in Marre and Briggs, 33, 34.

10. http://www.un.org/esa/population/publications/adoption2010/child_adoption.pdf, xvii.

11. Peter Selman, "Global Trends in Adoption," *Adoption Advocate 44*. National Council for Adoption, February 2012. Since 2004, there has been a 50 percent drop in international adoptions to the United States, the primary destination country. Elizabeth Bartholet and Paul Barrozo, "Amid Disaster, Haitian Orphans Find Homes," Briefing for NPR broadcast, Jan. 20, 2010 (on file with author).

12. David Smolin, "Child Laundering: How the Intercountry Adoption System Legitimizes and Incentivizes the Practices of Buying, Trafficking, Kidnapping and Stealing Children," *Wayne Law Review* 52, (2006): 115–32; Barbara Demick, "A Family in China Made Babies Their Business," *Los Angeles Times*, Jan. 24, 2010.

13. The United States banned new adoptions from Cambodia in 2002, Vietnam in 2003 and 2008, Guatemala in 2008, and Nepal in 2010 (if abandonment cannot be verified). See US Department of State, "Notice: Update of Status of Adoptions in Cambodia," Mar.

19, 2012; Karen Russo, "Corruption Halts Vietnam Adoptions by Americans," *ABC News*, May 15, 2008; US Department of State, "Guatemala," Nov. 2009; and US Department of State, "Notice: U.S. Department of State Continues to Recommend Against Adopting from Nepal," Jan. 11, 2012.

14. In 2012, Haiti suspended new adoptions and Romania limited international adoptions to a child's relatives or Romanian citizens living abroad. See US Department of State, "Haiti: Alert: Temporary Suspension of New Adoption Cases," May 4, 2012, and "Notice: Romania New Adoption Law in Effect," Apr. 10, 2012.

15. US Department of State, "Top 5 Adopting Countries and States," Sep. 30, 2011.

16. US Department of State, "Alert: Russian President Vladimir Putin Signs Legislation to Ban Intercountry Adoption by U.S. Families into Law," Dec. 28, 2012.

17. Andrew Osborn, "Russia Suspends Adoptions by Americans," *Daily Telegraph*, Apr. 15, 2010, and "Kremlin Knocks U.S. for Silence on Adopted Child's Death," *Moscow Times*, Dec. 5, 2011.

18. Eleana Kim, "Wedding Citizenship and Culture: Korean Adoptees and the Global Family of Korea," in Toby Alice Volkman, ed., *Cultures of Transnational Adoption* (Durham: Duke University Press, 2005), 65.

19. Beth Kyong Lo, "Korean Psych 101," in Jane Jeong Trenka, Julia Chinyere Oparah, and Sun Yung Shin, eds., *Outsiders Within: Writings on Transracial Adoption* (Cambridge, MA: South End Press, 2006), 167. See also Indigo Williams Willing, "Beyond the Vietnam War Adoptions: Representing our Transracial Lives," in Trenka et al., 259.

20. Elizabeth Bartholet, "International Adoption: The Child's Story," *Georgia State University Law Review* 24, no. 2 (2007): 333.

21. Robert Mnookin and E. Szwed, "The 'Best Interests' Syndrome and the Allocation of Power in Child Care," in H. Geach and E. Szwed, eds., *Providing Civil Justice for Children* (London: Edward Arnold, 1983), 10, cited in Nigel Thomas and Claire O'Kane, "When Children's Wishes and Feelings Clash with Their 'Best Interests,'" *International Journal of Children's Rights* 6, no. 2 (1998): 137–54, 151.

22. Sang Nguyen, "Unicef Statement on Guatemalan Intercountry Adoption," Aug. 28, 2003, cited in Families Without Borders, *UNICEF, Guatemalan Adoption, and the Best interests of the Child: An Informative Study* (2003).

23. Jacqueline Bhabha, "Moving Babies: Globalization, Markets and Transnational Adoption," *Fletcher Forum of World Affairs* 28, no. 2 (2004): 181.

24. For some birth mothers, international adoption is an exit route from an impossible situation. See Barbara Yngvesson, "Going 'Home': Adoption, Loss of Bearings, and the Mythology of Roots," in Volkman, 42. For others it is a lifelong trauma. For a careful and nonsensationalist account of the sense of loss that afflicts birth mothers, see Laurel Kendall, "Birth Mothers and Imaginary Lives," in Volkman, 162–81, 165.

25. Institutionalized children in Russia, who number in the hundreds of thousands, suffer from high incidences of mental illness. According to a 2000 study by the Russian government, one in five children raised in orphanages go on to commit crimes, one in ten to commit suicide. See also, Darshak Sanghavi, "Adopted Boy's Return Highlights Problems in Russian Orphanages," *Washington Post*, Apr. 25, 2010.

26. Elizabeth Alice Honig, "Phantom Lives, Narratives of Possibility," in Volkman, 214.

27. For an overview of the deportation of thousands of British children to places like Australia, see Margaret Humphreys, *Empty Cradles* (London: Corgi Books, 2011).

28. For a discussion of the illegal separation of Aboriginal children from their families from 1939 to 1953 in Australia, see Cameron Raynes, *The Last Protector: The Illegal Removal of Aboriginal Children from Their Parents in South Australia* (Kent Town: Wakefield Press, 2009).

29. Rebekka Göpfert and Andrea Hammel, "Kindertransport: History and Memory," *Shofar: An Interdisciplinary Journal of Jewish Studies* 23, no. 1 (2004): 21–27.

30. Toby Alice Volkman, "Introduction: Transnational Adoption," *Social Text 74*, vol. 21, no. 1 (2003): 2. This positive assessment of alternative nonbiological child-rearing patterns is true of other historical antecedents of adoption too, e.g., wet-nursing in nineteenth-century France, and family care for children of migrant mothers since World War II. See Bhabha and Shutter, *Women's Movement*.

31. Peter Selman, "The Movement of Children for International Adoption," in Marre and Briggs, 36.

32. Kathryn Joyce, *The Child Catchers: Rescue, Trafficking, and the New Gospel of Adoption* (New York: Public Affairs, 2013).

33. Under US immigration law, a child can be adopted only from a non–Hague Convention country if he or she has "orphan status," meaning has "no parents" or has "a sole or surviving parent who is unable to care for the child and has, in writing, irrevocably released the child for emigration and adoption." A child is considered to have no parents if "both are determined to have died, disappeared, deserted, abandoned or have been lost or separated from the child." US Department of State, "Who Can Be Adopted."

34. Jacobs, supra note 2. An illustrious case in point is the famous hairdresser Vidal Sassoon, placed in an orphanage with his brother by their mother, after the father died leaving the family in penury. "Stylist Who Snipped Salon Rituals and Built a Global Brand," *Financial Times*, May 13, 2012, 2.

35. This term is preferred to "surrender," which suggests defeat. Barbara Melosh, *Strangers and Kin: The American Way of Adoption* (Cambridge, MA: Harvard University Press, 2002), viii.

36. "Catholic Leaders Embrace Plan to Bring Orphans In," *McClatchy Newspapers*, Jan. 20, 2010.

37. "Canada Trying to 'Fast-Track' Haitian Adoptions: Kenney," *CBC News Canada*, Jan. 20, 2010.

38. Ginger Thompson, "Case Stokes Haiti's Fear for Children, and Itself," *New York Times*, Feb. 1, 2010.

39. Ibid., "After Haiti Quake, the Chaos of Adoption," *New York Times*, Aug. 3. 2010. For a compelling critique of US policy in respect to Haitian adoptions after the 2010 earthquake, see Kathryn Joyce, *The Child Catchers: Rescue, Trafficking and the New Gospel of Adoption* (Public Affairs, 2013).

40. Center for Adoption Policy, *Best Practices in International Adoption: Proposed Framework* (2010), 3.

41. US Department of State, "Table 4: Convention Adoptions and Average Number of Days to Completion by Convention Country," *FY 2011 Annual Report on Intercountry Adoption*, Nov. 2011, 4.

42. "Profile: Zoe's Ark," *BBC News*, Oct. 29, 2007.

43. Signe Howell, *The Kinning of Foreigners: Transnational Adoption in a Global Perspective* (New York: Berghahn Books, 2006), 190.

44. Judith S. Modell, *A Sealed and Secret Kinship: The Culture of Policies and Practices in American Adoption* (New York: Berghahn Books, 2002), 91–107.

45. Claudia Fonseca, "Transnational Connections and Dissenting Views: The Evolution of Child Placement Policies in Brazil," in Marre and Briggs, 154–73.

46. Trenka et al.

47. Kendall, 162–81; Anne Cadoret, "Mothers for Others," in Marre and Briggs, 271–82.

48. Fonseca, 154–73, 159.

49. Françoise-Romaine Ouellette, "The Social Temporalities of Adoption and the Limits of Plenary Adoption," in Marre and Briggs, 69–86; Judith Schachter, "International Adoption: Lessons from Hawai'i," in ibid., 52–68; Chantal Collard, "The Transnational Adoption of a Related Child in Quebec, Canada," in ibid., 119–137, 128.

50. Signe Howell, "Return Journeys and the Search for Roots: Contradictory Values Concerning Identity," in Marre and Briggs, 264.

51. Jessaca B. Leinaweaver, "The Medicalization of Adoption in and from Peru," in Marre and Briggs, 197.

52. Khabibullina, 175.

53. Bartholet, "International Adoption," 374–75.

54. Emily Noonan, "Adoption and the Guatemalan Journey to American Parenthood," *Childhood* 14, no. 3 (2007): 301; Judith L. Gibbons, Samantha L. Wilson, and Alicia M. Schnell, "Foster Parents as a Critical Link and Resource in International Adoptions from Guatemala," *Adoption Quarterly* 12, no. 2 (2009): 59–77.

55. Kay Johnson, *Wanting a Daughter, Needing a Son: Abandonment, Adoption, and Orphanage Care in China* (St. Paul: Yeong & Yeong, 2004).

56. "Manufacturing Abandoned Infants," Southern Metropolis News (Nanfang Dushi Bao) (China), July 1, 2009.

57. Demick.

58. As I noted in chapters 1 and 2, caution is necessary when ascribing a single motive to individuals' migration and family-formation decisions. A more realistic view is that multiple, complex, and interconnected factors determine people's key life choices, including the decision to adopt a child internationally.

59. US Department of State, "Intercountry Adoptions in the United States for FY2009."

60. Sanghavi.

61. Jacobs, supra note 2.

62. Michael Freeman, "Article 3: The Best Interests of the Child," in A. Alen et al., eds., *A Commentary on the United Nations Convention on the Rights of the Child* (Leiden, The Netherlands: Martinus Nijhoff Publishers, 2007), 64.

63. Volkman, "Introduction: Transnational Adoption," in Volkman, 19.

64. N. V. Prisiahnaia, "Orphan Children: Adjusting to Life after the Boarding Institution," *Russian Education and Society* 50, no. 12 (2008): 24.

65. Mary Margaret Gleason et al., "Epidemiology of Psychiatric Disorders in Very Young Children in a Romanian Pediatric Setting," *European Child and Adolescent Psychiatry* 20, no. 10 (2011): 527–35; Anna T. Smyke et al., "Placement in Foster Care Enhances Quality of Attachment among Young Institutionalized Children," *Child Development* 81, no. 1 (2010): 212–23. However, other studies show that at least some children can overcome the effects of profound institutional privation from infancy to three years of age, and can develop normal psychological functioning if they are later placed in a good adoptive family. Michael Rutter, Jana Kreppner, Thoman O'Connor, and the English and Romanian Adoptees study team, "Specificity and Heterogeneity in Children's Responses to Profound Institutional Privation," *British Journal of Psychiatry* 179 (2001): 97–103.

66. See *David Banda* case, supra note 9, at 16.

67. AIDS has orphaned more than 16 million children, 14.8 million of whom live in sub-Saharan Africa. UNAIDS, *Report on the Global AIDS Epidemic 2010*, 112.

68. UN, *Child Adoptions: Trends and Policies*, SST/ESA/SER.A/292 (2009), 66, 130,., 31, 129. See also Mary Ann Davis, "Intercountry Adoption Flows from Africa to the U.S.: A Fifth Wave of Intercountry Adoptions?," International *Migration Review* 45, no. 4 (2011): 784–811, 805.

69. Melissa Fay Greene, "What Will Become of Africa's AIDS Orphans?," *New York Times Magazine*, Dec. 22, 2002.

70. US Department of State, "Intercountry Adoptions 2011."

71. Indrias Getachew, *Ethiopia: Steady Increase in Street Children Orphaned by AIDS* (UNICEF, 2006).

72. US Department of State, "Intercountry Adoptions 2011."

73. Ethiopian Ministry of Finance and Economic Development and UN, *Investing in Boys and Girls in Ethiopia: Past, Present and Future 2012*, 93.

74. US Department of State, "Intercountry Adoptions 2011."

75. Mehair Taddele Maru, "On International Adoption of Ethiopian Children," *Reporter*, June 27, 2009.

76. Accreditation and Adoption Accredited Bodies, "General Principals and Guide to Good Practice: Guide No. 2," Hague Conference on Private International Law, 2012: 90–97.

77. Pauline Turner Strong, cited in Laura Briggs and Diana Marre, "Introduction: The Circulation of Children," in Marre and Briggs, 1.

78. Bhabha and Schmidt, *SAA (US)*.

79. Jane Perlez, "With U.S. Busy, China Is Romping with Neighbours," *New York Times*, Dec. 3, 2003.

80. Kathryn Joyce, *The Child Catchers: Rescue, Trafficking, and the New Gospel of Adoption* (New York: PublicAffairs, 2013).

81. "Baby Smugglers Sentenced to Death," *BBC News*, Nov. 30, 2003.

82. Michael Leidig, "A Trade that No One Seems Prepared to Admit Exists," *Sunday Telegraph*, Nov. 30, 2003.

83. Viviana A. Zelizer, *Pricing the Priceless Child: The Changing Social Value of Children* (New York: Basic Books, 1985), 5–6.

84. Nguyen, "Guatemalan Intercountry Adoption."

85. Optional Protocol to the Convention on the Rights of the Child on the Sale of Children, Child Prostitution and Child Pornography, GA Res. 54/263, Annex I, 54 UN GAOR Supp. (No. 49), 7, A/RES/54/263, Vol. III, May 25, 2000, Art. 3 [Sale of Children Protocol].

86. Siddharth Kara, *Sex Trafficking: Inside the Business of Modern Slavery* (New York: Columbia University Press, 2009).

87. In the case of international adoption, the "strangers" are the adoptive parents, but they are still strangers at the time of transport.

88. The Internet has even been used to challenge restrictive adoptive rules: in Guatemala, the locus of extensive adoption profiteering, four hundred "adoption attorneys" opposing more stringent adoption controls galvanized support from adoptive parents online. Hugh Dellios and Bonnie Miller Rubin, "Guatemala Grapples with Black Market for Adopted Babies," *Chicago Tribune*, Oct. 4, 2003, 3.

89. Human Rights Council, *Report of the Special Rapporteur on the Sale of Children, Child Prostitution and Child Pornography, Najat Maalla M'jid,* A/HRC/19/63, 23 Dec. 2011.

90. Jacobs, supra note 2.

91. Debora L. Spar, *The Baby Business: How Money, Science, and Politics Drive the Commerce of Conception* (Boston: Harvard Business School Press, 2006).

92. The population of Romanian and Chinese orphanages expanded because of government policies, not the adoption market. But demand, not supply, drove the surge in transnational adoption,.

93. Dellios and Rubin.

94. Diana Lary, *Minnan Migrations: The People of Southern Jufian on the Move, Past and Present* (Vancouver: University of British Columbia, 2003), 20. The sale of organs is another example of what is perceived as a lesser evil.

95. Sue Ferguson, "A New Community Comes of Age: As the First Chinese Adoptees Reach Puberty, Researchers Are Taking Stock," *Canadian Business and Current Affairs*, Feb. 24, 2003.

96. Families Without Borders, 8.

97. Richard A. Posner and Elisabeth Landes, "The Economics of the Baby Shortage," *Journal of Legal Studies* 7, no. 2 (1978): 323–48.

98. Rayhan Demytrie, "Tajik Women Who Buy and Sell Babies," *BBC News Tajikistan*, Jan. 28, 2009.

99. Kay Johnson, telephone conversation with author, Apr. 30, 2010.

100. Paradoxical as it seems, one can think of coercion and consent going together in many of the situations reviewed in this chapter.

101. Richard Falk, *Predatory Globalization: A Critique* (Cambridge: Polity Press, 1999).

102. Sophie Arie, "I Gave Away Son so He Could Escape Squalor: Albanian Mother Denies Selling Her Child to Couple," *Guardian*, Oct. 14, 2003, 19.

103. Raymond Bonner, "For Poor Families, Selling Baby Girls Was Economic Boon," *New York Times*, June 23, 2003, A3.

104. See Schuster Institute for Investigative Journalism (Schuster Institute), Brandeis University, "News Reports of Adoption Irregularities in Cambodia," Feb. 22, 2011.

105. Norimitsu Onishi, "Korea Aims to End Stigma of Adoption and Stop 'Exporting' Babies," *New York Times*, Oct. 8, 2008; Shane Green, "The Seoul Providers," *Sydney Morning Herald*, Dec. 17, 2003.

106. See Schuster Institute, "News Reports of Adoption Irregularities in Guatemala," Mar. 7, 2012. See also Letta Taylor, "Robbing the Cradle: Adoptions Under Fire in Guatamala," *Newsday*, Oct. 26, 2003. ("They said my baby would go to a family in the United States and have a better life," recalled Mendoza, 17. "When I told them I wanted to keep him, they said, 'If you don't sign, we'll kill you.'")

107. "World Briefing: Romania: Adoption Dispute with Europeans," *New York Times*, Feb. 5, 2004.

108. *Lakshmi Kant Pandey v. Union of India and Others* (1984) 2 SCC 244.

109. *Bengt Ingmar Eriksson v. Jamnibai Sukharya Dhangda*, decided June 8, 1987, Notice of Motion No. 1738 of 1985 in Misc. Petition No. 570 of 1980 (Bombay Original Side), cited in Asha Bajpai, *Child Rights in India: Law, Policy and Practice* (New Delhi: Oxford University Press, 2003), 69–70.

110. Bajpai, 70.

111. Catherine Elton, "In El Salvador: A Disappeared Son Returns," *Christian Science Monitor*, Mar. 5, 2001.

112. In Argentina, the National Commission for the Right to Identity (CONADI) has taken a lead role. Reed Lindsay, "Children of the Disappeared Step Forth: Argentina's 'Dirty War' Gives Us More Secrets as the Victims of Baby Theft Unearth Their Real Identities," *Observer*, June 8, 2003. In El Salvador, several human-rights organizations, including Physicians for Human Rights, in partnership with the Salvadorean organization Pro Busqueda and Amnesty International, have called for greater political attention to the continuing problem. See PHR, "Physicians Launch DNA Testing to Reunite 'Disappeared' Salvadorean Children with Parents," May 31, 1995. Amnesty International, *El Salvador: Where Are the "Disappeared" Children?* (2003).

113. An increasing number of children are taken from their undocumented biological parents and then placed for adoption with American families. In one recent case, a Guatemalan woman lost rights to her five-year-old son after she was imprisoned in an immigration sting; the boy's adoption by a Missouri couple is expected to proceed. Susan Redden, "Judge Terminates Guatemalan Woman's Rights to Child, Allows Carthage Couple to Adopt," *Joplin Globe*, July 18, 2012.

114. See Bajpai, 61–64.

115. CRC, Art. 21(b).

116. David Smolin, *Abduction, Sale and Traffic in Children in the Context of Intercountry Adoption*, paper presented at the Special Commission of The Hague Conference on Private International Law, The Hague, Netherlands, June 2010, 11.

117. "UNICEF's Position on Inter-country Adoption," UNICEF, July 22, 2010.

118. Families Without Borders, 7.

119. Dellios and Rubin.

120. Kim, 63. See also UN, *Child Adoptions*, 69–74.

121. Korean Ministry of Health & Welfare, "Policies: Children, Support for Children in Need."

122. Fonseca, 162.

123. Barbara Yngvesson, "Refiguring Kinship in the Space of Adoption," in Marre and Briggs, 105.

124. Bartholet, "International Adoption," 339–40, 333–34.

125. Howell, "Return Journeys," 258.

126. "Hague Intercountry Adoption Convention Outline," Hague Conference on Private International Law, January 2013, 2.

127. "Recognizing that intercountry adoption may offer the advantage of a permanent family to a child for whom a suitable family cannot be found in his or her State of origin . . ." Convention on Protection of Children and Co-operation in Respect of Intercountry Adoption, May 29, 1993, S. Treaty Doc. No. 105–51 (1998), 1870 UNTS 182, Preamble [hereafter Hague Convention].

128. Hague Convention, Art. 4(b).

129. Paulo Barrozzo, presentation at Adoption Policy Conference, New York Law School, Mar. 6, 2009.

130. The UN has appointed a Special Rapporteur on the Sale of Children, Child Prostitution and Pornography who has documented egregious cases and produced reports. In addition, the CRC Sale of Children Protocol entered into force on Jan. 18, 2002.

131. Melosh, *Strangers and Kin*, 3–4.

132. Transnational adoption may be an easier option for unorthodox family types because US birth mothers favor married couples. See Marilyn Gardner, "One + One Makes a Family," *Christian Science Monitor*, Mar. 23, 2003.

133. Barbara Yngvesson, "Negotiating Motherhood: Identity and Difference in 'Open' Adoptions," *Law and Society Review* 31, no. 1 (1997): 31, 66.

134. Mary Wiltenburg and Amanda Paulson, "All in the (Mixed-race) Family: A US Trend," *Christian Science Monitor*, Aug. 28, 2003.

135. "America's Children: Key National Indicators of Well-being, 2011: Adoption," Federal Interagency Forum on Child and Family Statistics. See also Multiethnic Placement Act (MEPA), 42 U.S.C. §§ 671 (18), 1966b (2006) (prohibiting child-welfare agencies from delaying or denying adoptions based on race but allowing race as a factor in placement decisions under certain narrow circumstances).

136. Astrid Trotzig, quoted in Barbara Yngvesson, "Placing the 'Gift Child' in Transnational Adoption," *Law & Society Review* 36, no. 2 (2002): 247, 248, 227.

137. Mary Lyndon Shanley, *Making Babies, Making Families* (Boston: Beacon Press, 2001).

138. Yngvesson, "Refiguring Kinship," 109.

139. Caroline Legrand, "Routes to the Roots: Toward an Anthropology of Genealogical Practices," in Marre and Briggs, 249.

140. Betty Jean Lifton, *Journey of the Adopted Self: A Quest for Wholeness* (New York: Basic Books, 1994), 68.

141. Lifton, *Adopted Self*, 189.

142. J. Feinberg, "The Child's Right to an Open Future," in William Aiken and Hugh LaFollette, eds., *Whose Child? Children's Rights, Parental Authority and State Power* (Totowa, NJ: Littlefield Adams, 1980), cited in Thomas and O'Kane, "When Children's Wishes," 140.

143. CRC, Arts. 7, 8.

144. Kay Johnson, "Chaobao: The Plight of Chinese Adoptive Parents in the Era of the One-child Policy," in Volkman, 117.

145. Adoption Law of the People's Republic of China (adopted on Dec. 29, 1991), Arts. 5, 18, 21.

146. Volkman.

147. The *Nystrom* case, a decision of the ICCPR's Human Rights Committee, challenges the notion that a person who has lived the vast majority of his life in a country of which he happens not to be a citizen (in Nystrom's case, all but the first twenty-four days of his life, a situation analogous to that of infant adoptees) cannot be justifiably held to consider it their "home country." *Nystrom v. Australia*, CCPR, Comm. No. 1557/2007, 18 Aug. 2011.

148. This concept of "home" may well be as artificial and inappropriate as the one used to justify deportation of long-settled immigrants following criminal convictions. See Jacqueline Bhabha, "Get Back to Where You Once Belonged: Identity, Citizenship and Exclusion in Europe," *Human Rights Quarterly* 20, no. 3 (1998): 592–627.

149. Kim, 53.

150. See Trenka et al., and Volkman.

151. Kim, 54.

152. Homi K. Bhabha, *The Location of Culture* (New York: Routledge, 1994).

153. Aihwa Ong, *Flexible Citizenship: The Cultural Logics of Transnationality* (Durham: Duke University Press, 1999).

154. Howell, "Return Journeys," 256–57.

155. Ibid., 257.

156. Kim, 69.

157. Jacqueline Bhabha and Wendy Young, "Not an Adult in Miniature: Children as Refugees," *International Journal of Refugee Law* 11 (1999): 84–125; Bhabha and Crock; and Wendy Ayotte, *Separated Children Coming to Western Europe: Why They Travel and How They Arrive* (Save the Children, 2000).

158. Susan Moller Okin, *Justice, Gender, and the Family* (New York: Basic Books, 1989). Several scholars also recognize the failures of some families to provide the necessary nurturing to their children. See, generally, Elisabeth M. Ward, "Utilizing Intercountry Adoption to Combat Human Rights Abuses of Children," *Michigan State University College of Law Journal of International Law* 17, no. 3 (2008–2009): 729. This article advocates reform of the intercountry adoption system to provide greater protections to children who suffer human-rights abuses by their families.

159. Concern about corruption and inadequate legal safeguards for transnational adoption in Romania led the Romanian government, rather than the United States or any other receiving country, to restrict adoptions. US Department of State, "Update on Romanian Moratorium on International Adoption," Jan. 2004.

160. Betty Jean Lifton, *Lost & Found: The Adoption Experience* (New York: Harper Perennial, 1988); Betty Jean Lifton, *Twice Born: Memoirs of an Adopted Daughter* (New York: St. Martin's Griffin, 1998).

161. Shanley, 13, 15.

162. See Carolyn Lisa Norris, *The Banning of International Adoptions in Romania: Reasons, Meaning, and Implications for Child Care and Protection* (Boston: Boston University Press,

2009); Harry de Quetteville, "EU Forces Romania into Ban on Foreign Adoptions," *Telegraph*, June 17, 2004.

163. Eleana Kim, "Our Adoptee, Our Alien: Transnational Adoptees as Specters of Foreignness and Family in South Korea," *Anthropological Quarterly* 80, no. 2 (2007): 497, 502.

164. 1989 Law on Marriage and Family (allowing adoptions within Cambodia regardless of nationality of adoptive parent) and "Can Expats Adopt Cambodian Children?," *Cambodian Law Blog*, June 9, 2011; "Cambodian Adoption Ban 'Unlawful,'" *BBC News*, Apr. 20, 2005.

165. "Guatemala halts foreign adoptions," *BBC News*, May 6, 2008.

166. US Department of State, "Putin Signs Legislation to Ban Intercountry Adoption."

167. Pam Belluck and Jim Yardley, "China Tightens Adoption Rules for Foreigners," *New York Times*, Dec. 20, 2006.

168. David M. Smolin, "Child Laundering and the Hague Convention on Intercountry Adoption: The Future and Past of Intercountry Adoption," *University of Louisville Law Review* 48, no. 3 (2010): 441, 490.

169. Shanley, 19.

170. The United States recently changed its laws to enable children adopted overseas by US citizens to get their citizenship automatically, within forty-five days of entering the United States, rather than requiring adoptive parents to comply with additional qualifying procedures after the child enters. See Child Citizenship Act of 2000, Pub. L. No. 106–395, 114 Stat. 163 (2000), codified at 8 U.S.C. §§ 1431–33. Indeed, for all countries that have ratified the CRC, nationality passes from adoptive parent to adopted child just as readily as it passes from biological parent to natural child. CRC, Art. 21.

171. For the case of "Oscar W.," see Human Rights Watch, *Costly and Unfair: Flaws in US Immigration Detention Policy* (2010), 4.

172. Gardner, "One + One Makes a Family."

173. This is true for each of the top twenty countries of origin of "orphans" adopted in the United States in 2002. See US Department of State, "Immigrant Visas Issued to Orphans Coming to the U.S.: Fiscal Years 2000–2005."

174. Patrick McDermott, "Disappeared Children and the Adoptee as Immigrant," in Trenka et al., 105–14.

175. Adoption of Children Act (Cap 26:01), Section 3(5).

176. This mirrors the argument about exceptionally compassionate circumstances in deportation cases, and the assessment of need in family-reunion cases, such as the ECHR case, *Gul v. Switzerland*. See chapter 1, note 100.

177. Jessica Leinaweaver, "Medicalization of Adoption in and from Peru," 197.

178. See Elizabeth Bartholet, *Nobody's Children: Abuse and Neglect, Foster Drift, and the Adoption Alternative* (Boston: Beacon Press, 1999).

179. Jacobs, supra note 2.

180. And here too there is a market—Canadian wombs are apparently cheaper to rent than American ones. Aaron Derfel, "More Americans Renting Canadian Wombs: Prof: At Least $6,000 Cheaper," *National Post (Canada)*, Oct. 24, 2003.

181. Auksuole Cepaitiene, "Children, Individuality, Family: Discussing Assisted Reproductive Technologies and Adoption in Lithuania," in Marre and Briggs, 208–22.

182. Martha Field suggests that both surrogate and birth mothers should always have the option of retaining their children at or following birth, despite contrary contractual arrangements. See Martha A. Field, *Surrogate Motherhood: The Legal and Human Issues* (Cambridge, MA: Harvard University Press, 1988), 151.

183. See CRC, Arts. 7 and 8. See also Hague Convention, Art. 30 (but note it only requires access to information "in so far as is permitted" by the laws of the state of origin; this does not ensure adequate access to birth-registration information for an adopted child).

Chapter 4. Targeting the Right Issue: Trafficked Children and the Human Rights Imperative

1. "Traffickers Buying Romanian Orphans for Begging for 3,000," *Austrian Times*, Nov. 10, 2010.

2. Carole Vance, "Sexual Rights and Agency," keynote address, Sex Work in Asia: Health, Agency, and Sexuality Conference, Harvard University, Oct. 1, 2010.

3. Gross exploitation of domestic child servants by diplomats or wealthy émigré families is a common form of trafficking within the United States. See Louise Shelley, *Human Trafficking: A Global Perspective* (Cambridge, UK: Cambridge University Press, 2010), 251.

4. This is common in Europe, where access to permanent status for trafficking victims in the destination state is as rare as any form of social or economic support in the home country. Shelley, 215.

5. Helga Konrad, "Trafficking in Human Beings: A Comparative Account of Legal Provisions in Belgium, Italy, the Netherlands, Sweden and the United States," in Christien L. van den Anker, ed., *Trafficking and Women's Rights* (New York: Palgrave Macmillan, 2006), 118.

6. Immigration Law Practitioners Association, UK, cited in Alexis A. Aronowitz, *Human Trafficking, Human Misery: The Global Trade in Human Beings* (Westport, CT: Praeger Publishers, 2009), 158.

7. US Department of State report on human rights practices in Albania, 2005, cited in Shelley, 215. For more recent efforts by Albania, see Group of Experts on Action against Trafficking in Human Being, *Report Concerning the Implementation of the Council of Europe Convention on Action against Trafficking in Human Beings by Albania*, First Evaluation Round (2011).

8. This is a highly lucrative side business for lawyers working in the overall trafficking network. One Harvard-educated lawyer and his New York law firm earned over $10 million in fees in the 1990s by filing false political-asylum claims to secure the entry of exploitable Chinese workers. Shelley, 106.

9. Aronowitz, 63.

10. Shelley, 212.

11. Women's Refugee Commission, *The Struggle between Migration Control and Victim Protection: The UK Approach to Human Trafficking* (2005), 26.

12. End Child Prostitution, Child Pornography and Trafficking of Children for Sexual Purposes (ECPAT) International, *[Ireland] Country Progress Card* (2010), 7, citing Speech by Denis Naughten TD at the Dignity & Demand Conference Royal College of Physicians, Nov. 5, 2009.

13. Mark Townshend, "Trafficked Children Condemned to a Nightmare by State Neglect," *The Guardian*, May 28, 2011.

14. ECPAT UK and the Anti-Trafficking Monitoring Group (ATMG), *Wrong Kind of Victim? One Year On: An Analysis of UK Measures to Protect Trafficked Persons* (June 2010), 50, 24; and Tom Brady and Shane Phelan, "Kids in HSE Care Ended Up Working in Brothels," *Irish Independent*, June 3, 2011.

15. Anne Gallagher suggests that the human rights engagement with antitrafficking work has prevented "an uncritical acceptance of the strange legal fiction . . . that 'trafficking' and 'migrant smuggling' are two completely different crimes involving helpless, virtuous victims on the one side, and foolish or greedy adventurers, complicit in their own misfortune, on the other." Gallagher, 3.

16. UNHCR, *Refugee Protection and Mixed Migration: The 10-Point Plan of Action*, Feb. 2011, 6.

17. USCIS, *Children's Asylum Claims* (1998); UK Home Office Border & Immigration Agency, "Processing Asylum Applications from a Child," *Special Cases: Guidance* (2005); and UNHCR, *Guidelines on International Protection No. 8: Child Asylum Claims under Articles 1(A)2 and 1(F) of the 1951 Convention and/or 1967 Protocol relating to the Status of Refugees*, HCR/GIP/09/08, Dec. 22, 2009 [*2009 Guidelines on Child Asylum Claims*].

18. The act was passed in 2000, and then reauthorized in 2003, 2005, 2008, and 2011. See Jacqueline Bhabha and Susan Schmidt, "From Kafka to Wilberforce: Is the U.S. Government's Approach to Child Migrants Improving?," *Immigration Briefings* No. 11–02, Feb. 2011, 1–30.

19. See Office of the UN High Commissioner for Human Rights (OHCHR), *Recommended Principles and Guidelines on Human Rights and Human Trafficking*, E/2002/68/Add.1, May 20, 2002; Council Framework Decision of 19 July 2002 on Trafficking Human Beings, 2002/629/JHA, OJ L 203/1, Aug. 1, 2002; South Asian Association for Regional Cooperation (SAARC) Convention on Preventing and Combating Trafficking in Women and Children for Prostitution, SAAROCPCT/WD/ l/REV.3/98; and Council of Europe Convention on Action against Trafficking in Human Beings, May 16, 2005, CETS 197 16.V.2005 [European Trafficking Convention]. For a full discussion of the difference emphases and goals of these legislative initiatives, see Gallagher, 42–46.

20. Sale of Children Protocol. See chapter 3, note 81.

21. Article 6(4) of the Protocol to Prevent, Suppress and Punish Trafficking in Persons, Especially Women and Children [Palermo Protocol], supplementing the UN Convention against Transnational Organized Crime, Nov. 15, 2000, GA Res. 55/25, Annex II, UN GAOR, 55th Sess., Supp. No. 49, at 53, A/RES/55/25 (Vol. I) (2001).

22. European Trafficking Convention, Art. 5. The European Union is also strengthening its child-specific asylum procedures in the 2005 EU Asylum Procedures Directive, to oblige member states to take into account children's best interests and special needs when arriving at a decision about their case (Amendment 39 to Art. 13[1][3]); and to ensure that interviews with children are conducted by child welfare experts (Amendment 45 to Art. 14[3][e]). See Council Directive 2005/85/EC of 1 December 2005 on Minimum Standards on Procedures in Member States for Granting and Withdrawing Refugee Status.

23. EU Trafficking Directive.

24. For a list of relevant international instruments, see Human Rights Council, *Report Submitted by the Special Rapporteur on Trafficking in Persons, Especially Women and Children, Joy Ngozi Ezeilo*, A/HRC/10/16, 20 Feb. 2009, para. 20.

25. In the United States, for example, there are documented cases in which victims of "domestic minor sex trafficking" have been arrested, prosecuted, criminalized, and revictimized by the justice system. Human Rights Council, *Interim report of the Special Rapporteur on Trafficking in Persons, Especially Women and Children, Joy Ezeilo*, A/65/288, 9 Aug. 2010, para. 20 [*Report A/65/288 (2010)*].

26. Shelley, 259.

27. ECPAT UK reports that the United Kingdom still lacked a comprehensive framework for reporting trafficking children. *The Child Protection System in England: Written Evidence Submitted by ECPAT UK* (Nov. 15, 2011).

28. UNICEF, *Action to Prevent Child Trafficking in South Eastern Europe: A Preliminary Assessment* (2006), 14, 23.

29. Beyond these economic realities, the notion of parents as masters, and children as property, remains deeply rooted. For an analysis of traditional theories of parental rights, including the ambivalence between protection and control, see Woodhouse, "Hatching the Egg: A Child-centered Perspective on Parents' Rights," 14 *Cardozo Law Review* 1747 (1993).

30. Shelley, 177.

31. Goździak, "Identifying Child Victims," 253.

32. Habiba Nosheen and Anup Kaphle, "For Nepali Girls Abducted into Indian Brothels, Where Is Home?," *Atlantic*, Nov. 30, 2011.

33. Human Rights Council, *Report of the Special Rapporteur on Trafficking in Persons, Especially Women and Children, Joy Ngozi Ezeilo*, A/HRC/17/35, 13 Apr. 2011, para. 21; and UN General Assembly, *Trafficking in Persons, Especially Women and Children: Note by the Secretary-general*, A/64/290, 12 Aug. 2009, para. 31.

34. Jacqueline Bhabha, "Demography and Rights: Women, Children and Access to Asylum," *International Journal of Refugee Law* 16, no. 2 (2004), 227–43.

35. Julia O'Connell Davidson, "Moving Children? Child Trafficking, Child Migration, and Child Rights," *Critical Social Policy* 31, no. 3 (2011): 461–64; Jennifer M. Chacón, "Tensions and Trade-offs: Protecting Trafficking Victims in the Era of Immigration Enforcement," *University of Pennsylvania Law Review* 158 (2010): 1640–41; and Clare Ribando Seelke and Alison Siskin, *Trafficking in Persons: U.S. Policy and Issues for Congress* (CRS, 2008), note 9 at 3.

36. See UNICEF's *Guidelines*, 2.5 (Right to Information).

37. Child protection must be a central strategy for border-control personnel. This may include preventing or delaying a child's exit if the circumstances appear to warrant it; discriminatory exit bans against whole groups based on age and/or gender, however, violate fundamental human-rights principles. See International Council on Human Rights Policy, *Irregular Migration, Migrant Smuggling and Human Rights: Towards Coherence* (2010), 95.

38. Shortcomings of "rescue" strategies include non-identification of trafficked children at borders, inadequate long-term protection measures and failure to emphasize economic and social reintegration upon return. See Janie Chuang, "Rescuing Trafficking from Ideological Capture: Prostitution Reform and Anti-Trafficking Law and Policy," 158 *University of Pennsylvania Law Review* 1655 (2010): 1655–728.

39. UNICEF, *Action to Prevent Child Trafficking*, 23.

40. Gallagher, 24.

41. For the latter approach see Kara, 224–26. Some advocates do stress the need for social interventions to strengthen vulnerable local communities—see, e.g., the "social-ecological" model of prevention, described in the public health literature—and there has been a corresponding emphasis on capacity building at the programmatic level. Roy Ahn et al., *Sex Trafficking of Women and Girls in Eight Metropolitan Areas Around the World: Case Studies Viewed through a Public Health Lens*, MGH Division of Global Health and Human Rights, Report for Humanity United (2009), 6–8, 194, 198; Jonathan Todres, "Moving Upstream: The Merits of a Public Health Law Approach to Human Trafficking," *North Carolina Law Review* 89, no. 2 (2011): 447; and UNICEF Innocenti Research Centre, *South Asia in Action: Preventing and Responding to Child Trafficking: Summary Report* (2008).

42. Catherine A. MacKinnon, "Trafficking, Prostitution and Inequality," *Harvard Civil Rights–Civil Liberties Law Review* 46, (2011): 271–309; Robert Uy, "Blinded by Red Lights: Why Trafficking Discourse Should Shift Away from Sex and the 'Perfect Victim' Paradigm," *Berkeley Journal of Gender, Law & Justice* 26, (2011): 204–19; and Jacqueline Berman, "The Left, the Right, and the Prostitute: The Making of U.S. Anti-trafficking in Persons Policy," *Tulane Journal of International and Comparative Law* 14 (2006): 269–93.

43. Some commentators have attributed this inconsistency to a "reductivist narrative" on trafficking: "But what's enthralled the media, the Christian right and the Bush administration is not the demanding, multi-layered narrative of migrants, but the damsels in distress, the innocents lured across borders [for prostitution]." Jennifer Block, "Sex Trafficking: Why the Faith Trade Is Interested in the Sex Trade," *Conscience*, Summer–Autumn 2004, at 32, 33, cited in Chuang, "Rescuing Trafficking," 1697.

44. Data based on reporting states only. UN Office on Drugs and Crime (UNODC), *Global Report on Trafficking in Persons* (Feb. 2009), 49.

45. Although the ILO no longer distinguishes between forced labor and trafficking for statistical purposes, the impact of this change may be slight since the ILO's definition of "forced labor" only includes labor that is the product of "coercion or deception." The most recent estimate, based on new data sources and methodologies, updates the 2008 estimate of 12.3 million victims of forced labor, of whom 2.4 million were trafficked. ILO, *Global Estimate of Forced Labour Results and Methodology 2012* (2012), 13, 19–20; ILO, *Action Against Trafficking in Human Beings* (2008), 3.

46. Ambassador-at-Large Luis C deBaca, US Department of State Office to Monitor and Combat Trafficking in Persons, Remarks at "Freedom Here & Now: Ending Modern Slavery" Event, May 8, 2012, in Minneapolis, MN. See also Alison Siskin and Liana Sun Wyler, *Trafficking in Persons: U.S. Policy and Issues for Congress* (CRS, 2010), 7 at note 7 (noting the 800,000 annual estimate dates from 2003).

47. Elzbieta M. Goździak, "On Challenges, Dilemmas, and Opportunities in Studying Trafficked Children," *Anthropological Quarterly* 81, no. 4 (2008): 903–24.

48. ILO, *Every Child Counts, New Global Estimate on Child Labour* (2002), 6.

49. While UNICEF and others suggest up to 50 percent of trafficking victims are children, this is likely based on 2008 ILO estimates. ILO, *Forced Labour 2012*, 14; and ILO, *Tackling Child Labour: From Commitment to Action* (2012), 15.

50. See O'Connell Davidson, "Moving Children," 455.

51. Note that this calculation excludes some 726,000 children engaged in state-imposed or military forms of forced labor. ILO, *Forced Labour 2012*, 13–15.

52. US Department of Justice, *Characteristics of Suspected Human Trafficking Incidents, 2008–2010* (2011), 6.

53. Ibid.; US Department of Labor, *2011 Findings on the Worst Forms of Child Labor* (2011); US Department of Labor, *2010 Findings on the Worst Forms of Child Labor* (2010); and Cameron Newman, *Trafficking in Humans*, 28, 81.

54. ILO, "Asia and the Pacific", www.ilo.org/ipec/Regionsandcountries/Asia/lang—en /index.htm.

55. Barack Obama, President, Presidential Proclamation—National Slavery and Human Trafficking Prevention Month, Jan. 4, 2010.

56. George W. Bush, President, Statement on Signing the Trafficking Victims Protection Reauthorization Act of 2005.

57. *TIP Report 2010*, 2.

58. See Ann Jordan, *Slavery, Forced Labor, Debt Bondage, and Human Trafficking: From Conceptual Confusion to Targeted Solutions*, Issue Paper 2 (Center for Human Rights & Humanitarian Law, 2011); and Karen E. Bravo, "The Role of the Transatlantic Slave Trade in Contemporary Anti-Human Trafficking Discourse," *Seattle Journal for Social Justice* 9, no. 2 (2011): 555–97, 569.

59. *TIP Report 2012*.

60. Kara, 111.

61. Gallagher, 177. The preferred view among scholars is that the notion of "slavery," as defined in Article 1 of the 1926 League of Nations Convention to Suppress the Slave Trade and Slavery, refers only to situations where "any or all the powers attaching to the right of ownership are exercised by the master." League of Nations, *Slavery: Report of the Advisory Committee of Experts, Third (Extraordinary) Meeting of the Advisory Committee*, LN Doc. C.189 (I).M.145.1936.VI, Apr.. 13–14, 1936, at 24–25, cited in Gallagher, note 208 at 180–81. Precisely because the term was intended to be used narrowly, later international treaties introduced the notion of "institutions and practices similar to slavery" to expand the scope of abolitionist intervention.

62. See Anti-Slavery International, "Bonded Labour," www.antislavery.org.

63. For a discussion of whether the concept of trafficking could be extended to intergenerational bonded labor, in exactly the situation mentioned in the text, and a suggestion that "harboring" might cover it, see Gallagher, 31. I agree with her reasoning that it is preferable to resist this expansion of the concept of trafficking, because it makes the three-part definition of trafficking discussed below redundant in parts.

64. Ahn et al., 6.

65. For indicators characteristic of trafficked persons, see Aronowitz, Appendix 3, 215–19.

66. Kara, 39–41.

67. This analogy was developed by Carole Vance, supra note 2.

68. Nicholas Kristof and Sheryl WuDunn, *Half the Sky, Turning Oppression into Opportunity for Women Worldwide* (New York: Knopf, 2009).

69. UN Convention against Transnational Organized Crime.

70. Palermo Protocol, Art. 3(a).

71. Not all exploited children are trafficked: a child who applies for and accepts an exploitative job offer and keeps the earnings, such as they are, is not trafficked; a child who decides to travel abroad alone in search of work is not trafficked just because the working situation ends up being exploitative. But sometimes the distinction is elusive, see UNICEF, *Action to Prevent Child Trafficking*, 19.

72. Refugee Convention, Art. 31.

73. CRC, Art. 22.

74. The Palermo Protocol makes it clear that trafficking victims may be eligible for refugee protection, Art. 14; the merits of each case, of course, have to be considered according to the criteria in the refugee definition, discussed in detail in chapter 6.

75. IOM, *Trafficking in Unaccompanied Minors in the EU* (2002), 23 [*Minors*].

76. UNICEF, *Child Trafficking Guidelines*.

77. IOM, *Minors*, 27.

78. Myron Weiner, Neera Burra, and Asha Bajpai, *Born Unfree: Child Labour, Education, and the State in India* (Oxford: Oxford University Press, 2006), 14.

79. See Janie Chuang, "United States as Global Sheriff: Using Unilateral Sanctions to Combat Human Trafficking," *Michigan Journal of International Law* 27, no. 2 (2006): 437, 438.

80. Gallagher, 4.

81. US Government Accountability Office, *Better Data, Strategy, and Reporting Needed to Enhance U.S. Antitrafficking Efforts Abroad* (2006).

82. See the work of Palantir (www.palantir.com) and of Polaris (www.polarisproject.org) for examples of the fast-growing possibilities in the field of social-media-based trafficking investigation.

83. Given the difficulties in accurately counting the cases of child-labor exploitation, this calculation is open to challenge. See UNODC, *Promoting Health, Security and Justice* 23 (2010):

> The most commonly reported purpose of human trafficking is sexual exploitation (79 per cent), followed by forced labour (18 per cent), but many types of trafficking may be underreported, in part because they are largely "invisible"—including forced or bonded labour, domestic servitude and forced marriage, organ removal, and exploitation of children for begging, the sex trade and warfare.

84. Aronowitz, 60, 76, 57.

85. The US Secretary of Homeland Security has discretion to waive the "good moral character" disqualification for T visa applicants under Trafficking Victims Protection Reauthorization Act of 2008, Section 107. INA § 245(I)(6), codified at 8 USC § 1255(I)(6).

86. The Protocol does not go further and encourage states to provide permanent residence or long-term protection to trafficking victims, or to treat them on a par with refugees. The host state is only required to try and provide for the trafficking victim's physical safety while he or she is within its territory. See Palermo Protocol, Art. 6(5).

87. European Trafficking Convention, Art. 10(1).

88. Ibid.

89. UNODC, *Global Report 2009*, 8.

90. *TIP Report 2012*, 44.

91. US Department of Justice, *Attorney General's Annual Report to Congress on U.S. Government Activities to Combat Trafficking in Persons: Fiscal Year 2005* (2006), 3. This figure remains the most recent government estimate to date.

92. US Department of Justice, *Attorney General's Annual Report 2010* (2011), 30.

93. Despite antitrafficking legislation in the United Kingdom, child victims continue to disappear from state care, and female victims face ingrained skepticism of their asylum claims. See Sarah Left, "Hundreds of Children Go Missing in London," *Guardian*, May 3, 2005.

94. Palermo Protocol, Art. 6(2) (3).

95. Compare Palermo Protocol, Arts. 7, 8.

96. US Departments of Justice, Homeland Security, Labor, Health and Human Services and State, and the US Agency for International Development.

97. Jacqueline Bhabha and Christina Alfirev, *The Identification and Referral of Trafficked Persons to Procedures for Determining International Protection Needs*, PPLAS/2009/03 (UNHCR, 2009).

98. Amelia Gentleman, "Katya's Story: Trafficked to the UK, Sent Home to Torture," *The Guardian*, Apr. 18, 2011.

99. Ibid., citing Sally Montier of the Poppy Project. See also IOM, *The Causes and Consequences of Re-trafficking: Evidence from the IOM Human Trafficking Database* (2010).

100. Gentleman.

101. OM, *Minors*, 38.

102. Ibid., 53.

103. Ibid., 46.

104. Sylvain Dessy and Stéphane Pallage, "Some Surprising Effects of Better Law Enforcement against Child Trafficking," *Journal of African Development* 8, no. 1 (2006):115–32.

105. Belgium, Italy, the Netherlands, Spain, France, and Greece provide victims with assistance and temporary residence permits in exchange for cooperating with the prosecution of their traffickers. Anne T. Gallagher, "Recent Legal Developments in the Field of Human Trafficking: A Critical Review of the 2005 European Convention and Related Instruments," *European Journal of Migration and Law* 8, no. 2 (2006), note 13, at 167. However, few tailor these measures to child victims, consistent with their obligations under Council Directive 2004/81/EC of 29 April 2004 on the residence permit issued to Third Country nationals who are trafficking victims or who have been the subject of an action to facilitate illegal immigration, and who cooperate with the competent authorities.

106. USCIS, "USCIS Victims of Trafficking Form I-914 (T) and Victims of Crime Form I-918 (U) Visa Statistics (FY2002–Jan. FY2012)," Mar. 21, 2012.

107. *TIP Report 2012*, 15.

108. US Department of Justice, *Attorney General's Annual Report: 2005*, 3.

109. US Department of Homeland Security, "ICE Total Removals through June 16, 2012."

110. Beth Simmons, *Mobilizing for Human Rights, International Law in Domestic Politics* (New York: Cambridge University Press, 2009), 358.

111. IOM, *Minors*, 32. 17.

112. Jacqueline Bhabha and Nadine Finch, *Seeking Asylum Alone: Unaccompanied and Separated Children Seeking Refugee Protection in the UK* (Cambridge, MA: President and Fellows of Harvard University, 2006), 30–31.

113. Shelley, 180, 54.

114. Some scholars note positive developments with respect to community-based efforts to identify and provide resources to victims of trafficking. See Aronowitz, 149, and Shelley, 175, 202.

115. In the United States, adult trafficking victims must be willing to assist with the investigation of the trafficker before receiving federal services or benefits. Trafficking Victims Protect Act, § 107, codified at 22 USC §§ 7105(b)(1)(E) & (c)(1). Child victims are not subject to this requirement but in practice are vulnerable to aggressive tactics by prosecutors. See Micah N. Bump, "Treat the Children Well: Shortcomings in the United States' Effort to Protect Child Trafficking Victims," *Notre Dame Journal of Law, Ethics & Public Policy* 23, no. 1 (2009): 73, 83–95.

116. Jhumka Gupta et al., "HIV Vulnerabilities of Sex-Trafficked Indian Women and Girls," *International Journal of Gynecology and Obstetrics* 107, no. 1 (2009): 30–34, cited in Ahn et al., 8.

117. IOM, *Minors*, 42.

118. Ahn et al., 29.

119. Susie B. Baldwin et al., "Identification of Human Trafficking Victims in Health Care Settings," *Health and Human Rights: An International Journal* 13:1 (2011).

120. Palermo Protocol, Art. 9(2).

121. Shelley, 29.

122. UNODC, *Global Report 2009*, 6, 47.

123. Ahn et al., 26.

124. La Strada International, "European Network against Trafficking in Human Beings."

125. Ibid., "Projects—Human Rights Impact Assessment."

126. Polaris Project, National Human Trafficking Resource Center.

127. See, e.g., Kara, 177; E. Benjamin Skinner, *A Crime So Monstrous: Face-to-Face with Modern-day Slavery* (New York: Free Press, 2008), 292; and Anthony M. De Stefano, *The War on Human Trafficking: US Policy Assessed* (New Brunswick: Rutgers University Press, 2007).

128. Albert O. Hirschman, *Exit, Voice, and Loyalty: Responses to Decline in Firms, Organizations, and States* (Cambridge, Mass.: Harvard University Press, 1970).

129. IOM, *Minors*, paras. 3.3, 29.

130. Ibid.

131. Ibid., 10.

132. Michele Decker, Sex Work in Asia: Health, Agency, and Sexuality Conference, Harvard University, Oct. 1, 2010 (notes on file with author).

133. See Natalie M. McClain and Stacy E. Garrity, "Sex Trafficking and the Exploitation of Adolescents," *Journal of Obstetric, Gynecologic, and Neonatal* Nursing 40 (2011): 243–52; and Michele Decker et al., "Forced Prostitution and Trafficking for Sexual Exploitation among Women and Girls in Situations of Migration and Conflict," *Women, Migration, and Conflict* (2009): 63–86.

134. See Kara, 111, and Shelley, 251.

135. Amy Farrell, “Improving Law Enforcement Identification and Response to Human Trafficking,” in John Winterdyk, Benjamin Perrin, and Philip Reicheleds, eds., *Human Trafficking: Exploring the International Nature, Concerns, and Complexities* (Boca Raton, FL: CRC Press, 2011), 188; and Goździak, “Identifying Child Victims,” 245–55.

136. See Ahn et al., *Sex Trafficking*; Baldwin et al., “Identification of Human Trafficking.”

137. See the Palermo Protocol, Art. 9(5); *Report A/65/288 (2010)*, para. 13 ; and UNICEF, *Combating Child Trafficking: Handbook for Parliamentarians* (2005), 17.

138. UNODC, *An Introduction to Human Trafficking: Vulnerability, Impact and Action* (2008), 114.

139. Palermo Protocol, Art. 9(4).

140. European Commission, *Action Plan on Unaccompanied Minors (2010–2014)*, Communication from the Commission to the European Parliament and the Council, COM(2010) 213/2, 6 [*Action Plan 2010–2014*].

141. Council of the European Union, *Council Conclusions on Unaccompanied Minors*, 3018th Justice and Home Affairs council meeting, Luxembourg, 3 June 2010, 10630/1/10 REV 1, para. 29.

142. IMF Dissemination Standards Bulletin Board, “Economic and Financial Data for the Republic of Moldova.”

143. Thousands of Moldovan victims are trafficked for sex into Russia, Turkey, United Arab Emirates, Italy, and beyond. Kara, 110–12.

144. World Bank, *World Development Indicators* (2011), 73 [*World Development Indicators 2011*].

145. Ibid., 49. “Decent work” includes safe working conditions, adequate rest, and adequate compensation; see ILO, “Decent Work Agenda.”

146. *World Development Indicators 2011*, 72–74, 48–50.

147. Economist Intelligence Unit, *Country Report: Somalia* (May 2012), 3, 14.

148. *World Development Indicators 2011*, 53, 40.

149. Government of India, *Literates and Literacy Rate by Residence*, Provisional Population Totals Paper 2 of 2011: Gujarat.

150. Indira Hirway and Neha Shah, “Labour and Employment under Globalisation: The Case of Gujarat,” *Economic & Political Weekly* 46, no. 22 (2011): 59, 64.

151. Alba Collective, www.albacollective.org.

152. Orla Kelly and Jacqueline Bhabha, “Beyond the Education Silo? Tackling Adolescent Gender Equity in Rural India,” unpublished manuscript on file with the author.

153. Among girls ages fourteen to seventeen, 37 percent were engaged and 12 percent were married (versus 27 percent and 3 percent of boys, respectively). Ibid. See also Jacqueline Bhabha, “Child Marriage and the Right to Education: Evidence from an Ongoing Study in Rural Gujarat, India,” Evidence Submitted to the United Kingdom All-Party Parliamentary Group on Population, Development and Reproductive Health, Apr. 2012.

154. Bhabha, *Shanu*, 32.

Chapter 5. Under the Gun: Moving Children for War

1. Tristan McConnell, “Liberia’s Former President Becomes the First African Head of State to Go on Trial for War Crimes Monday,” *Christian Science Monitor*, June 4, 2007.

2. Michael Wessels, *Child Soldiers: From Violence to Protection* (Cambridge, MA: Harvard University Press 2006), 205.

3. The three former rebel leaders were convicted of committing war crimes, including the use of child soldiers, and crimes against humanity during Sierra Leone's 1991–2002 war. They were commanders of the Armed Forces Revolutionary Council (AFRC), former government soldiers who split from the army and joined rebels from the Revolutionary United Front (RUF) against Sierra Leone's government and the pro-government paramilitary group, the Civil Defense Forces (CDF). See Special Court for Sierra Leone, Trial Chamber II, SCSL 04–16-T, June 20, 2007, para. 1244.

4. All the charges arise out of just two conflicts, the civil war in Sierra Leone and the ongoing thirty-year conflict in the Democratic Republic of Congo (DRC). See Special Court for Sierra Leone; Coalition to Stop the Use of Child Soldiers (Coalition), *Child Soldiers: Global Report 2008* (2008), 32; International Criminal Court (ICC), "Thomas Lubanga Dyilo Sentenced to Fourteen Years of Imprisonment," ICC-CPI-20120710-PR824, July 10, 2012; and Human Rights Watch, "DR Congo: Militia Leader Guilty in Landmark Trial," Mar. 10, 2009.

5. Human Rights Watch, *"Even a 'Big Man' Must Face Justice": Lessons from the Trial of Charles Taylor* (2012), 12–15.

6. Six of these conflicts are currently subject to international legal proceedings: the ICC is investigating five: the DRC, Uganda, the Central African Republic, Côte d'Ivoire, and Sudan; a joint UN/Extraordinary Chamber in the Courts of Cambodia is investigating the sixth. See ICC, "Situations and Cases," www.icc-cpi.int/Menus/ICC/Situations+and+Cases/. See also Coalition, 2–3, 15.

7. Theresa Betancourt et al., "High Hopes, Grim Reality: Reintegration and the Education of Former Child Soldiers in Sierra Leone," *Comparative Education Review* 52:4 (July 2008).

8. Wessels, *Child Soldiers*, 13. Historically, countries engaged in protracted conflicts have witnessed very significant proportions of child soldiers. For example, in Peru's Shining Path insurgency movement, thousands of children were forcibly recruited on both sides of the conflict, and some 12.8 percent of all victims were children. Salvador Herencia Carrasco, *Transitional Justice and the Situation of Children in Colombia and Peru*, UNICEF Innocenti Working Paper No. 2010–16 (2010), 6–8. In Colombia during the 1990s, an estimated 30 percent of guerilla units consisted of children, and within urban units, 85 percent were under eighteen years of age. Human Rights Watch, *"You'll Learn Not to Cry": Child Combatants in Colombia* (2003), 19–21.

9. For a comprehensive description of the brutal and pervasive impact of contemporary war on children, see UNICEF, *Machel Study Ten-year Strategic Review: Children and Conflict in a Changing World*, A/62/228 (2009).

10. P. W. Singer, *Children at War* (New York: Pantheon Books, 2005), 73–74 (quoting testimony of a sixteen-year-old youth).

11. UNICEF, "Fact Sheet: Child Soldiers," www.unicef.org/emerg/files/childsoldiers.pdf.

12. Graça Machel, *The Impact of War on Children: A Review of Progress* (London: Hurst & Co., 2001) 7. Note, however, that because the use of children extends beyond combat, many scholars prefer the term "children associated with armed forces and groups" (CAAFAG). Theresa Betancourt, "Child Soldiers: Reintegration, Pathways to Recovery, and Reflections from the Field," *Journal of Development and Behavioral Pediatrics* 29:2 (Apr. 2008), 139.

13. Betancourt et al., "High Hopes," citing UNICEF, *Paris Principles: Principles and Guidelines on Children Associated with Armed Forces or Armed Conflict* (2007), 7.

14. See Sharanjeet Parmar, "Realizing Economic Justice for Children: The Role of Transitional Justice in Post-conflict Societies," in Sharanjeet Parmar et al., eds., *Children and Transitional Justice: Truth-telling, Accountability and Reconciliation* (Cambridge: UNICEF and the Human Rights Program at Harvard Law School, 2010), 376–78. For a discussion of factors influencing children's involvement in war as victims, witnesses, and perpetrators, see International Bureau for Children's Rights, *Children and Armed Conflict: A Guide to International Humanitarian and Human Rights Law* (2010), 267–76.

15. Tristan Anne Borer, John Darby, and Siobhan McEvoy-Levy, *Peacebuilding after Peace Accords: The Challenges of Violence, Truth, and Youth* (South Bend, IN: University of Notre Dame Press, 2006), 42, cited in Parmar et al., 382.

16. Graça Machel, *Impact of Armed Conflict on Children,* Report of the Expert of the Secretary-General, Ms. Graça Machel, U.N. Doc. A/51/306 (1996), para. 34.

17. Singer, *Children at War,* 102.

18. Child Friendly Version of the Sierra Leone Truth and Reconciliation Commission [TRC] Report, 2004, cited in Philip Cook and Cheryl Heykoop, "Child Participation in the Sierra Leonean Truth and Reconciliation Commission," in Parmar et al., 106. Just as some children "choose" to embark on trafficking-fueled journeys, so some children "choose" to volunteer for participation in war. Many factors account for this, including the protection vacuum and social disintegration facing children living in war-affected societies. A small study of demobilized former child soldiers in Colombia found that 70 percent had voluntarily enlisted in the armed forces, 40 percent of them because they were attracted by the uniform and the weapons they would receive. Katie Naeve, *Right, Duty of Privilege? The Impact of Reintegration Programs for Former Child Soldiers in Colombia*, Policy Analysis Exercise Harvard Kennedy School, May 2012, Appendix pages 5–6. On file with author.

19. In fact, the ILO counts involuntary military service as a type of forced labor. See ILO, *Global Estimate*, 13.

20. Jean-Hervé Jézéquel argues that military enlistment is a strategy some youth adopted to escape social marginalization, "Les Enfants Soldats d'Afrique, un Phénomène Singulier", cited in Parmer, 382.

21. Children toiling in the diamond mines of Sierra Leone are a case in point; see *Digging in the Dirt: Child Miners in Sierra Leone's Diamond Industry* (2009), cited in Parmar, "Economic Justice," 376.

22. See Michael Wessells, "Supporting the Mental Health and Psychosocial Well-Being of Former Child Soldiers," *Journal of the American Academy of Child and Adolescent Psychiatry* 48:6 June 2009, 588.

23. See Parmar, "Economic Justice," 394–95.

24. In cases of fragile states such as Sierra Leone and Liberia, international accountability mechanisms have focused on preventing future recruitment and instituting retrospective judicial mechanisms. In cases of violent secessionist movements within strong states such as India and Nepal, states refuse to categorize the wars as internal armed conflicts but instead consider them only internal struggles to maintain law and order, domestic security issues

from which international humanitarian intervention is excluded. In either situation, the needs of states take precedence over the interests of the humanitarian victims, particularly children. For an argument about the increasing irrelevance of international humanitarian law to child soldiers caught up in internal or "localized conflicts," see Mukul Saxena Vimug, "Left Out by the Pied Piper: The UN Response to Children in Localized Conflict Settings," 9(1) *Northwestern Journal of International Human Rights*, 59–81.

25. Wessels, "Mental Health," 588.

26. UN Office of the Special Representative of the Secretary-General for Children and Armed Conflict, "Children and Armed Conflict," June 15, 2007.

27. Disarmament, Demobilization and Reintegration (DDR) activities have become the gold standard for postconflict transitions to peace, including the rehabilitation of former child soldiers, but gaps remain with respect to specific subpopulations. Save the Children has argued that DDR processes have largely failed girls involved in armed conflicts, despite that girls constitute up to 40 percent of the child-soldier population, because they have been a "shadow army." "Although the international community has developed a formal process designed to help children leave armed groups and go back to their families after a conflict ends, it is drastically under-funded. And, because of *their invisibility* and the discrimination they suffer, it is girls who particularly lose out." Save the Children, *Forgotten Casualties of War: Girls in Armed Conflict* (2005), vi.

28. Sissela Bok, "The New Ethical Boundaries," in Jennifer Leaning, Susan M. Briggs, and Lincoln C. Chen (eds.), *Humanitarian Crises: The Medical and Public Health Response* (Cambridge, MA: Harvard University Press, 1999), 188.

29. The recent spate of compelling autobiographical accounts by former child soldiers has made some impact—Ishmael Beah's *A Long Way Gone* was a best seller for months, and he was a prominent speaker on the international lecture circuit and at international policy forums for about a year after the book was first published. Emmanuel Jal published a book in February 2009 titled *War Child: A Child Soldier's Story*, about his experience as a child soldier in Sudan. But public attention to the enduring problems of former child soldiers in Sierra Leone and Uganda has waned as the acute phase of these conflicts has abated.

30. International Bureau for Children's Rights, 48–49.

31. International Criminal Law & Practice Training Materials, *Module 4: International, Hybrid and National Courts Trying International Crimes*, 3.

32. The Geneva Conventions have been supplemented by further agreements, including the Additional Protocols of 1977 relating to the protection of victims of armed conflicts; a series of conventions from 1954 to 1997 relating to the use of conventional, biological, and chemical weapons; and the 2000 Child Soldiers Protocol to the CRC.

33. International Criminal Law & Practice Training Materials, 3.

34. Leila Nadya Sadat, *The International Criminal Court and the Transformation of International Law: Justice for the New Millennium* (2002).

35. An analogy in the field of economic and social rights might be drawn to the innovative work of the Ethical Globalization Initiative (EGI), which operated from 2002 to 2010 under the leadership of former UN High Commissioner for Human Rights, Mary Robinson. The EGI partnered with international, national, and local stakeholders on joint

initiatives targeting climate justice, corporate responsibility, trade and decent work, the right to health, and women's leadership.

36. Effective as of July 1, 2012, 121 countries are parties to the Rome Statute. ICC, *The Court Today* (May 2012).

37. Investigations are active in Uganda, the Democratic Republic of the Congo, the Central African Republic, the Darfur situation in Sudan, Kenya, Libya, and Côte d'Ivoire. Monitoring is under way in Afghanistan, Colombia, Georgia, Honduras, Nigeria, the Republic of Korea, and Guinea. ICC, *The Court Today* (May 2012).

38. Statement by Luis Moreno Ocampo, press conference in relation to the surrender to the Court of Mr. Thomas Lubanga Dyilo, Mar. 18, 2006.

39. David Smith, "Thomas Lubanga Sentenced to Fourteen Years for Congo War Crimes," *The Guardian*, July 10, 2012.

40. Human Rights Watch, "ICC: Congolese Rebel Leader Gets Fourteen Years," July 10, 2012.

41. Protocol Additional to the Geneva Conventions of 12 August 1949, and relating to the Protection of Victims of Non-International Armed Conflicts (Protocol II), 8 June 1977, Art. 4(3)(c): "children who have not attained the age of fifteen years shall neither be recruited in the armed forces or groups nor allowed to take part in hostilities."

42. CRC, Art. 4(3)(c).

43. This recommendation was followed. Under the leadership of the Special Representative, Olara Otunnu, a series of Security Council Resolutions was passed establishing a framework for monitoring violations of the prohibition on child soldier recruitment. See Security Council resolutions on "Children and Armed Conflict": 1379 (2001); 1460 (2003) and 1612 (2005).

44. The incongruous mismatch between the CRC's generic definition of a child as "every human being below the age of 18" (CRC, Art. 1) and the convention's adoption of the Protocols' lower age limit of 15 (Art. 38) for the prohibition on recruitment and direct participation of children in armed conflict, one of the most dangerous and potentially rights violative of all activities, gave rise to a vigorous and ultimately successful campaign to establish consistency around the higher threshold. In 2000, the Child Soldiers Protocol was adopted (entering into force in 2002) raising to 18 the minimum age for compulsory recruitment and participation in hostilities, and requiring states parties to take "all feasible measures" to raise the minimum age of voluntary recruitment to 18. The United States, which has not signed on to the CRC as a whole, nevertheless ratified this Optional Protocol.

45. Convention Concerning the Prohibition and Immediate Action for the Elimination of the Worst Forms of Child Labour, 2133 UNTS 161, ILO No. 182, June 17, 1999, Art. 3(a) [Worst Forms of Child Labour Convention].

46. Child Soldiers Protocol, Art. 1.

47. Parmar, "Economic Justice," 390–91.

48. Wessells, "Mental Health," 589.

49. Theresa Betancourt et al., "Psychosocial Adjustment and Mental Health Services in Post-conflict Sierra Leone: Experiences of CAAFAG and War-affected Youth, Families, and Service," in Stephen Parmentier, Jeremy Sarkin, and Elmar Weitekamp (eds.), *New Series on Transitional Justice* (Antwerp, Belgium: Intersentia, in press), 379.

50. International Bureau for Children's Rights, 186.

51. Report of the Secretary-General on the establishment of a Special Court for Sierra Leone (2000), Annex S/2000/915, para. 15(c); Human Rights Watch, *Big Man*, 16.

52. Christina M. Carroll, "An Assessment of the Role and Effectiveness of the International Criminal Tribunal for Rwanda and the Rwandan National Justice System in Dealing with the Mass Atrocities of 1994," 18 *Boston University International Law Journal* (2000) 163–200, cited in Estelle R. Higonnet, "Restructuring Hybrid Courts: Local Empowerment and National Criminal Justice Reform," 23(2) *Arizona Journal of International and Comparative Law* (2006) 347–435, 358. This article, on which the following section relies heavily, provides an excellent analysis of the functioning and potential of hybrid courts. For a discussion of the efficacy of the SLSC in affecting change on the ground, see also Jane Stromseth, *Accountability for Atrocities: National and International Responses* (Ardsley, NY: Transnational Publishers 2003).

53. Apart from Sierra Leone, some examples of hybrid courts include those in Kosovo, East Timor, and Cambodia.

54. The ICC can only try crimes committed in signatory states after the statute went into effect. Due to resource constraints it can only try a small proportion of the most senior figures responsible.

55. Higonnet, 385.

56. *Prosecutor v. Brima et. al.*, SCSL-04-16-T, Trial Chamber, Judgment, June 20, 2007, para. 1250, quoting Exhibit D-37, Osman Gbla, "Research Report: The Use of Child Soldiers in the Sierra Leone Conflict," para. 9.

57. Ibid., citing Exhibit D-37, paras. 35–37.

58. Cook and Heykoop, "Child Participation," 165.

59. For an example of a case where this happened to a young girl in the DRC, see Save the Children, *Forgotten Casualties*, 14.

60. Jeremy Waldron proposes a useful defense of this universalistic approach against radical cultural relativism in a different context. Discussing the meaning of "cruel, inhuman or degrading" treatment, he dismisses the relativist challenge to establishing a standard by drawing a distinction between "meaning" and "norm." See Jeremy Waldron, "Cruel, Inhuman and Degrading Treatment: The Words Themselves," HLS WIP Aug. 8, 2008, p. 43 (notes 137–38). All cultures have a notion of what is inhuman or degrading, though the norms they introduce to give meaning to these terms might be different. Similarly, all cultures have a notion of what is destitution or deprivation, though the standards at which these thresholds are judged no doubt vary.

61. Higonnet, 387–88.

62. Human Rights Watch, *Big Man*, 40–43.

63. Ibid., 33–38.

64. "A drastic acceleration of trials is required, or the Court will simply run out of money and friends." Cockayne, 628.

65. Human Rights Watch, *Big Man*, 12.

66. Both treaties have active treaty bodies composed of highly regarded international experts who receive and review periodic reports from ratifying states. Shadow reports

submitted by advocacy groups provide the presiding experts with ammunition for cross-examination of government witnesses. This process, while it does not lead to binding judgments or enforceable decisions, nevertheless provides some outside scrutiny of a state's performance and an opportunity to engage in constructive dialogue about progress or lack of progress toward appropriate human-rights benchmarks.

67. For a concise history of this long campaign, see W. Warren H. Binford, "School Lessons in War: Children at Tuol Sleng and the Rise of International Protections for Children in War," 16(28) *Willamette Journal of International Law and Dispute Resolution* (2008), 30–75.

68. Louis Henkin et al., *Human Rights*, 2nd ed. (New York: The Foundation Press, 2009).

69. Human Rights Watch, *Big Man*, 1.

70. Cockayne, 647. See also International Bureau for Children's Rights, 226: "Following international concern about the role played by the illicit diamond trade in fuelling conflict in Sierra Leone, the Security Council adopted resolution 1306 on 5 July 2000, imposing a ban on the direct or indirect import of rough diamonds from Sierra Leone, not controlled by the Government of Sierra Leone, through a Certificate of Origin regime."

71. "Sierra Leone: Amputees Still Waiting for Reparations Almost Ten Years On," *IRIN News*, Oct. 24, 2011.

72. UNDP, *Human Development Report 2011: Sustainability and Equity: A Better Future for All*, 130 [*Human Development Report 2011*].

73. See David Keen, *Liberalization and Conflict*, 26 International Political Science Review 73, 78–79 (Jan. 2005).

74. CRC, Arts. 3, 12, 28(1), 24, 25, 24(3).

75. Ibid., Art. 38(3). See also Child Soldiers Protocol, Art. 2.

76. See CRC, Arts. 34, 36. See also Sale of Children Protocol, Art. 1.

77. See CRC, Art. 32. See also Convention Concerning Minimum Age for Admission to Employment, 1015 UNTS 298, ILO No. 138, June 26, 1973, Arts. 1, 3; and Worst Forms of Child Labour Convention, Art. 1.

78. See generally CRC; ICCPR; and the International Covenant on Economic, Social and Cultural Rights, 999 UNTS 171, Dec. 16, 1966 [ICESCR].

79. CRC, Art. 1.

80. For an excellent discussion of issues related to child citizenship, see "The Child as Citizen," special editor, Felton Earls, *The Annals of the American Academy of Political and Social Science*, vol. 633, Jan. 2011. See also the discussion in chapter 2 above, and in particular references to children's partial, fractured, or "semi" citizenship.

81. Forty eight percent of Sierra Leone's six million people are under age eighteen. See UNICEF, *The State of the World's Children 2012: Children in an Urban World*, 110 [*SOWC 2012*].

82. *Human Development Report 2011*, 130.

83. Government of the Republic of Sierra Leone, *Millennium Development Goals Progress Report 2010*, 8.

84. *SOWC 2012*, 106.

85. Sierra Leone, *Millennium Development Goals*, 16.

86. UNICEF, *Progress for Children: A Report Card on Adolescents*, no. 10, Apr. 2012, 25.

87. Mohamed Fofanah, "Sierra Leone Facing Facts of Teenage Pregnancy," *IPS News Agency*, Apr. 3, 2011.

88. UNICEF, *Progress for Children*, 14–15.

89. World Bank, *Africa Development Indicators 2011*, 113.

90. Save the Children, *Fighting Back: Child and Community-led Strategies to Avoid Children's Recruitment into Armed Forces and Groups in West Africa* (2005), cited in Parmar, "Economic Justice," 383.

91. Parmar, "Economic Justice," 376–81, 377.

92. *Second Annual Report of the President of the Special Court of Sierra Leone* (2003–2004), 41.

93. Tim Ensor, Tomas Lievens, and Mike Naylor, *Review of Financing of Health in Sierra Leone and the Development of Policy Options* (Oxford Policy Management, 2008), 17.

94. World Bank, *Education in Sierra Leone: Present Challenges, Future Opportunities* (2007) 104.

95. Ibid., *Report on Development Assistance to Sierra Leone 2004–2005*, 27.

96. Saudamini Siegrist, "Child Rights and Transitional Justice," in Parmar et al., 6.

97. Gerald N. Rosenberg, *The Hollow Hope: Can Courts Bring about Social Change?* (Chicago: University of Chicago Press. 1991), 5–7.

98. Simmons, 112–55. See also Alicia Ely Yamin, "Power, Suffering and the Courts: Reflections on Promoting Health Rights through Judicialization," in Alicia Ely Yamin and Siri Gloppen (eds.), *Litigating Health Rights: Can Courts Bring More Justice to Health?* (Cambridge, MA: CMI and the Human Rights Program at Harvard Law School, 2011), 333–69.

99. Courts may embrace social justice goals through their decisions, but producing sustained societal change requires a much broader set of social, political, and economic inputs. For a full exploration of the complex legacy of the landmark case of *Brown v. Board of Education*, see Martha Minow, *In Brown's Wake* (New York: Oxford University Press. 2010). For an interesting analysis of the Indian Supreme Court's anti-child-labor decisions, see Modhurima Dasgupta, "Public interest litigation for Labour: How the Indian Supreme Court Protects the Rights of India's Most Disadvantaged Workers," *Contemporary South Asia*, 16:2 (2008), 159–70. More recently, India has banned the employment of children under fourteen in circuses. See *Bachpan Bachao Andolan v. Union Of India & Others*, 5 SCC 1, 18 Apr., 2011.

100. See the debate between Human Rights Watch and Physicians for Human Rights: Kenneth Roth, "Defending Economic, Social and Cultural Rights: Practical Issues Faced by an International Human Rights Organization," 26 *Human Rights Quarterly* (2004) 63–73; Leonard Rubenstein, "How International Human Rights Organizations Can Advance Economic, Social and Cultural Rights: A Response to Kenneth Roth," 26 *Human Rights Quarterly* (2004) 845–65.

101. Rosenberg, 313.

102. UNAMSIL completed its mandate in December 2005 and was succeeded by the United Nations Integrated Office for Sierra Leone. "Sierra Leone—UNAMSIL—Facts and Figures," United Nations Mission in Sierra Leone, www.un.org/en/peacekeeping/missions/past/unamsil/facts.html.

103. Wessels, *Child Soldiers*, 166.

104. Save the Children, *No Place like Home? Children's Experiences of Reintegration in the Kailahun District of Sierra Leone* (2004), 13.

105. John Williamson, *Reintegration of Child Soldiers in Sierra Leone* (USAID, 2005), 4.

106. See Theresa S. Betancourt, "High Hopes," 565, and Macartan Humphreys and Jeremy M. Weinstein, "Demobilization and Reintegration," *Journal of Conflict Resolution* 51:4 (2007) 531–67.

107. Save the Children, *No Place*, 11.

108. The TRC was "a nonjudicial process, aimed at uncovering root causes of the conflict and the nature and extent of the human rights violations that were committed." International Bureau for Children's Rights, 305.

109. Cook and Heykoop, "Child Participation," note 4 at 164.

110. Ibid., 161, 179.

111. Beah, 163.

112. Betancourt et al., "*Psychosocial Adjustment*," 11.

113. Save the Children, *No Place*, 19, 21, 17.

114. Save the Children, *No Place*, 13.

115. Ibid., 21.

116. Wessels, *Child Soldiers*, 205.

117. Ibid., 199–200.

118. Studies of war-affected youth indicate that longitudinal variations in psychosocial and mental health outcomes depend not only on wartime exposures but on a range of individual, familial, and societal postconflict factors as well. Betancourt et al. have shown that former child soldiers in Sierra Leone who experience persistently serious mental-health problems are more likely to be older (i.e., longer involvement in war), to have lost a caregiver during war, to have suffered family abuse and neglect, to have experienced social stigma, and to live in communities that are less protective of children and free from criminality. "Trajectories of Internalizing Problems in War-affected Sierra Leonean Youth: Examining Conflict and Post-conflict Factors," *Child Development* (in press).

119. Colin MacMullin and Maryanne Loughry, "Investigating Psychosocial Adjustment of Former Child Soldiers in Sierra Leone and Uganda," *Journal of Refugee Studies* 17(4) 469. Betancourt et al., "Psychosocial Adjustment," 379–411.

120. Save the Children, *Fighting Back*.

121. Since the passage of the Act, concerns persist that children's rights have not been fully translated into programming and services. Under 1 percent of the country's budget is allocated to the Ministry of Social Welfare, Gender and Children's Affairs, and in a recent survey of fifty-two African countries, Sierra Leone was ranked second to last in composite budgeting for children's health, education, and social protection. See African Child Policy Forum, *The African Report on Child Wellbeing 2011: Country Brief, Sierra Leone* (Nov. 2010). See also UNICEF, *State of the World's Children 2010: Child Rights*, 29; Amnesty International, "Annual Report: Sierra Leone 2011"; and Abibatu Kamara and Jessica McDiarmid, "Sierra Leone: Child Rights Exist Only on Paper," *Inter Press Service Africa*, Sep. 12, 2011.

122. UNICEF, "Sierra Leone Approves the National Child Rights Bill," June 7, 2007, www.unicef.org/media/media_39951.html.

123. *Human Development Report 2011*, 130, 161.

124. US Department of State, *2011 Human Rights Reports: Sierra Leone*, May 24, 2012.

125. Betancourt et al., "Psychosocial Adjustment."

126. Parmar, "Economic Justice."

127. See, e.g., Nung Wong, "Discerning an African Post-colonial Governance Imbroglio: Colonialism, Underdevelopment and Violent Conflicts in the Democratic Republic of Congo (DRC), Liberia and Sierra Leone," *African & Asian Studies* 11, no. 1/2 (Jan. 2012): 66–94, and Sylvia Ojukutu-Macauley and Andrew K. Keili, "Citizens, Subjects or a Dual Mandate? Artisanal Miners, 'Supporters' and the Resource Scramble in Sierra Leone," *Development Southern Africa* 25, no. 5 (Dec. 2008): 513–30.

128. Wessels, *Child Soldiers*, 165.

129. Theresa Betancourt and Timothy Williams, "Building an Evidence Base on Mental Health Interventions for Children Affected by Armed Conflict," *Intervention* (Amstelveen) 2008; 6(1): 39–56.

130. The sensational "Kony 2012" YouTube video about Ugandan warlord Joseph Kony reached ninety-two million views within months of its release, but was criticized by many for masking the complex socioeconomic factors underlying the conflict in Uganda.

131. This paradox, of notable progress on the legal and judicial front, combined with remarkable stagnation on the social and economic terrain, is not a unique feature of post-conflict Sierra Leone. In Bosnia, Rwanda, and East Timor, similar trends are discernible. UNDP, *International Human Development Indicators*, http://hdr.undp.org/en/data/profiles/.

Chapter 6. David and Goliath: Children's Unequal Battle for Refugee Protection

1. Words of Pedro, a detained, unaccompanied minor. M. Aryah Somers, Pedro Herrera, and Lucia Rodriguez, "Constructions of Childhood and Unaccompanied Children in the Immigration System in the United States," *UC Davis Journal of Juvenile Law & Policy* 14, no. 2 (2010): 319.

2. CRC, Preamble.

3. Bruce Finley, "Death of a Deportee," *Denver Post*, Apr. 5, 2004, A1.

4. Bruce Finley, "Deportee's Slaying Spurs Reform Push: Advocates Say Teen's Fear of Gangs Unheeded," *Denver Post*, Apr. 8, 2004, A1.

5. CRC, Art. 3(1). The United States however has not ratified the CRC, one of only two countries (the other being Somalia) not to do so. As a result its provisions are not binding on US officials. However, the "best interests of the child" principle has long been recognized in US child-welfare law and practice. See, e.g., The Adoption and Safe Families Act of 1997, Public Law 105–89, 111 Stat. 2115 (Nov. 19, 1997).

6. Of an estimated 230,000 Mexicans displaced by drug-cartel violence, roughly half are thought to have fled to the United States. Norwegian Refugee Council, *Forced Displacement in Mexico Due to Drug Cartel Violence*, Internal Displacement Monitoring Centre Briefing Paper, Dec. 31, 2010, 1. Yet in FY2011, the United States approved just 104 of 6,133 asylum requests (1.6 percent) made by Mexican nationals. US Department of Justice, "Immigration Courts FY 2011 Asylum Statistics," www.justice.gov/eoir/efoia/FY11AsyStats-Current.pdf.

7. Julia Preston, "Losing Asylum, Then His Life," *New York Times*, June 28, 2010.

8. Guy Goodwin-Gill, "Unaccompanied Refugee Minors: The Role and Place of International Law in the Pursuit of Durable Solutions," *International Journal of Children's Rights* 3 (1995): 405–16, 413.

9. Atle Grahl-Madsen, *The Status of Refugees in International Law* vol. 1 (Leyden: A.W. Sijthoff, 1966), 135.

10. UNHCR defines a separated child as one who is under the age of eighteen and "who is separated from both parents and [is] not being cared for by an adult who, by law or custom, is responsible to do so." UNHCR, *2009 Guidelines on Child Asylum Claims*, 121. The CRC Committee also provides definitions of unaccompanied and separated children: "'Unaccompanied children' (also called unaccompanied minors) are children, as defined in article 1 of the Convention, who have been separated from both parents and other relatives and are not being cared for by an adult who, by law or custom, is responsible for doing so"; "'[s]eparated children,' as defined in article 1 of the Convention, who have been separated from both parents, or from their previous legal or customary primary caregiver, but not necessarily from other relatives. These may, therefore, include children accompanied by other family members." *CRC General Comment* 6, paras. 7, 8.

11. Following common international usage, I use the term "separated" to cover both unaccompanied and separated child asylum seekers.

12. In 2009, asylum applications by separated children rose 13 percent across twenty-two EU states. France saw an increase of 94.5 percent, and Belgium, Sweden, and the Netherlands saw increases of 57 percent, 48 percent, and 42 percent, respectively. European Migration Network, *Policies on Reception, Return and Integration Arrangements for, and Numbers of, Unaccompanied Minors—An EU Comparative Study* (May 2010), 15, 123.

13. Finland is a case in point. A comprehensive investigation into asylum procedures was carried out in 2010 after the authorities noted the dramatic multiplication in unaccompanied child asylum-seeker arrivals: from 70 in 2002 to 706 in 2008. See Annika Parsons, *The Best Interests of the Child in Asylum and Refugee Procedures in Finland* (Helsinki: Vähemmistövaltuutettu, 2010), 12.

14. Bhabha and Schmidt, "From Kafka," 6.

15. See Linda Kelly Hill, "Immigration: The Gangs of Asylum," *Georgia Law Review* 46, (2012): 639, and Lindsay M. Harris and Morgan M. Weibel, "Matter of S-E-G-: The Final Nail in the Coffin for Gang-Related Asylum Claims?," *Berkeley La Raza Law Journal* 20, (2010): 5.

16. Bhabha and Schmidt, *SAA (US)*,18.

17. Ibid., 71–75; US Department of Homeland Security, *Immigration Enforcement Actions: 2010* (2011), 4; and CPPP, *A Child Alone*. In 2011, the United States returned 14,237 unaccompanied children to Mexico without investigating their eligibility for asylum. National Migration Institute figures, cited in *PICUM Bulletin*, Feb. 29, 2012.

18. In February 2012, the UK Home Office paid compensation and legal costs amounting to £2 million per child in a case concerning forty asylum seekers wrongly detained as adults. Diane Taylor, "£2m Paid Out over Child Asylum Seekers Illegally Detained as Adults," *Guardian*, Feb. 17, 2012.

19. Bhabha and Crock, 66.

20. UNHCR, *Statistical Yearbook 2010*, 9, 15, 48–49. In addition, there are 4.8 million Palestinians within the UNRWA mandate, and 27 million internally displaced persons. See Milner and Loescher, 3.

21. Daniel Steinbock, Everett Ressler, and Neil Boothby, *Unaccompanied Children: Care and Protection in Wars, Natural Disasters and Refugee Movements* (Oxford: Oxford University Press, 1988).

22. P. Stromberg, "Going Home . . . but to an Uncertain Future," *Refugees* (UNHCR, 1997), 19–21.

23. See Machel, *Impact of Armed Conflict*, paras. 1, 250. See also Geraldine van Bueren, "Opening Pandora's Box: Protecting Children Against Torture or Cruel, Inhuman or Degrading Treatment or Punishment," *Law and Policy* 17, no. 4 (1995): 389.

24. See *The Application of the Convention on the Prevention and Punishment of the Crime of Genocide (Bosnia and Herzegovina v. Serbia and Montenegro)*, [2007] ICJ Rep. 43, para. 291; *Prosecutor v. Radislav Krstic*, Case No. IT-98–33-A, Appeal Judgment, Apr. 19, 2004, paras. 31–33; and *Prosecutor v. Radislav Krstic*, Case No. IT-98–33-T, Trial Judgment, Aug. 2, 2001, para. 117.

25. See Tara Gingerich and Jennifer Leaning, *The Use of Rape as a Weapon of War in the Conflict in Darfur, Sudan*, prepared for USAID/OTI (2004).

26. Omar Khadr, now in his late twenties, was detained for nine years. John Swaine, "Canadian Ex–Child Soldier Pleads Guilty at Guantanamo," *Telegraph*, Mar. 28, 2011.

27. Children account for 31 percent of 850,200 asylum seekers. UNHCR, *Statistical Yearbook 2010*, 12, 48.

28. While living conditions vary by situation, camp-based refugees often face high risks to their health and well-being, including acute malnutrition, lack of adequate water and sanitation, and massive underenrollment in school, particularly among girls. Such difficulties are compounded by inadequate security and a lack of employment opportunities. Bart de Bruijn, *Human Development Research Paper 2009/25: The Living Conditions and Well-being of Refugees* (UNDP, 2009), 21–22, 25, 38.

29. "The camp is the space that opens up when the state of exception starts to become the rule. In it, the state of exception, which was essentially a temporal suspension of the state of law, acquires a permanent spatial arrangement that, as such, remains constantly outside the normal state of law." Giorgio Agamben, *Means Without End: Notes on Politics*, trans. Vincenzo Binetti and Cesare Casarino (Minneapolis: University of Minnesota Press, 2000), 16.

30. UNHCR, *Statistical Yearbook 2010*, 25.

31. Milner and Loescher, 3.

32. UNHCR, "Dadaab—World's Biggest Refugee Camp Twenty Years Old," Feb. 21, 2012.

33. IRIN, "Kenya: Overcoming Cultural Obstacles to Girls' Education in Dadaab," Apr. 11, 2012.

34. See, e.g., Elizabeth Cooper, "What Do We Know about Out-of-school Youths? How Participatory Action Research Can Work for Young Refugees in Camps," *Compare* 35, no. 4 (2005): 464; and Caitlin Crowley, "The Mental Health Needs of Refugee Children: A Review of Literature and Implications for Nurse Practitioners," *Journal of the American Academy of Nurse Practitioners* 21, no. 6 (2009): 322–31.

35. Sandy Ruxton, *Separated Children and EU Asylum and Immigration Policy* (Separated Children in Europe Programme, 2003), 14.

36. Between 1999 and 2002, 3,689 separated/unaccompanied children applied for asylum in Canada, and 285 applied for asylum in Australia. More recent numbers are unavailable as neither country publishes regular statistics on the number of separated children arriving in the country. Fiona Martin and Jennifer Curran, "Separated Children: A Comparison of the Treatment of Separated Child Refugees Entering Australia and Canada," *International Journal of Refugee Law* 19, no. 3 (2007): 446–48.

37. See Bhabha and Schmidt, Appendix 1, Table 1, "From Kafka," 18.

38. See Leanne Weber and Sharon Pickering, *Globalization and Borders: Death at the Global Frontier* (New York: Palgrave Macmillan, 2012).

39. The European Court of Human Rights, reviewing EU interdiction practices in the Mediterranean, ruled in 2012 that states have an obligation to ensure that intercepted migrants are not treated in inhuman or degrading ways, and that they are not permitted to engage in collective expulsion of would-be migrants attempting to reach European shores by interdicting them en masse. *Hirsi Jamaa and Others v. Italy*, no. 27765/09, ECHR (2012), para. 43, quoting UNHCR, *Note on International Protection*, A/AC.96/951, Sep. 13, 2001, para. 16:

> International human rights law has established *non-refoulement* as a fundamental component of the absolute prohibition of torture and cruel, inhuman or degrading treatment or punishment. The duty not to *refoule* is also recognized as applying to refugees irrespective of their formal recognition, thus obviously including asylum-seekers whose status has not yet been determined. . . . This includes rejection at the frontier, interception and indirect *refoulement*, whether of an individual seeking asylum or in situations of mass influx.

40. Bhabha and Crock, 59.

41. Jose, interviewed by Joanne Kelsey, interpreted by Andrea Pantor, on Nov. 7, 2004, for Bhabha and Schmidt, *SAA (US)*, 6.

42. Bhabha and Crock, 41.

43. Adam Clymer and Lizette Alvarez, "The Elián Gonzalez Case: The Overview," *New York Times*, Apr. 27, 2000.

44. "Shipwreck Orphan Released from Detention," *ABC News (Australia)*, Feb. 24, 2011.

45. See Ines Keygnaert, Nicole Vettenburg, and Marleen Temmerman, "Hidden Violence Is Silent Rape: Sexual and Gender-Based Violence in Refugees, Asylum Seekers and Undocumented Migrants in Belgium and the Netherlands," *Culture, Health & Sexuality* 14, no. 5 (2012): 505, and Margaret Lay and Irena Papadopoulos, "Sexual Maltreatment of Unaccompanied Asylum-Seeking Minors from the Horn of Africa," *Child Abuse & Neglect: The International Journal* 33, no. 10 (2009): 728.

46. See European Agency for the Management of Operational Cooperation at the External Borders of the Member States of the European Union (FRONTEX), *Unaccompanied Minors in the Migration Process*, Reference nr: 18477 (2010), 5, 27.

47. *CRC General Comment* 6, and para. 1.

48. Ibid., para. 29.

49. For the changes in US policy toward separated child asylum seekers, see Bhabha and Schmidt, "From Kafka"; for Spain, see Daniel Senovilla Hernández, "Unaccompanied and

Separated Children in Spain: A Policy of Institutional Mistreatment," in Bhabha, *Children Without a State*, 151–75.

50. The Young Center for Immigrant Children's Rights in Chicago (formerly the Immigrant Child Advocacy Project) is an innovative effort to partly address this failing. While it does not offer guardianship services as such, the Center provides a guardian ad litem to a growing number of separated child asylum seekers for the duration of their immigration proceedings and related care and custody processes. Started in 2004, it is currently collaborating with the US Department of Homeland Security's Office for Refugee Resettlement to expand into a national program. Bhabha and Schmidt, "From Kafka," 11. See Young Center, www.theyoungcenter.org.

51. *CRC General Comment 6*, para. 21.

52. Bhabha and Crock, 76.

53. *CRC General Comment 6*, para. 36.

54. Vera Institute of Justice, *Promoting Justice in the Immigration System: Legal Access for Unaccompanied Children* (July 2009).

55. In the United States, some recent innovations in the nonprofit sector have improved unaccompanied child asylum seekers' legal access. Kids in Need of Defense (KIND), an organization established by UNHCR with support from philanthropist Angelina Jolie, is one of several entities dedicated to securing legal representation for this population. See KIND, www.supportkind.org.

56. Bhabha and Crock, 78.

57. A 2002 study found that in the United States, asylum seekers with legal representation were four to six times more likely to be granted asylum than those without. Jonathan Jacobs and Andrew Schoenholtz, "*The State of Asylum Representation: Ideas for Change*," *Georgetown Immigration Law Journal* 16, no. 4 (2002): 739. Representation not only increases the chances of a child being granted asylum but also of a child appearing in court when required to be there for the hearing. Bhabha and Schmidt, "From Kafka," 21.

58. Bhabha and Crock, 130.

59. Ibid., 77.

60. Ibid., 97, 134.

61. Ibid., 30, 85.

62. UNHCR, *Handbook on Procedures and Criteria for Determining Refugee Status under the 1951 Convention and the 1967 Protocol Relating to the Status of Refugees*, 1979, HCR/IP/4?Eng/REV.1 (reissued Jan. 1992), 219 [*Handbook*].

63. Bhabha and Finch, 56, 57.

64. See note 18 above.

65. Erroneous classification of minors "can negatively affect detention conditions, physical and mental health, access to available and appropriate legal counsel, access to age-specific forms of protection like [Special Immigrant Juvenile Status], and the possibility of being reunited with family." Bhabha and Schmidt, *SAA (US)*, 117. See also Jacqueline Bhabha and Susan Schmidt, "Kafka's Kids: Children in U.S. Immigration Proceedings Part I: Seeking Asylum Alone," *Immigration Briefings* 07–01(1) (Thomson West, Jan. 2007).

66. Bhabha and Crock, 84.

67. Women's Refugee Commission, *Halfway Home*.

68. International Detention Coalition, *Captured Childhood* (2012).

69. *ID & Others v. Home Office* [2005] EWCA Civ 38, 111 at note 19, cited in Bhabha and Crock, 60.

70. Children's Commissioner for England, *The Arrest and Detention of Children Subject to Immigration Control: A Report Following the Children's Commissioner for England's Visit to the Yarl's Wood Immigration Removal Centre* (2009).

71. Bhabha and Crock, 60, 93.

72. Human Rights Watch, "Detained and Deprived of Rights: Children in the Custody of the U.S. Immigration and Naturalization Service," *Forced Migration Review* 10, no. 4 (G) (1998): 3.

73. Bhabha and Crock, 78, 97, 92.

74. *ABC News (Australia)*, supra note 44.

75. See Children's Commissioner for England, *Arrest and Detention of Children*.

76. "Children 'to Remain' at Dungavel," *BBC News*, May 17, 2010.

77. *Kanagaratnam v. Belgique*, no. 15297/09, ECHR (2011).

78. *Muskhadzhiyeva and Others v. Belgium*, no. 41442/07, ECHR (2010).

79. Rod McGuirk, "Australia Criticized over Child Asylum Seeker Plan," *Associated Press*, June 2, 2011.

80. This principle is articulated in chapter 6 of the UNHCR *Handbook*, a "soft law" document that, though not legally binding, has been characterized as a source of useful guidance in adjudicating asylum claims. See *INS v. Cardoza-Fonseca*, 480 U.S. 421, 49 at note 22 (1987).

81. UNHCR, *Statistical Yearbook 2010*, 45.

82. Bhabha and Young, "Not Adults in Miniature," 91.

83. In the United Kingdom, for example, despite a sizable number of unaccompanied child-asylum applications and access to free legal representation for children seeking asylum, only 15 percent of child refugee claims succeed at first instance (if one is to go by Home Office figures). More unaccompanied children succeed on appeal, but the majority receive temporary protection, which expires when they turn eighteen. See UK Home Office, *Monthly Asylum Statistics—Dec. 2010* and Bhabha and Crock, 22, 124.

84. The United Kingdom has developed an Asylum Policy Instruction on Children, and is now also bound by EU guidelines on unaccompanied and separated child asylum seekers, including relevant provisions of the Asylum Procedures Directive 2005/85/EC (Art. 17), the Reception Conditions Directive 2003/9/EC (Art. 19), the Temporary Protection Directive 2001/55/EC (Art. 16), and the Qualification Directive 2004/83/EC (Art. 30). In Australia, the High Court confirmed, in the case of *Applicant S v. Minister for Immigration and Multicultural Affairs (MIMIA)*, [2004] 206 ALR 242, that persecutory behavior has to be determined within the framework of human-rights law taking into account the extent to which discrimination is involved. Bhabha and Crock, 3, 155.

85. See *Canada (Minister of Citizenship and Immigration) v. Patel*, 2008 FC 747, para. 45.

86. UNHCR, *Handbook*, 52, 15 (para. 56).

87. See, e.g., Guy S. Goodwin-Gill and Jane McAdam, *The Refugee in International Law* (Oxford: Oxford University Press, 2007), 356–65; Kay Hailbronner, "New Techniques for

Rendering Asylum Manageable," in Kay Hailbronner, David Martin, and Hiroshi Motomura, eds., *Immigration Controls: The Search for Workable Policies in Germany and the United States* (Oxford, Providence, RI: Berghahn Books, 1998), 159–99; and Arthur C. Helton, "Persecution on Account of Membership in a Social Group as a Basis for Refugee Status," *Columbia Human Rights Law Review* 15, no. 1 (1983): 39, 67.

88. *Kahssai v. INS*, 16 F.3d 323, 329 (9th Cir. 1994).

89. *Hernandez-Ortiz v. Gonzales*, 496 F.3d 1042 (9th Cir. 2007).

90. *Matter of [name not provided]*, A76–512–001 (Oct. 18, 2000) (Chicago, IL) (Zerbe, IJ). For a discussion of forced marriage, arranged marriage, and child marriage as grounds for asylum, see Jenni Millbank and Catherine Dauvergne, "Forced Marriage and the Exoticization of Gendered Harms in the United States Asylum Law," *Columbia Journal of Gender and Law* 19, no. 3 (2011).

91. *Matter of Juan Carlos Martinez-Mejia*, A 76 312 250, 5–6 (BIA Jan. 20, 1999) (unpublished).

92. See *Matter of Dennis Reyes-Diaz* (EOIR Aug. 2, 2001) (unpublished); *Matter of Brus. Wilson Fuentes-Ortega*, A78–677–043 (BIA Nov. 6, 2002) (unpublished); *Matter of Santos Ramon Zepeda Campos* (IJ Dec. 28, 2000) (Phoenix, AZ); and *Matter of Aurelio Mauricio Lopez*, A78–677–018 (BIA Nov. 28, 2001) (unpublished).

93. *Escobar v. Gonzales*, 417 F.3d 363 (C.A.3, 2005). *Escobar* has been adopted by the First Circuit; see *Mejilla-Romero v. Holder*, 600 F.3d 63, 29 (1st Cir. 2010), vacated on rehearing, 614 F.3d 572 (2010).

94. See, e.g., *Patel v. Canada*, supra note 84.

95. *Matter of [name not provided]*, (IJ Mar. 13, 1998) (Chicago, Ill.) (IJ Zerbe).

96. *Bian v. Canada (Minister of Citizenship and Immigration)*, IMM-1640–00, 11 Dec. 2000.

97. For a discussion of cultural essentialism in asylum advocacy, see, e.g., Michelle A. McKinley, "Cultural Culprits," *Berkeley Journal of Gender, Law and Justice* 24 (2009): 91–165; Makau Mutua, "Savages, Victims and Saviors: The Metaphor of Human Rights," *Harvard International Law Journal* 42, no. 1 (2001): 201, 203; and Sherene H. Razack, *Looking White People in the Eye: Gender, Race, and Culture in Courtrooms and Classrooms* (Toronto: University of Toronto Press, 1998), 88–129.

98. See *Matter of A and Z*, A72–190–893, A72–793–219 (IJ Dec. 20, 1994) (Arlington, VA) (Nejelski, IJ) and discussion of this case in Jacqueline Bhabha, "Embodied Rights: Gender Persecution, State Sovereignty and Refugees," *Public Culture* 9, (1996): 3–32, 17.

99. See Mutua, supra note 97.

100. *Matter of A and Z*, 14.

101. See James C. Hathaway, *The Law of Refugee Status* (Toronto: Butterworths, 1991), 8–9.

102. See, for instance, a decision by the Canadian Immigration and Refugee Board awarding asylum to a Somali girl who faced the prospect of female circumcision if returned; criticizing this "torturous custom," the Board ruled that the applicant's status as a "minor female from Somalia" qualified her for protection under the Refugee Convention. *Khadra Hassan Farah, Mahad Dahir Buraleh, Hodan Dahir Buraleh*, Immigration and Refugee Board of Canada, 10 May 1994. Additional countries where female circumcision has been the basis of grants of refugee status to children (or at the very least, reconsiderations of their claims)

include the United States, the United Kingdom, Germany, Austria, France, and Sweden. See, e.g., *In re Kasinga*, 21 I&N Dec. 357, 365 (BIA 1996); *FK (Kenya) v. Secretary of State for the Home Department* [2010] EWCA Civ 1302; *2007/01/0284 v. Independent Federal Asylum Board (UBAS)*, Administrative Court, 23 Sep. 2009; *Emily Collins and Ashley Akaziebie v. Sweden*, no. 23944/05, ECHR (2007); *A v. Federal Republic of Germany*, High Administrative Court Hessen, Judgment of 23 Mar. 2005, 3 UE 3457/04.A; *Mlle Diop Aminata*, 164078, Commission des Recours des Réfugiés (CRR), France, 17 July 1991.

103. See *Bian v. Canada*, supra note 95.

104. *Cruz-Diaz v. INS*, 86 F.3d 330 (4th Cir. 1996).

105. *Uthayakumar v. Canada (Ministry of Citizenship and Immigration)* IMM 2949–98, 18 June 1999.

106. *Canjura-Flores v. INS* 784 F.2d 885, 887 (9th Cir. 1985). The Board's position was reversed by the Court of Appeal, which accepted the applicant's evidence that young people were likely to be sought out by government forces. See also the case of a Chilean child turned down by Canadian Refugee Status Advisory Committee because decision makers did not consider that a twelve- to thirteen-year-old could be perceived as a threat by the Chilean regime, described in G. Sadoway, "Refugee Children Before the Immigration and Refugee Board," 35 *Immigration Law Reporter* 106 (1997): 110.

107. See *Salaam v. INS*, 229 F.3d 1234 (9th Cir. 2000). The board had refused asylum on the grounds that it was "not plausible" that the petitioner was a leading member of the Free Nigeria Movement at age eighteen. The Ninth Circuit found that this statement was "based on [the] entirely unsupported assumption [that] . . . 'important' organizations do not have young leaders."

108. According to a report on decision making on separated-child cases in the Netherlands: "Even where a separated child has been picked up by the police because he accompanied his father to a demonstration, the conclusion is that the arrest is simply the result of being present at a demonstration by chance." Ruxton, *Separated Children*, 80.

109. See Thomas Spijkerboer, *Gender and Refugee Status* (London: Ashgate Publishing, 2000), 65–74.

110. See *Sooriyakumaran v. Canada (Minister of Citizenship and Immigration)*, IMM-4099–97, 10 Jan. 1998.

111. See, e.g., Ellen Laipson et al., *Seismic Shift: Understanding Change in the Middle East* (Henry L. Stimson Center, 2011).

112. UNHCR Catalogue, German Case Signature CAS/ DEU/108, May 11, 1992. TA3–24983 v. Canada, Immigration and Refugee Board, Feb. 2, 2005.

113. Since March 2011, more than five hundred children have been killed in Syria. UN Human Rights Council, A/HRC/19/69 (Feb. 22, 2012).

114. *Civil v. INS*, 140 F.3d 52 (1st Cir. 1998).

115. See Viviana Zelizer, *Pricing the Priceless Child: The Changing Social Value of Children* (Princeton: Princeton University Press, 1985).

116. See Sharon Stephens, "Children and the Politics of Culture in 'Late Capitalism,'" in Sharon Stephens, ed., *Children and the Politics of Culture* (Princeton: Princeton University Press, 1995), 3.

117. *Ramirex Rivas v. INS*, 899 F.2d 864 (9th Cir. 1990).

118. *Khassai v. INS*, 16 F.3d 326 (9th Cir. 1994).

119. "Children may also be subjected to specific forms of persecution that are influenced by their age, lack of maturity or vulnerability. The fact that the refugee claimant is a child may be a central factor in the harm inflicted or feared. This may be because the alleged persecution only applies to, or disproportionately affects, children or because specific child rights may be infringed." UNHCR, *2009 Guidelines on Child Asylum Claims*, para. 18.

120. *In re R-A-*, 25 I&N Dec. 906 (BIA 1999). Courts have also recognized the discrimination and persecution faced by children born in violation of China's "one-child policy." See, e.g., *Shi Chen v. Holder*, 604 F.3d 324, 328 (7th Cir. 2010) and *Chen Shi Hai (an infant) by His Next Friend Chen Ren Bing v. Minister for Immigration and Multicultural Affairs* [2000], 201 CLR 293 (Austl.).

121. See, e.g., *Moreno v. Canada (Minister of Employment and Immigration)* [1994] 1 FC 298; *Negusie v. Holder*, 555 U.S. 511 (2009); France, CNDA, 20 Dec. 2010, Mr. N., n°10004872; and *O (a minor) v. Refugee Appeals Tribunal and Minister for Justice, Equality and Law Reform* [2010] IEHC 151.

122. See, e.g., *Bueckert v. Canada* (Minister of Citizenship and Immigration) [2011] FC 1042; *Aguirre-Cervantes v. INS*, 242 F.3d 1169 (9th Cir. 2001) (opinion vacated on rehearing en banc and remanded, 273 F.3d 1220 (9th Cir. 2001); and *Secretary of State for the Home Department v. Fatemah Firouz Ranjbar*, Immigration Appeal Tribunal, no. HX/70912/94, 28 June 1994.

123. See, e.g., Sweden—Migration Court (Administrative), 17 Mar. 2011, UM 206–11 and *LQ (Afghanistan) v. Secretary of State for the Home Department* [2008] UKAIT 00005.

124. See *[Names Not Provided] v. Minister* [2011] Immigration and Refugee Board of Canada—Refugee Protection Division, RPD File No. VA9–01475, VA9–01476, VA9–01477, VA9–01478, VA9–01479, para. 13 (Can.).

125. See note 110 above. See also UNHCR, *Guidance Note on Refugee Claims Relating to Female Genital Mutilation* (2009), 7–8.

126. See, e.g., *Gomez-Guzman v. Holder*, no. 11–3006, 2012 WL 2161636, at *3 (6th Cir. June 15, 2012) (unpublished); *Siliadin v. France* (2006) 43 EHRR 16; *Zhu (L.W.) v. Canada (Minister of Citizenship and Immigration)*, IMM-2746–00, 13 Aug. 2001; and *Bian v. Canada*, supra note 96.

127. See, e.g., *A B v. Secretary of State for the Home Department*, no. CC/64057/2002, 18 Feb. 2003; *In Re Ji-Zhu Mai*, A74–206–787 (BIA Mar. 20, 2001); and *Y.C.K. (re)* [1997] CRDD. No. 261 No. V95–02904.

128. A Canadian court has recognized that a forced polygamous marriage of a fourteen-year-old in accordance with the customary laws of *kuzarira* and *lobola* in Zimbabwe could constitute persecution. See *In W. (Z.D.) (Re) Convention Refugee Determination Decision* [1993] CRDD No. 3, no. U92–06668 . See also Finland—10/0642/1, Helsinki Administrative Court, 28 May 2010; *W.H. v. Swiss Federal Office for Migration*, Oct 9, 2006; and *Matter of [Name Not Provided]*, A76–512–001 (IJ Oct. 18, 2000)(Chicago, IL)(Zerbe, IJ).

129. See *Fatemah Firouz Ranjbar* case, note 121 above.

130. The case concerned a Pakistan boy suffering from autism and subjected to relentless insults at home; see Letter opinion by Robert Esbrook, A78 -642–794 (Chicago Asylum Office, Feb. 21, 2001) WL 78 No. 13 INTERREL 604.

131. *Tchoukrova v. Gonzales*, 404 F.3d 1181 (9th Cir. 2005). The court found that disabled Russian children and their parents could constitute a particular social group. Although the case was vacated and remanded by the Supreme Court (and eventually withdrawn by the petitioner), it has been cited in numerous decisions in the First, Third, Seventh, and Ninth Circuits.

132. Kaethe Weingarten, *Common Shock: Witnessing Violence Every Day: How We Are Harmed, How We Are Healed* (New York: Dutton, 2003).

133. *E.D. v. Refugee Appeals Tribunal* [2011] IEHC 354.

134. Bhabha and Crock, 161 (emphasis added). This principle has also been upheld by Canadian courts: "Children, because of their distinct vulnerabilities, may be persecuted in ways that would not amount to persecution of an adult. It is incumbent on the [Refugee Protection Division] to be empathetic to a child's physical and mental state and to be aware of the fact that harming a child may have greater consequences than harming an adult." *Kim v. Canada (Minister of Citizenship and Immigration)*, 2010 FC 149.

135. *Case G.005*, EOIR, Phoenix, Az., Mar. 20, 2003.

136. *O (a Minor) v. Refugee Appeals Tribunal and Minister for Justice, Equality and Law Reform* [2010] IEHC 151.

137. *ABC (A Minor) (Afghanistan) v. Secretary of State for the Home Department.* [2011] EWHC 2937.

138. *Hernandez-Ortiz v. Gonzales*, 496 F.3d 1042 (9th Cir. 2007).

139. Bhabha and Crock, 161.

140. *Ahota v. Canada (Minister of Employment and Immigration)* (1994) 80 F.T.R. 241.

141. Jeffrey D. Corsetti, "Marked for Death: The Maras of Central America and Those Who Flee Their Wrath," *Georgetown Immigration Law Journal* 20, no. 3 (2006): 407.

142. Report of the International Human Rights Clinic, *No Place to Hide: Gang, State and Clandestine Violence in El Salvador*, Human Rights Programme, Harvard Law School, Feb. 2007.

143. Youth within the age range of eight to eighteen years may be particularly vulnerable to recruitment. See USAID, *Central America and Mexico Gang Assessment Report* (Bureau for Latin American and Caribbean Affairs Office of Regional Sustainable Development, Apr. 2006), 15.

144. *Case of Edwin Jovani Enamorado*, Nov 22. 1999, EOIR.

145. See *Castellano-Chacon v. INS*, 341 F.3d 533 (6th Cir.2003).

146. *Matter of S-E-G-*, 24 I&N Dec. 579, (BIA 30 July 2008), 581, 580, 587.

147. *Matter of E-A-G-*, 24 I&N Dec. 591 (BIA 30 July 2008).

148. See, e.g., *Mendez-Barrera v. Holder*, 602 F.3d 21, 26–27 (1st Cir. 2010); *Contreras-Martinez v. Holder*, no. 08–2323 (4th Cir. 2009); *Cruz-Alvarez v. Holder*, 320 F. App'x 273, 274 (5th Cir. 2009); *Ramos-Lopez v. Holder*, 563 F.3d 855 (9th Cir. 2009); and *Gomez-Benitez v. Attorney General*, no. 07–13999 (11th Cir. 2008). The Sixth and Seventh Circuits are exceptions to this general trend. See *Urbina-Mejia v. Holder*, 597 F.3d 360 (6th Cir. 2010) and *Benitez Ramos v. Holder*, 589 F 3d. 426 (7th Cir. 2009). However, the Sixth Circuit has stopped short of recognizing all teenagers who resist gang recruitment as members of a particular social group, see *Escobar-Batres v. Holder*, no. 09–3748 (6th Cir. 2010).

149. See UNHCR, *Organized Gangs*.

150. *Valdiviezo-Galdamez v. Attorney General*, 663 F.3d 582 (3rd Cir. 2011). For a discussion of this case, see Dorothy A. Harbeck et al., "Vanishing Visibility: How Particular Social Group Requirements Have Changed in the Third Circuit's Asylum Cases," 59 *Federal Lawyer* 48 (Mar. 2012).

151. Preston, "Losing Asylum."

152. Immigration and Refugee Board of Canada, *Guideline 3: Child Refugee Claimants: Procedural and Evidentiary Issues* (1996); USCIS, *Guidelines for Children's Asylum Claims* (1998); UK Home Office Border & Immigration Agency, "Processing Asylum Applications from a Child," *Special Cases: Guidance* (2005); and UNHCR, *2009 Guidelines on Child Asylum Claims*.

153. UNHCR, *Organized Gangs*, para. 19.

154. Parsons, *Best Interests*, 5.

Chapter 7. Demanding Rights and a Future: Adolescents on the Move for a Better Life

Earlier versions of parts of this chapter were published as an article in the *Human Rights Quarterly* 2009, volume 13 ("Arendt's Children: Do Today's Migrant Children Have a Right to Have Rights?").

1. Hannah Arendt, *The Origins of Totalitarianism* (San Diego: Harcourt, 1966), 291–92.

2. This region is commonly referred to as MENA—Middle East and North Africa.

3. International Finance Corporation, *Education for Employment: Realizing Arab Youth Potential*, 2011.

4. The terms "child," "adolescent," "youth," and "young person" overlap but differ. Only the first is defined in international law: "a person under the age of 18," CRC, Art. 1. The other terms lack an agreed-upon, universally applicable definition; however, some consensus exists about their common usage. UNICEF, together with UNFPA, WHO, and UNAIDS, defines an "adolescent" as a person between ten and nineteen; the UN defines "youth" as persons between fifteen and twenty-four. No official definition of "young person" exists. This chapter will use the terms interchangeably. Most unaccompanied child migrants are in fact adolescents; and many reports on independent youth migrants do not specify their exact age.

5. Between 1993 and 2012, there were 16,136 deaths directly related to European border control. In 2011 alone, 1,500 refugees and migrants drowned en route to Europe in the Mediterranean, turning it into a "nautical graveyard." Leanne Weber and Sharon Pickering, *Globalization and Borders: Death at the Global Frontier* (Basingstoke: Palgrave Macmillan, 2011).

6. Gaia Pianigiani, "Twenty-five Migrants Found Dead in Boat Near Italy Coast," *New York Times*, Aug. 1, 2011.

7. *PICUM Bulletin*, July 4, 2011.

8. Amnesty International, *Italy: Amnesty International Findings and Recommendations to the Italian Authorities Following the Research Visit to Lampedusa and Mineo* (2011).

9. Some experts refer to this blurring of legal categories within contemporary migration flows as the "asylum-migration nexus." See Alexander Betts, "Towards a Mediterranean

Solution?: Implications for the Region of Origin," *International Journal of Refugee Law* 18, no. 3–4 (2006), 652–76.

10. UNICEF, *Evidence Gap*, 3–4.

11. See Shahin Yaqub, *Independent Child Migrants in Developing Countries: Unexplored Links in Migration and Development*, UNICEF Innocenti Working Paper No. 2009–01 (2009).

12. WRC, *Forced from Home: The Lost Boys and Girls of Central America* (2012), 4.

13. There were an estimated 7.5 million child migrants in Europe in 2010, many from Eastern Europe and North Africa. UN DESA, *Trends in International Migrant Stock: Migrants by Age and Sex* (UN Database, POP/DB/MIG/Stock/Rev.2011). There are no reliable figures on the number of *undocumented* child migrants in Europe, as the available data are based on border apprehension figures and likely underreport the phenomenon.

14. Dinesh Singh Rawat, "UN General Assembly Debates International Migration and Development," *ABC Live*, May 20, 2011.

15. Around 11.2 million undocumented migrants live in the United States, and the government spent over US$17 million on immigration enforcement in 2011. Jeffrey S. Passel and D'Vera Cohn, *Unauthorized Immigrant Population: National and State Trends 2010* (Pew Hispanic Center, 2011), 1; US Department of Homeland Security, *FY 2011: Budget in Brief* (2011), 17. In Europe, approximately 570,000 irregular migrants were apprehended in 2009, and the EU border agency FRONTEX budgeted €88,410,000 for immigration enforcement in 2011. European Commission Home Agency, "Immigration," http://ec.europa.eu/home-affairs/policies/immigration/immigration_illegal_en.htm; FRONTEX, *Budget 2011*.

16. Statement for the Record, The Honorable Michael Chertoff, Secretary, US Department of Homeland Security, before the United States House of Representatives Committee on Homeland Security, July 17, 2008, cited in Daniel Kanstroom, *Aftermath: Deportation Law and the New American Diaspora* (Oxford University Press: forthcoming), 98.

17. UN General Assembly, *International Migration and Development. Report of the Secretary-General*, 18 May 2006, A/60/871, 44–45. See also Home Office and DWP, *The Economic and Fiscal Impact of Immigration*, CM 7237 (2007).

18. Save the Children, *General Recommendations for EU Action in Relation to Unaccompanied and Separated Children of Third Country Origin* (2009).

19. Arendt did not envisage the cosmopolitan collectivity that constitutes the national population in many of the states to which child migrants travel today. But her insight is no less relevant: multicultural polities today generate de facto statelessness through border-control regimes rather than race laws. For an interesting reflection on this point, see Butler and Spivak, 62–66.

20. ICCPR.

21. ICESCR.

22. International human-rights treaties include the 1989 CRC and the 1990 Convention on the Rights of Migrant Workers and their Families. Regional and national provisions include the European Commission, *Action Plan 2010–2014* and the US Special Immigrant Juvenile Visa scheme.

23. Arendt, *Totalitarianism*, 270.

24. Nando Sigona and Vanessa Hughes, *No Way Out, No Way In: Irregular Migrant Children and Families in the UK* (ESRC Centre on Migration, Policy and Society, 2012), 6.

25. Women's Refugee Commission, *Halfway Home*, 10.

26. Sigona and Hughes, supra note 26, viii.

27. Cynthia Menjivar, "Liminal Legality: Salvadoran and Guatemalan Immigrants' Lives in the United States," *American Journal of Sociology* 111 (2006), 999–1037, cited in Kara Cebulko, "Documented, Undocumented and Somewhere 'In-between': The Effects of Documentation Status on Children of Brazilian Immigrants" (unpublished draft on file with author).

28. Sigona and Hughes, supra note 24.

29. Cebulko, 11.

30. Many nouns and adjectives are used to describe individuals who lack a legal migration status: alien, immigrant, migrant, entrant, noncitizen, foreigner, illegal, unlawful, irregular, and undocumented. The term "unauthorized migrant" will be preferred here where accurate ("undocumented" may not be, e.g. for those who overstay visas) over more value-laden alternatives.

31. Jeffrey S. Passel and Paul Taylor, *Unauthorized Immigrants and Their US-Born Children* (Pew Hispanic Center, 2010), 1.

32. Kanstroom, *Deportation Nation*. In some US states, notably Illinois and California, legislation has been passed allowing undocumented students access to school and scholarship programs to finance their education, but in other states, such as Indiana, Alabama, and Wisconsin, opposing legislative initiatives have been initiated.

33. See US Department of Homeland Security, "Secretary Napolitano Announces Deferred Action Process for Young People Who Are Low Enforcement Priorities," June 15, 2012.

34. H.R. 1751, 111th Cong. § 4(a) ("special rule for certain long-term residents who entered the United States as children") (2009); S. 3992 111th Cong. §4 ("cancellation of removal of certain long-term residents who entered the United States as children") (2010).

35. Cebulko, 13, 12.

36. Stephen Legomsky, "Undocumented Students, College Education, and Life Beyond," in Bhabha, *Children Without a State*, 217–35.

37. Roberto G. Gonzales, "Learning to be Illegal: Undocumented Youth and Shifting Legal Contexts in the Transition to Adulthood," *American Sociological Review* 76, no. 4 (2011): 602–19.

38. Thronson, "Thinking Small," 239.

39. Sigona and Hughes, supra note 28.

40. Ibid., 8.

41. *PICUM Bulletin*, Aug. 29, 2011.

42. France Terre d'Asile, "Mineurs isolés étrangers: le devoir impérieux de protéger," July 26, 2011.

43. *PICUM Quarterly Newsletter*, Aug.–Nov. 2011, 17.

44. Martin Rank, "Schulen müssen nicht mehr petzen," *TAZ*, July 8, 2011, cited in *PICUM Bulletin*, Aug. 29, 2011.

45. *PICUM Bulletin*, Sep. 12, 2011.

46. Brownlees and Finch, 23.

47. Louis Henkin, *The Age of Rights* (New York: Columbia University Press, 1996).

48. See UDHR, Arts. 12, 16; CRC, Arts. 5, 9, 10, 16, 22, 37; ECHR, Arts. 8, 12; ACHR, Arts. 11, 17; African Charter, Arts. 18; ICCPR, Arts. 17, 23; ICESCR, Art. 10.

49. CRC Committee, *General Comment 7: Implementing Child Rights in Early Childhood*, CRC/C/GC/7/Rev.1, Sep. 20, 2006.

50. Economic pressures, poor housing, and other living circumstances, including insecure immigration status, are closely associated with high levels of family stress and less effective parenting skills. New Economics Foundation, *Backing the Future: Why Investing in Children Is Good for Us All* (2009), 12.

51. See CRC, Art. 28(c); ICESCR, Art. 13(b), (c); and UN Committee on Economic, Social and Cultural Rights, *General Comment 13: The Right to Education (Art. 13 of the Covenant)*, E/C.12/1999/10, Dec. 8, 1999; UN Educational, Scientific and Cultural Organisation (UNESCO), Convention Against Discrimination in Education, 429 UNTS 93, Dec. 14, 1960, Art. 4. See also UNICEF, *The State of the World's Children 2011: Adolescence—An Age of Opportunity* and World Bank, *Constructing Knowledge Societies: New Challenges for Tertiary Education* (2002).

52. See Annette Bernhardt, *Research on Informal Work in the US*, background memo prepared for the WIEGO Workshop on Informal Employment in Developed Countries, Harvard University, Oct. 31–Nov. 1, 2008.

53. Women's Refugee Commission, *Halfway Home*; Bhabha and Schmidt, *SAA (US)*.

54. Elena Rozzi, "Transitions to Adulthood: Between Socio-cultural Differences and Universal Rights" in Jacqueline Bhabha, ed., *Coming of Age: Reframing the Approach to Adolescent Rights* (Philadelphia: University of Pennsylvania Press, forthcoming).

55. Francesco Vacchiano, "Bash n 'ataq l-walidin ('To Save My Parents'): Personal and Social Challenges of Moroccan Unaccompanied Children in Italy," in Kanics et al., 120.

56. Migrant adolescents whose asylum applications are rejected but who cannot return to their home countries exemplify this situation. In Norway, approximately four hundred adolescents lack protection, access to health care or education, because they have no legal status and no viable strategies for enforcing their basic rights. Norway International Network, "Effort Grows to Revive 'Nansenpass,'" Oct. 10, 2011.

57. For discussion of "co-production" decision-making strategies, see Action for Children, *Backing the Future: Why Investing in Children Is Good for Us All* (2009), 42.

58. Brownlees and Finch, 8.

59. US Department of Health and Human Services, Office of Refugee Resettlement, *Report to Congress FY 2008* (2011), iv.

60. Nicola Mai, "Marginalized Young (Male) Migrants in the European Union," in Kanics et al., 72.

61. M. Suárez-Orozco et al., "Growing Up in the Shadows: The Development Implications of Unauthorized Status," *Harvard Education Review* 81, no. 3 (2011).

62. This qualification references the discussion about choice and agency among adolescents facing severe structural constraints on their access to livelihood and basic resources. Labeling these forms of income-generating activity as "self-harming" obscures the structural forces blocking less dangerous choices. See O'Connell Davidson, *Global Sex Trade*.

63. Mai, 72–73.

64. James C. Scott, *Seeing Like a State: How Certain Schemes to Improve the Human Condition Have Failed* (New Haven: Yale University Press, 1998).

65. Ibid., paras. I.1, and I.2.

66. *Plyler v. Doe*, 457 US 202 (1982).

67. Jacqueline Bhabha, "Inconsistent State Intervention and Separated Child Asylum Seekers," *European Journal of Migration and Law* 3, (2001): 283–314.

68. Tom Tancredo, quoted in VOA News, "Health Care for Illegal Immigrants in USA Remains Point of Contention," Apr. 28, 2006.

69. See Bob Dane, "Dictionary's 'Anchor Baby' Decision Is Definition of Foolish," *Fox News*, Dec. 9, 2011; David Vitter, "Close the 'Birthright Citizenship' Loophole," *CNN*, Feb. 15, 2011; and Julia Preston, "State Lawmakers Outline Plans to End Birthright Citizenship, Drawing Outcry," *New York Times*, Jan. 5, 2011.

70. Liz Fekete, *They Are Children Too: A Study of Europe's Deportation Policies* (London: Institute of Race Relations, 2007), 14.

71. Fabrizio Gatti, "Lampedusa, la prigione dei bambini," *L'Espresso*, Sep. 9, 2011.

72. Joanna Kakissis, "Reclaiming Xenophobia: The Rise of Ultra Nationalism in Greece." *Time*, October 31, 2012. Retrieved from http://world.time.com/2012/10/31/reclaiming-xenophobia-the-rise-of-ultra-nationalism-in-greece/; Robert Amsterdam. "Xenophobic Nationalism Clouds Hungary's Elections." Huffington Post Blog. March 28, 2010. Retrieved from http://www.huffingtonpost.com/robert-amsterdam/xenophobic-nationalism-cl_b_516324.html; B.C. "Slovaki for Slovaks?" The Economist, March 7, 2013. Retrieved from http://www.economist.com/blogs/easternapproaches/2013/03/slovakia.

73. This is the approach recommended by UNHCR, the CRC Committee, and other experts. See UNHCR, *Handbook*, para. 196, and *CRC General Comment 6*, para. 39. For a full discussion, see Terry Smith and Laura Brownlees, *Age Assessment Practices: A Literature Review & Annotated Bibliography* (UNICEF, 2011).

74. "Asylum Seekers Policy 'Unlawful,'" *BBC News*, Jan. 26, 2007.

75. Thomas Hammarberg, Commissioner for Human Rights of the Council of Europe, "The Rights of Children in Migration Must Be Defended," Presentation to Save the Children Sweden Conference, Warsaw, Mar. 20, 2007.

76. Children's Commissioner for England, *Arrest and Detention of Children*.

77. "Migrant Children Detention to End, Government Says," *BBC News*, May 26, 2010.

78. *PICUM Bulletin*, Feb. 2012.

79. Women's Refugee Commission, *Forced from Home: The Lost Boys and Girls of Central America* (2012), 21.

80. *Selmouni v. France*, no. 25803/94, ECHR (1999) (emphasis added).

81. Marine Vassort, *Paroles d'Errance* (Marseille: Editions P'tits Papiers, 2006), 13 (author's translation).

82. Defence for Children International, "European Committtee of Social Rights: Eviction of Undocumented Children from Dutch Reception Centers Should be Banned," Feb. 28, 2010.

83. Bhabha and Finch, 56.

84. *CRC General Comment 6*, paras. 19, 22(d), 23, 31(iii), 46; European Commission, *Action Plan 2010–2014*. See also Council of the European Union, *Council conclusions*, paras. 20–21.

85. See, e.g., CRC Committee, *Concluding Observations: Belgium*, CRC/C/15/Add.178, June 13, 2002, para. 18; *Concluding observations: Denmark*, CRC/C/15/Add.33, Feb. 15, 1995, para. 14; and *Concluding Observations: Italy*, CRC/C/15/Add. 198, Mar. 18, 2003, para 20.

86. Sylvia da Lomba, quoted in Ryszard Cholewinski, *Study on Obstacles to Effective Access of Irregular Migrants to Minimum Social Rights* (Strasbourg: Council of Europe, 2005), 17.

87. Human Rights Watch, *Nowhere to Turn: State Abuses of Unaccompanied Migrant Children by Spain and Morocco*, 14, no. 3 (2002).

88. *Siliadin v. France*, no. 73316/01, ECHR (2005).

89. UDHR, Arts. 2, 4, Art. 5.

90. "Motherhood and childhood are entitled to special care and assistance. All children, whether born in or out of wedlock, shall enjoy the same social protection," Ibid., Art. 25(2).

91. The UDHR presents children as at once rights holders and bearers of adult responsibilities. Article 26 on education makes this approach clear: "Everyone has the right to education. . . . Parents have a prior right to choose the kind of education that shall be given to their children."

92. See CRC Art. 14 (1) and (2) for an example of the CRC's careful balancing act between children and parental rights. States parties are required to respect the child's freedom of thought, conscience, and religion, but also the rights and duties of parents to provide direction to the child. A similar compromise between parental guidance and child agency is reflected in Article 29 on factors relevant to shaping the form of education a child should receive. The UDHR approach stating the privileged position of the parent as ultimate arbiter is replaced by a more nuanced position: "States Parties agree that the education of the child shall be directed to . . . the development of respect for the child's parents, his or her own cultural identity, language and values." CRC, Art. 29(c).

93. "States Parties shall take all appropriate measures to ensure that school discipline is administered in a manner consistent with the child's human dignity." Ibid., Art. 28(2).

94. "State Parties shall take all effective and appropriate measures with a view to abolishing traditional practices prejudicial to the health of children." Ibid., Art. 24(3).

95. South Sudan is the third country that has not ratified the CRC.

96. CRIN, "Convention on the Rights of the Child," www.crin.org/resources/treaties/CRC.asp?catName=International+Treaties&flag=legal&ID=6.

97. Martin Guggenheim, *What's Wrong with Children's Rights* (Cambridge, MA: Harvard University Press, 2006), xi.

98. Charter of Fundamental Rights of the European Union, 2000/C 364/01, 7 Dec. 2000, Art. 24.

99. European Commission, *Towards an EU Strategy on the Rights of the Child*, Communication of 4 July 2006, COM(2006) 367 final, para. 1.1.

100. Those with specific child-related briefs include the Special Rapporteur on the Sale of Children, Child Prostitution, and Child Pornography; Special Rapporteur on Trafficking in Persons, especially Women and Children; Special Representative for Children and Armed Conflict; and Special Representative for Violence Against Children.

101. UNICEF is mandated "to advocate for the protection of children's rights, to help meet their basic needs and to expand their opportunities to reach their full potential." Its programs are explicitly guided by the CRC, and it has special responsibility under Art. 45 to monitor the implementation of the Convention and Optional Protocols.

102. The Australian Human Rights and Equal Opportunities Commission's (HREOC) report on detention of unaccompanied minors seeking asylum is a good example of this approach. HREOC, *A Last Resort? National Inquiry into Children in Immigration Detention* (2004).

103. The primary EU pronouncement on the rights of migrant children and adolescents is the 1997 Council Resolution on Unaccompanied Minors (see Introduction, note 9). Although nonbinding, the resolution is an important soft-law reference point for domestic and regional policy makers. It recognizes the extreme vulnerability of this population and recommends appointment of a guardian and access to legal representation as soon as an unaccompanied minor is identified. Several EU directives on asylum and immigration also make reference to the specific needs of minors, including unaccompanied children and adolescents. While these standards are not as protective as those developed by the CRC Committee—for example, the directives permit states to return unaccompanied children to their countries of origin without first establishing that this is in their best interests—they do stipulate that minors require special care and protection, and that officials dealing with them should receive specialist training. For a detailed discussion of EU provisions, see *The Legal Status of Unaccompanied Children within International, European and National Frameworks: Protective Standards vs. Restrictive Implementation*, eds. Daniel Senovilla and Philippe LaGrange (PUCAFREU, 2011).

104. See CRC Committee, *General Comment 3: HIV/AIDS and the Rights of the Child*, CRC/GC/2003/3, Mar. 17, 2003, and CRC Committee, *General Comment 4: Adolescent Health and Development in the Context of the Convention on the Rights of the Child*, CRC/GC/2003/4, July 1, 2003.

105. *Nsona v. The Netherlands*, 63/1995/569/655, ECHR (1996); *Mubilanzila Mayeka and Kaniki Mitunga v. Belgium*, no. 13178/03, ECHR (2006).

106. Hungarian Helsinki Committee, *Stuck in Jail: Immigration Detention in Hungary (2010)*, Apr. 2011, cited in *PICUM Bulletin*, May 9, 2011.

107. An optional protocol establishing a complaints procedure for violations of children's rights was introduced by the UN on December 19, 2011, so this situation is set to change. CRIN, "UN Adopts Complaints Mechanism for Children," Dec. 19, 2011.

108. CRC Committee, *Reservations, Declarations and Objections Relating to the Convention on the Rights of the Child—Note by the Secretary-General*, CRC/C/2/Rev.3, July 11, 1994.

109. Oona Hathaway, "Do Human Rights Treaties Make a Difference?" *Yale Law Journal* 111, no. 8 (2002).

110. CRC, Art. 37.

111. Het Belang van Limburg, "Illegalen met kinderen worden opnieuw opgesloten," May 4, 2011, cited in *PICUM Bulletin*, May 9, 2011.

112. UN Economic and Social Council, Commission on Human Rights, *Migrant Workers: Report of the Special Rapporteur, Ms. Gabriela Rodríguez Pizarro, submitted pursuant to Commission on Human Rights Resolution 2002/62*, E/CN.4/2003/85, Dec. 30, 2002.

113. *CRC General Comment 6*, paras. 24, 33–39.

114. The EU Resolution standard is somewhat weaker than that established by the CRC because it permits member states to provide representation by welfare organizations or non-specified "other appropriate representation." 1997 Council Resolution on Unaccompanied

Minors, Art. 3(4). As Senovilla et al. point out, this more generic terminology is unsatisfactory because it suggests that something less than legally trained representation may be an adequate protection for unaccompanied minors. Senovilla and LaGrange, *Legal Status of Unaccompanied Children*, 22.

115. In the United States, there are voluntary, nonprofit organized systems that do provide a form of guardianship and legal representation in some cases. See the Chicago-based Young Center, supra note 48, and the Washington, DC-based KIND, supra ch. 6, note 50.

116. INS Office of General Counsel Memo: Elian Gonzalez Jan. 3, 2000. See chapter 1, notes 39–40.

117. The United Kingdom announced its decision to remove its reservations to Articles 22 and 37(c) in September 2008.

118. Bhabha and Finch, 60.

119. Parliamentary Assembly, Council of Europe, *Resolution 1810 (2011) on unaccompanied children in Europe: Issues of Arrival, Stay and Return*, para. 1. See also Terry Smith, *Separated Children in Europe: Policies and Practices in European Union Member States: A Comparative Analysis* (2003).

120. Emphasis added. Amnesty International, *Invisible Children—The Human Rights of Migrant and Asylum-Seeking Minors Detained upon Arrival at the Maritime Border in Italy* (2006).

121. Recall Arendt's reflection on an identical problem in a different historical moment:

> The full implication of the identification of the rights of man with the rights of peoples in the European nation-state system came to light only when a growing number of people and peoples suddenly appeared whose elementary rights were as little safeguarded by the ordinary functioning of nation-states in the middle of Europe as they would have been in the heart of Africa. (Arendt, *Totalitarianism*, 291)

122. See Benhabib, 52.

123. According to Seyla Benhabib: Arendt's "moral cosmopolitanism founders on [her] legal and civic particularism." Ibid.,66.

124. Kenneth Cmiel (2004), cited in Emily Haffner-Burton, "Can the Human Rights Movement Achieve Its Goals?" (unpublished manuscript on file with author).

125. Jack L. Goldsmith and Eric A. Posner, *The Limits of International Law* (Oxford: Oxford University Press, 2005), 132.

126. Haffner-Burton and Ron.

127. Beth Simmons, *Mobilizing for Human Rights: International Law in Domestic Politics* (Cambridge: Cambridge University Press, 2010), 4–5.

128. CRC, Art. 3.

129. UNHCR, *Handbook*, para. 196.

130. Bhabha and Crock, 82–85.

131. Brownlees and Finch, 43.

132. For a general discussion of age determination with the UK asylum system, see Bhabha and Finch, 55–65.

133. *R (on the application of B) v. London Borough of Merton* [2003] EWHC 1689, 14 July 2003.

134. CRC, Arts. 3, 12.

135. Royal College of Paediatrics and Child Health, *The Health of Refugee Children—Guidelines for Paediatricians* (1999), para. 5.6.

136. Brownlees and Finch, 44.

137. Ibid., 24.

138. CRC, Art. 12.

139. See, e.g., Gerison Lansdown, *Evolving Capacities and Participation*, prepared for Canadian International Development Agency, Child Protection Unit (2004).

140. Women's Refugee Commission, *Prison Guard or Parent?: INS Treatment of Unaccompanied Refugee Children* (2002); HREOC, *National Inquiry*.

141. See, e.g., Olga Byrne, *Unaccompanied Children in the United States: A Literature Review* (Vera Institute of Justice, 2008); Christopher Nugent, "Whose Children Are These? Towards Ensuring the Best Interests and Empowerment of Unaccompanied Alien Children," *Boston University Public Interest Law Journal* 15 (2006): 219, 221; and David B. Thronson, "Kids Will Be Kids? Reconsidering Conceptions of Children's Rights Underlying Immigration Law," *Ohio State Law Journal* 630, (2002): 979, 980.

142. Human Rights Watch, *Nowhere to Turn*, 15.

143. Giorgio Agamben, *Homo Sacer* (Stanford: Stanford University Press, 1995), 169–70.

144. See note 107 above.

145. This category applies to a very diverse group of children whose parents leave home in search of work or safety, often planning to reunify by returning home or sending for their children to join them.

146. *Mayeka and Mitunga v. Belgium*, supra note 105.

147. This figure is based on the number of unaccompanied minors registered with Belgium's Guardianship Service and does not reflect undetected and unregistered children. European Migration Network, *Unaccompanied Minors in Belgium: Reception, Return and Integration Arrangements* (2009).

148. ECHR, Arts. 3, 5(1), 5(4), 8.

149. Belgian law of December 24, 2002, Title XIII, Chapitre 6, Guardianship on the Unaccompanied Foreign Minors.

150. "Canary Islands Face Migrant Crisis," *Al Jazeera*, July 26, 2007.

151. Rutvica Andrijasevic, "Lampedusa in Focus: Migrants Caught between the Libyan Desert and the Deep Sea," *Feminist Review* 82 (2006): 120–25.

152. *Pretty v. United Kingdom*, no. 2346/02, ECHR (2002), para. 52.

153. Ruth Farrugia and Kristina Touzenis, "The International Protection of Unaccompanied and Separated Migrant and Asylum-seeking Children in Europe," in Kanics et al., 21–55.

154. CRC Committee, *Concluding Observations: Denmark*, supra note 85.

155. Maria Ahmed, "Peers Want Equal Status for Asylum-Seeking Children," *Community Care*, Dec. 6, 2007.

156. Brownlees and Finch, 24.

157. Save the Children Italia, "L'Identificazione dei minori vittime di tratta e sfruttamento" (draft report on file with author).

158. For an excellent collection of first-person narratives by children in these circumstances in France, see Vassort, supra note 81.

159. Arendt, *Totalitarianism*, 279.

160. Vassort, supra note 81.

161. Ibid., 11 (translation from French by author).

162. "A los niños les mataron los pájaros," *El Mirador De Tanger*, Dec. 19, 2007.

163. French patois abbreviation of "adolescents."

164. See Television Suisse Romande, "L'Exil a 15 Ans," Dec. 21, 2007.

165. Sigona and Hughes, supra note 26.

166. See Sharlene Swartz, *The Moral Ecology of South Africa's Township Youth* (New York: Palgrave Macmillan, 2009).

167. Progetto Equal PALMS (Percorsi di accompagnamento al lavoro per minori stranieri non accompagnati), *Pratiche di Accoglienza I: Aggancio, inserimento, mediazione e rimpatrio* (Save the Children Italy, 2006), 7.

168. Personal communication, UNICEF meeting on "Children on the Move," Zurich, Switzerland, November 29–30, 2007.

169. Ireland has faced a similar problem, see chapter 4, note 12.

170. Mai, "Marginalized Young," 76, 13.

171. Salvatore Fachile, *L'Identificazione dei Minori Vittime di Tratta e Struttamento*, Programma AGIS 2005—Development of a Child Rights Methodology to Identity and Support Child Victims of Trafficking, Progetto—JLS/2005/AGIS/045 (unpublished draft on file with author), 33, translation by author.

172. "Senegal tiene dificultades para aceptar a sus menores acogidos en Canaria," *El Dia*, Dec. 31, 2007.

173. ICESCR, Arts. 13(1)(a), 12 (1); CRC, Art. 24.

174. Ibid., Arts. 2(2), 13; CRC, Art. 28.

175. For a survey of six EU member states, see Senovilla and LaGrange, *Legal Status of Unaccompanied Children*, 38.

176. Article 19 section 2(a) of Consolidated Text 286/98 on Immigration.

177. PICUM, *Undocumented Children in Europe: Invisible Victims of Immigration Restrictions* (2009), 11. Noncompulsory educational facilities are a different matter altogether. In 2007, the municipality of Milan issued a circular excluding undocumented children from access to state kindergartens and nursery schools; eventually the courts ruled that the measure was unconstitutional. Ibid., 47. Educational facilities for adolescents over sixteen are also outside the compulsory framework and are regularly inaccessible to undocumented youth, both in the European Union and in the United States. For the former, see PICUM, *Undocumented Children*, 37; for the latter, see Legomsky, "Undocumented Students," 217–35.

178. PICUM, *Undocumented Children*, 16.

179. Sigona and Hughes.

180. See chapter 1, note 139.

181. PICUM, *Undocumented Children*, 28.

182. See US Department of Homeland Security, "Secretary Napolitano."

183. Antonella Inverno, quoted in PICUM, *Undocumented Children*, 32, 25.

184. Vassort, supra note 81, 46–47.

185. PICUM, *Undocumented Children.*

186. Z. Medarik and A. Kopitar, *The Risk Group of Unaccompanied Minors: Protection Measures in an Enlarged European Union*, Country Report Poland (Koper, Slovenia: University of Primorska, 2007). See also Agnieszka Kosowicz, "Dzieci cudzoziemskie mają prawo do edukacji w Polsce," *Polskie Forum Migracyjne*, Mar. 30, 2007.

187. PICUM, *Undocumented Children*, 26.

188. Brownlees and Finch, 45.

189. *Plyler v. Doe*, 457 US 202 (1982). In 1973, the Supreme Court held in *San Antonio Independent School District v. Rodriguez*, 411 US 1 (1973), that education was not a human right; following this ruling the Texas education code was amended to allow school districts to charge tuition for undocumented children in primary and secondary schools. M. A. Olivas, "*Plyler v. Doe*, the Education of Undocumented Children, and the Polity," in David A. Martin and Peter H. Schuck, eds., *Immigration Stories* (New York: Foundation Press, 2005), 197–220, 198. Nine years later, the Supreme Court reversed in *Plyler.*

190. Olivas, *Plyer*, 230.

191. Ibid., 228.

192. Passel and Cohn, *Unauthorized Immigrant Population*, 1.

193. Passel and Taylor, 1.

194. US Department of Health and Human Services, Office of Refugee Resettlement, *DHS UAC Apprehensions Placed in ORR/DUCS Care, FY 2009 by State*. See also Chad C. Haddal, *CRS Report to Congress, Unaccompanied Alien Children: Policies and Issues* (2007), 26–27.

195. According to a 2006 Pew Research Center survey, 71 percent of Americans felt that the children of illegal immigrants should be allowed to attend public schools. Andrew Kohut and Roberto Suro, *No Consensus on Immigration Problem or Proposed Fixes: America's Immigration Quandary* (Pew Hispanic Center, 2006).

196. Pew Hispanic Center, *2007 National Survey of Latinos: As Illegal Immigration Issue Heats Up, Hispanics Feel a Chill*, Dec. 13, 2007.

197. Elizabeth de Ornellas, "Immigrants Feel the 'Shadow of Fear,'" *Daily Tar Heel*, Oct. 30, 2007.

198. Kirk Semple, "U.S. Warns Schools Against Checking Immigration Status," *New York Times*, May 6, 2011, cited in *PICUM Bulletin*, May 23, 2011.

199. Mayra Cuevas-Nazario, "Texas School District Turns Away Students from Mexico," *CNN*, Sep. 11, 2009.

200. Gonzales, 608.

201. International law provisions can be found at: UDHR, Art. 25; CRC Art. 24(1); ICESCR, Art. 12 (1). Regional provisions include the European Social Contract, Art. 13, and, in relation to the prohibition on cruel, inhuman, or degrading treatment, ECHR, Art. 3.

202. ICESCR, Art. 12.

203. Human Rights Watch, *Nowhere to Turn*, 2. See also, PICUM, *Undocumented Children*, 45–68.

204. PICUM, *Undocumented Children*, 52, 55.

205. Sigona and Hughes, 10.

206. Richard Brown, Nadereh Pourat, Steve Wallace. "Undocumented Residents Make Up Small Share of California's Uninsured Population," UCLA Health Policy Fact Sheet, March 2007, 1.

207. Robert Verkaik, "Battle to Halt Deportation of Girl, Three, Puts Spotlight on UK Asylum Policy," *Independent*, Jan. 2, 2008.

208. See *International Federation of Human Rights Leagues v. France*, European Committee on Social Rights, Complaint No. 13/2003.

209. See *International Federation of Human Rights Leagues v. France*, European Committee of Social Rights, Complaint No. 14/2003.

210. PICUM, *Undocumented Children*, 55, 59.

211. *ZH (Tanzania) v. Secretary of State for the Home Department* [2011] UKSC.

212. *London Borough of Harrow v. Nimco Hassan Ibrahim and Secretary of State for the Home Department*, ECJ 23 Feb. 2010, Case C-310/08; *Maria Teixeira v. London Borough of Lambeth and the Secretary of State for the Home Department*, ECJ 23 Feb. 2010, Case C-480/08.

213. See chapter 2, notes 91–95.

214. CRC, Arts. 23, 24, 28, 29; ICESCR, Arts. 11, 12, 13; Convention against Discrimination in Education, ratified by Spain in 1969. The Committee on Economic, Social and Cultural Rights has interpreted the principle of nondiscrimination to extend "to all persons residing in the territory of a State party, including non-nationals, and irrespective of their legal status." *General Comment 13*, para. 34, cited in Human Rights Watch, *Nowhere to Turn*, 24. For domestic Spanish law, see Organic Law 8/2000 of 22 December, Reforming Organic Law 4/2000, of 11 January, Regarding the Rights and Freedoms of Foreign Nationals Living in Spain and Their Social Integration, 22 Dec. 2000.

215. Human Rights Watch, *Nowhere to Turn*, 20.

216. E.g., David Kennedy, "When Renewal Repeats: Thinking Against the Box," in Janet Halley and Wendy Brown, eds., *Left Legalism/Left Critique* (Durham: Duke University Press, 2002).

Index

Human Rights and Crimes against Humanity

Eric D. Weitz, Series Editor

Echoes of Violence: Letters from a War Reporter by Carolin Emcke

Cannibal Island: Death in a Siberian Gulag by Nicolas Werth. Translated by Steven Rendall with a foreword by Jan T. Gross

Torture and the Twilight of Empire: From Algiers to Baghdad by Marnia Lazreg

Terror in Chechnya: Russia and the Tragedy of Civilians in War by Emma Gilligan

"If You Leave Us Here, We Will Die": How Genocide Was Stopped in East Timor by Geoffrey Robinson

Stalin's Genocides by Norman M. Naimark

Against Massacre: Humanitarian Interventions in the Ottoman Empire, 1815–1914 by Davide Rodogno

All the Missing Souls: A Personal History of the War Crimes Tribunals by David Scheffer

The Young Turks' Crime against Humanity: The Armenian Genocide and Ethnic Cleansing in the Ottoman Empire by Taner Akçam

The International Human Rights Movement: A History by Aryeh Neier

Child Migration and Human Rights in a Global Age by Jacqueline Bhabha